The Bosch book of
The Motor Car
Its evolution and engineering development

The Bosch book of
The Motor Car

Its evolution and engineering development

Written by John Day B.Sc.(Eng.), C.Eng., M.I.Mech.E.

Illustrated by Barry Rowe

Collins
GLASGOW · LONDON

1973 Alfa Romeo Montreal

CREDITS

The publishers would like to thank the following individuals and organisations for their kind permission to reproduce pictures in this book and for their help in supplying material.

Alfa Romeo (G.B.) Ltd
Armstrong Patents Company Ltd
Associated Engineering Ltd
Audi NSU (GB) Ltd
Automotive Products Ltd
Biscaretti Museum, Turin
Blaupunkt GmbH.
B.M.W. Concessionaires GB Ltd
Borg-Warner Ltd
Bosch Archives, Stuttgart
British Leyland Motor
Corporation Ltd
Britover (Continental) Ltd
Neill Bruce
Chrysler United Kingdom Ltd
Citroën Cars Ltd
City Museum, Birmingham
Conservetoire Nationale des Arts
et Metiers, Paris
Daf Motors (G.B.) Ltd
Daimler Benz, Stuttgart
John Day
Joyce Day
Deutsches Museum, Munich
J. Arthur Dixon
L. A. C. Dopping-Heppenstall
Dunlop Ltd
Ian Dussek
Ferodo Ltd
Fiat (England) Ltd
Ford Motor Company Ltd
General Motors Ltd
G. N. Georgano
Girling Ltd
GKN Group Services Ltd
Glasgow Transport Museum
Geoffrey Goddard
Betty Haig
JCB Sales Ltd

Jean Ames
Jensen Motors Ltd
Light Steam Power
Lotus Group of Companies
Maranello Concessionaires Ltd
Mercedes-Benz (Great Britain) Ltd
Michelin Tyre Company Ltd
Motorola Ltd
National Motor Museum
Osterreichischer Automobil-
Motorrad-und-Touring Club
Pirelli Ltd
Charles Pocklington
Reliant Motor Company Ltd
Renault Ltd
Ricardo & Co (Engineers) Ltd
Robert Bosch GmbH, Stuttgart
Andrew Rodger BA.
Rolls Royce Motors Ltd
Barry Rowe
Royal Automobile Club
Saab (Great Britain) Ltd
Science Museum, London
Bruce Scott
Skoda (Great Britain) Ltd
Smiths Industries Ltd
Stratford Motor Museum
Tony Stone Associates Ltd
Tecalemit Group Services Ltd
J. Walter Thompson Company Ltd
Triplex Safety Glass Ltd
Trojan Ltd
Vauxhall Motors Ltd
V.K.D. Ltd
Volkswagen (G.B.) Ltd
Volvo Concessionaires Ltd
D. J. Wakeley
Wilmot Breeden (Holdings) Ltd
Zenith Carburettor Co Ltd

First published in 1975

Third impression 1976

Published by
William Collins Sons and Company Limited,
Glasgow and London

Printed in Spain by Mateu Cromo, S. A. Pinto (Madrid)
ISBN 0 00 435016 2

**Created and designed by
Berkeley Publishers Limited**

1935 MG P.B. cockpit

FOREWORD

The Bosch Book of the Motor Car is the history of the car not by make and model but through its component parts: an original concept of Charles Stainsby developed with the enthusiastic support of the Publishers and author John Day.

The motor car has evolved from the horseless carriage to the functional transport which the mass of the population now enjoys. Man has solved the problem of how to become more mobile only to find he now needs to be protected from some of the consequences: atmospheric pollution, overcrowded roads and the accelerating drain on natural resources.

The central technical challenge in the resultant search for greater reliability, greater safety and greater efficiency is to produce components at prices people can and will afford to pay. Our own Company is part of a worldwide Group which has been meeting and solving these challenges since before the turn of the century, along with many other pioneers.

All who work within the motor industry today owe their livelihoods and opportunities to a long line of inventors and engineers who, indirectly, have created the roots from which The Bosch Book of the Motor Car could grow. It is upon the results of their work and their efforts that John Day has been able to build our story of the motor car's archaeology, with the help of Barry Rowe's illustrations and many drawings and photographs not previously easily available to the public.

Environmental considerations, safety requirements, the economics of fuel supply, drivers' more pressing needs for information about road conditions and the functioning of their vehicles, coupled with service factors, all provide stimuli for further development.

New problem solving will bring new challenges. I believe that the more complete our understanding of the motor car's short but complex history, the better will be our perspective.

Bernard Mills

Managing Director,
Robert Bosch Limited,
Watford, Hertfordshire
England

1928 8-litre Hispano Suiza Boulogne

CONTENTS

THE ENGINE-Heart of a Car

The engine is the heart of a car. Indeed, it has always been the heart of the whole matter, ever since man first dreamed of a conveyance that was not muscle powered. Surviving sketches and models testify to this aspiration. Some method of mechanical propulsion is needed. Every small boy in a soapbox on wheels comes wistfully to the same conclusion.

With the development of the steam engine midway through the 18th century motor car aspirants looked towards steam for the breakthrough in self propulsion.

As long ago as 1769 a strange looking carriage, powered by steam, was built by a French military engineer, Nicholas Joseph Cugnot, to tow guns for the artillery. This carriage was three-wheeled and its boiler stuck out in front as there was nowhere else for it to be fitted.

On trial in Paris it was reported to have shown itself able to cover six miles in an hour, if only its built-in energy crisis would have let it run for more than ten or twelve minutes. A second version was so unmanageable it demolished a wall. It was locked up and Cugnot given a state pension to keep him out of trouble. However, despite the unfortunate conclusion this was a milestone along the road of car development.

Britons were to the fore in these 18th-century experiments. Some, notably the Englishman Thomas Newcomen, and the Scotsman James Watt, fathers of the steam engine,

Cugnot's celebrated gun-towing steam carriage, made in 1769. The carriage was three-wheeled and is said to have reached a speed of six miles an hour.

Left: Richard Trevithick, who built the first powered road vehicle in England. Right: Scotsman James Watt, who was highly sceptical that a steam-driven road vehicle was possible.

used heat to make the pressure of the atmosphere, and later the pressure of steam, move a piston in order to provide power.

Others, like John Barber, another Englishman, thought of using the pressure of heated air to drive their engines. So there were two schools of thought. One was concerned with an external combustion engine in which fire heated a boiler. The second involved an internal combustion engine in which the fire took place directly inside the engine.

Barber realized that a high pressure was needed for a useful amount of work to be done. So he pumped inflammable gas, made from coal or oil, together with air into an exploder chamber. This was lit by a match or candle and "rushed out with great rapidity in one continued stream of fire".

The gas "issued out with amazing force and velocity against a fly wheel". The flywheel was fitted with vanes round the rim and the rush of the gas turned the wheel. This invention of 1791 was probably the first internal combustion engine and, incidentally, the first gas turbine.

Steam, however, was to be the preoccupation for a considerable while. During the first half of the 19th century steam coaches became popular and no doubt would have won even greater popularity had it not been for the opposition they provoked from the conservative horse-owning fraternity.

The use of horses, in fact, was dying hard. Those who had a vested interest in the animal, particularly in its commercial use, proved a formidable opposition. The Red Flag Act of 1865 was really more than the new-fangled steamer could stand. There seemed little future in a form of transport fettered by the fact that someone carrying a warning flag had to *walk* (not run!) about 60 yards (55 metres) in front.

Yet steam carriages had made a point. Ordinary people had taken to the steam bus services. There was a public for powered road transport.

Steam vehicles also performed other useful pioneering services. They advanced knowledge of the behaviour of wheels, springs and steering beyond the limit of horse-drawn transport.

It was not, however, until some 80 years after John Barber pointed the way that the internal combustion

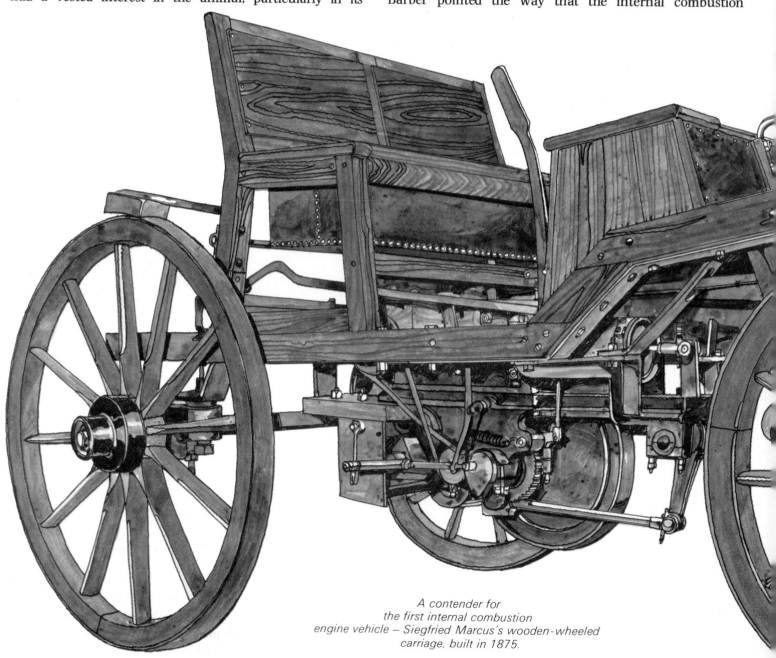

A contender for the first internal combustion engine vehicle – Siegfried Marcus's wooden-wheeled carriage, built in 1875.

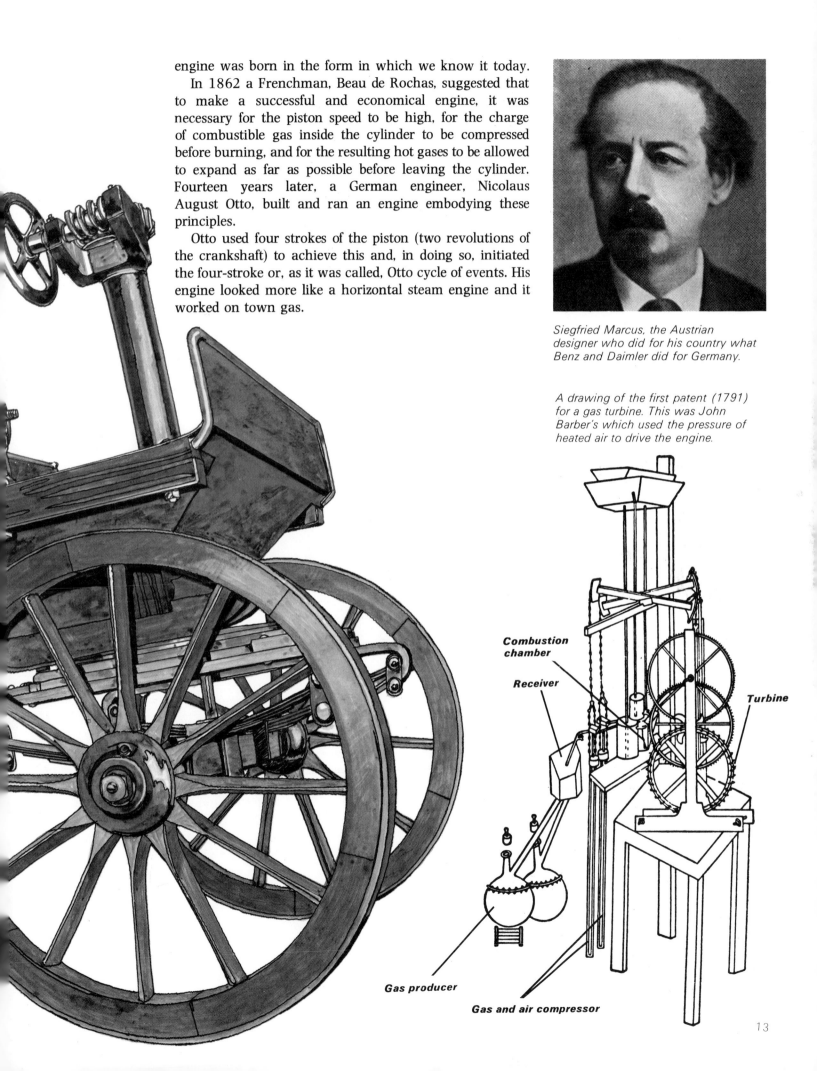

engine was born in the form in which we know it today.

In 1862 a Frenchman, Beau de Rochas, suggested that to make a successful and economical engine, it was necessary for the piston speed to be high, for the charge of combustible gas inside the cylinder to be compressed before burning, and for the resulting hot gases to be allowed to expand as far as possible before leaving the cylinder. Fourteen years later, a German engineer, Nicolaus August Otto, built and ran an engine embodying these principles.

Otto used four strokes of the piston (two revolutions of the crankshaft) to achieve this and, in doing so, initiated the four-stroke or, as it was called, Otto cycle of events. His engine looked more like a horizontal steam engine and it worked on town gas.

Siegfried Marcus, the Austrian designer who did for his country what Benz and Daimler did for Germany.

A drawing of the first patent (1791) for a gas turbine. This was John Barber's which used the pressure of heated air to drive the engine.

Combustion chamber

Receiver

Turbine

Gas producer

Gas and air compressor

THE ENGINE/Heart of a Car

The 1886 Daimler, the chassis of which owed a lot to the horse carriage.

Earlier attempts by Isaac de Rivaz (France 1807), Samuel Brown (London 1826), Lenoir (France 1862) and Siegfried Marcus (Vienna 1875) had produced gas engine powered vehicles that could move themselves. Edward Butler, an Englishman, built and ran a two-cylinder petrol-driven tricycle in 1885.

But for the truly significant advance of the motor car in the closing years of the 19th century, the honours go to two Germans, Carl Benz and Gottlieb Daimler. Benz and Daimler, operating separately, built compact engines running on volatile inflammable liquids such as light petroleum spirit and naptha. Both of these engines were soon developed for motor vehicle propulsion.

Benz hailed from Karlsruhe, but Mannheim was to be the scene of his great endeavours. He had worked with a firm of locomotive makers in Karlsruhe. In Mannheim he started his own machine shop.

He came from a comparatively humble background. His father, who was an engine driver, died when Carl was

two, and his story was one of struggle and of frustration; a story, in fact, that was often common among innovators.

In 1885, Benz built his famous three-wheeler. It was steered with a tiller and propelled by a single-cylinder gas engine modified to use liquid fuel. Sales, however, were not initially encouraging.

Daimler also had locomotive engineering training. He travelled to France and England, always on the look-out for power development, before becoming technical director of Otto and Langen's Deutz Gas Engine Works. Later he started his own business near Stuttgart and did much of his work in association with the talented William Maybach who had shared his enthusiasms ever since 1862.

Benz and Daimler made cars powered by internal combustion engines for sale, so it can be said in the modern context that they were the true founders of a way of life. Plaything, status symbol or necessity, whatever the meaning of a car to mid-20th-century man — it all really began with these two inventors.

In the 1899 Daimler engine a cylinder (**1**) with a combustion chamber (**2**) at the top provides the space in which the burning and expanding gases can push on a piston (**3**) which, through a connecting rod (**4**), turns a crankshaft (**5**) to provide rotary power. Fuel from pipe (**6**) goes into a carburettor which has a chamber (**7**) where fuel is kept at a constant level by float (**8**). This level is such that air, from an inlet (**9**) passing through a passage (**10**) can draw fuel from the jet (**11**) to form a mist.

This petrol-air mist passes through an inlet valve (**12**) to the combustion chamber. The flow is produced by the descent of the piston, which causes a partial vacuum in the cylinder, and the pressure of the air in the manifold (**13**) forces open the valve (**12**) against its spring (**14**). When the piston begins to ascend, the vapour in the cylinder is compressed and becomes hotter.

At about the top of the piston stroke the vapour is combustible enough to be ignited by the temperature of a platinum tube (**15**), which is heated by a petrol burner (**16**). When the gas ignites, it burns extremely rapidly – almost like an explosion – and the expansion forces the piston back down the cylinder to drive the crankshaft for a power stroke. As the piston ascends for the second time, gears (**17**) rotate a cam (**18**), lifting a pushrod (**19**) to open an exhaust valve (**20**) and allow the burnt gas to escape through an exhaust pipe (**21**).

Then the cycle of four strokes – inlet, compression, power and exhaust – begins again. The combustion causes the engine to heat up, and it is cooled by a flow of water through pipes (**22**) connected to a jacket surrounding the hot parts of the engine.

This Daimler engine has no throttle control on the carburettor and no control over the exact moment when the vapour starts to burn. So the engine runs at more or less constant speed. To ensure that a sudden increase in speed does not take place when the load is removed or lightened, a governor operates on a linkage (**23**) to remove the rod (**19**) from the cam follower (**24**), and so prevents the exhaust valve from opening. If the valve does not open, the burnt gas cannot get out to make way for a fresh charge, and the engine stops firing until it slows and the exhaust valve is allowed to open again.

Benz (top) and Daimler (bottom), the famous contemporaries who put the motor car on the road.

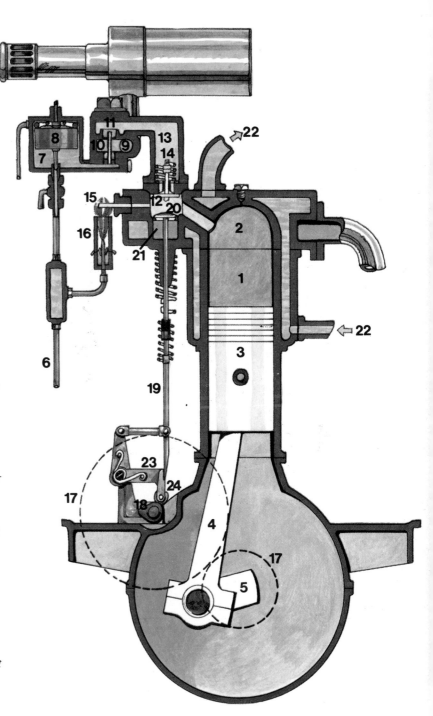

The Daimler engine of 1899 was a good example of design at the turn of the century. Except for the fact that it did not possess electrical ignition, this Daimler engine displayed both the method of working and the main components of most four-stroke internal combustion engines that were to follow.

Although this 1899 Daimler engine was basically correct in its operation, experience soon showed that engines could be made far more efficient, powerful and flexible, as can be seen from the engine of the modern car. To achieve this it was first of all necessary to introduce as much fuel, air and mixture into the cylinder as possible.

The fuel had to be mixed with just the right amount of air and it had to be in the best conditions for burning. Once burnt it had to work on the piston for as long as possible. Then it had to be released from the cylinder rapidly to make space available for the next charge.

Moreover, all these things had to take place as quickly as possible and at the same time the engine had to be kept cool enough so that its parts were not destroyed by excessive heat. Finally, the engine had to be strong enough structurally to stand up to the power it developed.

A modern family-car engine of comparable size to the 1899 Daimler will run at something like ten times the speed, if necessary, and will develop about ten times the power. Also, it will be infinitely more reliable.

If an engine is to run faster, the events must be timed much more accurately than in the early engines. For instance, inlet valve operation cannot be left to the piston sucking it open. The valve must be opened mechanically.

THE ENGINE / Heart of a Car

Within a year or so of the Daimler engine, a little known American petrol-driven tradesman's tricycle, the Columbia, had both valves operated by separate cams on a camshaft driven at half the crankshaft speed. The half speed of the camshaft results from the need for the lump (or lobe) of the cam to push the valve-operating rod only once in two revolutions of the crankshaft, in other words once in four strokes of the piston – the complete cycle.

In those very early days, the valves were often extremely troublesome, since the materials available at the time were unable to stand up to the hammering the valves received when the spring snapped them shut. They were equally vulnerable to the high temperatures at which the

A splendid example of a turn of the century car – the 1904 Napier, which had conical spokes to its steering wheel and a bulb horn in the centre. The Napier was built by a long established firm of ships' engine builders and was built at the suggestion of the famous racing driver Selwyn Frances Edge. The 1904 18 horsepower, six-cylinder Napier was a forerunner of the British six-cylinder cars.

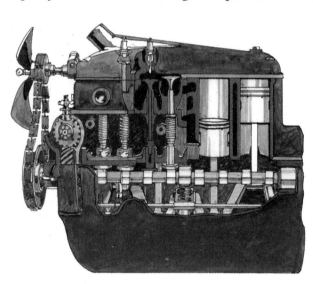

The side valve arrangement of the Morris Cowley engine. This was a classic arrangement which lasted for more than 40 years.

valves had to work. Consequently, engines were designed in such a way that valves could be changed within a few minutes at the side of the road.

Engines with non-mechanically operated, or automatic, inlet valves had these valves situated in a complete unit in a cage which contained a light closing spring and included the valve seating. The unit could easily be unscrewed from the cylinder.

The inlet valves were over the exhaust valves so that once the inlet cage had been screwed out, the corresponding exhaust valve could be removed upwards through the hole. The exhaust valve was released by pulling out a cotter (or pin) below a collar (or washer) under the valve spring. When the inlet valve came to be operated mechanically, it was moved to a position alongside the exhaust valve which is now usually smaller than the inlet valve.

Screwed caps were then provided over each valve. The designers of those days knew very little about the importance of the shape of the combustion chamber to its efficient operation. Because they were more concerned with easy design and manufacture, they put the valves vertically side by side and opened them with a camshaft mounted at the side of the crankshaft. Thus the camshaft could be driven very simply with just one gear on the crankshaft and a meshing gear on the camshaft.

This produced the classic side-valve engine, which remained in fashion for something like 60 years. It was solid, reliable and easy to maintain but it lacked power.

A variation of the side-valve was the T-head, where the two valves were still vertical, but the inlet and exhaust were on opposite sides of the cylinder. As well as requiring two camshafts, this gave an even worse shape to the combustion chamber.

In 1902, the Maudslay Motor Company of London, built, for their first car, a twenty-horsepower, three-cylinder engine in which they retained automatic inlet valves. But they moved years ahead of their time by putting the exhaust valve operating camshaft over the top of the cylinder head, in which the valves were mounted in a vertical position with their heads down.

Other uncommon features for 1902 were a cylinder head which could be removed from the cylinder block and a camshaft which, complete with its worm gear drive and the rockers which transferred the motion from cams to valves, could be swung out of the way merely by releasing three nuts.

Two years later Napier and Son, like Maudslay a long established firm renowned for high quality engineering, produced a fifteen-horsepower four-cylinder engine. The inlet valves were once again over the exhaust valves but were operated mechanically by rockers, pivoted on brackets on the cylinder head and rocked by pushrods which were operated by cams on the single camshaft in the crankcase.

Early in the history of engines, it became obvious that

there were drawbacks in using a platinum tube, kept incandescent by a naked flame, as a means of igniting the fuel and air mixture. It could not be relied upon to fire the charge at exactly the right moment and the flame could be blown or jolted out too easily or could even set light to stray oil and petrol under the engine cover.

The answer to these problems was to start the burning with an electric spark. This had none of the failings of tube ignition, although in its early days the spark could be pretty temperamental. The story of the production and timing of the spark is described in Section Six.

In the decade spanning the turn of the century, many firms originally founded for other purposes, together with many more new firms, began to join in the exploitation of the motor car. After this initial enthusiasm, the basic

THE ENGINE / Heart of a Car

design of the engine settled down. This second period, a period almost of entrenchment, was prolonged by the First World War and its aftermath until the early 1920s. By then the design of engines owed much to scientific experiment which had been brought about partly by pre-war motor racing and wartime flying.

Considerable knowledge became available on the actual process of combustion. One of the leading authorities on the subject was Sir Harry Ricardo who had looked deeply (quite literally) through a quartz window, to see what happened inside the engine as the charge burned within the combustion chamber.

Harry Ricardo, knighted in 1948, had a distinguished career in engineering research, beginning in the early 1900s. His own research establishment, near Shoreham Airport in Sussex still develops internal combustion engines.

Sir Harry Ricardo and the shed in which he did research on the internal combustion engine.

At Cambridge University the young Ricardo so impressed his professor that he was kept on as a research assistant. Together the two men worked on the problem of detonation in an engine. Later, Ricardo joined a firm of engineering consultants where he used to do his own research in a shed at the works. One of the endearing aspects of this brilliant man was his loyalty to this particular shed. Wherever he went thereafter the shed went with him.

While working for the government during the First World War, Ricardo designed the two types of engine used in British tanks. In the early 1920s he introduced the Ricardo turbulent cylinder head for side-valve engines. It became an absolute essential for this kind of engine. The Ricardo Comet cylinder head is even today fitted on a number of Diesel engines.

Ricardo was one of the first to research the combustion process within an engine. The burning of the compressed air and fuel mixture starts from the sparking plug and the flame travels through the combustion chamber until all

the charge has burned. In a modern engine, the charge is compressed from just below atmospheric pressure to around 170 pounds per square inch.

As the burning takes place, the heat released raises the pressure to some four times this figure and expands the gases to push down the piston. By the time the exhaust valve starts to open, the pressure will have dropped to the region of 70 pounds per square inch and will continue to drop as the gases escape down the exhaust pipe. The inlet valve is opened, the piston descends and a fresh charge of unburnt mixture rushes in to fill the vacant space.

In practice, because these events occur at anything up to 3,000 times each minute and because the gases have what is known as inertia (a disinclination to get moving but, once moving, a momentum which tends to keep them moving), the valves are opened and closed early and late respectively.

That is, the inlet valve opens before the piston reaches the top of its travel before the suction stroke (before top dead centre – or B.T.D.C.) and closes after the bottom of the suction stroke (after bottom dead centre – or A.B.D.C.). The exhaust valve opens before bottom dead centre (B.B.D.C.) of the power stroke and closes after top dead centre (A.T.D.C.) of the exhaust stroke.

Also, because the charge takes time to burn, the spark is timed to flash just before the piston reaches the top of the compression stroke. The timing of these operations is usually expressed in degrees of crankshaft rotation and a typical example, the Ford Cortina 1300, has the following timing :–

> Inlet opens 17 degrees B.T.D.C.
> Inlet closes 51 degrees A.B.D.C.
> Exhaust opens 51 degrees B.B.D.C.
> Exhaust closes 17 degrees A.T.D.C.
> Ignition timing 10 degrees B.T.D.C.

The fuel and air mixture does not burn all at once. That is to say, it does not explode as it would do if the fuel were mixed with pure oxygen. Since air contains about four-fifths nitrogen, which does not burn, the burning is damped and the flame has to travel progressively from the spark to the furthest point of the combustion chamber.

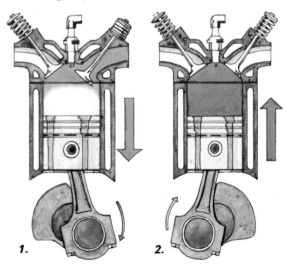

1. 2.

A photograph of a modern overhead valve cylinder head. The 1974 Alfa Romeo Alfetta.

In view of this, two desirable requirements become obvious. First, the spark must be in the best place to get the flame going. Secondly the flame should have the shortest possible distance to travel for complete burning.

That is another point where the design of the 1899 Daimler was wrong, in that the ignition took place a long way from the combustion chamber. With the later side-valve engines, the sparking plug was often situated over the centre of the cylinder which, at first sight, seems to be a good position.

However, the scientific approaches of Ricardo showed that, if the incoming charge could be made turbulent, so that the flame not only spread but could be swept round the combustion chamber, the burning would be faster and more even. The interior of the combustion chamber

was sloped and the piston, as it rose, swept the charge into a pocket over the valves. This, therefore, became the best position for the sparking plug.

When gases are compressed, they increase in temperature unless they can lose heat to the surrounding walls. In an engine, the walls are already warm from the last firing stroke and events are occurring rapidly, with the result that the charge temperature increases. The increase is proportional to the degree to which the gas is compressed. This is currently to about one-eighth of its original volume, that is the compression ratio (the ratio of the gas volume before compression to the volume after) is eight to one.

For each fuel there is a temperature, produced by the degree of compression, at which the gas will ignite without the aid of a sparking plug. This is known as detonation, the

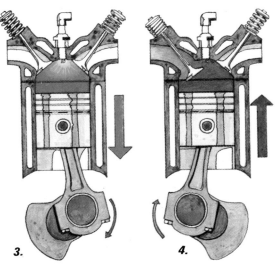

Left: The four-stroke cycle.
1: *Induction stroke in which the gas/air mixture is drawn into the cylinder.*
2: *The compression stroke in which the mixture is compressed.* **3**: *Combustion stroke in which the mixture is burnt.*
4: *The exhaust stroke in which the gases are pushed out through the exhaust valve.*

3.   4.

Right: The Ricardo side valve cylinder head which produced turbulence in the region of the spark plug. This raised the efficiency of the side valve engine.

The wedge-shaped combustion chamber has valves on the sloping roof and spark plug on the steep side. This gives a short flame path.

The bath-tub chamber has the same advantages as the wedge-shaped chamber. The spark-plug is on the side slope and pinking is minimised.

In the compact hemispherical chamber the spark-plug is set between the valves. Large valves can be used, which allow good 'breathing'.

The chamber-in-piston has a combustion space in the head of the piston. The cylinder head is flat. The spark-plug is to one side of the valves.

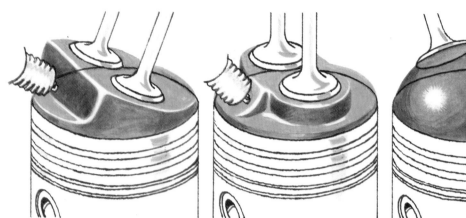
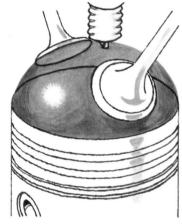

problem which concerned Ricardo and Hopkinson. While it is possible to take advantage of the phenomenon (the diesel engine works on this principle), it is a certain spoiler of petrol engines.

Another cause of detonation, often known as "pinking" from the sound it produces, is the speed at which the flame spreads within the charge. If the rate at which the pressure wave of the hot gas expansion travelling from the spark is faster than the rate at which the flame burns through the gas, the pressure wave hits the far wall of the combustion chamber and produces a metallic "pink", while the pressure rise tends to ignite the rest of the charge.

Obviously, both these conditions are unwanted, as they produce undesirably high pressures in the combustion chamber. Designers began to produce cylinder heads with chambers avoiding these pitfalls as far as possible.

The shape of the combustion chamber also has a considerable effect on the compression ratio which can be used with a particular fuel without starting detonation. Also, since the power output increases with the compression ratio, the aim is to employ as high a ratio as possible without having to use very elaborate and expensive fuels.

One method of designing the inside of the cylinder head is to place the sparking plug near the exhaust valve in an area of relatively large volume. This starts the burning process in the hottest part of the combustion space at a time when the piston is still rising. As the flame front travels across the space it meets the gas still being compressed and then travels on to a third space where detonation is most likely to occur.

Providing this space still has an adequate volume and is kept relatively cool by the inlet valve (which is itself cooled by the incoming charge), detonation in the super-compressed gas can be avoided. Examples of this are

shown in the F-heads of Rover and Rolls-Royce cars, where an overhead inlet valve is above the piston and a side exhaust valve is either vertical or inclined at about 45 degrees. The combustion chamber is wedge shaped and the sparking plug is positioned to provide the shortest possible flame travel. Other and widely used examples of the wedge head have both valves in the cylinder head and the plug positioned towards the short, vertical, side of the wedge. These wedge chambers provide a degree of turbulence in the mixture as it is compressed, which assists in even burning and provides a degree of plug and valve cooling.

Another type of combustion chamber is the inverted bath tub, which allows the valves to be vertical and over the cylinder centre. This head does not allow such a high compression ratio to be used, as there is far less turbulence. What there is has to be generated by the direction of the flow of the incoming mixture.

Ideally the combustion chamber should be spherical with the sparking plug at the centre of the sphere, since this shape provides the maximum chamber volume with the minimum area through which heat can be lost from the fuel when burning.

However, this shape cannot provide a sufficiently high compression ratio, while a sparking plug projecting deep into the hot area would have a short life. As a compromise, a hemispherical chamber is used when the greatest power and efficiency is desired. Although the hemispherical head has a greater area for a given volume, it allows the plug to be positioned for very short flame travel. When the compression ratio is increased by using a domed-top piston, the piston crown comes close to the head surface to give a good degree of "squish" and turbulence.

As compression ratios rise the space remaining within

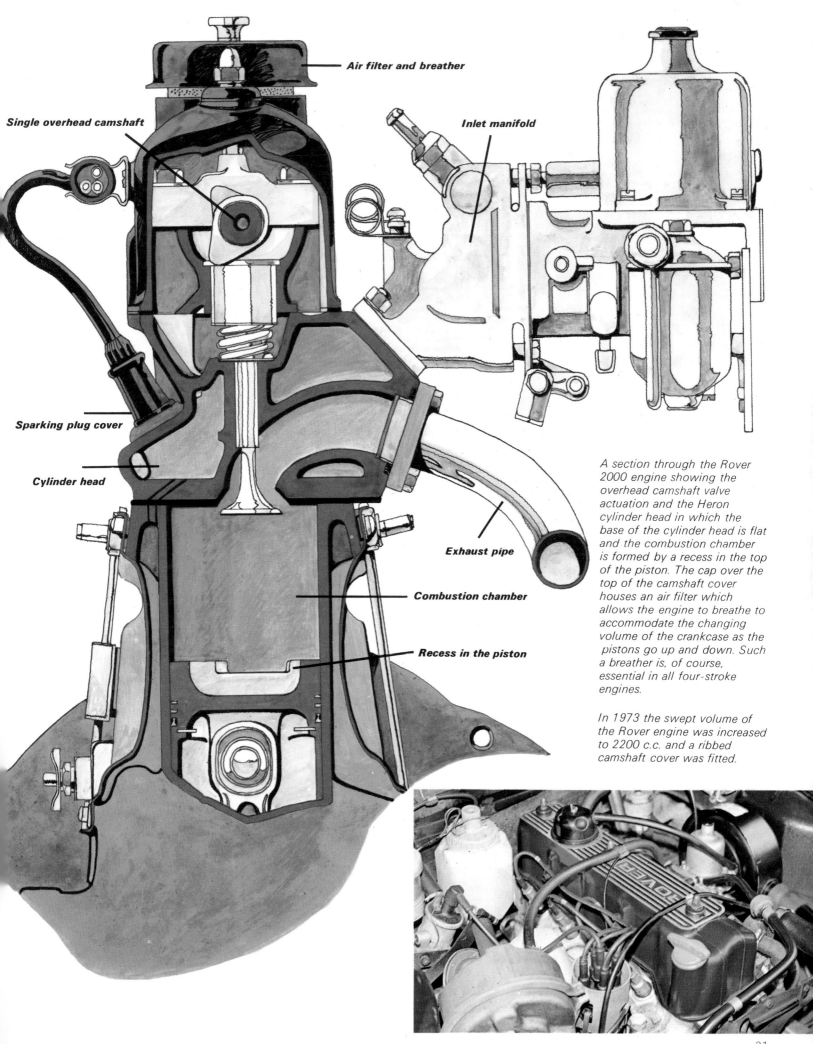

Air filter and breather

Single overhead camshaft

Inlet manifold

Sparking plug cover

Cylinder head

Exhaust pipe

Combustion chamber

Recess in the piston

A section through the Rover 2000 engine showing the overhead camshaft valve actuation and the Heron cylinder head in which the base of the cylinder head is flat and the combustion chamber is formed by a recess in the top of the piston. The cap over the top of the camshaft cover houses an air filter which allows the engine to breathe to accommodate the changing volume of the crankcase as the pistons go up and down. Such a breather is, of course, essential in all four-stroke engines.

In 1973 the swept volume of the Rover engine was increased to 2200 c.c. and a ribbed camshaft cover was fitted.

the head diminishes until there is barely room for the valves to open to their fullest extent. Provision has to be made by cutting recesses in the piston crown to prevent valves and piston meeting at full stroke.

An extension of this is the Heron head, first developed in the early 1920s and later used on the Rover 2000, Jaguar V12 and Ford engines. In this configuration the base of the cylinder head is flat and almost solely devoted to two large valves and the sparking plug, while the combustion space is machined in a thickened piston head. This provides an efficient chamber shape at the expense of heavier pistons and greater piston cooling problems.

The valves must be of the largest diameter possible to allow the easiest and greatest flows of gas both in and out of the cylinder, but the dimensions of the combustion chamber limit the valve sizes. With the hemispherical head, the greatest valve area which can be provided is achieved by the use of four smaller valves (two inlet and two exhaust) or occasionally by one inlet and two exhaust.

This brings the problem that the valves are not only angled to the centre-line of the engine, but are also angled in a plane at right angles to the centre-line. Thus all the valve stems have to point towards the centre of curvature of the hemisphere, making for great difficulty in designing valve operating mechanisms.

A compromise for high performance engines is to modify the hemisphere into a pent-roof shape in which the valve stems lie in planes, one on each side of the engine centre-line. This makes the valve mechanism design much easier and the overall loss of efficiency is quite small.

As well as being helped by valve area, the greatest and smoothest gas flows result when the passages leading from the outside of the head to the valves, that is the inlet and exhaust ports, are as straight and as short as possible. With the earliest engines nobody bothered very much about such matters. It was a wonder how the gases ever found their way round the tortuous passages to get in and out of the engine.

Later, as more people began to think of mass gas flows, the passages were made shorter and straighter, even to the extent, on overhead valve engines, of turning the inlet port face upwards, so that the mixture could be helped on its way by gravity. Many engine designs have downward sloping ports to assist in this way, a scheme which helps to solve this problem without appreciably increasing the height of the power unit.

A further modification is to bring the incoming mixture to the cylinder bore at a tangent, so that the mixture swirls round above the piston and continues to swirl out through a tangential exhaust port.

When the inlet and exhaust ports are on opposite sides of the cylinder head, it is known as a cross-flow head, since the gases come in from one side and go out at the other. This design became popular, particularly with the Ford Cortina in which this flow was combined with a Heron type combustion chamber.

Rover P.3 1948–9

The F-head, such as those fitted to the Rover P.3 (above) and the contemporary Rolls Royce. In this configuration the inlet valve in the cylinder head was actuated by a push rod and rocker system from the camshaft midway along the side of the cylinder block. The exhaust valve at approximately 45 degrees to the vertical was in the cylinder block and was actuated from the same camshaft through another rocker. This arrangement was yet another way of ensuring turbulence in the region of the sparking plug and exhaust valve. This turbulence is necessary to increase the rate of flame spread in the air/gas mixture. This system was, in fact, a combination of both an overhead valve and a side valve arrangement and was subsequently superseded.

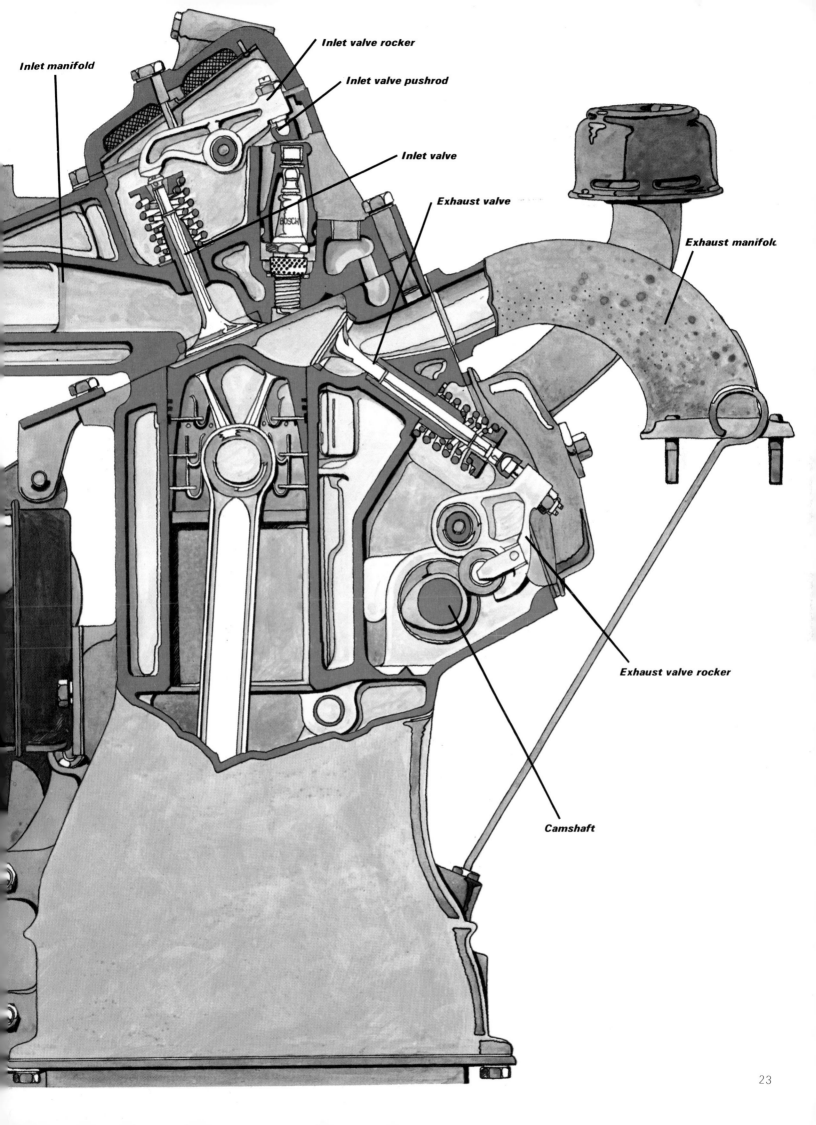

Inlet manifold

Inlet valve rocker

Inlet valve pushrod

Inlet valve

Exhaust valve

Exhaust manifold

Exhaust valve rocker

Camshaft

23

VALVES

The valves themselves play an important part in the combustion process. They must let through the greatest amount of gas in the time they are open and, when shut, they must effectively provide a seal against the pressures resulting from the expansion of the burning gases. These pressures can be as high as 1,000 pounds per square inch or more, and the valves must operate in a temperature momentarily higher than that needed to melt iron.

Early valves were virtually flat discs of good quality steel, forged with a long stem or screwed on to a stem. As engine speeds increased, the springs used to shut the valves were made stronger to do so more quickly. The stem was flared into the valve head to make the junction stronger and to provide a kinder surface for the more rapidly flowing gas.

Over this period new materials became available which were better able to cope with the pounding that valves receive at high temperatures. Valves were less liable to lose their heads, and the flames less likely to eat away at the seatings, particularly when the heads became distorted.

For a long time, the angle of the valve seating remained static at 30 or 45 degrees. Then the angles of the two seatings, those of the valve and the cylinder head, were made slightly different so that they became the same when the valve was at working temperature.

A later improvement was the use of special heat resisting materials such as Stellite, an alloy of cobalt, chromium, tungsten and molybdenum. These became necessary when the anti-detonating properties, or octane ratings, of fuels were increased by the addition of leaded compounds such as tetraethyl-lead, which tended to attack steel.

Similar problems were met in the seatings in the cast iron cylinders or cylinder heads and also in the more recent aluminium cylinder heads. These were met by screwing or pressing alloy steel inserts into the cylinder or head to provide valve seatings.

A tappet is positioned between the surface of the rotating cam and the end of the valve stem. Its purpose is to prevent a rubbing action on the valve stem, which would produce a sideways force likely to wear the stem and its guide and allow the valve to tilt and not seat correctly. This reduces gas leakage.

The tappet also gives a means of adjustment between the cam and valve stem, so that a clearance can be set which allows the valve to seat fully under the pull of the valve spring. At the same time it provides for the variations in dimension between the cam and the valve seat, due to thermal expansion of the cylinder block and the valve.

For a long period there were doubts as to whether it was desirable for tappets to rotate. A compromise was reached whereby the valves themselves were allowed, or made, to rotate to even out wear.

Although the valve must be free to seat under spring action, the clearance which allows that is a prime source of clattering from the engine. This fact was recognized as

long ago as 1910 by the Frenchman, Amédée Bollée, one of those rare sons who follow in a distinguished father's footsteps with almost equal distinction.

Amédée Bollée senior had been a great steam-car innovator. He was also, by most accounts, an estimable character and the soul of honesty and family devotion, qualities not necessarily suited to the commercial side of a thrusting infant industry.

The family fortune was based on bell-foundries. The Bollées came from a line of itinerant bell-founders. They had established themselves in the Le Mans area when Amédée began experimenting with "horseless carriages" in the foundry environs.

In January, 1873, he produced L'Obéissante (The Obedient One), a steam carriage which enraptured visitors when it was exhibited in Paris two years later. Two further models followed. They were La Mancelle in 1878, with the engine under the bonnet, a feature not to be seen again for sixteen years, and La Rapide in 1881, astonishingly speedy for its time.

But those who enthused about his models were somewhat tardy in following through with orders and the disillusioned designer returned to bell-casting. It is said that

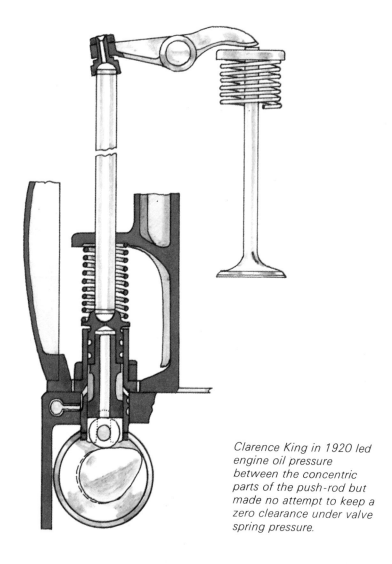

Clarence King in 1920 led engine oil pressure between the concentric parts of the push-rod but made no attempt to keep a zero clearance under valve spring pressure.

Amédée Bollée's 1873 steam carriage L'Obiéssante. L'Obiéssante had a number of original features which were not to be found again in the motor vehicle for a number of years.

he even harboured feelings of guilt for having turned his back upon bells.

In Amédée junior's engine, the tappet was in two pieces, held apart by a light spring. The gap between the two pieces was within the tappet guide and was fed with pressure oil obtained from the engine lubricating system.

The oil came through a ball valve, thus preventing the oil holding the two tappet pieces apart from being squeezed back into the system under the pressure of the valve spring when the valve was opened. This was the forerunner of the later "Zero lash" tappets which came into vogue in America on General Motors cars in the early 1930s.

In 1920, Clarence King of Vauxhall Motors applied a similar idea to the operating mechanism of both pushrod and overhead camshaft operated valves. But he was content to omit the ball valve and let the oil pressure merely deaden the sound without automatically adjusting the tappet clearance to zero.

One of the disadvantages of the hydraulic self-adjusting tappet is a tendency to pump itself up at high speeds, resulting in an adjustment which prevents the valve from seating. In 1968 Ford devised a double valve seating system which avoided this.

Another interesting combination, developed in 1947 by Bernard Samuelson, was the use of a screwed piston to vary the volume of trapped oil in a hydraulic tappet. His method adjusted the lift of the valves and consequently altered the valve timing.

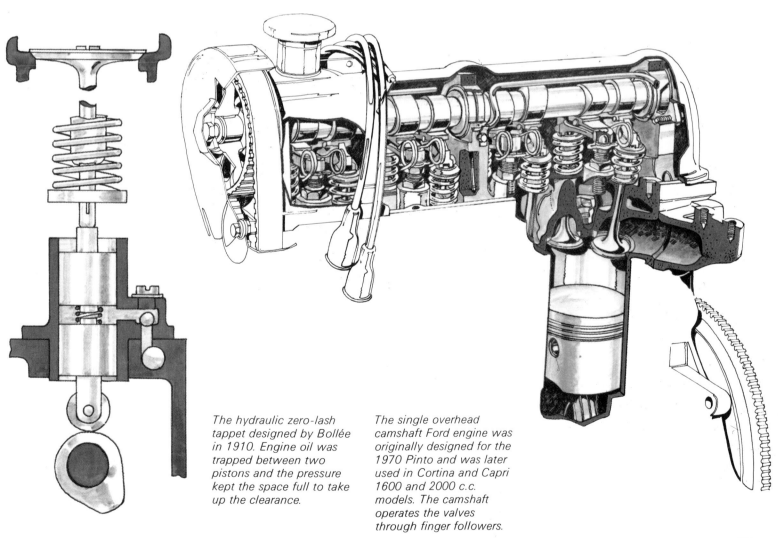

The hydraulic zero-lash tappet designed by Bollée in 1910. Engine oil was trapped between two pistons and the pressure kept the space full to take up the clearance.

The single overhead camshaft Ford engine was originally designed for the 1970 Pinto and was later used in Cortina and Capri 1600 and 2000 c.c. models. The camshaft operates the valves through finger followers.

Introduced in 1973, The Triumph Dolomite Sprint gained nearly 40 per cent more power by the incorporation of an ingenious four-valve cylinder head.

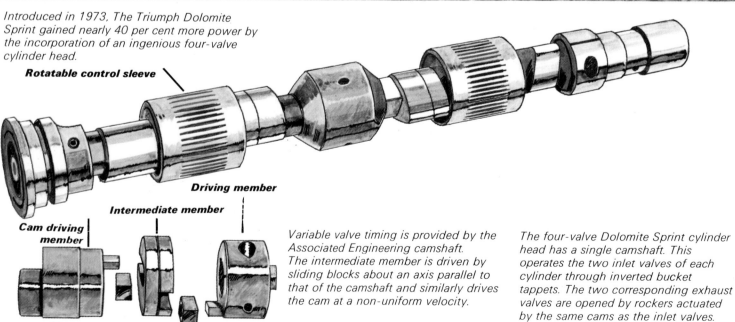

Rotatable control sleeve

Driving member

Intermediate member

Cam driving member

Variable valve timing is provided by the Associated Engineering camshaft. The intermediate member is driven by sliding blocks about an axis parallel to that of the camshaft and similarly drives the cam at a non-uniform velocity.

The four-valve Dolomite Sprint cylinder head has a single camshaft. This operates the two inlet valves of each cylinder through inverted bucket tappets. The two corresponding exhaust valves are opened by rockers actuated by the same cams as the inlet valves.

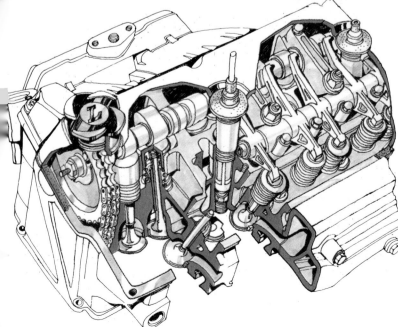

Instead of the "hit and miss" governing system of the 1899 Daimler and many other engines of that period, where the exhaust valve mechanism had an extra member between the cam follower and valve stem, which could be moved out of the way to prevent the exhaust valve opening and so stop the engine from firing until the speed had dropped, other designs made use of a tapered cam. This could be slid along the camshaft by a governor, or other control, to vary the lift of the exhaust valve and so affect the speed.

These older ideas of varying the timing of valves have recently come back to prominence in the cause of anti-pollution, where complete and efficient combustion is essential to prevent too much of the wrong kind of gases escaping down the exhaust pipe. It is relatively easy to tune an engine for one particular speed. But, when the speed variation is of the order of one to six, some means of enabling the timing of the valves to be varied is an attractive development.

While such devices, in unsuccessful forms, date back for many years, two firms, Fiat and Associated Engineering have recently developed new systems. Associated Engineering's system permits variation both of the moment and the duration of opening of a valve. These are inter-related as the cam profile remains the same.

Reference to the valve timing figures quoted earlier for the Ford Cortina (page 18), will reveal that both the inlet and exhaust valves are opened for the same angular movement of the crankshaft (i.e 248 degrees). Thus both the inlet and exhaust cams are of the same shape but at different positions around the camshaft so that they operate at different times.

In designing the cylinder head of the Triumph Dolomite Sprint engine, with four valves per cylinder, space for the valve-operating gear became a little cramped. To solve this, C. Spencer King re-introduced the idea of using each cam to operate both an inlet valve (directly, via a tappet) and an exhaust valve (by means of a rocker). The idea of one cam for both valves was pioneered by Zurcher in 1903.

VALVE SPRINGS

The obvious way to snap a valve shut rapidly and securely on its seating is to use a spring, a system employed on nearly all poppet valve internal combustion engines since their first few faltering chuffs.

As engine speeds increased, the acceleration of the valve from its seat and, of course, that end of the spring attached to the valve, increased greatly until a point was reached when the coils of the spring began to accelerate on their own. This occurred when the frequency of the valve opening was the same as the natural vibration frequency of the spring, a condition known as surge.

If the spring was made heavier to stop this, it only reduced the frequency and surge occurred at lower engine speeds. If the spring was lighter it could not shut the valve properly. A number of remedies were tried. Alvis used nine small springs clustered round the valve stem. Other manufacturers such as Daimler, Benz and Leyland used blade or leaf springs. Some used springs shaped like hairpins, with the advantage that the coils kept cooler at the expense of space. Panhard even used bars in torsion to shut the valves.

However, since all springs have a natural vibration frequency, the problem still remains. A fairly early solution, which is still major current practice, was to put two springs of different frequency together, one inside the other. If one spring began to surge, the other would still maintain the valve operation.

DESMODROMIC VALVES

Some designers concluded that the common spring was not good enough to stand up to high-speed work and they devised complicated systems to open and shut the valves mechanically. A form of desmodromic valve gear appeared in 1913 when Samuel White and Company, the shipbuilders, used a cam with a groove in its side face, into which a hooked end of the valve stem was fitted. The device had been used earlier on a few special engines and on rotary aero-engines.

By 1918 the idea had grown of using two cams on shafts above and below a valve-operating rocker (Cat-

Below: Desmodromic valve gear was fitted to the 1945 Mercedes-Benz 300 SLR. This gear shut the valves mechanically through a second cam and rocker.

Right: The 1903 Clement. The 1902 model was the first production car in which both inlet and exhaust valves were opened by an overhead camshaft.

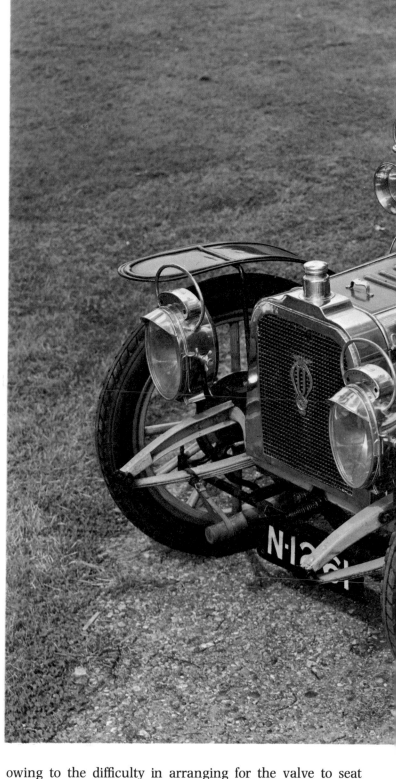

taneo). In the same year, S. J. Burt used a forked rocker, which contacted two points on the cam.

Desmodromic valve gear was experimented with over the following years and in 1945 Mercedes-Benz used it on the engines of their 300 SLR sports car. In this arrangement the camshaft was directly over the valve stem and had an opening and closing cam for each valve.

The opening cam acted on a tappet and the closing cam on a lever having one arm bearing on the surface of the closing cam, and another arm forked to pass each side of a flattened portion of the valve stem and bear under the head of the stem end.

The desmodromic gear has never found much favour

owing to the difficulty in arranging for the valve to seat in the cylinder head in a gas tight fashion without excessive stress on the stem and operating levers.

VALVE GEAR

Although the position of the valves changed slowly over the years from side by side to both in the cylinder head, as a greater understanding of the combustion process grew, there were occasional examples of non-contemporary valve locations. For example, in 1902 Adolphe Clément devised an engine with both valves vertical in the head and operated by a single camshaft above the engine, in other words an overhead camshaft or O.H.C. engine.

Clément was a rugged Parisian individualist who had graduated to car production after considerable experience of manufacturing bicycles. His racing bicycles were especially well known, as Clément always seemed interested in this aspect of his business. His sons took to the track with his models when he went over to cars.

One of them, Albert, was killed practising for a French Grand Prix. But this still did not prevent his father from entering other models in the race. Most makers of that period were still using a side exhaust valve and an overhead automatic inlet valve. With side valves the operation was as simple as it could be. All that was needed was a gear on the crankshaft end meshing with a gear of twice

the diameter on the camshaft (to produce half the speed).

With the move of the valves to the cylinder head, the camshaft could still be driven and located in the same way, motion being transmitted by pushrods to rocking levers carried in bearings on the cylinder head. These were encased in a rocker cover to keep out dust and to keep in oil and noise.

The oil became something of a problem, since it could drain down the valve stems and get into the cylinder, aided by the suction on the inlet side. A multiplicity of devices was developed to prevent excess drainage. These varied from simple systems like felt washers to helical springs made from thin, flat steel to enclose the valve stems. There were, in addition, some fairly elaborate types of oil seal.

As the distances from the cam followers to the rockers, particularly on engines with long strokes, needed long and slender pushrods, the camshafts gradually moved upwards. The simple system of two gears was superseded by a chain drive to save the use either of very large gears or of a train of gears.

This worked well. However, the advent of the hemispherical cylinder head with its valves angled to the cylinder axis, made it easier to put the camshaft over the valves, as Clément had done. This design also removed trouble caused by pushrods bending under the compression load of opening the valves.

To avoid the side thrust of the cam wiping across the end of the valve stem and to provide some system of adjustment of the tappet clearances, a rocker was used, with the cam bearing on a pad around mid-length and an adjusting screw bearing on a hardened cap over the valve stem. In some instances, such as the M.G.s of the 1930s, the adjustment was made by eccentric bushes for the rocker bearings.

Another system used, particularly where there are two camshafts (one for each row of valves), is an inverted flat-ended cylinder or bucket. This is guided in a bearing in the cylinder head. The cam bears on the bucket with the valve stem inside the bucket. Adjustment is provided usually by fitting, inside the bucket, thin circles of steel (shims) whose thickness is chosen to give the desired clearance.

Once the camshaft had moved above the cylinder head, there were problems of driving it. Some makers, such as Alfa Romeo, preferred a long train of small gears, particularly when two camshafts were to be driven.

These tended to be noisy in operation, owing to the fluctuations in torque load as the cams moved round to open the valves against the springs and then, as the valves began to shut, when the springs began to rotate the cams. The clattering came as the clearances between gear teeth were taken up, first in one direction and then, as the cycle continued, in the other.

Just as the chain drive allowed the camshaft to be positioned higher up the crankcase, so it proved suitable for use with both single or double overhead camshafts. The single O.H.C. engine, designed by John Weller for A.C. in 1919, had an inverted tooth chain, with gear tooth projections on the chain engaging with gear shaped sprockets on the crankshaft and camshaft. Later versions of this engine, which continued in production until 1963, used conventional roller chains. All versions of the engine had their chains tensioned by a curved blade spring pressing on a considerable length of the outside of the chain to prevent whipping.

Weller was an engineering genius who will also be remembered for his part in launching a famous firm – A.C. Cars. At the turn of the century, he got together with just the right man to complement his gifts – a prosperous butcher with the rosily optimistic name of John Portwine.

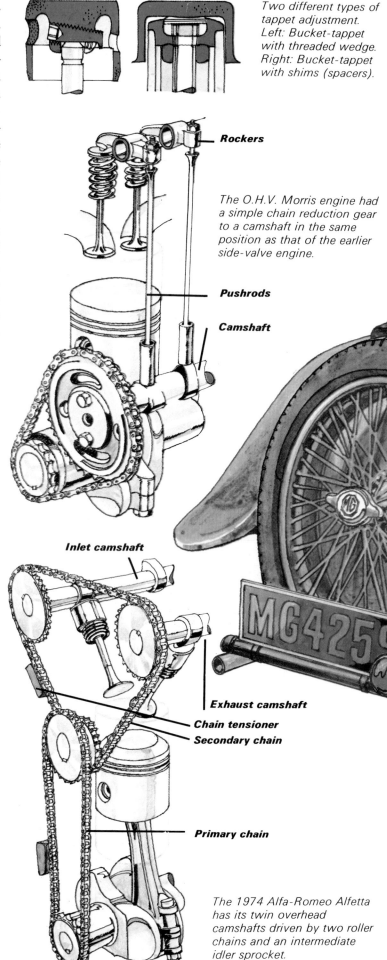

Two different types of tappet adjustment. Left: Bucket-tappet with threaded wedge. Right: Bucket-tappet with shims (spacers).

Rockers

The O.H.V. Morris engine had a simple chain reduction gear to a camshaft in the same position as that of the earlier side-valve engine.

Pushrods

Camshaft

Inlet camshaft

Exhaust camshaft

Chain tensioner

Secondary chain

Primary chain

The 1974 Alfa-Romeo Alfetta has its twin overhead camshafts driven by two roller chains and an intermediate idler sprocket.

Both the MG and Morris Minor below had single overhead camshaft engines. A pair of bevel gears drove the vertical armature shaft of the dynamo mounted in front of the engine. Another pair of bevel gears, with a two to one ratio, drove the camshaft from the top of the armature shaft.

It was the dawn of an era when motor manufacturing firms mushroomed at an extraordinary rate. Every little business with some degree of mechanical involvement, if only a way with lawnmowers, nurtured the vision of building and selling a horseless carriage.

Weller and Portwine started a small engineering concern with Portwine looking after the business side and his partner attending to the nuts and bolts. It says much for Portwine's shrewdness that when, in 1904, they built their famous Autocarrier (its abbreviation gave the firm its name) the aim was not grandiose but strictly functional.

This tricar began life as a commercial vehicle but was soon extended to passenger use. A.C. was to go on to achieve four-wheel successes, an outstanding reputation with light cars, and records galore at Brooklands.

The Weller tensioner was used for various applications, and the usual versions had the blade held in a bowed shape by a tension spring between the ends. It was necessary to maintain this tension both for taking up slack in the chain, which would otherwise have affected valve timing, and to absorb torsional fluctuations in the camshaft.

Other tensioners include small idler sprockets loaded by springs at the back of the chain. Sometimes both systems are used in the same engine, an example being the drive for the two overhead camshafts of the Jaguar XK 120. This has a Weller-type tensioner for the first chain, which drives a double intermediate sprocket at half crankshaft speed. The second sprocket takes drive, by means of a V-shaped loop, round the two camshaft sprockets, and a tensioner (idler) sprocket inside the bottom of the V.

Another form of chain tensioner developed by Austin in 1944 used synthetic rubber rings in grooves formed in the sprockets, so that the links, and not the rollers, of the chain ran on the elastic material. This not only kept the chain tensioned but considerably reduced the noise.

A further system of overhead camshaft drive, employed

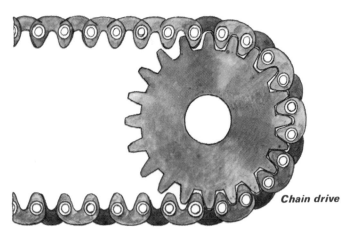

Chain drive

Right: The largest of the pre-Derby Bentleys. An eight litre straight-six with a single, eccentric driven, overhead camshaft. Only 100 of these 220 horsepower cars were made in 1931.

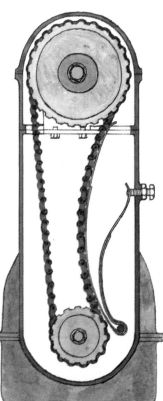

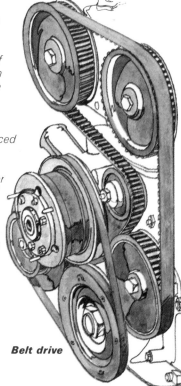

John Weller, the brains of the original AC partnership, designed the blade spring type of chain tensioner used on his and other cars since 1919 (left).

The inverted tooth chain on the early ACs (above) was later replaced by a roller chain.

After the roller chain came the toothed rubber belt (right), quieter and needing no lubrication. This belt was nothing more than a version of the inverted tooth chain with greater flexibility.

Belt drive

Blade spring tensioner

by Bentley in the eight-litre of 1931 and by N.S.U. in the much later Prinz of 1958, used a system of eccentrics and connecting rods to provide a smooth and silent camshaft operation.

A vertical shaft driving the camshaft through a worm gear was used for the 1902 Maudslay and a similar vertical shaft with bevel gears at both ends was used in the O.H.C. Morris Minor of 1929 and the M.G. cars derived from it. In the latter examples the driving shaft was also used as the armature shaft of the dynamo and was equipped with a flexible joint at its upper end to allow for inevitable cylinder expansion.

In the search for a quiet and cheap camshaft drive, the advent of the inextensible toothed belt in 1945 was welcomed first by Goggomobil and then by Fiat and Vauxhall, among many others.

These belts are made from oil-resistant synthetic rubbers moulded over a core of inextensible nylon or steel wires and have gear teeth moulded on their inner surfaces. These teeth engage teeth on gears on the crankshafts and camshafts. Since these belts work efficiently without lubrication, they do not require expensive oil-tight casings and can be left uncased or merely covered by a light guard.

ROTARY VALVES

The poppet valve is still the most popular type and has outlived all other types for reciprocating internal combustion engines. Continual developments over some 80 years has overcome the original drawbacks of noise, poor combustion chamber shape, constant need for clearance adjustment, bouncing and spring breakages at high speeds.

Today the poppet maintains its advantages of simplicity, with protection of the sealing surface against the heat of combustion over at least the worst part of the cycle and of the lack of sliding sealing surfaces needing lubrication. But many experimenters have had ideas for devices which are more attractive mechanically in having smoother motions.

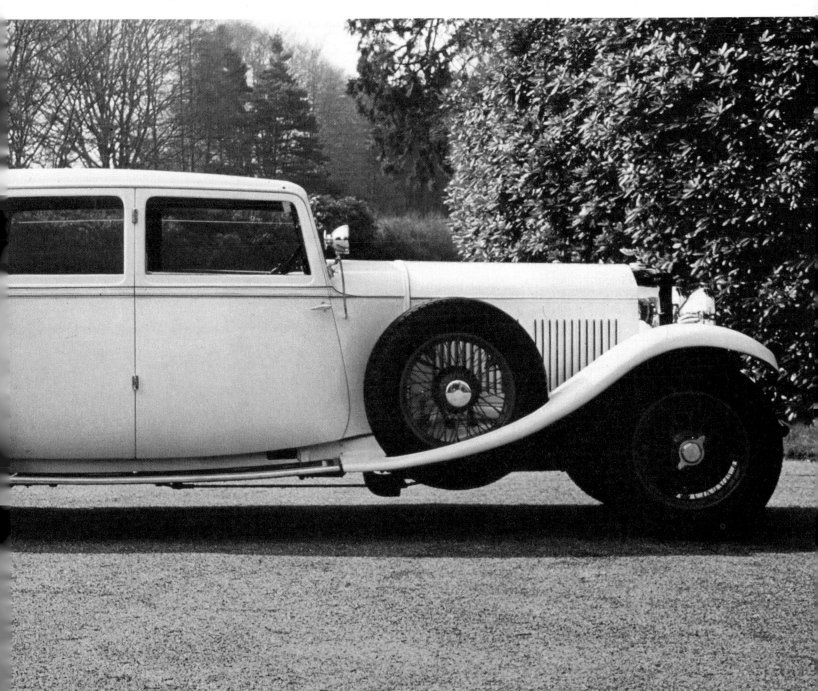

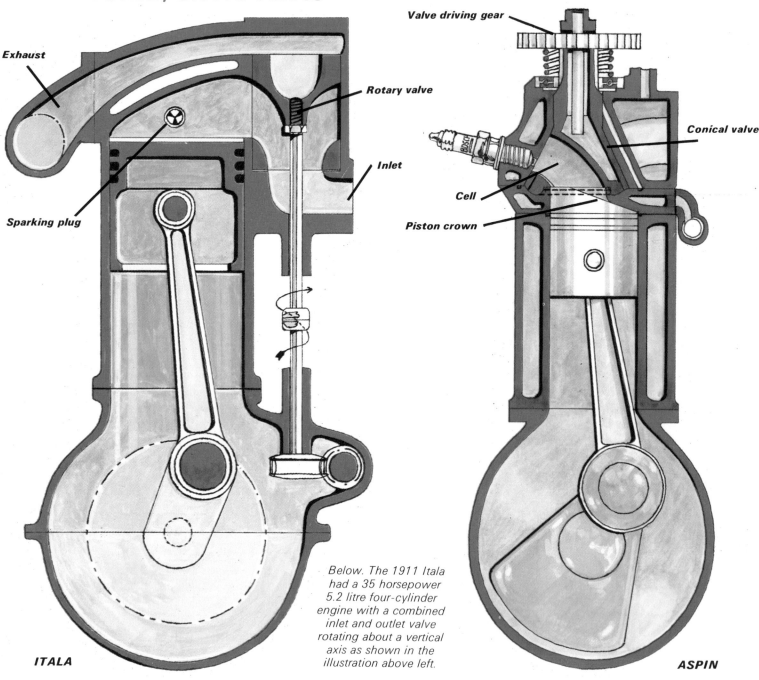

Exhaust

Rotary valve

Inlet

Sparking plug

ITALA

Valve driving gear

Conical valve

Cell

Piston crown

ASPIN

Below. The 1911 Itala had a 35 horsepower 5.2 litre four-cylinder engine with a combined inlet and outlet valve rotating about a vertical axis as shown in the illustration above left.

Early engines, which were stationary and often run on town gas to drive workshop machinery, followed steam practice and used flat sliding valves. As engine speeds and gas temperatures increased these proved unsuitable.

Edward Butler used rotating valves with holes or ports cut in them in his tricycle of 1887. They were driven to allow the ports to open to the combustion chamber at the proper times. After this many rotary valves were tried, mostly without success. But three that are worth noting are the Itala of 1911, the Aspin of 1936 and the Cross of 1923, which broadly represent the three main types.

The earliest of these, the Itala, was the only one of the three examples which really went into production. It was used from 1911 to 1922 and had a rotating cylindrical valve at the side of the combustion chamber. Each valve served a pair of cylinders and had openings at each end, leading to ports on opposite sides. The inlet ports were at the bottom of the valve and the exhaust ports at the top. The valve rotated to line up with the appropriate ports in

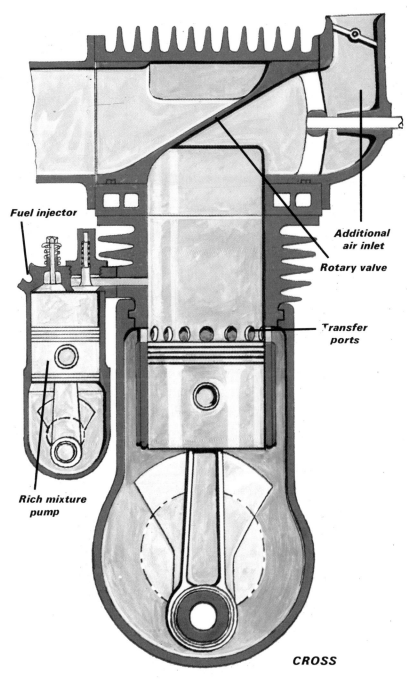

Fuel injector

Additional air inlet

Rotary valve

Transfer ports

Rich mixture pump

CROSS

THE ITALA rotating cylindrical valve was at the side of the combustion chamber and each valve served a pair of cylinders. A slot led from each combustion chamber to a port in the valve housing. The valve was driven through a vertical shaft, by worm gearing, from an engine speed driven shaft parallel to the crankshaft. Openings in the ends of the valve led to rectangular ports in the side of the valve. The inlet mixture flowed from the bottom of the valve, turned through a right-angle and through a curved passage to the combustion chamber. The exhaust gas followed the same path in reverse, but was led out of the top of the valve. To serve two cylinders, two valve ports were cut diametrically opposite each other in the valve wall.

THE ASPIN valve was conical and formed the combustion chamber in the cylinder head. It had a major diameter slightly greater than the cylinder bore and rotated at half engine speed. This conical valve had a cell, or port, leading from an eccentric position in the base of the cone to an opening in the conical wall. The cell was the combustion chamber and the wall opening

faced the inlet port, the sparking plug and the exhaust port in order. On the compression stroke, the gas was turbulently forced into the cell. The cell rotated to throw the gas against the plug as it sparked. Since flame travels against, and at a similar speed to, a moving gas mixture the flame and its front had no definite direction due to the turbulence. Since there was no definite flame front, there was no opportunity for detonation. In addition as soon as combustion began the sparking plug was shielded and could not overheat to cause pre-ignition.

THE CROSS rotary valve was similar to the Itala, but was positioned over the top of the cylinder with its axis. parallel to the crankshaft. In the original 1923 design of the Cross engine fuel was injected into a reciprocating air compressor to give a rich mixture. This mixture was weakened by additional air from throttle controlled crankcase transfer ports and from a main air inlet through the valve. This gave a degree of supercharging and a fuel injection system in which the mixture strength was set by controlling the air flow through the transfer and valve ports.

the combustion chamber at the correct times for gas flow.

The Aspin valve formed the top of the cylinder head and rotated to uncover the inlet and exhaust ports and the sparking plug. This valve was notable for avoiding problems of detonation and as soon as combustion began it shielded the sparking plug again so that the plug could not overheat to cause pre-ignition. In fact, engines were run with compression ratios twice as high as conventional engines using the same fuel. This interesting design became dormant through lack of development in valve sealing and because of the onset of the Second World War.

The third form of rotary valve, which R. C. Cross began to develop in 1923, was similar to the Itala but was positioned at the top of the combustion chamber with its axis parallel to the crankshaft. Development was carried out on this design for some fifteen years and in the late 1930s, it was showing considerable promise. But again events overtook this fascinating design, and it has not yet been used on a production vehicle.

SLEEVE VALVES

While some of the earliest engines followed steam practice in using either flat-faced or cylindrical reciprocating valves (which were doomed to eventual failure because they could not provide a combustion chamber of efficient shape), a second school of thought devised and developed sleeve valves which were cylinder liners, with ports cut in them, moving up and down.

But first, C. Y. Knight, an American publisher, devised an engine in 1905 in which the cylinder, as well as the piston, reciprocated and the cylinder head remained stationary.

A complicated gear and double crank mechanism in the bottom of the crankcase lowered the cylinder on the suction stroke to allow a ring of ports in the bore to coincide with the inlet pipe. As the piston rose on the compression stroke, the cylinder rose with it until the ports were closed. Then the piston went on alone to compress the charge. The cylinder remained stationary during the firing stroke and, when the piston was near bottom dead centre, it uncovered a row of exhaust ports fitted in the cylinder wall.

More exhaust was provided by further cylinder movement to uncover additional exhaust ports in the cylinder head as the piston rose. The movement of the cylinder was also used to provide a blast of compressed air into the combustion chamber to facilitate the scavenging of exhaust gases.

Three years later, Knight had a much less complicated idea when he used two concentric sleeves between the piston and cylinder bore. In fact, the inner sleeve was the bore in which the piston worked. Both sleeves were given reciprocating motion by a pair of eccentrics, or cranks, on a half-speed shaft, which corresponded to a camshaft.

This design provided admission and exhaust through the cylinder wall area of the combustion space, and allowed a relatively free design of combustion chamber shape and sparking plug position. Moreover it allowed excellent cooling of the cylinder head. The double-sleeve valve engine was used with success in the Daimler-Knight of 1908 and was renowned for its silent and efficient operation, the reason for this being that it had no noise-generating cams, tappets or poppet valves.

The sleeve valve engine had the advantages of fewer parts, much less mechanical noise and, once the problems of lubricating all the sliding sleeve surfaces had been solved, an ability to run reliably for long periods. Its main drawbacks were a rather high oil consumption and a limitation on engine speed because of the inertia loadings of the sleeves.

J. H. K. McCollum of Toronto devised an engine in 1909 with only one cylindrical distributing valve, or sleeve. This had a combined reciprocating and oscillating motion and surrounded the water-cooled cylinder head of the engine. Two annular passages outside the valve formed the main inlet and exhaust passages, and these had radial ports leading to two rows of openings in the cylinder bore. The linkwork for these movements was very complicated and would never have allowed high-speed smooth running.

Later the same year, P. Burt of Argylls Limited used the same idea of a combined reciprocating and oscillating motion in the drive for a single sleeve positioned in the cylinder, between the bore and the piston. The sleeve was driven at half crankshaft speed and the ports in their elliptical orbit uncovered the inlet, remained closed and uncovered the outlet as shown in the diagram far right.

The 15–30 Argyll was built in Glasgow between 1909 and 1914 but eventually the cost of lawsuits over patent rights in its Burt-McCallum single-sleeve valve engine caused the end of manufacture.

The shape of the port openings was designed to produce the correct timing of events and the fastest opening and closing times. Although the single-sleeve valve was used only on the Argyll and one Vauxhall model, it was employed extensively in aircraft engines until the advent of the gas turbine which proved to be more efficient.

TWO-STROKES

Another form of engine which has been used consistently in smaller sizes is the two-stroke in which, as the name suggests, the four phases of the engine cycle are condensed into one crankshaft revolution, or two strokes of the piston. The fundamental idea of valving in this engine is the uncovering and covering of ports in the cylinder walls by the piston itself.

The cycle of events is generally credited to Sir Dugald Clark but two of his contemporaries, Robson and Fielding, were working on the same lines between 1877 and 1881. The most common type of two-stroke engine that evolved owed something to all three. Clark produced the two-stroke cycle by using a separate pump to scavenge the cylinder of exhaust gases, and Robson used Clark's cycle and employed the underside of the piston to scavenge the cylinder. Fielding devised a transfer port, where the

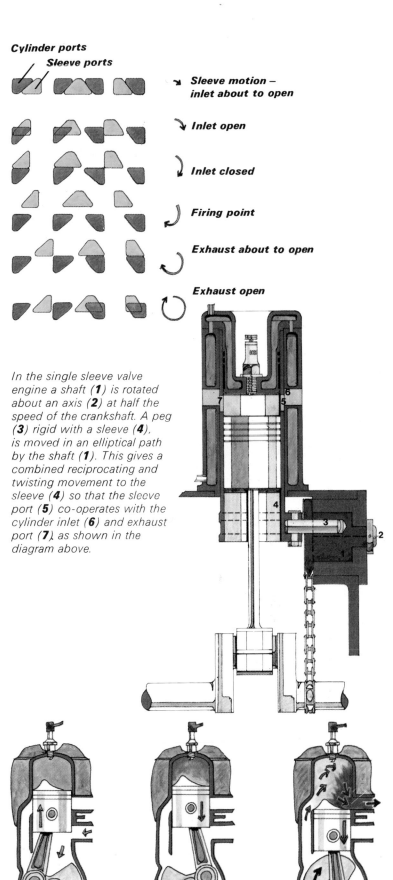

Cylinder ports
Sleeve ports

Sleeve motion –
inlet about to open

Inlet open

Inlet closed

Firing point

Exhaust about to open

Exhaust open

In the single sleeve valve engine a shaft (1) is rotated about an axis (2) at half the speed of the crankshaft. A peg (3) rigid with a sleeve (4), is moved in an elliptical path by the shaft (1). This gives a combined reciprocating and twisting movement to the sleeve (4) so that the sleeve port (5) co-operates with the cylinder inlet (6) and exhaust port (7) as shown in the diagram above.

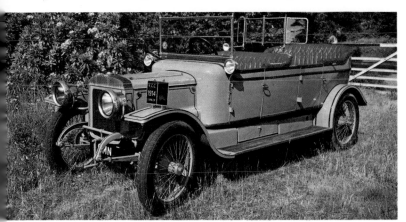

This 1914 English Daimler followed its 1909 ancestor in having a Knight double-sleeve valve engine and a worm drive rear axle. These were often called Silent-Knights.

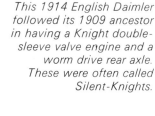

The Two-Stroke Cycle

As the piston ascends mixture is drawn through the inlet port into the crankcase. The descending piston pushes this mixture up through the transfer port to the combustion chamber. The piston rises on the compression stroke, the

sparking plug ignites the fuel mixture and the piston goes down on the power stroke. The new charge from the transfer port sweeps across the combustion space to push the burnt gas out through the exhaust port.

incoming mixture was moved from the crankcase to the combustion chamber by the descent of the piston.

In the two-stroke cycle, as the piston ascends on the compression stroke, the increasing volume in the crankcase and under the piston draws the mixture into the crankcase below the piston. The descent of the piston forces the mixture up through a transfer passage, which opens into the cylinder bore and is uncovered by the piston crown as it descends.

The piston ascends for the compression stroke and descends on the firing stroke to uncover the exhaust port towards the end of its stroke and, at the same time, again open the inlet port of the transfer passage.

In earlier engines a deflector on the piston crown directed fresh mixture from the transfer passage up to the cylinder head on one side of the bore. The flow of fresh gas went across the combustion chamber top to sweep the spent gas down and out of the exhaust port.

Later designs employed a flat-top piston and directed the gas flow with more careful thought about the shape and direction of the several passages. Often the device used a port in the piston skirt to control gas flow into the transfer passage, a scheme which helped to cool the piston crown

interior. These ideas had first been mooted by the German, Schnuerle. Other designs, few of which went into serious production for cars, used positive displacement compressors and valves to aid the gas flow.

An early engine to employ two pistons sharing a common combustion chamber and with the pistons moving together was devised by R. Lucas in 1904. He used a two-year-old idea of his own, whereby neat fuel was drawn into the transfer passage after a fuel valve had been opened by air inlet suction. This was one of the early forms of fuel injection.

By 1909 Lucas had designed an engine with two crankshafts geared together to run in opposite directions and have their centre-lines offset to the centres of the parallel cylinder bores, there being a common combustion chamber above the two cylinders.

As the two pistons descended together on the firing stroke, one opened the exhaust ports in its cylinder bore and the other opened the inlet ports to allow the charge in the crankcase to swirl into that bore across the combustion chamber and push out the exhaust gases. As the pistons rose for compression, the air inlet valve was sucked off its seating, opening the fuel valve, and the next

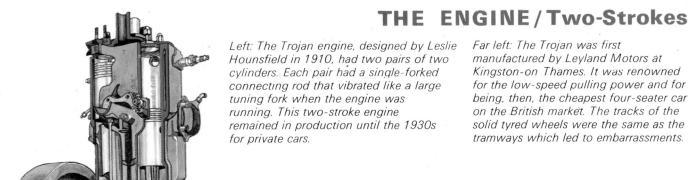

Left: The Trojan engine, designed by Leslie Hounsfield in 1910, had two pairs of two cylinders. Each pair had a single-forked connecting rod that vibrated like a large tuning fork when the engine was running. This two-stroke engine remained in production until the 1930s for private cars.

Far left: The Trojan was first manufactured by Leyland Motors at Kingston-on Thames. It was renowned for the low-speed pulling power and for being, then, the cheapest four-seater car on the British market. The tracks of the solid tyred wheels were the same as the tramways which led to embarrassments.

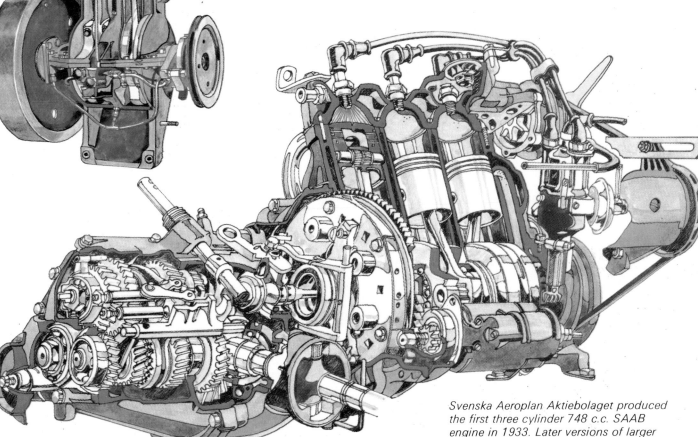

Svenska Aeroplan Aktiebolaget produced the first three cylinder 748 c.c. SAAB engine in 1933. Later versions of larger capacity with three tuned carburettors were very successful in international rallies.

charge was admitted to the crankcase. This engine was made by David Brown and Company.

A somewhat similar double piston system of working was used for many years in the Trojan car from 1922

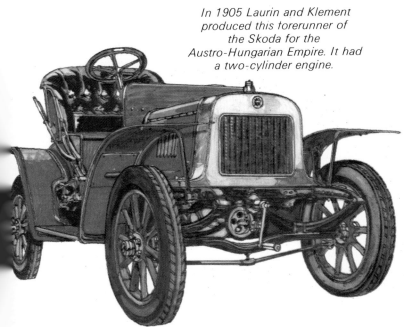

In 1905 Laurin and Klement produced this forerunner of the Skoda for the Austro-Hungarian Empire. It had a two-cylinder engine.

onwards. The Trojan engine had two pairs of cylinders side by side and dispensed with the spring-loaded inlet valves for air and fuel. Each pair of cylinders used a V-shaped connecting rod which sprang open and shut to some degree as the pistons moved up and down the bores.

The piston timing was such that the exhaust opened before the inlet ports on the down stroke and closed the exhaust before the inlet on the up stroke. A wire gauze in the transfer passage acted as a flame trap to stop the crankcase charge catching alight.

Ricardo turned his attention to the two-stroke in 1909. He used a separate pumping cylinder, arranged at an angle to the main cylinder, to draw in and compress the charge which, at a predetermined pressure, opened a flap valve in the main cylinder head when its piston was in the region of bottom dead centre.

His engine, known as the Dolphin, was used in Hampton and Weston light cars. A similar charging pump was used in the D.K.W. two-strokes of 1928 and in the Trojan of 1947. More conventional two-stroke engines of three cylinders powered the Saab 92 and D.K.W. Sonderklasse from 1950 and 1953 onwards, and continue to be used in the Wartburg.

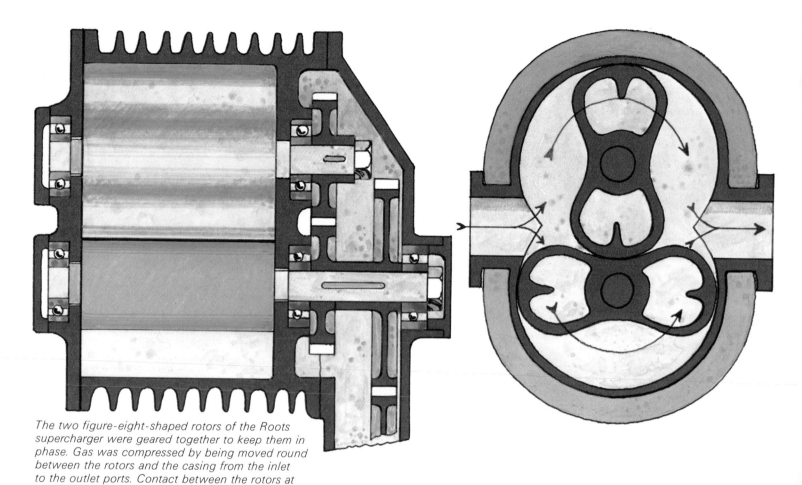

The two figure-eight-shaped rotors of the Roots supercharger were geared together to keep them in phase. Gas was compressed by being moved round between the rotors and the casing from the inlet to the outlet ports. Contact between the rotors at the centre prevented back flow of gas.

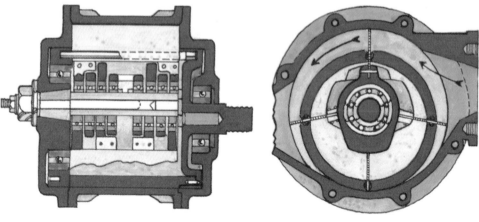

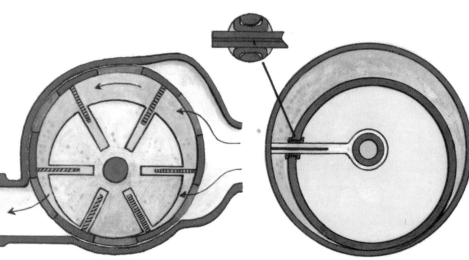

Left: The Centric supercharger had four vanes pivoted to a central rotor and passing through an eccentric sleeve. The volume between the vanes, sleeve and casing changed to compress the gas.

Below left: Six radially-sliding vanes in an eccentric rotor provided the volume change in the Cozette supercharger. left: Only one blade, pivoted on the axis of an eccentric rotor was used in the Powerplus design, right.

Right: Without the bodywork, the Mercedes 38/250K with its supercharged engine looks even more rugged and powerful. This was possibly the ultimate sports car of the mid 1930s.

SUPERCHARGERS

It will be realized that the use of a pumping cylinder could, and did, result in the charge being introduced to the combustion chamber at a pressure higher than that of the normal atmosphere. Therefore more mixture could be available to provide more power per firing stroke.

This point had not been overlooked by designers of four-stroke engines and supercharging, as it was known, was experimented with as far back as the turn of the century, although with reciprocating pumps.

Ten years later rotary pumps were being tried but none of these reached production cars until at least the mid-1920s, when superchargers were first used on sports cars.

The supercharger, in producing greater power from a given engine size, has its disadvantages. These are mainly in the much greater amount of heat generated in the engine and in the carry-over of the oil needed to lubricate the blower, besides the power needed for driving it.

Just as the air is heated by the compression within the cylinder, so it is heated by compression in a supercharger. Although these pumps increased the pressure by only a few pounds per square inch, the increased heat and the additional final pressure within the combustion chamber required either an improvement in the anti-detonation properties of the fuel or a lowering of the engine compression ratio.

Broadly speaking, two types of compressor were used. One was the Centric or Cozette, which had rotors with radially sliding vanes working within an eccentric casing. The other was the Roots originally designed on a much larger scale by Jones in 1859 for ventilating coal mines, which had two intermeshing rotors of figure eight shape.

The Roots-type supercharger was used mounted vertically in front of the engine of the 1924 Mercedes 15/70/100, which later developed into the legendary SS and SSK from 1929 to 1934. Unlike other cars such as Lea Francis, Frazer-Nash and A.C., which compressed the fuel/air mixture, the Mercedes blew into the carburettor. Moreover, in the interests of fuel economy and engine life, the blower was driven through a disc clutch which was engaged only when the throttle pedal was fully depressed.

With the advent of wartime fuel shortages and low octane ratings, the supercharger was largely abandoned except for a few firms which fitted them as extras to standard engines. Larger capacity engines to produce the required higher power were more the fashion.

A more recent form of supercharging is the use of the turbo-blower in which a turbine, driven by the gases on their way down the exhaust system, powers a centrifugal fan or blower, thus aiding the mixture on its way between the carburettor and inlet ports. In 1971, Ralph Broad developed a system in which the use of a turbo-charger was rendered optional by a switch on the facia and a solenoid-operated changeover valve passed unpressurized air to the carburettor when extra power was not wanted.

CARBURATION

Petrol is a hydrocarbon, which means that it is one of the family of chemicals composed of hydrogen and carbon. It usually contains additional chemicals, or additives, which modify the manner and rate at which it burns. When considering the way in which fuel burns, it is easier to think of weights rather than volumes. One pound of petrol contains 0·84 pounds of carbon and 0·16 pounds of hydrogen. This requires three pounds of oxygen to achieve exact and complete combustion and, since air consists of only one-fifth oxygen to four-fifths of nitrogen, a weight of fifteen pounds of air is required to burn one pound of petrol.

When the whole of the fuel is burned, the exhaust gas contains 2·7 pounds of carbon dioxide, 1·3 pounds of water and twelve pounds of nitrogen. However, combustion is never complete. Since air contains other gases in small quantities and petrol is a more complex chemical mixture than outlined above, the exhaust also contains carbon monoxide, oxides of nitrogen, some unburnt petrol vapour and other impurities.

As well as in the theoretically ideal ratio of fifteen to one, petrol and air will burn with rich mixtures containing only eight parts of air and with weak mixtures having as much as twenty four parts of air by weight. This was fortunate for the pioneers of the internal combustion engine. For their first way of mixing the fuel and air (carburetting) was to allow a wick to soak up the fuel and to pass the air over the soaking wick so that the resultant flow was a fuel-laden air.

This was known as a wick carburettor and had a variable inlet for extra air, enabling the mixture strength to be kept within the limits in which it would burn in the engine. Such a device was susceptible to road shocks because bumps in uneven roads splashed the petrol further up the wick and produced mixture strengths too rich for continuous running.

In 1885, Daimler devised a surface carburettor in which a float, free to rise and fall with the level of the fuel in a container, had a conical depression at its centre. A vertical inlet pipe was fixed to the bottom of the depression to form an air inlet. It extended through the container lid and it had transverse holes near the fixing point. The top of the container was sealed off, except at the point where the inlet pipe projected through it, and was connected to the engine inlet port.

When the engine began its suction stroke, air was drawn through the inlet pipe to bubble through the transverse holes below the fuel level and the resulting fuel-wet air was drawn into the cylinder. Although this surface carburettor was not upset too much by road shocks, it did not provide a particularly accurate mixture strength.

In 1887, Edward Butler invented a carburettor which made use of facts discovered by an Italian, Venturi, while experimenting in the 1790s with the way fluid flows in pipes. Venturi found that if the velocity of a fluid was increased by reducing the bore of a pipe smoothly and the bore was gently increased to its original size, the rate of

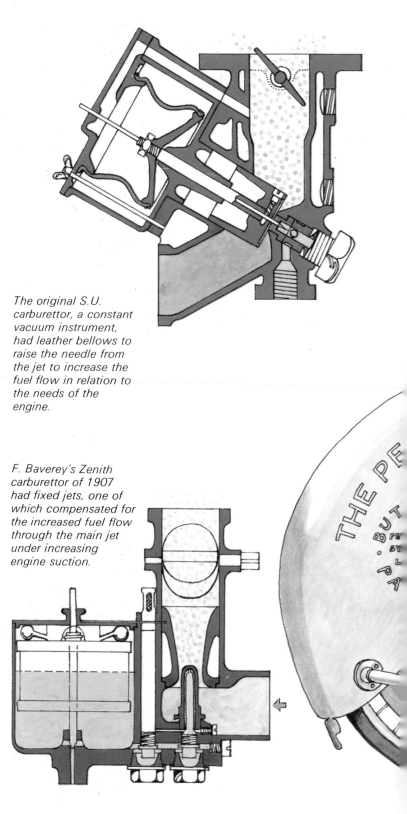

The original S.U. carburettor, a constant vacuum instrument, had leather bellows to raise the needle from the jet to increase the fuel flow in relation to the needs of the engine.

F. Baverey's Zenith carburettor of 1907 had fixed jets, one of which compensated for the increased fuel flow through the main jet under increasing engine suction.

fluid flow was virtually unaltered. The pressure in the fluid was found to decrease in relation to the decreased cross-sectional area of the pipe at the measurement point. Therefore if the inlet air is flowing under atmospheric pressure into a pipe having a reduction of area, then the pressure will be less than atmospheric at the reduction and will be proportional to the reduction in area.

In Butler's carburettor the fuel level was kept constant by means of a ball float like that in a household cistern. A duct from the float chamber led to an opening, or jet, which

As well as a float chamber, Butler included an adjustment for the fuel flow through the main jet and a Venturi shape choke to increase the suction on that jet.

Among the many original ideas on Edward Butler's 1887 tricycle was a variable jet carburettor and the first use of a ball valve, or float chamber, to maintain a constant level of fuel in the jet.

protruded into a pipe forming part of the inlet air passage to the engine. This jet was slightly above the fuel level and the inlet passage had a contraction or choke in the region of the jet.

An adjusting screw was provided to vary the flow of the fuel through the jet and another one to vary the area of the choke. When the inlet valve opened air was drawn along the choke passage and the pressure drop at the choke caused fuel to issue from the jet in a fine spray which mixed with the air to produce a combustible mixture. Un-

fortunately for Butler, his inventions were not noticed and, five years later, William Maybach, Gottlieb Daimler's associate, thought of the same idea. Maybach's carburettor was used on Daimler engines such as the 1899 engine shown earlier.

In all carburettors the ideal is to produce a fuel gas mixture rather than a mist of very fine droplets suspended in air. In doing this the fuel cools by providing the heat energy necessary for the change of state from liquid to gas. In consequence many of the early carburettors had water jackets coupled with the engine cooling system, to keep them warm and help the vaporization. Water jackets were later discarded in favour of bolting the carburettor to the exhaust manifold to create a hot-spot to warm the carburettor.

As long as motorists were content to travel at fixed speeds decided by a governed one-speed engine and two or three gear ratios, these primitive fuel-vapour producing devices were adequate. However, many designs were produced to increase the efficiency of vaporization.

In the first decade of the century drivers began to think of variable engine speeds and designers were faced with the fact that the pressure reduction in a venturi choke was not directly proportional to the volume of air flowing through. As the engine speed increased and the air flow increased, the suction on the jet did not increase at the same rate to keep the fuel/air ratio at the best (or stoichiometric) ratio.

If a carburettor of the simple, single-jet type is adjusted to give the maximum amount of power at slow speed the mixture will be far too rich. Conversely, if the setting gives full power at high speed, then there could well be insufficient suction on the jet at low speed to get any fuel flow at all.

In carburettors with throttles, compensation is provided for this by two main systems. One is a variable jet controlled by the inlet pipe (or manifold) suction, as in the S.U. carburettor. The other is a compensating jet, which feeds additional fuel when the air speed decreases as in the Zenith carburettor.

The first of the S.U. type carburettors was devised and made by G. H. and T. C. Skinner in 1904. It operated by maintaining a constant air speed over the jet, which was varied in area according to the engine's requirements.

Behind this world-famed carburettor is yet another of those stories of small beginnings and much struggle which tinge the early automobile endeavours with their own kind of romance.

Skinners was a small family firm that started in London and S.U. stood for Skinners Union. Competition among the carburettor makers was fierce at the time when the family business was struggling to survive. Their commercial breakthrough came when W. R. Morris (later Lord Nuffield) held over them the umbrella of his early mass-production methods. Big orders and financial backing ensured the future of S.U.

The original S.U. carburettor had a water-jacketed vertical choke passage, or mixing chamber, curved through nearly a right angle. On the outside of the bend was a drilling at 45 degrees, which held a jet fed with fuel through a vertical passage. This passage was fed through a horizontal passage from a float chamber. In the chamber was a circular float which freely encircled a needle with a pointed lower end and a grooved collar at the upper end above the float. The pointed end rested in a conical seating at the end of the petrol pipe and, according to whether the needle was raised or lowered, allowed fuel to flow or not.

Two counterbalance weights were pivoted to the top of the float chamber, one end of each weight arm resting in the groove of the collar and the weights resting on top of the float. As the fuel rose in the float chamber, the float lifted the weights and their arms pushed the needle down to close off the petrol inlet. In this way the fuel level was kept constant.

On the other side of the mixing chamber was a cylinder of the same diameter as the choke. Sliding in this was a solid piston having at its lower (jet) side a thin tapered needle which poked into the jet. On the upper side of the piston was a rod connected to the bottom of a leather bellows whose top was sealed to the casing. The area inside the bellows was connected by a passage to a point just below the throttle valve while the area round the bellows was connected to the atmosphere.

When the disc of the butterfly throttle was nearly shut across the inlet pipe, the vacuum (or depression) led by the passage to the space inside the bellows was low. Thus the piston nearly closed the choke area and the thickest part of the needle was in the jet. Under these conditions the choke area was small and the area of the jet was small, allowing only a low fuel flow.

As the throttle opened for greater power demand, the depression increased and the bellows lifted the piston and

The updraught Zenith of 1914 had main and compensating jets. Adjustment for slow running mixture was made by rotating a tube that fed fuel to a port in the choke close to the closed edge of the butterfly throttle.

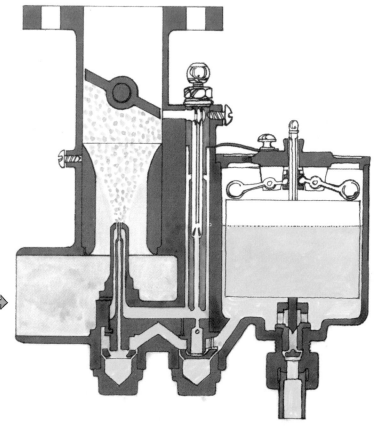

needle valve, so that the mixture strength remained constant throughout the working range.

The constant air speed over the jet was obtained by varying the choke area to keep the vacuum constant. This was done by the leather bellows which contracted as the vacuum within them increased. Contraction of the bellows raised the piston to increase the choke area and maintain the vacuum constant. At the same time the bellows pulled the taper needle farther out of the jet to give an increased petrol flow.

Other early carburettors which used diaphragms or pistons and jet needles were the Chenard-Walcker, the Winton and the Brotherhood-Crocker. The Krebs used an extra air valve actuated by a diaphragm to weaken the mixture with increasing speed and keep the strength constant. On the other hand, the Rover carburettor employed a piston to raise a conical perforated petticoat, which surrounded the jet, reducing the velocity of the air passing the jet. At the same time the perforations allowed more air to pass to the mixture outlet.

The S.U. carburettor has remained in use and still operates on the same principle, but has been modified to deal with the other carburation requirements. The jet is adjustable vertically to allow the correct setting of the mixture strength. On versions which followed the original one the jet could be raised and lowered by a linkage system attached to the bottom of the jet tube to allow for mixture enrichment when starting a cold engine. Around the same period, the leather bellows were replaced by an aluminium piston working in a dome of the same material.

As engines grew more lively in acceleration a damping device was fitted to the piston assembly. The piston guide rod was drilled down and oil and a small damper piston, attached to the top of the dome, were put in the guide rod.

When the S.U. carburettor was used on down-draught systems, where the choke tube was vertical, a spring was placed behind the piston to act against the suction, to close the piston across the choke, a force produced by the weight of the piston when the choke tube was horizontal.

In the latest version, the bottom of the jet tube is connected to the float chamber by a flexible pipe. There is thus no moving joint through which fuel can leak.

The early non-variable jet carburettor, which depended on compensating jets to maintain the desired mixture strength, is typified by the Zenith designed by François Baverey in 1907. It had a main jet, fed from a float chamber, at the bottom of a vertical mixing chamber.

As with the Maybach design, this jet provided an increasing fuel flow under increasing suction. To compensate for that, the main jet was surrounded by a second jet

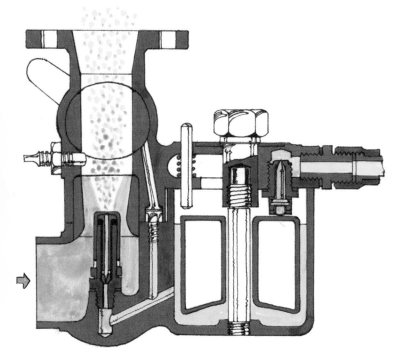

The Solex carburettor used an air bleed dependent on choke suction for compensation. The main jet was below the level of fuel and had a passage of large diameter leading to the narrowest part of the choke, with transverse holes drilled

above the jet proper. The jet was held in the fuel feed tube by a deep cap having a hole at its top and transverse air holes near its lower end. The jet being below the fuel level, the air passages ensured that the jet was relieved of surplus petrol at the tick-over speed, when the choke suction had a vacuum equal to the head of petrol over the jet.
As the engine speed increased, the fuel level above the main jet fell progressively and allowed more air bleed holes to be uncovered to reduce the suction acting on the jet.

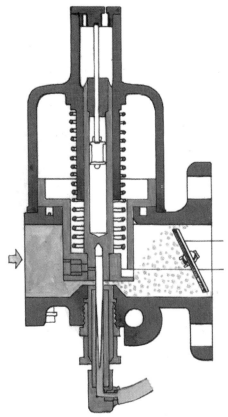

The modern S.U. carburettor has a metal piston within a light alloy dome in place of the original leather bellows and rapid fluctuations are damped by a dash-pot device in the piston rod. Earlier versions had a linkwork to lower the jet for cold-starting enrichment.

tube. This tube was fed from the bottom of a well which was open to the atmosphere at the top and was supplied with petrol from the float chamber through a small predetermined sized hole, or compensating jet.

As the area of the well was considerably greater than the area of the second jet tube, the fuel level in the well was determined by the height of the fuel in the float chamber and the size of the compensating jet connecting the chamber and the well. By this means the main jet flow increased with the throttle opening. However, the compensating system flow was reduced from the starting condition to continue more or less constant, thus off-setting the richness that the main jet alone gave.

In the 1914 Zenith carburettor the well contained a tube allowing slow running adjustment. The tube was open at both ends and fitted snugly into the well, which had a groove cut into its wall, leading from the bottom to an opening in the choke wall just by the point where the throttle butterfly came when closed. The lower end of the tube was angled so that, as it turned, more or less of the bottom part of the groove was exposed to the petrol in the well. This provided an adjustment for the amount of fuel reaching the opening in the choke wall and allowed the slow running speed of the engine to be set.

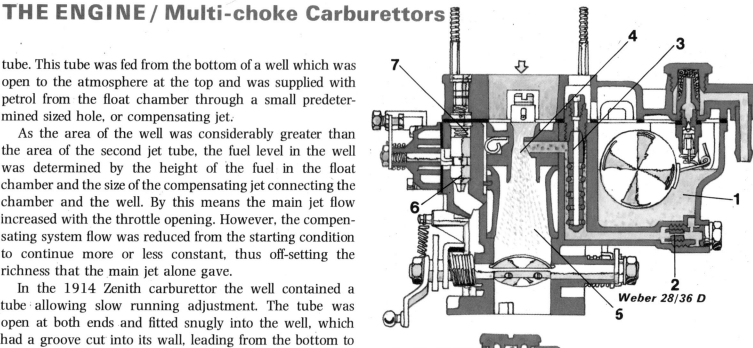

Weber 28/36 D

Zenith CDSET

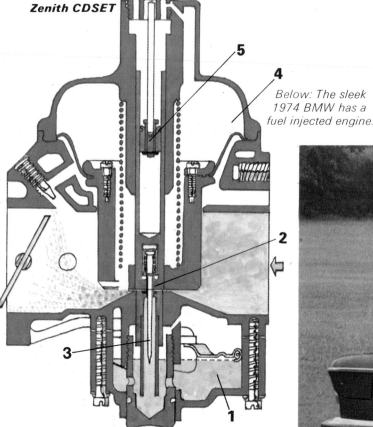

Below: The sleek 1974 BMW has a fuel injected engine.

Weber 28/36 D

In the modern multijet twin-choke carburettor the fuel passes from the float chamber (1) through the main jet (2) to fuel wells into which dip emulsifying tubes (3), fed with metered air. The emulsified fuel mixes with primary air in an auxiliary venturi (4) and is discharged into the main venturi (5). When the first throttle has opened at least half-way, a lost motion linkwork opens the second throttle and the siamesed carburettors work together.

As the primary throttle opens, a spring-loaded piston provides acceleration enrichment by pumping fuel to a jet just above the auxiliary venturi.

For starting, fuel passes to a plunger (6) through a separate starting jet and emulsifying system. The fuel/air mixture emerges below the shut throttle.

As the engine starts, the increased suction causes an air valve (7) at the top of the plunger to open and weaken the mixture. When the engine is warm the plunger is manually lowered to shut off the starting device. At idling, fuel passes to a jet to meet air coming from a calibrated inlet and passes to an orifice below the throttle. As speed increases, the suction at the

throttle edge also increases and draws fuel from a progression orifice, so that there is a clean transition from stage to stage. Opening of the second throttle induces flow from a similar orifice for smooth transition to double choke working.

Zenith CDSET

The fuel level in the float chamber (1) is controlled by twin floats. The jet (2) is a ring-shaped orifice between the jet tube and a tapered needle (3), of accurately calculated shape, moved by a diaphragm (4) in accordance with the suction existing in the choke tube. An oil dashpot (5) prevents the piston holding the needle rising too rapidly on sudden throttle openings, and provides acceleration enrichment. For cold starting, the fuel for an auxiliary carburettor is metered by a tapered needle which is controlled by a coolant temperature-sensitive spiral coil. A stepped cam and lever system provides a fast idling speed appropriate to the ambient temperature. When the engine coolant reaches normal temperature, the additional fuel jet is shut off. With no air flow through the choke, a further device gives a wider throttle opening and an even richer

mixture until the engine begins to turn.

For normal idling the mixture is supplied through the main jet under the control of the needle. A throttle by-pass valve opens to feed air into the mixing chamber just downstream of the piston at high manifold suction. Also, an idling trimming screw provides an initially slightly weak mixture for a new and stiff engine to help with pollution problems.

The tube played two other important roles. It gave a rich mixture for starting. When the tube fuel level was high – at the same level as it was in the float chamber – the strong suction set up near the edge of the throttle caused a heavy initial flow of fuel through the choke wall hole. Similarly, it provided a rich mixture for acceleration purposes when the sudden opening of the throttle increased the rush of air, and this was compensated by fuel being drawn out of the tube.

An alternative form of compensation was employed in the Solex carburettor in the form of an air bleed which was dependent on the suction in the choke. Stromberg and Claudel-Hobson carburettors also used air bleeds as a means of compensation in mixture strength.

In an ideal carburettor the mixture strength is required to be reduced (in comparison with the chemically correct strength) from some twenty per cent rich at very low engine loads to around twelve per cent weak in the region of 80 to 90 per cent of full load, and then to be enriched again to twenty per cent above the correct level at full load. A further requirement is a richer mixture strength for acceleration. This is usually provided by a pump worked by movement of the throttle linkwork.

Anti-pollution laws have added to the complexity of the modern carburettor. This is seen from the examples of the present day constant vacuum (Zenith CDSET) and multi-jet twin-choke (Weber 28/36 DCD) carburettors (see diagrams).

MULTI-CHOKE CARBURETTORS

Big capacity V8 engines produced by American manufacturers (nowadays such engines run up to eight litres) cause the problem of getting a large choke area to pass all the required air and simultaneously allow sufficient depression at low speeds. The difficulty is met by using four-choke carburettors. These are, in fact, a pair of twin-choke instruments in a single block, the twin choke being two carburettors of which one becomes effective only at wider throttle openings. The other provides the starting, slow running and compensating systems, as well as all the mixture at lower throttle openings.

The Weber 28/36 DCD, as fitted to Fiat and Ford GT engines, is a good example of a highly efficient modern multi-jet twin-choke carburettor. It satisfies the varying demands of relatively high performance engines and aids economy by ensuring that the first throttle has opened

about half way before a lost motion linkwork on the throttle spindles begins to open the second throttle below the parallel second choke. The two carburettors then work together to deliver mixture for the higher power demands.

More complex Weber carburettors may be fitted with automatic, thermostatically controlled chokes, pneumatically controlled differential opening of the throttles, systems for part throttle weakening for economy, means for heating the idling speed mixture, means for compensating for altitude and full air pollution control devices.

EMISSION CONTROLS

The peculiar geographical situation of Los Angeles, with its bowl configuration close to the sea, and its regular sunshine, together result in distressingly consistent smog formation. This has produced some very stringent legislation in the entire United States, which has been followed to a greater or lesser degree by the rest of the world. The intention of the legislation is to limit the amounts of certain, alleged, noxious emissions from car exhausts.

The main emissions against which this campaign rages are carbon monoxide (CO), unburnt hydrocarbons (fuel), oxides of nitrogen (NOX) and lead compounds. The first three of these are dependent upon the air/fuel ratio of the mixture being burnt in the engine, the CO and hydrocarbons falling in percentage as the ratio weakens. The NOX, however, increases with the weaker mixtures, as it is largely produced at the higher temperatures reached by burning weak mixtures. The best ratio is just below fourteen to one though the emissions are still too high.

Two systems are suggested to remove CO and hydrocarbons. One is to use a direct flame afterburner, which finally burns them in the exhaust systems. The other is to use a catalytic converter. This converter is a chamber containing an expensive coating, such as platinum, which changes the gases into acceptable compounds without itself changing. But the lead used in the fuel to improve its anti-detonating properties tends to clog up the catalyst.

Tests called for by the new laws are designed to simulate road driving conditions, and the primary means of meeting these tests is the use of weaker mixtures (hence the complicated design of modern carburettors) and the abolition of leaded fuels. The latter measure results in the use of lower compression ratios and, in consequence, the need for larger engines to produce the equivalent power. Obviously such engines use more fuel and so tend to cause greater pollution.

Unburnt fuel emission results from fuel which has been cooled on the port or cylinder walls, or shielded from the flame in a nook or cranny in the cylinder head. It is also caused through fuel spilling or vaporizing out of tank vents and other parts of the fuel system.

One source of hydrocarbon emission is a high suction, formed by a suddenly closed throttle, drawing off neat fuel, which is not burned. This can be minimized by a

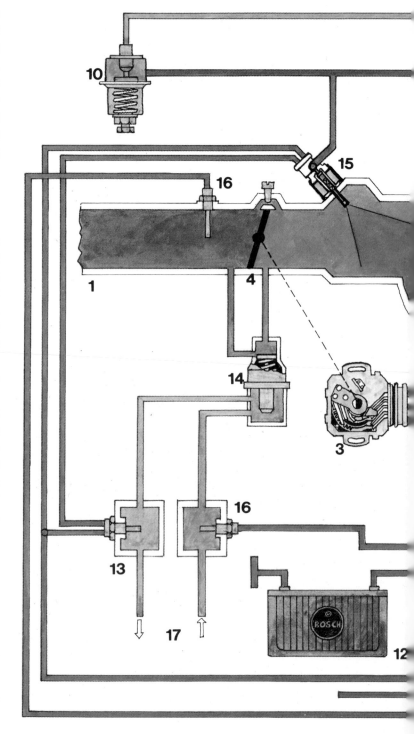

gulp-valve which, because it is sensitive to such sudden changes, adds extra air into the manifold.

Another preventive is to feed the crankcase fumes, which include exhaust gases that have got past the piston rings, back through a one-way valve to the inlet manifold. Yet another emission antidote is to retard the ignition still further at the lowest idling speed by an extra vacuum servo system, fed from the choke near the point where the throttle closes.

FUEL INJECTION

Even with the complex modern carburettors, which will provide correct mixture strength under all conditions,

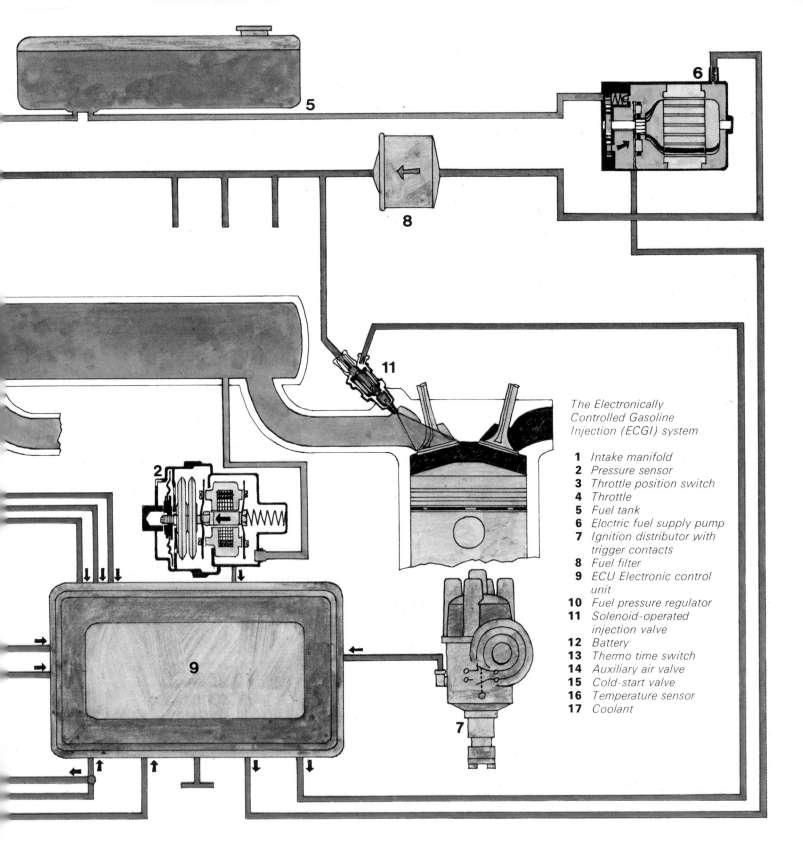

The Electronically Controlled Gasoline Injection (ECGI) system

1 Intake manifold
2 Pressure sensor
3 Throttle position switch
4 Throttle
5 Fuel tank
6 Electric fuel supply pump
7 Ignition distributor with trigger contacts
8 Fuel filter
9 ECU Electronic control unit
10 Fuel pressure regulator
11 Solenoid-operated injection valve
12 Battery
13 Thermo time switch
14 Auxiliary air valve
15 Cold-start valve
16 Temperature sensor
17 Coolant

there still exist the two limitations of restriction of air flow by the choke design, and the great difficulty of getting the same strength mixture to all the cylinders through a tortuous inlet manifold.

Separate carburettors for all cylinders have been tried but a more obvious solution is to squirt the correct amount of fuel either into the inlet ports or the manifold adjacent to the ports. This is known as fuel injection.

While fuel injection has been tried for petrol engines by many inventors over the past 70 years, it is only within the last twenty years that techniques have been available to meter the very small quantities of fuel needed for injection and to adjust these quantities for variations of speed, load, temperature and driver's demand. At present the benefits gained in economy, performance and ecology are about balanced by the additional cost of complex and extremely accurate mechanisms.

There have been a number of fuel injection systems based on different methods of injection and of fuel metering.

Liquid fuel may be injected directly into the cylinders or into the manifold near the inlet valve. The quantity of fuel may be proportioned to the engine operating conditions by varying the effective stroke of a pump, by varying the opening time of an injection nozzle fed from a constant pressure main, or by varying the rate of flow through an injection nozzle.

Just as in a carburettor, the ratio of fuel to air needs to be maintained in the region of the stoichiometric ratio. Thus the fuel volume must be proportioned to the mass air flow with enrichment for cold starting. The different systems to provide this are well illustrated by the three main lines of development taken by Bosch.

The first system, as used on the Mercedes 300SL in 1954, was based on the well-tried diesel pump. In this there was a separate pump for each cylinder. The pistons of these pumps were reciprocated through a fixed stroke by a camshaft and they could be rotated by a control rack engaging a gear ring clamped to each piston. The upper end of each piston was reduced from full diameter, along a helical line, to form a slanting control edge. By rotation of the piston the control edge shut off the fuel inlet at different proportions of the stroke and, in consequence, gave a variable volume discharge.

The speed of the engine was controlled by a butterfly throttle in the air intake to the manifold. This throttle was in a venturi having a vacuum pipe leading to a spring-loaded diaphragm connected to the end of the control rack. By this means the fuel volume injected into the cylinders was determined by the vacuum at the venturi. This vacuum is a measure of the engine load.

The connection between the diaphragm and control rack was adjusted by a bellows unit sensitive to ambient temperature and pressure and by an overriding cold-start enrichment control.

The injection nozzles, screwed into the cylinder head, had spring-loaded valves opening under the pressure of fuel delivery. Injection was timed early in the compression stroke to aid atomization and mixing with the air, and to assist in cooling the interior of the cylinder.

In 1967, Bosch, in collaboration with Volkswagen, began to produce the ECGI – electronically controlled gasoline injection-system. In this sophisticated system, fuel is injected into the inlet manifold near the inlet valve by solenoid operated valves. Since the nozzle area and the fuel pressure are kept constant, the fuel quantity is determined by the time the valve is open.

The timing of the start of injection is triggered by contacts activated by a cam on the ignition distributor shaft before the centrifugal advance mechanism. The current pulses are fed to an electronic control unit (ECU) which determines the duration of the injection.

Based on printed circuits, the ECU is an electronic calculator which contains between 250 and 300 components including some 30 transistors and 40 diodes. As well as the timing pulse, the ECU receives information on the intake manifold pressure and temperature, the engine temperature, the amount of opening of the throttle and the engine speed. By combining this information it determines the fuel needs of the engine and signals the timing and duration of the injection valve opening.

Since the fuel/air mixture is formed upstream of the inlet valve, it can be held there briefly and thus the exact

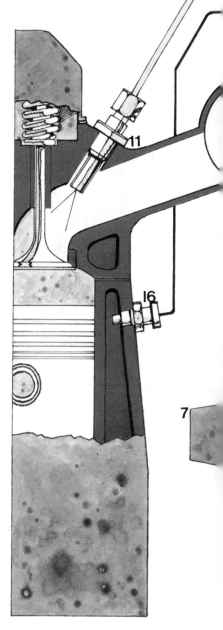

The K-Jetronic continuous-flow fuel injection system
1 air collector box
2 divergent air metering passage
3 flowmeter pressure plate
4 throttle
5 fuel tank
6 fuel pump
7 accumulator
8 filter
9 metering valve and distributor
10 fuel pressure regulator
11 fuel injector
12 plunger follower
13 idle adjustment screw
14 damping orifice
15 cold-start valve
16 temperature-time switch
17 throttle by-pass valve
18 warm-up valve

moment of injection is not critical. This allows the ECU to be simplified by connecting groups of injectors together electrically so that they open at the same time. As an example, for a six-cylinder engine the injectors for cylinders one, five and three will open together and those of the second group six, two and four will open together one crankshaft revolution later.

A separate cold-start valve not controlled by the ECU provides a highly atomized spray of fuel into the manifold near the air throttle to make up for fuel condensing on the cold interior of the engine. Once the engine starts, the warm-up enrichment is taken over by the injector valves.

Enrichment for idling, acceleration and full-load is initiated by a throttle-position switch that signals drivers demand conditions to the ECU.

In 1973, Bosch introduced a third system of fuel injection. This is a wholly mechanical metering system in which the fuel flow is proportioned to the air flow and is continually injected just upstream of the inlet valves. The continuous injection is a development of the grouping idea of the ECGI and gives the system its name K-Jetronic

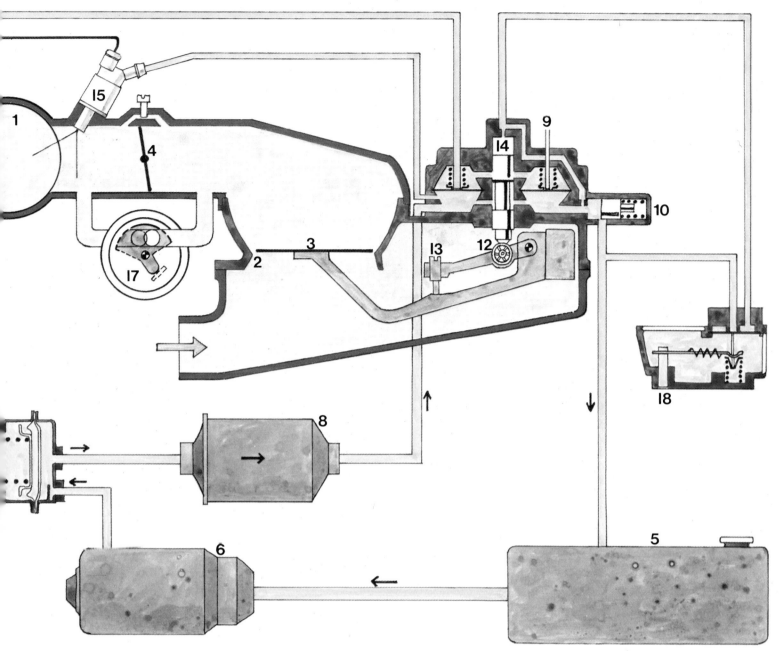

(K for Kontinuierlich or continuous).

The air flow passing into the engine in a given time, is measured by the position of a circular plate moving in a divergent conical air metering passage.

Since the pressure on the plate is dependent on the density and speed of the air, movement of the plate against a constant control force will be such that the air speed remains constant. The air flow is dependent on the air speed and the area through which it is flowing. Therefore with a constant air speed the plate moves in the divergent metering passage to a position where the area between the edge of the plate and the passage wall is proportional to the air flow.

The position of the plate at any particular air flow is transmitted to a valve that meters the flow of fuel to the injectors. All the injectors subsequently receive an equal share of the metered fuel.

Fuel is pumped to the system by a rotary electric pump at about 70 pounds per square inch and passes into an accumulator. The accumulator has a spring-loaded diaphragm on one side of a chamber and this damps out any fluctuations in pressure. It also provides a pressurized system for restarting when the engine is switched off for a few minutes. The fuel then passes a filter and goes to the metering valve. In the metering valve assembly, a spring-loaded diaphragm across each injector outlet ensures a constant differential pressure across the extremely accurately dimensioned metering port.

The fuel pressure is maintained constant by a relief valve that spills excess fuel back to the tank. A duct from the pressure side of this relief valve leads through a restrictor to the top area of the metering valve to damp fluctuations and balance the metering plate position.

Warming-up enrichment is provided by a thermostatically controlled valve, which reduces the pressure in the duct to the top of the metering valve.

A later system, the "L-Jetronic" (L for Luftmengenmessung or air flow measurement), came in 1973. Similar to the K-Jetronic system, the fluctuating air flow in the metering passage is translated to a varying electrical impulse by a potentiometer. Fuel is again injected intermittently into the inlet manifold.

FUEL FEED SYSTEMS

The fuel supply to the float chamber of the 1899 Daimler was as simple as can be imagined. The petrol tank was mounted well above the engine and, when the tap was turned on, the fuel flowed down the pipe.

This gravity feed remained in common use well into the second half of the 1920s and most cars carried their fuel tanks over the knees of the front seat occupants. As car bodies became lower the tank was relegated normally to the rear of the car although some, like the Model T Ford, kept it under the seat.

This lack of gravitational help required the use of pressure. In some cases, mainly in sports cars, a manual pump was used which pressurized the air above the fuel in the tank. On more expensive cars, such as with the Bugatti Brescia of 1922, an engine-driven pump was provided. Other makers cooled some of the exhaust gas and used its pressure to move the fuel.

Safer methods which found international favour were the Autovac and similar vacuum tank devices. These used the reduced pressure in the inlet manifold to draw petrol from the rear tank into a small tank mounted on the engine bulkhead, from which position gravity did the rest.

A pipe led from the manifold to a float-operated valve in the tank top. When the tank was empty, the suction drew fuel into the tank until it was full enough for the float to shut the suction pipe and open an air valve, which allowed

The early Bugattis, including this 1922 Bugatti Brescia T23, had rear mounted fuel tanks. Petrol was forced from the tanks to the higher float chambers by the pressure of air above the petrol. A hand pump provided air pressure for starting and the pressure in the tank was maintained by a small air compressor.

the fuel to flow to the carburettor by gravity. As fuel was used, the float fell and changed over the valves.

Mechanical engine-driven and electric fuel pumps superseded the Autovac, although both had been used before as, for example, the electric pump fitted to the Wills Sainte Claire of 1924.

The mechanical pumps, such as the widely used A.C., employ a special cam on the engine camshaft acting through a lever, to pull down a diaphragm against the force of a spring. The movement of the diaphragm creates suction which draws the fuel from the tank through a one-way inlet valve. A lost motion connection between the lever and diaphragm allows the latter to rise

Suction from the inlet manifold drew fuel up from the tank to the small container of the Autovac. From this small tank the fuel flowed under gravity to the carburettor.

under spring pressure and force fuel through an outlet valve and a filter to the float chamber of the carburettor. When the diaphragm reaches its upper limit of movement, the lever pulls it down again for a further stroke.

The electric pump operates in much the same fashion, but an electromagnet pulls the diaphragm against its spring and a rod, attached to the diaphragm, closes the switch supplying current to the magnet when the spring needs recompressing. As soon as the spring is compressed, the switch opens once more.

AIR FILTERS

With the increasing use of the car and the increasing expectations of engine life, it was realized in the 1920s that the amount of dust being drawn into the cylinders along with the air caused increased bore wear and carbon

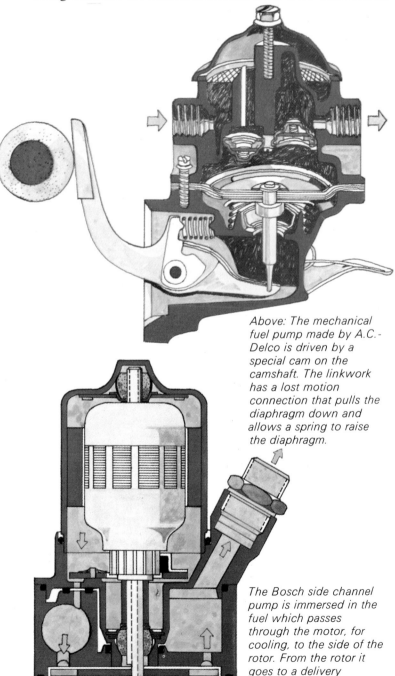

Above: The mechanical fuel pump made by A.C.-Delco is driven by a special cam on the camshaft. The linkwork has a lost motion connection that pulls the diaphragm down and allows a spring to raise the diaphragm.

The Bosch side channel pump is immersed in the fuel which passes through the motor, for cooling, to the side of the rotor. From the rotor it goes to a delivery chamber.

deposits, so filtration was necessary. The first filters were no more than gauze, but they soon developed into finer filters of special felt which could trap small particles. These filters became quite large, so that they could deal with the volume of air without obstructing the flow.

The next development was to turn the incoming air sharply just above a bath of oil. The dirt, being heavy, went

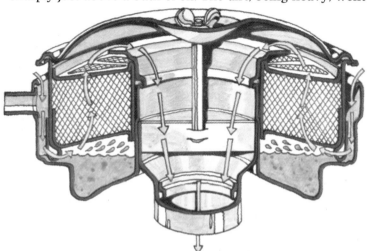

The A.C.-Delco air filter relies on the centrifugal force to throw dust particles into an oil bath before going through an oil washed gauze.

straight on and was trapped in the oil, while the air continued through a wire mesh on which oil caught the rest of the dirt. Some of these filters swirled the air round on entry in order to remove the larger particles of dirt by centrifugal action.

Later, development of pleated, resin-impregnated, paper filter elements enabled large areas of non-restrictive filtration to be achieved. One benefit of this was that there was a much longer life between replacement.

PISTONS

The pressure produced by burning the air/fuel mixture in the cylinder must be made to work. The piston does this. It is required to be as gas tight as possible in the cylinder bore yet still be able to slide freely and not to wear either itself or the cylinder bore too rapidly. Initially, pistons were made of cast iron, as in the 1899 Daimler. This is a metal with good bearing qualities when sliding in the cast iron cylinder. Unfortunately it is too heavy for high speeds, particularly as the piston has to change direction at each end of the stroke. By the end of the cast iron era, some very fine thin-section castings were being made but even these were too heavy. Steel was considered and examples of welded-up and forged or pressed steel pistons were subsequently made and used.

For a long time manufacturers were wary of using aluminium because it has an expansion with temperature of about two-and-a-half times that of cast iron, although it is only about a third of the weight. Some firms, like Talbot and Ford, used pistons with aluminium tops and cast iron skirts, to try to obtain the benefits of both metals, an expensive form of manufacture. Eventually, during the 1920s, aluminium became more generally used, aided by new alloys and a large number of designs to compensate for the different expansion rates. As the aluminium of the piston expands more than the iron of the bore, it is essential to provide enough clearance, when the engine is cold, to allow for this expansion.

The excessive clearance makes itself heard as piston slap when the piston rattles in the bore with the changing direction of force from the connecting rod. Some of the schemes suggested to alleviate this trouble were to make the piston oval, to split the skirt so that it could move inwards as the piston grew larger and to fit spring-backed piston rings towards the bottom of the skirt.

Mohle K-G of Germany introduced the Autothermic piston which had inserts of another metal cast between the gudgeon pin bosses and the walls so that the differences in expansion moved the skirt to keep the original clearance.

PISTON RINGS

The seal between the piston and the cylinder bore is maintained by cast iron piston rings which are located in grooves machined near the top of the piston. The rings are gapped to allow for thermal expansion Although at first sight the piston rings of the ancient Daimler may look like modern rings, the latest piston rings are thinner, made of better material and are of different shape.

More springiness can be imparted by using narrower and thinner rings, by making the inner and outer surfaces eccentric, so that the ring is thicker opposite the gap, and by hammering treatment of the inside of the ring opposite

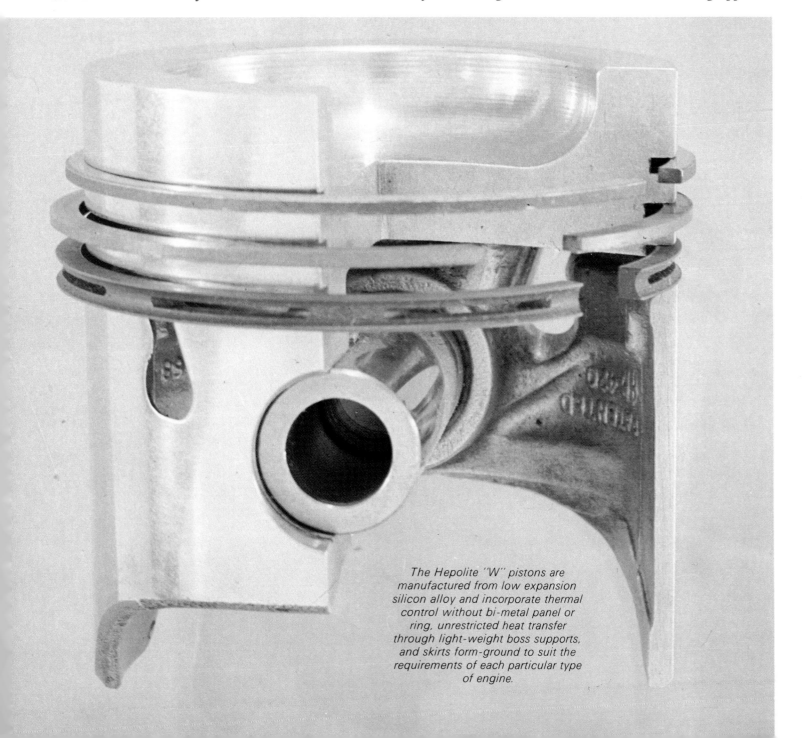

The Hepolite "W" pistons are manufactured from low expansion silicon alloy and incorporate thermal control without bi-metal panel or ring, unrestricted heat transfer through light-weight boss supports, and skirts form-ground to suit the requirements of each particular type of engine.

the gap area. This also results in the advantage of a more even pressure on the cylinder wall all round.

Whereas the older rings were cast in sand moulds, newer production is from tubes cast centrifugally in metal moulds. Also, the outer bearing surface of the ring is often plated with chromium and is slightly tapered to assist running-in and to give a good seal.

Often, the lowest ring has radial corners or an L-section to maintain a controlled amount of oil on the cylinder bore. Over the years there have been a great many designs to control the oil. If there is too much oil, there is excessive carbon formation in the engine; if there is too little oil, there is a risk of seizure.

Cord rings, for the control of oil and maintenance of a good seal in tapered and worn bores, were made of thin dished steel rings and were fitted four to a groove in a W fashion. Wellworthy made a Duaflex ring of two rounded-edge rings, held apart in the groove by a wavy spring and

prevented from rotating by a backing spring locked into one of the oil return holes drilled in the groove base. Often the lowest ring had a circumferential groove from which radial holes passed oil, scraped from the cylinder wall, to holes drilled in the piston from the ring groove.

GUDGEON PINS

The gudgeon pin, which holds the piston on the upper end of the connecting rod and allows it to rock about the axis of the little-end bearing, is a hardened tubular steel pin that has changed little over the years, although the means of stopping the pin from moving endways and cutting grooves in the bore have varied considerably.

In one system the pin was held by bolts passing into it from the gudgeon pin boss in the piston. In another design the pin was clamped in the connecting rod little-end, the latter being split, with a clamp bolt through it. This method successfully weakened the rod and caused expensive

Above: A sand-cast piston recessed to relieve expansion on the gudgeon pin axis. The piston had 3 compression rings and the gudgeon pin had brass end pads to prevent damage when the pin came into contact with the cylinder wall.

Centre: Many pistons in the late 1920s and early 1930s used a steel retaining band to prevent movement of the gudgeon pin. This example was fitted to the 1929/35 7 hp Jowett.

Top right: A bi-metallic piston manufactured from aluminium alloy in which skirt expansion is controlled by steel struts above and below each gudgeon pin boss. The use of two inserts on each side of the piston enables greater control to be exercised on the skirt expansion which varies along its length due to the temperature differential.

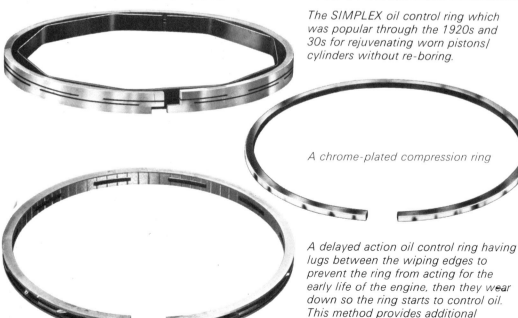

The SIMPLEX oil control ring which was popular through the 1920s and 30s for rejuvenating worn pistons/cylinders without re-boring.

A chrome-plated compression ring

A delayed action oil control ring having lugs between the wiping edges to prevent the ring from acting for the early life of the engine, then they wear down so the ring starts to control oil. This method provides additional lubrication during running-in.

noises when the rod broke and consequently let the piston hit the combustion chamber top!

A third way was to use soft brass pads at each end of the gudgeon pin and a fourth was to clamp the pin in the piston by making the hole slightly smaller than the pin and heating the piston to expand it and allow for the assembly of the pin.

Practically all modern engines rely on the pin being a good running fit in both the piston holes and a bronze bearing bush in the little-end of the connecting rod, with a spring ring, or circlip, positioned in a groove at the end of each piston boss hole.

CONNECTING RODS AND BEARINGS

The connecting rod and its other, big, end have also apparently changed little from the Daimler days, although the materials of the forged, H-section connecting rods have improved to cope with the demands of added loads, imposed as power has increased. A few engines have used aluminium alloy connecting rods, but the great majority of engines still use steel.

To enable the big-end to be assembled on the crankpin, the bearing is divided along a diameter, often at an angle to the connecting rod centre-line, for ease of assembly past the crankshaft. The cap so formed is secured by bolts having high tensile strength, the nuts of which are very securely locked.

The original type of bearing was a great lump of bronze, but an early development was to coat the actual bearing areas thickly with a soft alloy of tin, copper and antimony, first produced by Babbit in 1839.

The next development was to reduce the thickness of both bronze and Babbit metal and to produce bearing shells which could be slipped into place without the need for further fitting work. The actual bearing metals improved to deal with higher demands and the backing changed from bronze to steel.

One method of production is to coat a long steel strip with lead-bronze powder which is baked, or sintered, in place. The bi-metallic strip is then cut to short lengths which are pressed into accurately dimensioned semi-circular shells with small ears which rest in notches in the rod and its cap, to stop the shells moving around when in use. Other similar bearings have thin coatings of suitable metals flash-plated on the wearing area.

Some engines have used roller bearings but, as this entailed designing the crankshaft in such a way that it could be built up from a number of pieces, to allow the roller bearings to pass over the crankpins, it was used only on very expensive engines. Moreover, roller bearings are not ideal for use when they are subjected to heavy shock loadings, because the rollers tend to press grooves into their races under such conditions.

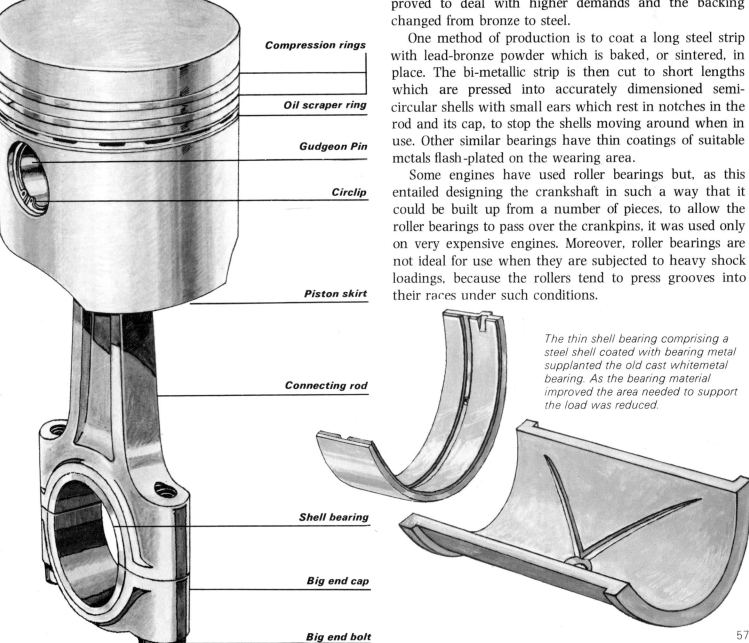

The thin shell bearing comprising a steel shell coated with bearing metal supplanted the old cast whitemetal bearing. As the bearing material improved the area needed to support the load was reduced.

Compression rings

Oil scraper ring

Gudgeon Pin

Circlip

Piston skirt

Connecting rod

Shell bearing

Big end cap

Big end bolt

CRANKSHAFTS

One of the problems which troubled early engine-makers was breakage of the crankshaft, the final link between the reciprocating pistons and the rotary power output at the end of the engine. The main reason for this was the lack of understanding of the complex forces involved and their momentarily great magnitude.

First, the shaft has to take the thrust from the connecting rod, which tends to both twist and bend it. The twist is due to the torque output, and the bending to the load being applied between the supporting main bearings.

In multi-cylinder engines the loads occur in order as the cylinders fire. At the same time, inertia type loads are at work, owing to the weight of pistons and connecting rods being started and stopped at the ends of their strokes. Unfortunately, it is not possible to balance all the forces acting on the shaft because of the masses of the crankpins and the connecting rods being offset from the crankshaft's rotational axis. This introduces further out-of-balance loads on the shaft.

A compromise is reached by adding some balancing masses and by using as many bearings as possible. Early crankshafts, as in the 1899 Daimler, had no balancing masses, and this lack was a great cause of engine vibration and frequent shaft breakage.

With multi-cylinder engines the crankshafts tended to bend so bearings were put at the centre as well as at the ends of the shaft. Some engines had bearings between each pair of cylinders or even between each cylinder, but this tended to make excessively long power plants. The compromise was to have two or three bearings and increased shaft diameters, although problems arose owing to the rise in rubbing speed between shaft and bearing.

With the coming of more accurate knowledge of the forces involved, and of bearing materials which would stand higher loads per unit area, the number of bearings increased again. In four-cylinder engines, three and five bearings are now common. In engines with more cylinders, even more bearings are used.

Because of the need for high strength, crankshafts came to be forged from high quality steels which gave a good grain structure along the shaft. However, in the mid-1950s, Ford changed to nodular cast iron, an alloy of iron, copper, chromium and silicon, with ideal properties for crankshafts. Other manufacturers followed suit.

A single-cylinder four-stroke engine has only one power stroke for every two revolutions of the crankshaft, an obvious cause of non-smooth running. To solve this and to keep the engine turning during the non-productive strokes of the cycle of operations, a heavy flywheel is secured to the crankshaft, acting as an energy storing and releasing device. Owing to its function, the use of a heavy flywheel prevents rapid changes of engine speed when the throttle is open or shut.

Using two cylinders, as with the Fiat 126, produces a firing stroke every revolution but also adds to the problem. If the two crankpins are arranged together, the firing is even. But the balance suffers because all the weight is on one side of the crankshaft, whereas if the crankpins are 180 degrees apart, the balance is much better but the firing becomes syncopated. The general practice is to even out the firing impulses and compensate as far as possible for the out-of-balance forces.

Another solution to the two-cylinder problem is to arrange the cylinders at 180 degrees to give a flat-twin. This was done by a number of light car makers, such as A.B.C., Jowett, Panhard and others. With two-stroke engines the problem is only half as difficult, as each piston produces a power stroke every revolution and a three-

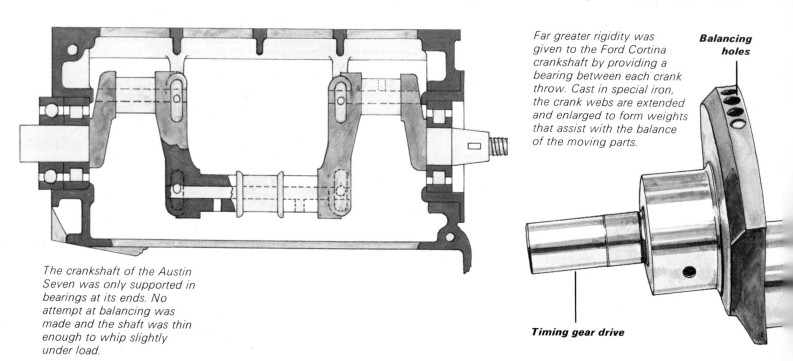

The crankshaft of the Austin Seven was only supported in bearings at its ends. No attempt at balancing was made and the shaft was thin enough to whip slightly under load.

Far greater rigidity was given to the Ford Cortina crankshaft by providing a bearing between each crank throw. Cast in special iron, the crank webs are extended and enlarged to form weights that assist with the balance of the moving parts.

Balancing holes

Timing gear drive

A Chrysler drop-head coupé of 1931 that found its way to England.

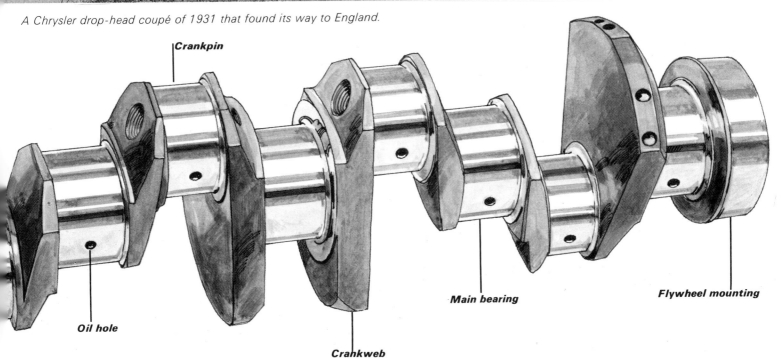

Crankpin

Oil hole

Crankweb

Main bearing

Flywheel mounting

The six-cylinder Napier of 1907 developed from the earlier cars built at the instigation of S. F. Edge. Edge later acclaimed the advantages of

cylinder two-stroke, like the Wartburg has the firing impulses of a six-cylinder four-stroke.

The crankshaft for an in-line four-cylinder engine, as first produced by the French firm of Panhard and Levassor in 1896 (Levassor won the first true motor race) has the crankpins for cylinders one and four on one side, and for two and three on the other side of the crankshaft axis. By this arrangement, when piston one is on its firing stroke, four must be on its suction stroke as this is the only other downward stroke. Pistons two and three will be moving upwards, which may be either compression or exhaust strokes. But these two must be different for even firing intervals. Therefore it is a matter of choice whether the firing order is one-three-four-two or one-two-four-three.

The first production six-cylinder engines of the London-built Napier of 1904, and subsequent straight-six engines, have pairs of cranks at 120 degrees, usually one and six, two and five, and three and four forming the pairs. The most popular firing order is one-five-three-six-two-four, although other sequences can be used.

Engines with eight cylinders in line, such as Zis, Daimler, Renault and Packard, can have crankshafts which are, in effect, two fours joined together, or the first and last pair of crankpins in one plane and the middle four pins in a plane at right angles, which produces even more choice of firing order.

Both six-and eight-cylinder engines tend to excessive bonnet length, particularly with modern concepts of body

six-cylinder engines for A.C. who still used their basic 1922 designed engine in the post-war Ace, below.

styling. They can be shortened by using two banks of cylinders, usually at 90 degrees. Taking the V8 as an example, the crankshaft can either be flat, that is a four with two connecting rods articulated to each crankpin, or the crankpins can be at 90 degrees with numbers two and three opposite each other, as introduced by Ford in 1932. Among the V6 engines are those of the Lancia Aurelia, Buick and the Ford Granada, while the V8 has been common among American cars from its production in 1915 by Cadillac and has been used by Rolls-Royce, Daimler, Mercedes-Benz and many others.

Just as two fours can be combined to give a V8, two two-cylinder engines can be combined to give a flat-four, which is the configuration of the Alfa Sud, Citroen GS,

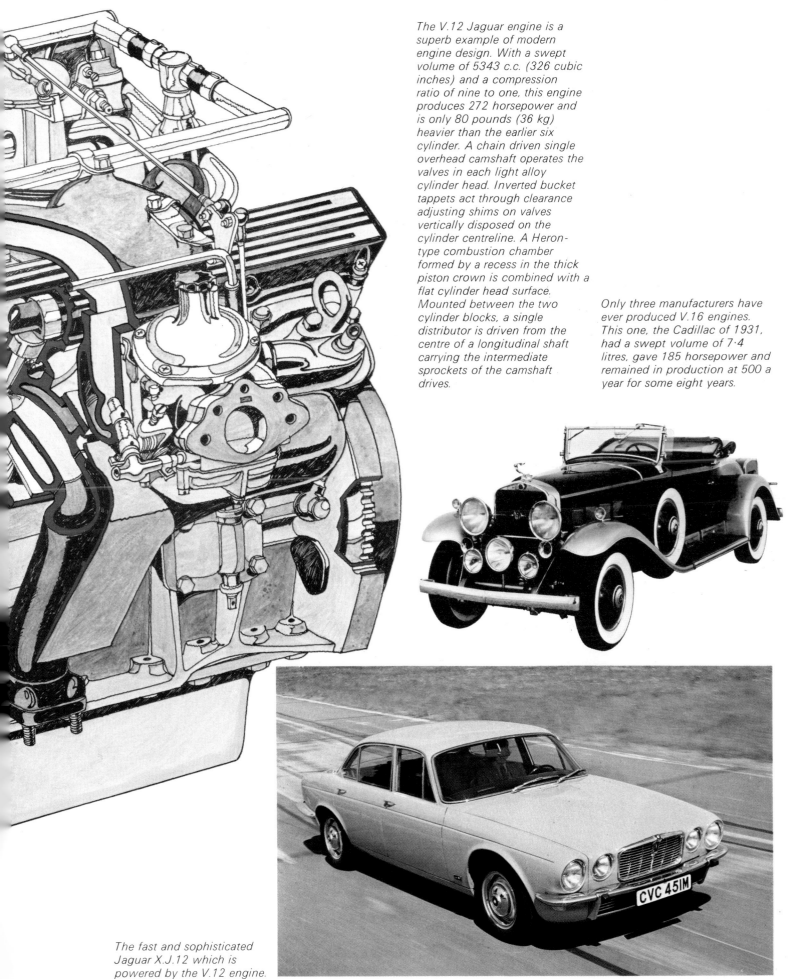

The V.12 Jaguar engine is a superb example of modern engine design. With a swept volume of 5343 c.c. (326 cubic inches) and a compression ratio of nine to one, this engine produces 272 horsepower and is only 80 pounds (36 kg) heavier than the earlier six cylinder. A chain driven single overhead camshaft operates the valves in each light alloy cylinder head. Inverted bucket tappets act through clearance adjusting shims on valves vertically disposed on the cylinder centreline. A Heron-type combustion chamber formed by a recess in the thick piston crown is combined with a flat cylinder head surface. Mounted between the two cylinder blocks, a single distributor is driven from the centre of a longitudinal shaft carrying the intermediate sprockets of the camshaft drives.

Only three manufacturers have ever produced V.16 engines. This one, the Cadillac of 1931, had a swept volume of 7·4 litres, gave 185 horsepower and remained in production at 500 a year for some eight years.

The fast and sophisticated Jaguar X.J.12 which is powered by the V.12 engine.

63

Jowett and Volkswagen. The Chevrolet Corvair was a flat-six. These are all short, rigid engines, taking up relatively little space and being fundamentally balanced.

Orthodox, but less common, are the V12s such as most Ferraris, the Jaguar XJ12, Daimler Double-Six, Rolls-Royce Phantom III and Lincoln Zephyr. Rarer was the V16 of the 1930 Cadillac, which had a wide angle between the two side-valve blocks served by a single camshaft.

Other configurations have been relatively few. Rumpler produced a six-cylinder engine in 1921 by combining three pairs of cylinders in arrow formation on a common crankcase, so that neither the balance nor the equal firing desires were satisfied. Another unorthodox cylinder layout was in the Enfield-Alldays of 1919 and the 1931 Zundapp, which followed aero-engine practice by having five cylinders all radial to the crankshaft.

THE CRANKCASE

The whole bottom half of an engine is the crankcase. It holds together all the pieces of the engine and the necessity for it to be extremely rigid is obvious. Not only does it provide a reaction to the stresses of the crankshaft and cylinders but it also forms the mounting for the various accessories such as the oil and water pumps, the dynamo, starter, and cooling fan. In a large number of installations the crankcase has acted as a strengthening member for the chassis or frame.

Many of the early engines had their cylinders mounted separately or, later, in one or two blocks on top of the crankcase. With the advance of mass production machining techniques, it became possible to make the cylinder block and crankcases from a single casting.

At the same time came a change from aluminium to cast iron as the material for this part of the engine, a necessity where the bores were machined directly in the cylinder block. On the other hand, when thin cast iron liners were used for the bores, as in the A.C. and Renault, aluminium could be used for the combined block and crankcase, resulting in a lighter engine.

A more recent development is exemplified in the 1971 Vega engine of General Motors, which has a die-cast aluminium crankcase and cylinder block in which the alloy has a silicon content that is exposed to electro-chemical etching to provide a good wearing surface for use in conjunction with iron plated pistons.

Since the bottom of the crankcase has to be open to allow assembly of the pistons, connecting rods and crankshaft, it is strengthened inside by ribs. The crankcase is divided transversely by the ribs which carry the main bearings.

Some crankcases are split along the axis of the crankshaft and in these, the lower part, or sump, carries some part of the load. Most of them extend well below the bearings, which are of generally similar design to the connecting rod big-end bearings, and the sump is a light steel pressing which is no more than a container for the oil. Other sumps are cast in aluminium with external fins to help cool the oil.

Bosses, or feet, which are cast integrally with the outside, enable the crankcase to be secured to the car chassis or body. Originally the engine was bolted directly to the chassis and, with the light and whippy tubular frameworks of those days, it provided a member which gave a beneficial effect of strength against twisting which was probably not appreciated fully by the designers!

The next school of thought decided to relieve the crankcase of such loads and bolted it to a separate sub-frame. It was considered that chassis of wood, strengthened with steel-plates, would not have sufficient strength.

When the flitched wood chassis was replaced by one of pressed steel channels, the crankcase was once more bolted to it rigidly. As public demand for smoothness began to grow, some thought was given to mounting the engine on rubber to prevent, or at least to reduce, the transmission

Produced in a purpose-built factory to the south of Naples, the Alfa Sud has a liquid-cooled flat-four engine driving the front wheels. It is noted for its smoothness, quietness and its ability to run at high engine r.p.m.

of out-of-balance vibrations from power unit to chassis.

This in itself is bound to produce its own problems. Once an engine is rubber-mounted it has a certain amount of freedom of movement longitudinally, vertically and transversely. Thus the power unit, usually including the clutch and gearbox, is subject to forces generated by the engine's lack of complete balance and the changing gas pressures, to forces generated by resistance to the torque being applied to the driving wheels (which changes direction between drive and over-run), to sideways forces generated by going round corners, and to vertical forces produced by moving up and down over uneven roads.

The engine movement produced by these forces can to a great extent be insulated from the chassis/body structure by designing and arranging the flexible mountings so that the engine can rock about its axes of minimum inertia (that is the axes about which the engine would rock without linear movement, if embedded in jelly). The principal of these axes is the longitudinal, which lies along a line sloping downwards rearwardly at around twenty degrees, passing through the crankshaft axis by the flywheel.

Chrysler introduced the idea of Floating Power by using rubber mountings, one fairly high at the front having two lines of damping at an angle to the vertical, and another under the gearbox with similar lines of action, all the lines meeting on the axis of minimum inertia.

These mountings are usually of synthetic rubber, which has a good resistance to the effect of heat and oil and possesses a degree of inherent damping. In some engine installations it has been found necessary to use additional means of damping, as for instance a strut connecting the top of the engine to the car body.

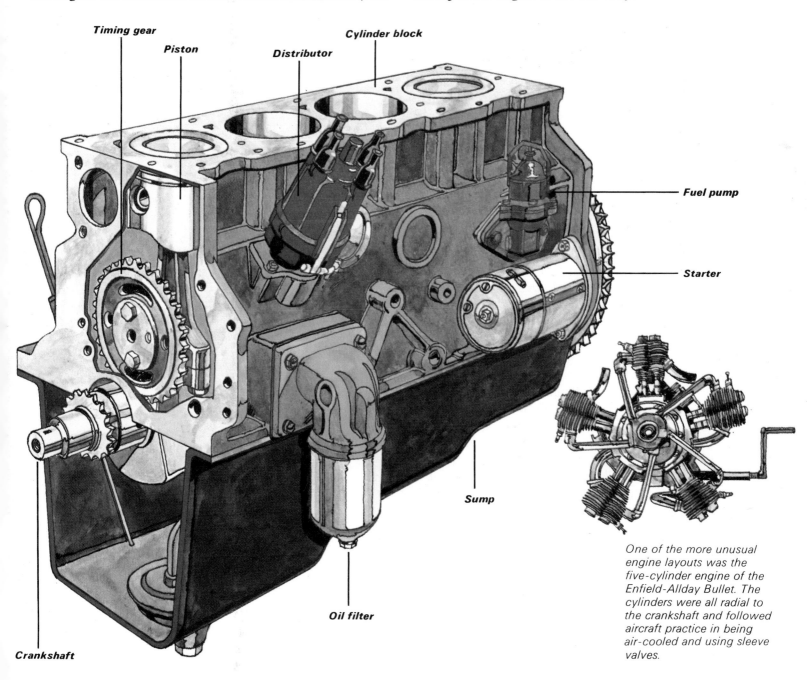

Timing gear

Piston

Distributor

Cylinder block

Fuel pump

Starter

Sump

Oil filter

Crankshaft

One of the more unusual engine layouts was the five-cylinder engine of the Enfield-Allday Bullet. The cylinders were all radial to the crankshaft and followed aircraft practice in being air-cooled and using sleeve valves.

The Mercedes Benz 130H originally designed by Dr Porsche
had a flat-four engine at the rear. When introduced to the
public the engine was water cooled and of greater capacity.
Although superseded by the more conventional 170V, the
130H was the forerunner of the Volkswagen.

Dr Ferdinand Porsche, who
worked for a number of
different car makers and
eventually headed his own
consulting office, is best
remembered for his design of
the Volkswagen.

COOLING SYSTEMS

The internal combustion engine derives its energy from the heat released from the burning of fuel and, ideally, none of that heat should be lost either from the engine or exhaust pipe. It is therefore unfortunate that the internal combustion engine uses only one-third of its fuel economically and the remainder merely heats the surrounding air.

Roughly the same amount of petrol is wasted in the cooling system as is used to drive the car, while even more disappears uselessly through the exhaust pipe.

The high temperatures generated within the combustion chamber, mean that the heat must be removed, or else the engine parts will either melt or become too soft to stand up to the stresses imposed. Early experimenters found this out the hard way, so that from the beginning all car engines have had some means of cooling.

The atmosphere can be used directly to cool the engine, or some intermediate medium in the form of a liquid (water being the cheapest and most readily available) can be employed to take heat more readily from a metal surface. The liquid can then give up its absorbed heat to the atmosphere.

Daimler relied on air cooling for his original motorcycle of 1885 and his subsequent two-cylinder engines, but even though he used a fan to blow through a casing covering the cylinder, he soon had to turn to liquid cooling.

Engines stayed just cool enough as long as they had only one or two cylinders which stuck out into the airstream and had a sufficient area of finning to catch a large flow of air. By 1902 H. H. Franklin began to sell air-cooled cars in North America. They were built to the design of J. Wilkinson and had a transverse four-cylinder engine. In 1908 a gear-driven fan helped the air flow, and two years later a fan was incorporated in the flywheel. They kept to air cooling until 1934, using vertical fins surrounded by an engine cowl.

Chevrolet produced a short-lived air-cooled engine in 1923 in which cooling fins of copper were welded to the cast iron cylinders. A big fan, mounted high at the front of the engine, blew air across the cylinder head and down the vertical copper fins.

In 1936, Ferdinand Porsche produced three air-cooled prototype cars. The following year Daimler-Benz made another 30 which were the forerunners of the Volkswagen, the "people's car", which was not available until 1949.

Porsche, born in 1875, the son of a tinsmith, was another of the giants of the German motor industry. If genius is a capacity for taking enormous pains, Porsche had this capacity to the ultimate degree.

He was a born inventive engineer of great imaginative sweep. Helicopters, airships, all manner of things, as well as cars seemed to be within his range, and he was simultaneously meticulous about the smallest detail.

Perfection was his aim and since this is an imperfect world and he was not the kind of man to suffer fools gladly, his life was littered with expressions of frustration — as for example, trampled hats.

His relationship with Adolf Hitler, whom he seems to

have treated as bluntly as he did everyone else, gave him the opportunity of achieving an object he had long had in mind — the building of a small, reliable car which the ordinary man could afford. Since Hitler also had the same notion, the People's Car was launched. However, the war intervened, and when Porsche died in 1951, he had not lived long enough to see the Beetle production exceed fifteen million — more than the ubiquitous Model T.

In the Porsche prototypes an engine-driven fan delivered cooling air to the two pairs of horizontal cylinders. It still does! Other successful air-cooled cars have been produced by Fiat, Citroën and Daf.

In his first car of 1885, Carl Benz started off with water cooling by jacketing the cylinder and leading the water through a grid-iron of tubes as a radiator. The Benz car and its successors relied on the fact that hot water, since it is less dense than cold water, always rises in a closed system. This causes a natural circulation system and is known as thermo-syphon cooling. With such a cooling system it is essential to have the top, or hot part, of the radiator, as high above the top, or hot part, of the cylinder jacket as possible, to aid the flow.

As radiators were lowered in the interests of car body fashion, it became necessary to aid the cooling water flow, either by fitting an engine-driven centrifugal pump in the bottom run of the cooling system piping, or to use an

impeller (often driven from the rear of the fan shaft) in the upper part of the system.

Because engines work more efficiently when they are hot, it was sensible to provide a means of restricting the flow of cooling air or water until a good working temperature was reached. Manually controlled radiator shutters were fitted to some cars, such as the driver-controlled roller blind thought up by Standard in 1922.

In 1916, the Detroit Motor Appliance Company had devised shutters worked by a thermostat in the cooling water. A similar thermostat shutter was fitted to the Straker Squire in 1920 and subsequently was fitted on Rolls-Royce, Salmson and other cars.

A thermostat was used to restrict the water flow for warming up in the Leyland of 1914, a device still employed in all liquid-cooled cars today. Early thermostats used metallic bellows, such as an aneroid barometer, filled with liquid, which expanded and contracted with temperature change to open and shut a valve in the top hose to the radiator. Later designs have a wax pellet embedded in a plastic casing to effect the same control movement, the wax thermostat being generally regarded as more reliable than the bellows type.

The best operating temperature for the internal combustion engine tends to be higher than the normal boiling point of water. Following aircraft practice, designers raised

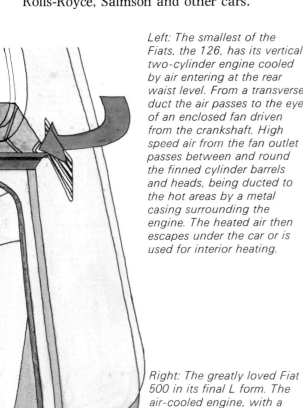

Left: The smallest of the Fiats, the 126, has its vertical two-cylinder engine cooled by air entering at the rear waist level. From a transverse duct the air passes to the eye of an enclosed fan driven from the crankshaft. High speed air from the fan outlet passes between and round the finned cylinder barrels and heads, being ducted to the hot areas by a metal casing surrounding the engine. The heated air then escapes under the car or is used for interior heating.

Right: The greatly loved Fiat 500 in its final L form. The air-cooled engine, with a complete disregard of freezing conditions and the ability to warm up rapidly, made this small car ideal for shopping and as a second vehicle.

Below: In 1920 the Straker Squire was fitted with thermostatically controlled shutters, like a venetian blind, to reduce the cooling capacity of the radiator and promote rapid warming-up from cold.

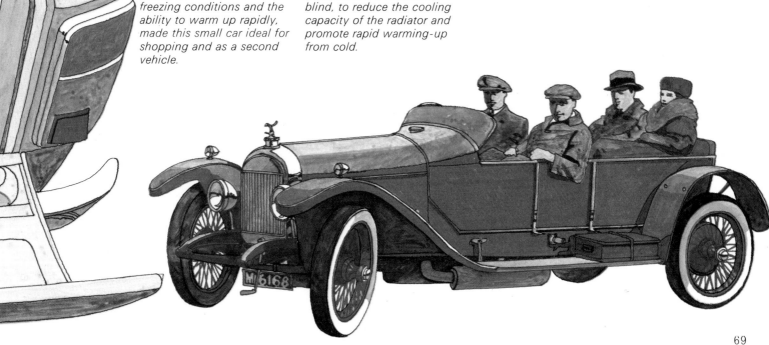

the boiling point by pressuring the cooling system. This was done by General Motors in 1954 by means of a radiator filler cap having a spring-loaded valve opening at a predetermined pressure to increase the boiling point by seven degrees to ten degrees centigrade. The valve has a second, inner, valve which opens when the system cools to prevent the forming of a vacuum in the system.

The Renault 4 of 1961 introduced the "sealed for life" cooling system in which an anti-freeze coolant was used. The overflow from the radiator, caused by high temperature coolant expansion, was led to a sealed header tank having an air space above the liquid. When the liquid cooled, it was drawn back into the radiator system so that, apart from leaks, there was no loss of fluid.

Primitive small bore tube radiators of the early days were soon found to have an insufficient cooling area for the slow flow of air. To increase radiator efficiency an engine-driven fan was added, while the tubes were wound with wire and, later, thin helical strips of metal, to provide a finned, or gilled tube. Another form of tube construction still in common use has a multiplicity of thin fin plates common to all the vertical tubes running between the top and bottom tanks of the radiator.

The honeycomb radiators on veteran and vintage cars comprised a large number of horizontal tubes which were expanded at their ends so that each tube presented a hexagonal shape. These tubes were soldered together at their ends to form what was, effectively, a rectangular core, in which the water could flow between the tubes as the air flowed through them. This provided an efficient heat exchanger but eventually the type became obsolete because of its vulnerability and cost of repair.

Another kind of radiator construction, the film type, became popular in the early 1920s. This produced a radiator similar to the honeycomb. But the water spaces were made from lengths of sinuous strip, soldered together to give a series of thin, wavy tube, water passages. These passages joined at their wave crests to form holes through which the water could flow. Later developments of this version used light alloy for the wavy strips, held together by an adhesive.

In the mid-1930s Murray Jamieson created a prototype sports car engine for E.R.A. which had the radiator fan blades spaced unevenly, with the aim of quieter operation. This fan was driven through a clutch designed to slip above a certain speed, so the fan did less work as air was rammed through the radiator by the car's forward motion.

A later application of this idea is the electrically-driven fan, controlled thermostatically to run only when the coolant temperature exceeds the desired figure. Other fans have thermostats which disengage friction clutches or control the quantity of a silicone oil used to provide a fluid friction drive in a viscous coupling.

An even simpler solution to this problem is to use flexible fan blades which automatically twist to decrease their angle as the engine speed rises.

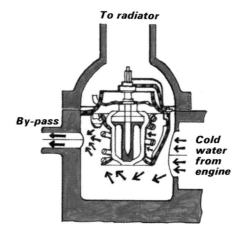

When the coolant is cold, the thermostat closes the passage between the engine and the radiator, allowing the coolant to rise to its working temperature.

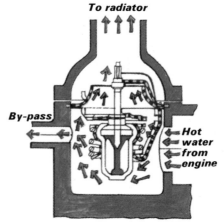

When the temperature rises above a predetermined figure, wax in the central capsule expands to force the capsule downwards and open the valve allowing coolant to flow to the radiator.

Right: An early product of one of the few remaining firms that date back to the start of the motor industry, the 1908 Renault was water-cooled and had its radiator mounted behind the engine as part of the dash. This layout was a Renault hallmark for some 30 years.

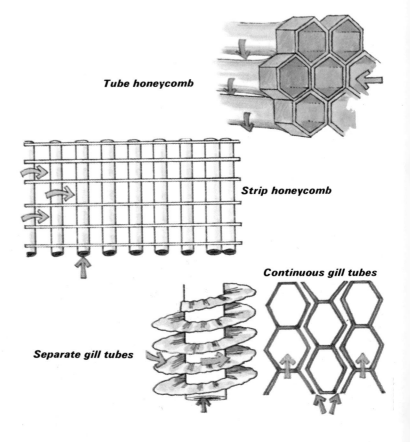

Tube honeycomb

Strip honeycomb

Continuous gill tubes

Separate gill tubes

LUBRICATION

Rubbing pieces of metal against each other is a sure way of wearing them out as the heat generated will destroy their surfaces, bringing rapid failure to the mechanism of which they are part. The quicker and harder they are worked, the more likely they are to be damaged unless they are held apart by some greasy substance. This problem is older than the use of metal in transport. As early as 3000 B.C. potters used fat to lubricate the bearings of their wheels.

Lubrication became a much more serious problem with the birth of the petrol engine. Although it was called a "high speed engine", the first form of petrol engine ran at no more than a tenth of the speed of its modern counterpart and its bearings were loaded relatively lightly.

Under those conditions, although lubrication was essential, the primitive practices already carried out in contemporary steam and gas engines were regarded as sufficient. The early Benz engine, with its exposed crankshaft, had a simple system to lubricate the main and big-end bearings and the cylinder wall. It consisted of large oil cups with adjustable needles, to dispense several drops of oil a minute. The other moving parts were lubricated only occasionally using the simple method of an oil can.

A slightly more complex system was to be seen on the Daimler engine with its enclosed crankcase. Oil was added to the crankcase periodically and the moving parts splashed it around. Eventually the oil found its way out of the crankcase, either through the bearings or the exhaust. So it either smothered the engine or fell on the road beneath.

This splash lubrication system continued to be used for many years, although refinements were gradually introduced. Initially it was supplemented by adjustable drip feeds, which were mounted on a dashboard oil tank. Veteran cars may be seen with rows of glass sight tubes, having flow adjusters above them, which allowed the driver to set the number of drops of oil carried down by pipes to the more important bearings. But a major advance came in the 1899 Mors with its V4 transverse engine, which had four variable-flow oil pumps which were driven indirectly by the camshaft.

Both Ford and Rhode cars showed improvements on a system of gravity feed, by using the flywheel to pick up oil from the sump and splash it into an open topped gallery whence oil passages led to the bearings.

With the drip-feed lubricator, adjustment of a needle valve regulated the rate at which drops of oil were fed to the bearings. These drops were visible in a glass tube below the reservoir bowl. When the engine was stopped the oil flow could be cut off by a lever on the lubricator top.

In time the flywheel was replaced by a pump, which picked up oil from the bottom of the crankcase (the sump) and fed it to the bearings or to jets, which squirted oil into holes in the connecting rod big-ends every time they came round. Such was the system in the Austin 7 of 1922, the car with which Herbert (later, Lord) Austin brought motoring to the British public just as Henry Ford did for Americans with his Model T.

William Morris, son of a humble Worcestershire farmer, was the other famous Englishman who thought in terms of mass production and achieved so much. Austin and Morris (now under the single banner of British Leyland) were the two names which spelt motoring to the British millions.

Austin, born in 1866, had the more academic background. As a teenager he was in Australia, when he had vague prospects of making a career in sheep-farming, but gravitated to its engineering side on shearing machines and maintained this interest on his return to England.

It was an almost inevitable next step in those days — inevitable for anyone of mechanical bent — to get involved with the new-fangled motor car; even, perhaps, to try

The ubiquitous Austin Seven appeared in many guises from the most popular and cheapest, the Chummy open four-seater to saloon and sports cars. Many firms made special bodies for their chassis such as Swallow Coachbuilding Company who were later to become Jaguar Cars Limited.

Sir Herbert Austin, who resigned from his position of General Manager of Wolseley in 1905 to form his own company, driving his 1922 Chummy. This firm was merged with its rival Morris to form the British Motor Corporation in 1952.

one's hand at designing one. In 1899 Austin's first production small car of $3\frac{1}{2}$ hp was a single-cylinder built under the Wolseley name by Vickers. By 1905 Wolseleys were tired of Austin's use of horizontal engines, and he left to form his own company.

Austin, like many of the pioneer designers, raced cars on the Continent. He did so with courage and tenacity, two of his outstanding characteristics. Another side of his character was his off-and-on irascibility.

Morris was a young Oxfordshire engineer who originally mended, hired and made bicycles. By 1913 he was producing light cars, one version of which sold for £175. This won good opinions and pointed towards the popularity that was to attend him most of the way.

Henry Ford, the "father figure" of mass production, had a harder job to win through than legend sometimes suggests. He designed a quadricycle in 1896, but years of experiment preceded the world-conquering "car for everyone", the Model T.

Two aspects of his story tend to be over-looked. He was a gambler willing to stake all on his aims, and he saw the value of racing his cars.

The early side of his activities is crowded out by the conventional image of assembly line initiator, tycoon, rugged individualist, and (in his later phase) querulous eccentric, but he once defeated the great Alexander Winton and in 1903 held the world speed record of 91·378 mph. It was the fame of his "999" racer that set him off and recommended his workaday models to the public.

In the 1920s, Ettore Bugatti, an Italian who built his car factory at Molsheim in France, produced cars of superb proportion and tremendous performance. They had a lubrication system in which the oil was sprayed into grooves in the disc webs of the crankshaft. The grooves had their open sides facing the crankshaft axis and from them oil holes were drilled which led to the crankpins.

Another splash lubrication system was to fit a curved trough below each crankpin into which a scoop at the bottom of the big-end would dip on each revolution.

Valve gear was usually left to look after itself in side-valve engines, existing in the oil mist created by the splashing of the crankshaft components and aided by the fluctuating pressure in the crankcase, caused by the rise and fall of the pistons and a certain amount of gas blowing past the piston rings.

Overhead valves qualified for more positive forms of lubrication, oil being pumped by internal passages or an external pipe to the rocker shaft and other working surfaces. Afterwards the oil drained back to the sump down the conveniently placed vertical holes housing the push-rods, or the camshaft drive. A wire gauze stopped the larger pieces of metal and carbon (picked up by the oil in its circulation) on their way back to the sump. From there the oil was sent on another journey round the engine.

An example of a modern car engine lubrication system is that of the Fiat 1500. Any new oil which is required is put into the engine through the filler cap on the rocker cover top. It flows down the pushrod tunnels in the cylinder block and into the deep forward end of the sump.

This engine has its oil pump driven by skew gears from

The 1924 Rhode was made in Birmingham by F. W. Mead and T. W. Deakin who had achieved a reputation for sidecars and the Medina cyclecar. The firm lasted ten years from 1921 to 1931

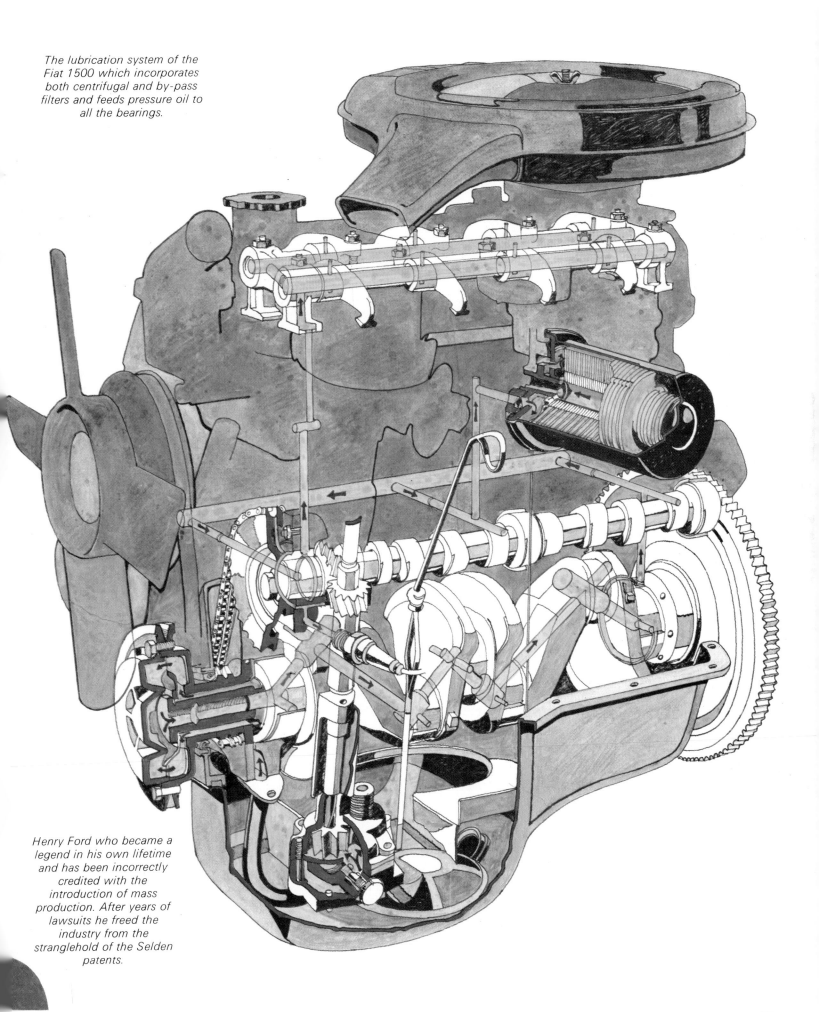

The lubrication system of the Fiat 1500 which incorporates both centrifugal and by-pass filters and feeds pressure oil to all the bearings.

Henry Ford who became a legend in his own lifetime and has been incorrectly credited with the introduction of mass production. After years of lawsuits he freed the industry from the stranglehold of the Selden patents.

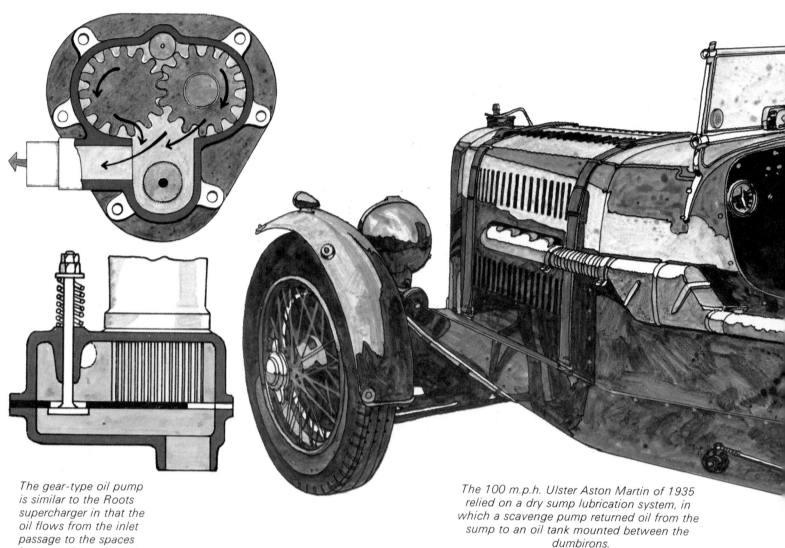

The gear-type oil pump is similar to the Roots supercharger in that the oil flows from the inlet passage to the spaces between the gear teeth and the casing. It is carried round the outside to the outlet passage where the pressure is regulated by a relief valve that spills excess pressure back to the inlet.

The 100 m.p.h. Ulster Aston Martin of 1935 relied on a dry sump lubrication system, in which a scavenge pump returned oil from the sump to an oil tank mounted between the dumbirons.

THE ENGINE / Oil Pumps

the camshaft. A large diameter gauze filter faces the bottom of the sump and is fitted with a horn-shaped tube leading to the suction side of the gear type oil pump. From the delivery side of the pump the oil is forced up to the front main crankshaft bearing. This particular type of engine is fairly unusual in having a centrifugal filter mounted on the front of the crankshaft.

The oil passes from this filter through diagonal drillings in the crankshaft with offshoots to feed the main and crankpin bearing surfaces. Oil reaching the rear main bearing escapes into a groove from which it is distributed to the camshaft bearings, the hollow rocker shafts, a pressure switch (which gives warning of low oil pressure) and a by-pass oil filter. Oil from the by-pass filter, which comprises a multi-leaved paper element designed to trap the smallest impurity, then drains back to the sump.

In many other systems the filter is of the full-flow type through which all the oil passes after leaving the pump. Thus all the oil is filtered on every passage through the

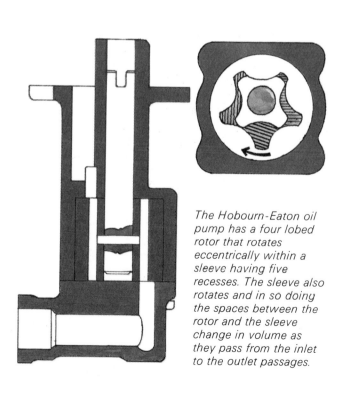

The Hobourn-Eaton oil pump has a four lobed rotor that rotates eccentrically within a sleeve having five recesses. The sleeve also rotates and in so doing the spaces between the rotor and the sleeve change in volume as they pass from the inlet to the outlet passages.

76

engine, and the centrifugal filter is not included. Pressure is regulated by a spring-loaded ball valve, which only opens under excess pressure to by-pass oil to the pump inlet or back to the sump.

The centrifugal filter operates as its name implies – by the oil being thrown outwards by a baffle. The oil then flows inwards to pass back down the centre of the crankshaft, leaving impurities sticking to the interior of the filter by virtue of their weight.

The lubricating oil has a secondary function, to conduct heat away from the bearings. It must not be allowed to become too hot itself, or it loses its lubricating qualities. In high performance cars particularly, sumps are sometimes provided with cooling fins. Others have a separate radiator or oil cooler, often mounted below the main (engine water cooling) radiator, as on the Rover 2000 TC.

Occasionally (as on the pre-1939 Aston Martins) a dry sump lubrication system is used. This has a second, scavenge pump, passing the oil from the bottom of the engine to an external tank. The tank on the Aston Martins was mounted between the chassis members forward of the front axle. This had the twin advantages of cooling the oil and reducing the overall height of the engine.

OIL PUMPS

Several kinds of pump are used to circulate oil under pressure. The gear type pump traps oil in the outer tooth spaces of two meshing gears. The oil is prevented from returning by the teeth of one gear filling the tooth spaces of the other where the gears mesh. Thus the oil is moved positively from one side of the pump to the other.

In another common variety of pump, the Hobourn-Eaton, a driven four-lobed rotor is mounted eccentrically in a rotatable ring with five internal lobes. With the rotor and ring rotating together, the spaces between the lobes increase in volume as they pass the inlet or suction port, and decrease as they pass the outlet port to force out the oil.

STARTER SYSTEMS

Because of its big horizontal flywheel at the rear, there were no problems in turning the engine of the 1885 Benz except those of the driver's strength and his ability to keep his fingers out of the spokes once it started to run. The Daimler did not have this facility, and consequently the nose of the crankshaft was extended to take a starting handle. Because it was necessary to ensure that once the engine had started, the handle did not whizz round and damage the hand that was turning it, a primitive form of freewheel was fitted.

This consisted of a crosspin in the handle engaging in a sloping angle slot in the end of the crankshaft. This release device was used as long as cars had starting handles.

On some cars the engine was not suitable to be started by a normal starting handle. The Trojan had a pull-up starting handle inside the body and, from 1913 to 1926, the Horstman had a foot starter. Even the first year's production of the Austin 7 had an internal hand starter.

An early form of self-starter used compressed air from a bottle charged by a compressor driven by the engine. Compressed air was fed to the cylinders in their firing order when a pedal was depressed. The distributing valve which controlled the operation was driven from the camshaft. In this system, used by Wolseley up to 1919, compressed air could also be used for inflating the tyres or raising the jack.

The first electric starter was fitted to the Arnold in 1898. This was a dynamo-cum-motor which could also provide additional power for hill climbing. But it was not until 1912 that Cadillac really began the use of electric starters. The dynamotor type of starter drove directly on to the crankshaft, whereas other starters were designed to drive a gear ring which was made integral with, or was bolted on to, the flywheel rim, consequently providing a gear reduction between the high speed electric motor and the low crankshaft turning speed.

The method of connecting the flywheel ring and the

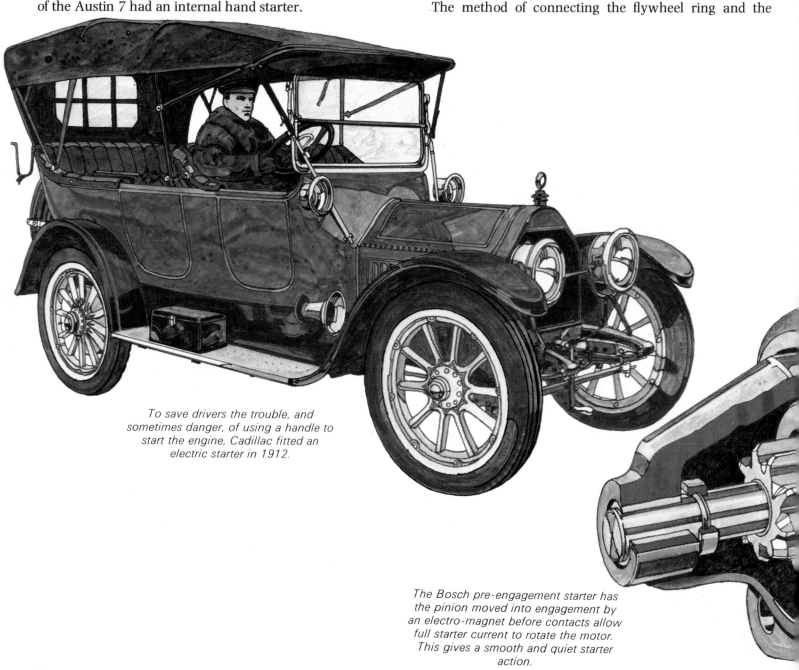

To save drivers the trouble, and sometimes danger, of using a handle to start the engine, Cadillac fitted an electric starter in 1912.

The Bosch pre-engagement starter has the pinion moved into engagement by an electro-magnet before contacts allow full starter current to rotate the motor. This gives a smooth and quiet starter action.

starter pinion, devised by Brooks and Holt in 1913, was similar to the Bendix invention of 1912 in America. In the Brolt method, the end of the starter-motor shaft was provided with a quick pitch screw thread which carried a mating threaded pinion. When the electric motor was started, the pinion was free and its inertia caused it to screw itself along the shaft and into engagement with the teeth of the ring gear on the flywheel. When the engine started, the pinion was turned faster than the starter motor so that it screwed itself back out of engagement.

Since 1914, the Bendix pinion has had a strong torsion spring to damp out the shock loading, both when the motor starts and when the pinion comes flying back as the engine fires.

In the Bosch pre-engaged starters, the pinion is engaged electro-magnetically with the flywheel ring just before the full current is supplied to the starter motor. This system is used to provide smoother and quieter engagement.

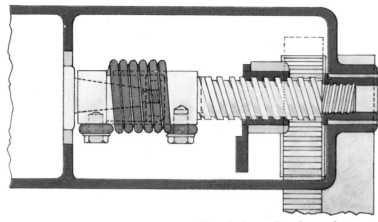

Even in its earliest form of 1914, the gearing for engaging the starter motor with the flywheel designed by Bendix had an inertia weight and quick thread screw for pinion engagement and a heavy spring to absorb shocks.

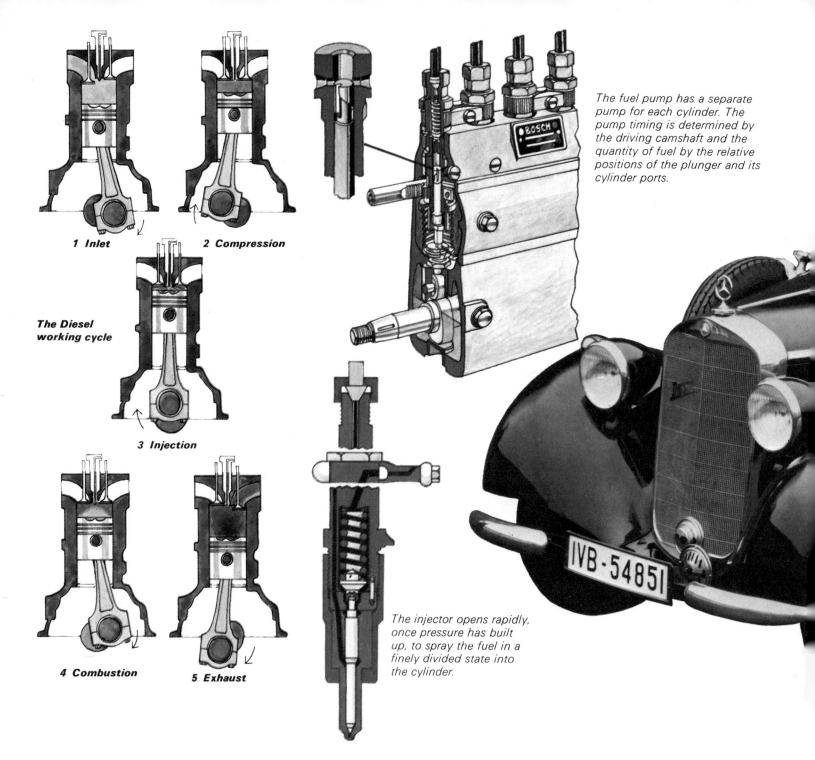

1 Inlet

2 Compression

The Diesel working cycle

3 Injection

4 Combustion

5 Exhaust

The fuel pump has a separate pump for each cylinder. The pump timing is determined by the driving camshaft and the quantity of fuel by the relative positions of the plunger and its cylinder ports.

The injector opens rapidly, once pressure has built up, to spray the fuel in a finely divided state into the cylinder.

IVB · 54851

DIESEL ENGINES

The petrol-burning reciprocating piston engine has been, and remains, the car's most popular and consistently used power unit. But it is by no means the only type. Well before the late 19th century, when it emerged as the most satisfactory form of motive power for road vehicles, engineers were working on alternatives. They have done so ever since, and there is still a lot of activity in this field.

More closely related to the petrol engine than most of the others, the diesel or compression-ignition engine is another form of reciprocating internal combustion engine which, in many respects, is similar to the petrol engine. It is widely employed in commercial vehicles, ships and railway engines, but has had relatively small use in cars.

The engine is named after Rudolf Diesel, a remarkable figure in the evolution of the internal combustion engine. Born in France in 1858, the son of a German father, Rudolf

became interested in the internal combustion engine as a young man. His research and experiments took him off the well-beaten track of the gas engine in the direction of compression ignition.

He produced the first "diesel" engine in 1892–3 when working with M.A.N. at Augsburg. It grew in favour mainly for industrial use, and Diesel prospered – particularly when he went to America. But his health – especially his mental health – suffered, and he died mysteriously when he vanished from a cross-Channel boat in September, 1913.

The diesel engine is at its best, and has been used most extensively, in its larger applications. Although it is more economical than the petrol engine, it has suffered from the penalties of greater weight, slow acceleration and a narrower speed range. It has, however, been offered as an alternative engine for Mercedes-Benz cars since 1931, in

The first production Diesel passenger car was the Mercedes 260D of 1935. The four-cylinder, 2·6 litre, engine produced 45 horsepower.

Rudolf Diesel, whose researches into the internal combustion engine were cut short when he disappeared from a cross-Channel ferry.

the Standard Vanguard since 1954, in the Land-Rover, and in various Fiats and Peugots.

In the four-stroke diesel cycle, air alone is admitted on the suction stroke and compressed on the compression stroke to about 500 pounds per square inch, as these engines run with compression ratios of from sixteen up to twenty-five to one. In consequence there is a great build-up of heat resulting from this compression, and the air reaches a temperature about 100 degrees centigrade above the point at which the fuel will burn – known as its ignition point.

Just before top dead centre, a very accurately metered quantity of fuel is injected into the combustion chamber in the form of a fine spray at a pressure of 2,000 to 3,000 pounds per square inch.

The fuel used is closely related to petrol but is a heavier type of hydrocarbon. It begins to burn immediately from the first moment of injection and continues to do so all the time it is being sprayed into the combustion chamber. The expanding gases force the piston down on the power stroke and are expelled on the exhaust stroke.

The compression-ignition engine is appreciably more economical than the petrol engine and has no need for carburetting or ignition devices. However, its apparent saving is cancelled out by expensive construction, caused by the extra rigidity required to withstand higher internal stresses produced, and the extreme accuracy and complication of the fuel injection pumps and nozzles.

These high costs might well have been accepted for passenger car use had it not been for the noticeable lack of smoothness as well as the higher level of noise in comparison with petrol engines of the same size.

STEAM ENGINE

Before the advent of the motor car, transport on land (other than that provided by actual animal power) meant the steam train. It is not surprising therefore that the first attempts to provide personal transport by mechanical power were concentrated on steam rather than the internal combustion engine.

Just as the first internal combustion engine designed to provide rotary power was a gas turbine, so the first steam engine to propel a vehicle was a steam turbine. This was the idea of Father Verbiest, who made a self-propelled steam vehicle in 1655 while on missionary duties in China. In 1763, Nicholas Cugnot, the French military engineer we have already mentioned, presented his steam tractor which smashed down a wall and was then impounded. There was another unhappy ending for the steam carriage of the Englishman Richard Trevithick. It burned out while parked outside an inn in 1801.

From then on, however, progress in steam was steady and devoted mainly to coaches and goods vehicles. Several small steamers were built privately but it was not until the end of the 19th century, when the railway was spreading through most developed areas of the world, that steam cars began to develop alongside the petrol car.

Bollée and de Dion, who were initially interested in steam, soon turned to petrol. But Serpollet, another Frenchman who devised a fast starting boiler in 1888, maintained his interest in steam for twenty years.

In America the steam car fared even better with 83 manufacturers producing steam cars, between 1860 and 1934, some of whose efforts are probably best forgotten. Models which will be remembered are the Stanley, in production from 1897 to 1925, the White (1901–1910), the Doble, the most advanced of all the designs (1914–1929), and perhaps the Delling (1923–1934), the last of the production steam cars.

The basic fuel was paraffin, used in a blow-lamp type of burner to provide the heat source. It heated a boiler which

The 1854 Bordino steam carriage, now in Turin, owes a lot to the earlier vehicles of Goldsworthy Gurney.

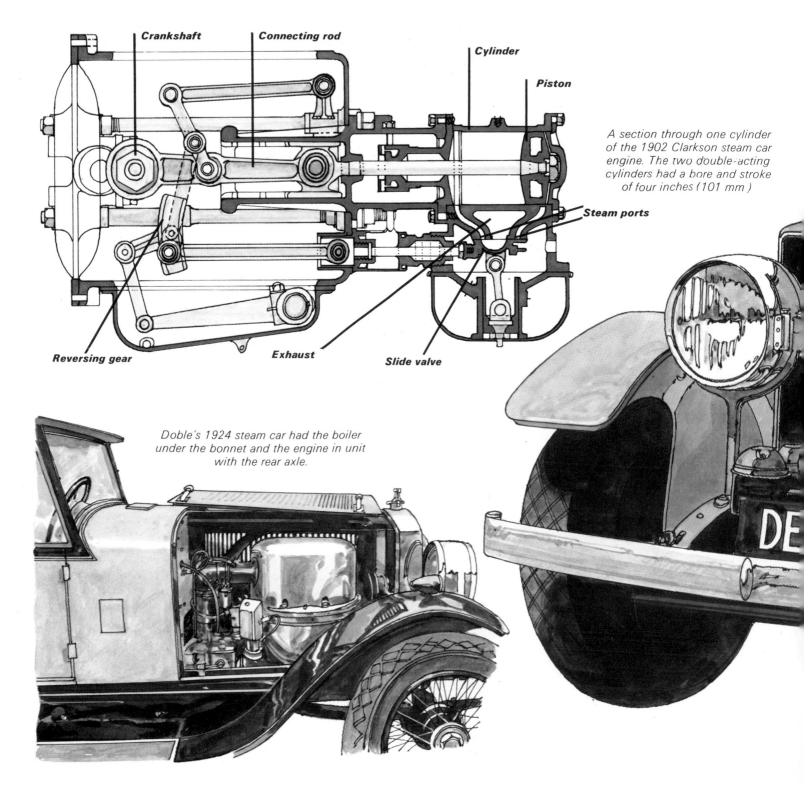

Crankshaft   Connecting rod

Cylinder

Piston

A section through one cylinder of the 1902 Clarkson steam car engine. The two double-acting cylinders had a bore and stroke of four inches (101 mm)

Steam ports

Reversing gear

Exhaust

Slide valve

Doble's 1924 steam car had the boiler under the bonnet and the engine in unit with the rear axle.

THE ENGINE / Early Steam

comprised multiple coils of small bore steel tubing, well lagged with asbestos and sheet steel and mounted under the bonnet of the vehicle.

As there was relatively little water in the coils, steam was raised quickly — in contrast to the lengthy process needed to get up steam for a coal-fired railway engine. The coils became so hot that the water, pumped in at the cold end, was flashed into steam in an instant. This led to the boilers becoming known as "flash boilers".

The steam was led to a two-cylinder engine coupled directly to the rear axle differential. In the engine each cylinder had a U-shaped valve, positioned in a valve chest full of high-pressure steam. The valve moved over three ports to connect the steam to one end of the cylinder,

and the exhaust to the other end, alternately. Steam was cut off from the cylinder inlet at a fraction of the piston stroke so that it could work on the piston as it expanded down to near atmospheric pressure. As steam worked on both sides of each piston, the effect was that of an eight-cylinder internal combustion engine.

Moreover, as the steam worked by gentle expansion, the engine was smooth and silent except for a soft chuff from the exhaust at slow speeds. There was no need for a clutch or a gearbox because the steam engine can develop full torque from a standstill and will therefore start as soon as steam is admitted.

In later versions, such as the Doble, the burner control became quite complicated. Within one minute of it being

Though conventional in appearance, the E13 Doble was silent and at least as fast as contemporary petrol-engined cars.

lit, steam was made available at 750 pounds per square inch. The expansive force of the steam was used more economically by feeding the second cylinder with the exhaust from the first. Thus the pressure was reduced in two stages. Additionally, the valve system was arranged not only to provide reverse, but also to allow variation of the time for which the steam was admitted to the cylinder working spaces. This gave control over the torque produced for starting and acceleration.

The great limitation of steam cars was their water consumption. So the Doble used what looked like a conventional car radiator to condense the exhaust steam which was returned as water to the tank. In the 1926 version of the Doble, a 30-gallon (135-litre) water tank would last

750 miles (1,200 kilometres) and its 26-gallon (120-litre) fuel tank for 250 miles (410 kilometres). The top speed was over 95 miles (150 kilometres) per hour, highly superior to most passenger cars of the time and 60 miles (95 kilometres) per hour was attained at only 900 rpm.

Impressive though these performance figures are, the fuel consumption of under 10 miles to the gallon (three and a half kilometres to the litre) points to a much less impressive level of specific efficiency.

Car manufacturers have continued to experiment with the steam engine but so far with little success. Recent research shows that, in the present state of knowledge, it is not practicable to produce anything which improves on the petrol engine for speed, economy and price.

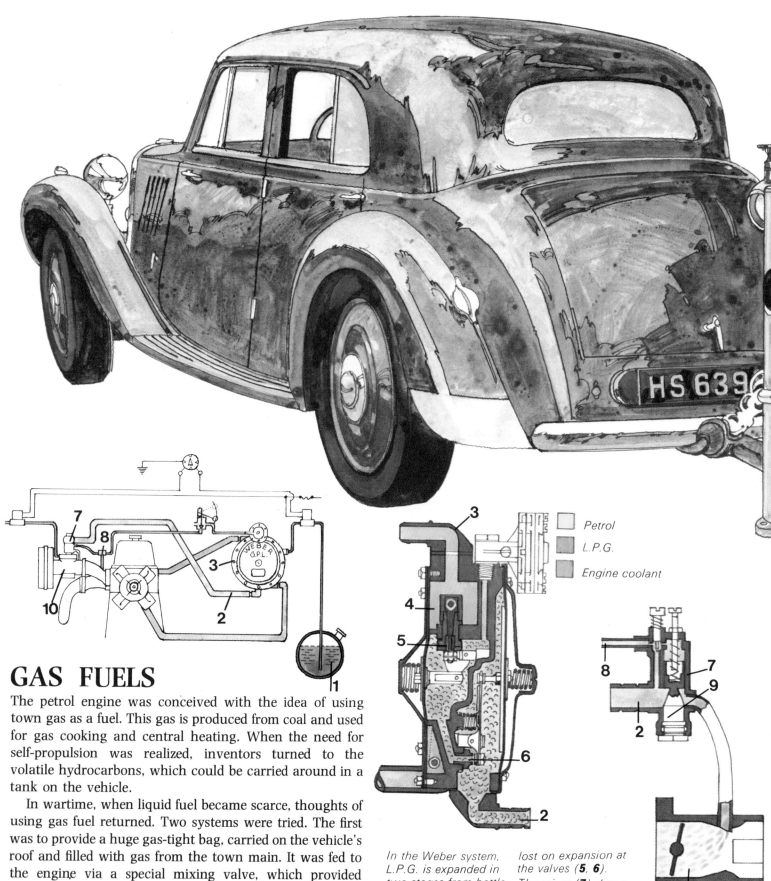

Petrol

L.P.G.

Engine coolant

GAS FUELS

The petrol engine was conceived with the idea of using town gas as a fuel. This gas is produced from coal and used for gas cooking and central heating. When the need for self-propulsion was realized, inventors turned to the volatile hydrocarbons, which could be carried around in a tank on the vehicle.

In wartime, when liquid fuel became scarce, thoughts of using gas fuel returned. Two systems were tried. The first was to provide a huge gas-tight bag, carried on the vehicle's roof and filled with gas from the town main. It was fed to the engine via a special mixing valve, which provided a combustible mixture of gas and air.

The second system was to tow a trailer carrying a gas-producing plant. This generated combustible gas by drawing or forcing a mixture of air and steam through a bed of incandescent anthracite or slack coal. It was a

In the Weber system, L.P.G. is expanded in two stages from bottle pressure (1) to atmospheric pressure (2) in the reducer (3). Engine coolant in a heat exchanger tube (4) replaces the heat *lost on expansion at the valves (5, 6). The mixer (7) draws the gas needed according to the inlet suction (8) acting on a spring-loaded metering valve (9) and feeds it to the carburettor (10).*

bulky device as it needed not only a solid fuel hopper feed, a shaking grate and a means of vaporizing water, but also a scrubber of considerable size to clean the gas before it could be mixed with air for use in the engine.

Another form of gas fuel is liquid petroleum gas, or L.P.G., a propane-butane mixture obtainable in pressurized gas cylinders. This can be used as a more direct alternative to petrol. Weber, the Italian carburettor manufacturing company, has a system in which a single fascia switch can effect a changeover from petrol to gas even when the engine is still running.

The main component of the L.P.G. system is a pressure-reducing and vaporizing unit which has two pressure-reducing valves, actuated by flexible diaphragms, in series. It is heated by engine-cooling water to compensate for the heat lost when the L.P.G. changes from liquid under pressure to gas at atmospheric pressure. Otherwise the system could freeze up.

A manually operated engine-starting device provides a correct mixture from the first stage of the main reducing valve directly to the inlet manifold. The main gas flow from the reducer-vaporizer unit leads to a mixing valve governing the flow according to the suction in the manifold and passing the measured quantity of gas to the minimum area section of the carburettor choke.

Compared with petrol, L.P.G. suffers a slight penalty in the form of lower maximum power. But it provides lower fuel consumption, greater engine flexibility, smoother, knockless acceleration and longer engine life because it leaves no carbon deposit when it burns. The major disadvantage involved with this form of fuel is the awkward need to carry the big gas cylinders.

ROTARY ENGINES

Throughout the whole of the period during which the reciprocating engine has been undergoing development, inventors have thought of obtaining rotary power from rotating components and not from pistons, which fly up and down with a complete reversal of direction on every half of a crankshaft revolution.

Many rotary-type engines have been conceived, still bearing in mind the Otto Cycle, requiring suction, compression, firing and exhaust phases. Between 1897 and 1908, an average of more than one a month of this sort of engine was invented.

In 1924 Felix Wankel joined the list and devoted his life to the rotary engine. Wankel, born in south-western Swabia, in Germany, had an unlikely rural background for a great engineer. He began work as a book salesman in Heidelberg. However, when still only 22 he started his own engineering workshop in the city.

He found in his experiments, as others had done before him, the great difficulty of sealing the rotor against the

The NSU Spyder of 1963 introduced the Wankel engine.

casing at the speeds, pressures and temperatures involved. But where others gave up, Wankel continued his work and, in 1929, took out his first patent.

In 1951 he went into partnership with N.S.U. to build a rotary engine. The first engine of this partnership was completed in April, 1954, the first N.S.U. prototype was tested in 1958, and the first production car with a Wankel rotary engine was shown at Frankfurt in 1963. This was the N.S.U. Spyder two-seater. The Ro80 followed another four years later.

In the Wankel engine a triangular piston has both rotational and orbital movements within a casing whose internal surface is shaped like a fat-waisted figure eight. This shape is called an epitrochoid. It is the path traced by a point on a circle whose interior is rolling (without slipping) on the outside of a smaller circle.

The piston, or rotor, is made with three points of contact — at the rotor tip seals. These are spaced from the first circle, which is in the form of an internally toothed gear. The smaller circle is an externally toothed gear which is fixed to the casing and mounted concentrically in relation to the driving shaft of the engine. Because the centre of the

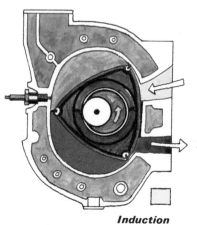
Induction

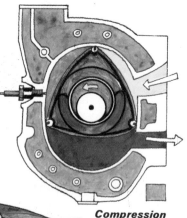
Compression

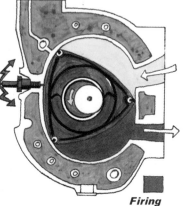
Firing

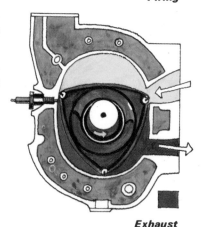
Exhaust

NSU Ro 80, a very advanced Wankel-engined car of 1967.

In the Wankel engine three cycles occur during the revolution of the rotor.

rotor is eccentric to the axis of the drive shaft, the shaft is rotated as the rotor turns.

As the engine runs, the three rotor tip seals rub against the inside of the casing, and the spaces between the sides of the rotor and the casing decrease and increase in volume twice for every revolution of the rotor.

In this way, the four strokes of the Otto Cycle can be reproduced for each revolution of the rotor and, because the rotor has three sides, there are three firing "strokes" per rotor revolution. Furthermore, as the gears are not of equal size and the rotor is mounted eccentrically, the driving shaft makes three revolutions for each rotor revolution.

Taken together, these two features result in there being one firing stroke for each driving shaft revolution. Thus a twin rotor engine is equivalent in its firing impulses to a four-cylinder, four-stroke reciprocating engine.

The construction of the Wankel engine is relatively simple, for there are no connecting rods and no valve gear with its driving mechanism. The casing, with its shape like a figure eight, does duty both as cylinder and crankcase. It carries the carburettor and exhaust pipe on one side and the sparking plug on the other. There are passageways for

cooling fluid between the inner and the outer surfaces.

The inner surface has to be machined very accurately and is coated with nickel containing minute particles of silicon carbide. This very hard material is Elnisil. To mate with this surface and provide a long life under all driving conditions, the tip seals are made of a softer material, with a combination of metal and ceramic called Ferrotic, a very hard material, in the centre. These seals are held in light spring contact with the casing. There are also side seals, situated near the curved faces of the rotor. These are spring-loaded into contact with the inner faces of the engine end covers carrying the bearings and stationary pinions.

The main driving shaft is virtually a crankshaft for an exceedingly short-stroke engine with large diameter crankpins. With a two-rotor engine, as in the Ro80, the crankpins or eccentrics are spaced 180 degrees apart. This compensates for most of the out-of-balance forces produced by the rotation of the shaft and rotors. The remainder are dealt with by a balance weight on a pulley which drives the accessories.

The bearings are lubricated by pumping oil through passages in the driving shaft. The oil helps to cool the rotors while being pumped through them on the way to the gears. Rotor seals are lubricated by dosing the inlet manifold with small quantities of oil metered in accordance with engine power output.

N.S.U. was first in the field with the Wankel. Now manufacturing licences have been taken up by many other companies. Licence holders may join a "Wankel Club" to exchange information, or they can operate independently.

Toyo Kogyo of Japan, maker of Mazda cars, was among the earliest licencees of the Wankel. It leads the world in production of the engine, having overcome the development problems with solutions sometimes differing from those employed by N.S.U.

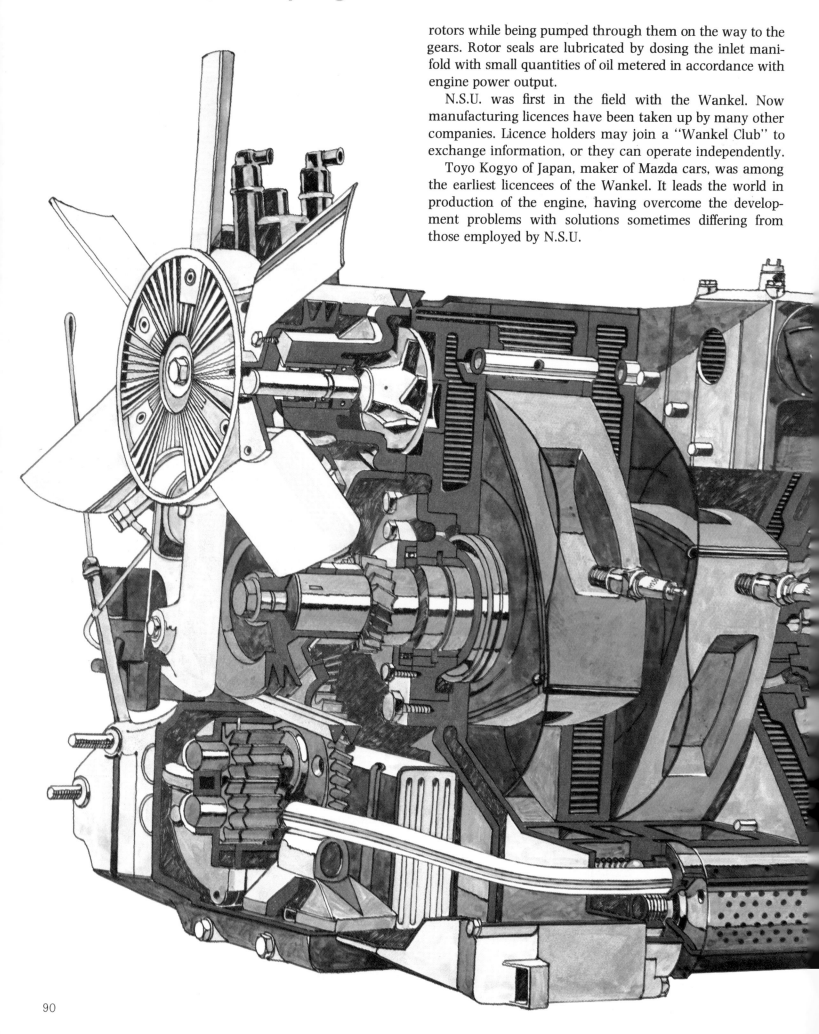

The Wankel engine is tolerant of low grade fuel, and an interesting development is a diesel version by Rolls-Royce. As well as having a level of mechanical silence and smoothness which is inherent in the rotary design, the Wankel engine is smaller in size and weight for a given ouput than a comparable reciprocating engine. The makers claim more efficiency than the piston engine and less pollution.

It is also said to be cheaper to produce in large volume production. But to date this claim has not been borne out by the cost of Mazda and Citroën cars with Wankel engines when compared with similar models (same bodies, equipment, running gear, and so on) using conventional engines. Also, the "greater efficiency" claim does not apply to fuel consumption, particularly at lower speeds. The design tends to lack low-speed torque and has less over-run braking effect.

However, considering the limited time in which Wankels have been in production, the design has made up a lot of lee-way on the reciprocating engine which started about 70 years earlier.

Two other rotary engines are at present under development. One, the Sarich, uses a lobed rotor and poppet valves. The other, the Anidyne, has two pairs of back-to-back pistons reciprocating in paths at right angles in a rotating cylinder block. So far, neither of these has reached the stage where it could be tried out practically on the road.

The NSU Ro80 twin rotor Wankel engine and transmission

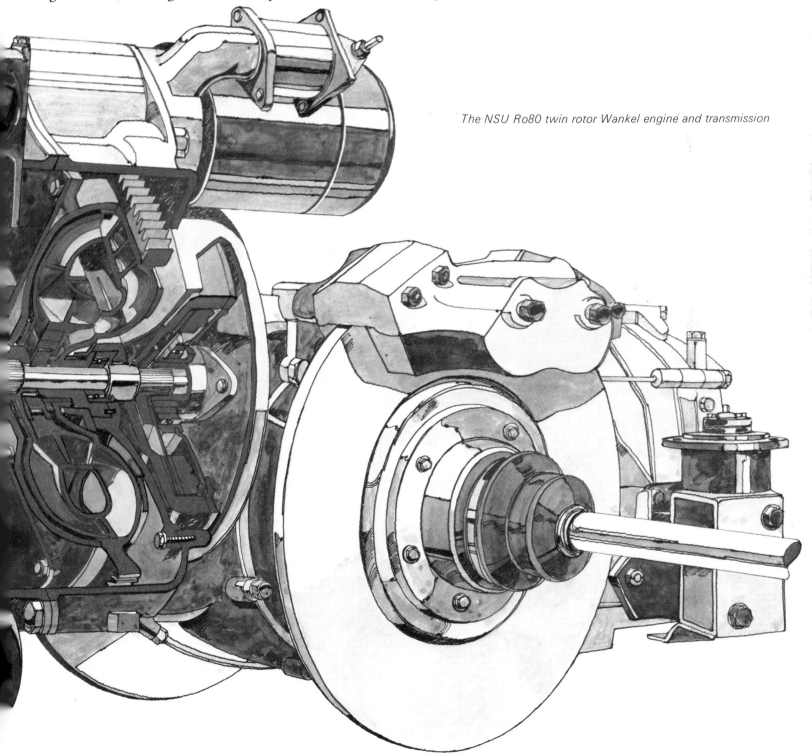

GAS TURBINES

The great impetus of jet aviation has made John Barber's 200-year-old idea for a gas turbine at long last a reality for motor vehicles.

For a long time the turbine principle had been applied successfully in other fields. Apart from stationary plant, it was used for several railway engines, notably on the Prussian state railway in 1920 as well as on the Swiss railway in the mid-1930s.

The gas turbine differs from all the engines considered so far in that power is developed continuously and not during one quarter of a complete cycle. This is most desirable, but it necessitates continuous compression of air and continuous burning.

Basically the engine comprises an air compressor (usually of the centrifugal type), a combustion chamber where the air is heated, and a vaned wheel, or turbine, on which the high velocity gases blast continuously to produce the power output.

Although axial flow compressors (multi-stage turbines which are driven instead of driving) can also be used to provide a non-pulsating air flow, the usual form of compressor has a single rotor with radial vanes. Air enters at the compressor eye, near the rotor centre, and is thrown outwards by centrifugal force to a surrounding chamber where the velocity energy is transformed largely into pressure energy.

This pressurized air is fed to one end of a combustion chamber, or flame tube, which has a fuel jet at the same end. Burning is similar to that in a big blowlamp. The temperature of the outer casing is kept down by giving the combustion chamber one or more perforated inner shells, forming annular ducts through which air is passed. This air is, of course, eventually heated by the flame before reaching the turbine.

The turbine has two annular rows of curved blades. The first is fixed to the casing and used to change the direction of the gas so that it flows on to the leading edges of the rotating turbine blades in the second row without shock. The rotating blades are curved in the opposite direction to the first blades, so that the reaction caused by reversing the gas direction drives the rotor and produces the power output.

By the suitable design of blade curvature, and entry and exit angles, and by addition of a further turbine stage, it is

Rover's T3 of 1956 was their third turbine-engined car.

Right: The Rover gas turbine

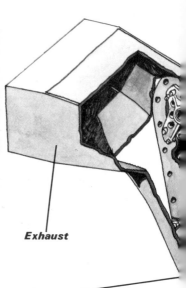

Exhaust

Heat exchanger

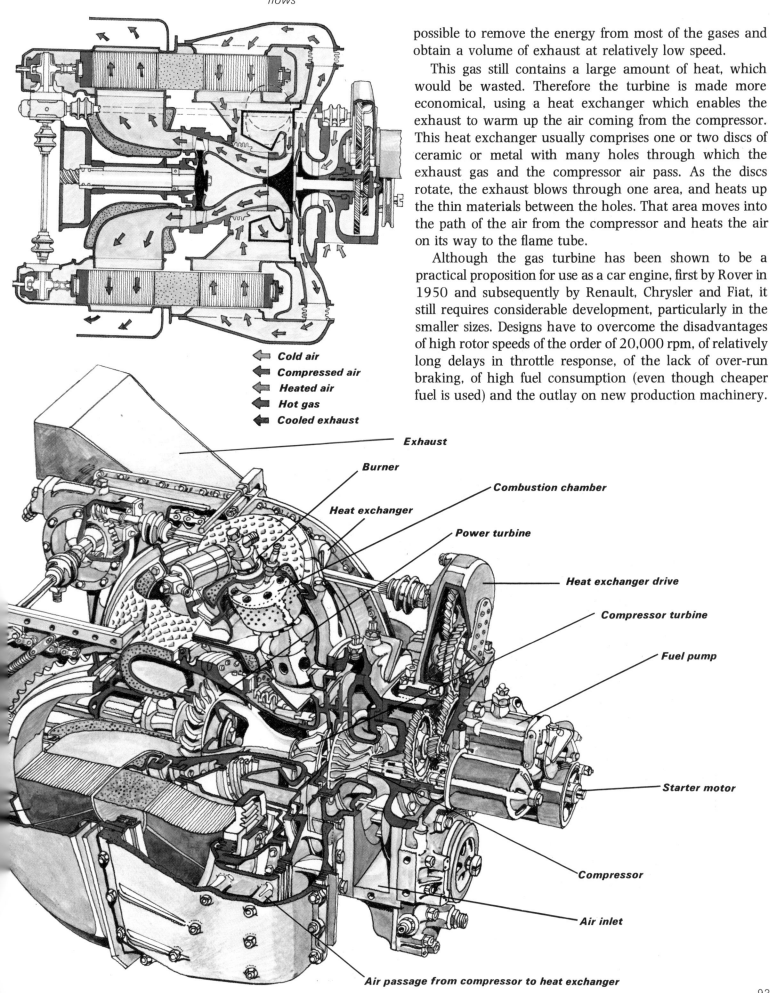

Horizontal section of the Rover gas turbine showing the gas flows

Cold air
Compressed air
Heated air
Hot gas
Cooled exhaust

Exhaust
Burner
Heat exchanger
Combustion chamber
Power turbine
Heat exchanger drive
Compressor turbine
Fuel pump
Starter motor
Compressor
Air inlet
Air passage from compressor to heat exchanger

possible to remove the energy from most of the gases and obtain a volume of exhaust at relatively low speed.

This gas still contains a large amount of heat, which would be wasted. Therefore the turbine is made more economical, using a heat exchanger which enables the exhaust to warm up the air coming from the compressor. This heat exchanger usually comprises one or two discs of ceramic or metal with many holes through which the exhaust gas and the compressor air pass. As the discs rotate, the exhaust blows through one area, and heats up the thin materials between the holes. That area moves into the path of the air from the compressor and heats the air on its way to the flame tube.

Although the gas turbine has been shown to be a practical proposition for use as a car engine, first by Rover in 1950 and subsequently by Renault, Chrysler and Fiat, it still requires considerable development, particularly in the smaller sizes. Designs have to overcome the disadvantages of high rotor speeds of the order of 20,000 rpm, of relatively long delays in throttle response, of the lack of over-run braking, of high fuel consumption (even though cheaper fuel is used) and the outlay on new production machinery.

TRANSMISSION-the use of power

Several thousand years ago, builders of wind and water mills found they needed to transmit the rotation of a horizontal driving shaft to a vertical driven shaft. In a watermill the wheel had a horizontal axis and the corn-grinding stones required a vertical axis. Further, the stones had to be driven at a higher speed.

These problems were solved by the use of shafts and toothed gears. Later, in the Industrial Revolution, when whole factories full of machines were driven from one engine, forests of cotton ropes and leather belts were used for the transmission of power.

The automobile pioneers, having used most of their inventiveness in producing an engine that would provide enough power to move itself, turned to the known ways of power transmission. Soon they were to realize the problems posed by weight and high speed.

Steam carriage builders had an easy time since the flexibility of steam allowed the driving axle to be the crankshaft. This cannot be done with the internal combustion engine for two main reasons. Firstly it cannot be set in motion just by opening a throttle. It has to be provided with some means, such as a clutch, which allows the engine to continue running when the car itself is stationary. Secondly, it develops little torque at low speeds and so has

to be provided with a torque-multiplying mechanism, or change-speed gear, to allow the car to accelerate from a complete standstill.

Because the clutch and the gearbox are difficult to fit to a sprung driving axle, some way of transmitting the power from the engine to the axle is required which will permit movement of the axle up and down in relation to the engine. Furthermore, since a vehicle has driving wheels which travel through different distances round corners (because they are spaced apart), a compensating gear or differential is needed to divide the power evenly between all the four wheels.

On the first of Carl Benz's vehicles of 1885 the engine was mounted with the crankshaft vertical to accommodate the large flywheel necessary for such a slow running engine. From the top of the crankshaft a pair of bevel gears drove a transverse shaft carrying a wide, flat pulley from which a narrower leather belt drove forwards to one or other of two pulleys mounted on bearings ahead of the engine.

One of the two pulleys was free to rotate on a bearing which was bolted to the chassis and, when the belt was on this pulley, the engine could run without moving the vehicle. The other pulley was rotatable about a second bearing and drove a differential, housed within that pulley,

which in turn drove two transversely extending shafts with sprockets at their outer ends to provide chain drive to the two rear wheels.

The option of the two pulleys, the fast and the loose, provided a form of clutch. The differential was known to be necessary from past experience with steam vehicles, and the flexibility of the chain drive allowed the rear axle to move under springing relative to the power unit. This primitive transmission did not allow a change of speed and had little ability to drive the car up hills. No doubt Benz was happy that his first vehicle could move under its own power at 10 mph (16 kilometres per hour).

In a later car of 1896 the engine was placed with the crankshaft horizontal and long enough to carry two wide, flat pulleys of different diameters. These drove by crossed leather belts to a double version of the original gearing, having the differential inside a single two-diameter pulley and the loose pulleys on each side. By shifting one belt at a time from a loose pulley to the appropriate step of the double pulley, two speeds and neutral were obtained. So a low gear was provided for hill-climbing.

Within a short time it became apparent that flat belt transmission had disadvantages. They slipped when wet or oily. They were limited in the ratios they could provide

in a small space (although some, such as the Canstatt Daimler of 1896, were made to give four speeds). They could not deal with increasing horsepowers, and did not last when used as a slipping clutch for starting from rest.

Emile Levassor, of the woodworking machinery firm which he ran with René Panhard in the Paris environs, was a typical example of the skilled engineer who drew upon an industrial inheritance when he turned his hand to cars (Panhard-Levassor was to become an illustrious name in the car world).

He used the things he knew to improve the transmission of his car. To this end he took the cone clutch and the sliding gear speed change from the machine tool industry to replace the driving belts.

He also put the engine in front, under a casing, with the crankshaft along the longitudinal centre line of the car, and drove an intermediate transverse shaft through forward and reverse bevel gears. This shaft was still connected to the rear wheels by chains. A year later, in 1895, his firm put the gears in a box in order to keep the oil in and the dirt out.

Levassor was also a brave and able racing driver. His performance in the race from Paris to Bordeaux and back in 1895 is one of the great stories of motor racing. For

Left: 1894 Panhard-Levassor with front engine and rear-wheel drive

Above: The intermediate shaft of the 1885 Daimler was belt driven from the engine shaft and carried pinions meshing with gear rings on the rear wheels.

Right: The gears of the steel-wheeled Daimler of 1889 were exposed to the elements and received little or no lubrication

almost 49 hours he drove the whole way solo, on solid tyres, to be first past the post. It has never really mattered that the judges awarded victory to another driver because of some quibble about the regulations. Levassor came to grief in another race the next year, and it has always been thought that his early death was due to the injuries he received in this race.

In 1899 the French firm of Renault made the final step in transmission layout. This was to set the fashion for most of the cars that followed. Louis Renault, founder of the firm, was in many ways the antithesis of Levassor. He was the comfortably off, gifted amateur who finds real fulfilment when a hobby becomes a profession. At the age of 21 he converted a motor tricycle into a small car which was extraordinarily advanced for its times. This proved so popular among his friends that he put the model into production.

His brothers, Marcel and Fernand, joined forces with him, but, although prosperity attended the firm almost from the outset, there were family tragedies. Marcel was killed racing and Fernand died in his early forties. Louis himself, who continued to run the business with his widowed mother, was jailed for collaborating with the German forces in 1944 and died soon after his release.

The Renault firm, which began with such flair and continued to flourish as a private concern, was nationalized in 1945. Louis Renault's original workshop still stands in the courtyard of the directors' building at Billancourt.

Renault's outstanding step forward in 1899 was his change from the intermediate shaft and final chain drive to the use of a propeller shaft, with universal joints, driving a bevel pinion which meshed with a crown wheel carrying a differential on the rear axle. So, by the turn of the century, the pattern of the main stream of transmission design was established for the future.

THE CLUTCH

The clutch provides the releasable connection between the engine, and the transmission and road wheels. Its prime purposes are to disengage the engine and to re-engage it smoothly with a gradually increasing torque, to allow the vehicle to move off from rest gracefully and comfortably rather than proceeding in a series of jerks.

With a simple belt drive, this was achieved, in some cases, by shifting the belt sideways to and from a pulley running loose on the driven shaft. In other models a roller, or jockey pulley, was pressed on the back of the belt to increase its tension and, in consequence, to increase its grip on the pulleys.

When the engine crankshaft and the gearbox input shaft were placed in line, as they were on the 1899 Daimler, a cone clutch was used. This had a tapered recess bored in the back face of the flywheel and a correspondingly taper-rimmed disc secured to the gearbox shaft. The disc was covered on its tapered face with leather, and the

entire gear shaft was urged forwards by a spring to push the leather cone into the flywheel recess. When lubricated with neat's foot oil, the leather gave a sweet engagement for commencing, and then the cones jammed home for full-power drive.

To make the initial engagement smoother a secondary, and smaller, cone clutch was added to the centre of the assembly. It was arranged to engage first on cones of a greater angle. The smaller cone on the gear shaft was spring-loaded to the main cone so that the latter could take over the major part of the drive at the moment that the clutch was fully engaged.

Disengagement was by pedal, which operated a forked lever pressing against a thrust collar on the gear shaft and acting against the engaging spring. Cone clutches of this type remained in fashion for a number of years despite various shortcomings. Among their disadvantages were their large size relative to their duties, their heavy flywheel effect which did not help gear changing, and the manner in which they would char their leather away if made to act as a variable speed gear.

Two other lines of thought at this time were the Weston-

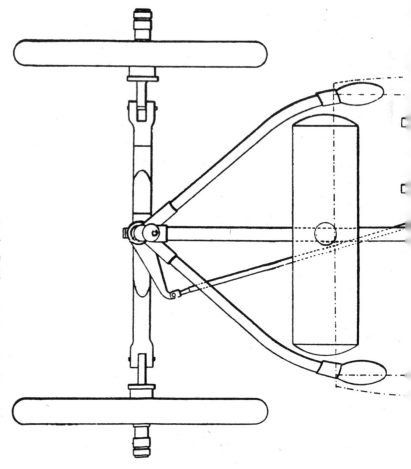

type multi-plate clutch and the Hele-Shaw clutch. The Weston-type clutch was conceived in 1863 and had a number of interleaved cast iron and phosphor-bronze discs. These were connected respectively by outer splines to the interior of a drum bolted to the engine flywheel and by inner splines to the driven shaft leading to the gearbox.

The plates were held pressed together by a spring in the end of the drum, and this spring could be compressed to release the pressure on the discs. An advantage of this type of clutch was its relatively small momentum when released. But it could drag, if not in the best condition, and it would seize solid if the oil (in which the plates had to run for sweetness) drained out. The Bugattis of the early 1920s employed this type of clutch, with the refinement of a toggle linkwork which added centrifugal pressure to the plates when the clutch was engaged and running at speed.

The Hele-Shaw clutch of 1903 was similar to the Weston but all the plates had annular conical rings formed in them which gave a combination of disc and cone clutch. Owing to the oil drag and the tilting of the plates, it was often necessary to provide a clutch stop. This stop was in effect a small brake which was applied to the driven

shaft at the moment when the clutch was released.

A development of the multi-plate clutch was the two-plate clutch as used on the Morris of the mid-1920s. The flywheel was hollow and contained three plain annular plates made to rotate with it by eight driving pins on which the plates could slide. Between these three driving plates were two driven plates, splined to a clutch centre which was secured on the output shaft, having two circular rows of holes containing cork inserts. Engaging pressure was applied by a row of springs between the flywheel and the inner plate, and disengagement by pulling the rearmost plate away from the pack. It was essential for this cork insert clutch to run in oil.

With the improvement of friction materials as pioneered by the Englishman Herbert Frood, particularly the moulded friction material which became available in 1921, the sticking disadvantages of the multi-plate clutch were overcome by the use of the single-plate dry clutch. This clutch is still in current use in modified form in most cars. Much of its development, from the late 1920s onward, was due to Borg and Beck.

The single driven plate has annular friction material

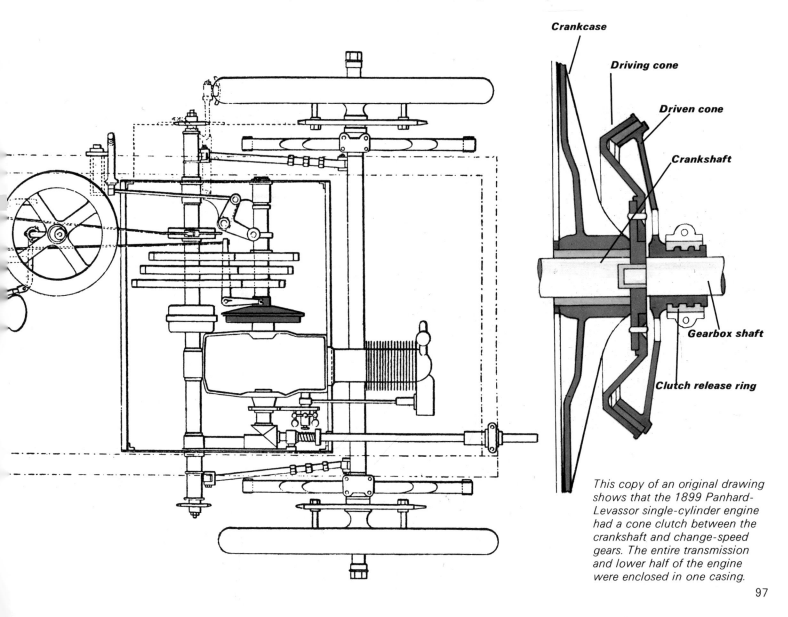

This copy of an original drawing shows that the 1899 Panhard-Levassor single-cylinder engine had a cone clutch between the crankshaft and change-speed gears. The entire transmission and lower half of the engine were enclosed in one casing.

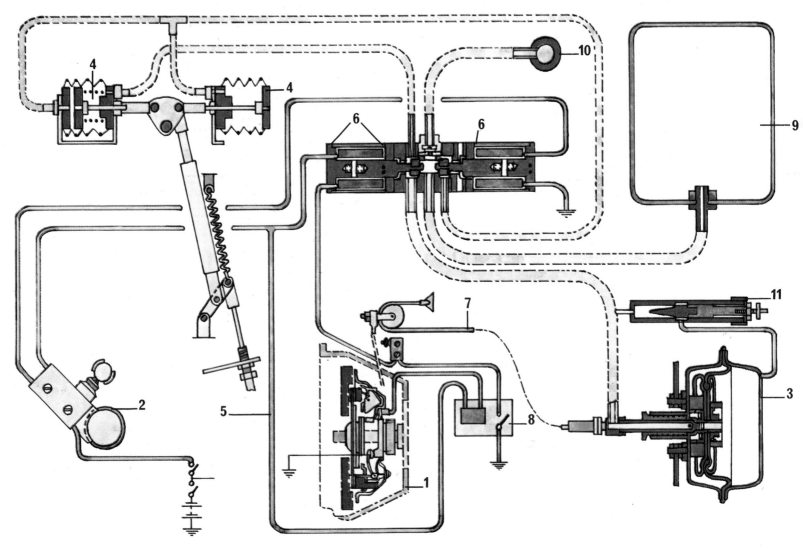

The Manumatic automatic clutch control

1	Centrifugal clutch	**6**	Throttle servomotors controlling
2	Gear lever switch		solenoids
3	Clutch-operating vacuum	**7**	Clutch withdrawal cable
	servomotor	**8**	Clutch speed-sensing switch
4	Throttle-operating vacuum	**9**	Vacuum reservoir
	servomotors	**10**	Engine inlet manifold
5	Cable from accelerator pedal	**11**	Clutch-engaging speed control valve

TRANSMISSIONS / The Clutch

facings riveted on each side and is sandwiched between a machined face on the rear of the flywheel and a presser plate carried (with freedom to move axially) in a pressed steel cover bolted to the flywheel. Six helical springs are supported in thimbles in the cover and bear on the back of the presser plate to provide engaging pressure.

Disengagement is by moving the presser plate rearwards against the helical springs. This is achieved by a system of radial levers hinged on the cover. The outer ends push against projections formed on the presser plate, and the inner ends on a clutch thrust bearing (a carbon ring bearing or a ball thrust bearing). Forward movement of the clutch pedal against the clutch thrust bearing, either directly or through a mechanical or hydraulic linkage, results in the rearward movement of the presser plate.

To give a cushioned, smooth engagement, the centre plate was made flexible by the use of radial slots, two dished laminations, or a wavy flexible construction behind the facings. Further cushioning was provided by mounting

the plate on a flanged hub to which it transmitted the drive through a circular row of springs, retained in rectangular openings in the plate and flange by two circles of D section wire.

In 1936 General Motors simplified the single dry-plate clutch considerably by using a corrugated conical disc pivoting on the cover. This acted between the thrust bearing and the presser plate in the same way as the release levers, and at the same time provided clutch engaging pressure. In later versions the disc (or diaphragm) was not corrugated, but was formed with inner radial fingers.

These diaphragms had their outer edge pushing against the rear of the presser plate and were fulcrumed on a round sectioned ring inside the cover, with the finger ends resting against the thrust bearing. This type of single dry plate diaphragm clutch is now almost universal.

To keep the necessary pedal pressure low when high clutch engaging pressures are employed, various types of centrifugal-force assisted clutches have been used. One of

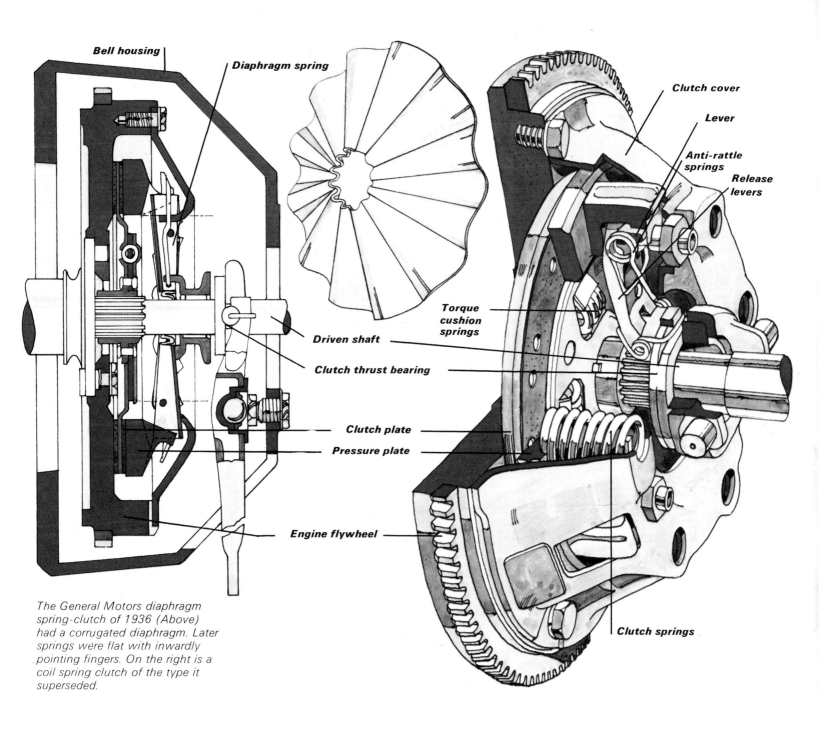

Bell housing

Diaphragm spring

Clutch cover

Lever

Anti-rattle springs

Release levers

Torque cushion springs

Driven shaft

Clutch thrust bearing

Clutch plate

Pressure plate

Engine flywheel

Clutch springs

The General Motors diaphragm spring-clutch of 1936 (Above) had a corrugated diaphragm. Later springs were flat with inwardly pointing fingers. On the right is a coil spring clutch of the type it superseded.

the simplest was to join a pair of toggle levers, between the cover and presser plate, with weights at the joints between the levers. Others used balls or rollers which moved outwards along wedging tracks as the rotational speed of the clutch increased. These centrifugally generated forces added their engaging thrust to main springs which could therefore be weaker in the interests of low pedal pressures.

From fairly early days the use of the clutch has been regarded as no better than a necessary evil by many drivers. To ease this burden, centrifugally-operated clutches, responsive to engine speed, have been employed to disengage the engine at idling speed and to provide a smooth, accelerator-responsive start from rest. The next step was to arrange a mechanism to disengage the centrifugal clutch when the gear lever was moved to select another ratio and to re-engage it when the required ratio had been obtained.

Many people tried this idea and, in 1951, Automotive Products produced what was to be known as the Manu-

matic control. In this system centrifugal weights engaged the clutch over a predetermined engine speed range when starting from rest. When the gear lever was moved, an electric switch (contained in the gear lever knob) and solenoid-system operated a vacuum servo to disengage the clutch through an over-riding release mechanism. A two-position switch sensed the relative speeds of the gearbox shafts and shut or opened the throttle, according to up or down shifts, to prevent racing or jerks during changes.

This system, and similar ones offered soon afterwards, suffered from several disadvantages. One was the complication caused by the fast idling speeds used for warming up, which were higher than the normal clutch-engaging speeds. Another was a tendency for the clutch to release when travelling downhill with the throttle shut. A method which substituted a fluid coupling or a torque converter for the centrifugal clutch, was used successfully by Volkswagen, Porsche and Fiat, among others, for several years. It had a separate friction clutch in the engine/gearbox drive.

FLUID COUPLINGS

The fluid coupling (a hydraulic centrifugal clutch), invented by Herman Fottinger in 1905, was developed by Vulcan of Hamburg for marine and diesel railway use with great success. It was not until 1926 that H. Sinclair had the idea of using the coupling on city buses. Four years later, Percy Martin pioneered the use of a fluid coupling in conjunction with a preselector gearbox on the Daimler Double-Six.

The fluid coupling is a self-contained hydraulic pump and turbine unit. It consists of two similar circular elements facing each other, the opposing faces having semicircular channels with radial vanes in them. One element, the impeller, is coupled to the engine, and the other element, the runner, to the gearbox. The circular ring-shaped space, called a torroid, is almost completely full of oil. When the impeller rotates, this oil is thrown outwards under centrifugal force. As it moves out, it follows the curve of the torroid and is projected into the runner, where it follows the curve of that half of the torroid inwards to join the impeller again at the inner diameter.

At the same time, the oil is moving round with the impeller by virtue of the radial vanes and thus has rotational

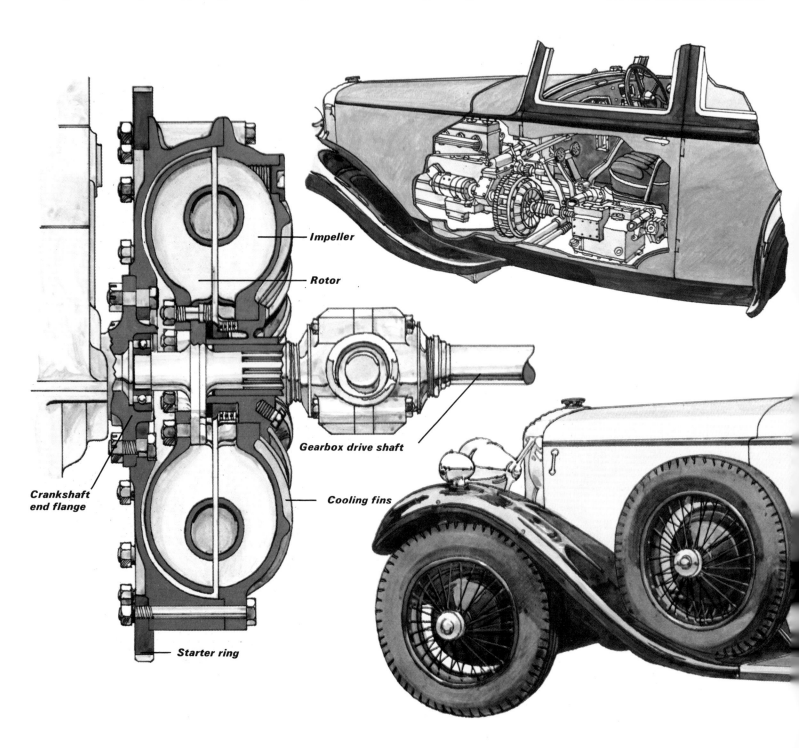

Impeller

Rotor

Gearbox drive shaft

Crankshaft end flange

Cooling fins

Starter ring

energy in the direction of rotation of the coupling. This energy is conveyed to the runner as the oil from the impeller meets the vanes in the runner. The path of the oil is best imagined as being in a helix with its axis bent round into a ring. As the same fluid is passing between the two elements, the torque input from the engine is equal to the torque output to the gearbox, although the speeds will be a little different.

This speed difference is apparent as slip. The slip is dependent on the rotational speed, and therefore the coupling acts as a centrifugal clutch with less slip as the engine speed increases, providing a smooth take-up in drive. At high speeds the slip is very small. As the engine speed is reduced to idling, the slip can reach almost 100 per cent, at which condition there is a very low drag torque which tends to make the vehicle creep if a gear is engaged at that point.

Since the coupling is not completely full, to allow for temperature expansion of the oil, there is a space at the centre of the flow. By putting two semi-torroidal channels in this space the coupling is made considerably more efficient because the oil is guided round its helical path.

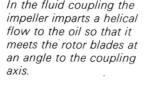

In the fluid coupling the impeller imparts a helical flow to the oil so that it meets the rotor blades at an angle to the coupling axis.

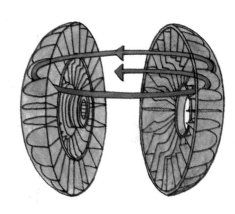

In place of the clutch, the 1932 Daimler Double 6-50 had a fluid coupling which drove a Wilson pre-selector gearbox. The third pedal operated the gearbox brake bands.

CHAIN DRIVE

Belts were able to transmit all the power from early engines, but began to slip more and more as power increased. For many engineers the next step was to chain-drive. In 1896, E. Hodgkinson devised an ingenious chain change-speed gear, with different size sprockets and a single chain that could be shifted sideways from one sprocket to another. As the chain was moved, the tension was released and a curved strip went round the sprocket to lift the chain from the teeth. The principle was similar in many ways to the Derailleur-type gears still used on many pedal cycles.

Another form of chain change-speed gearing had several chains between pairs of sprockets, the driving sprockets being on a transverse countershaft driven by the engine and the driven sprockets mounted on the rear axle. Speed changes were made by dog, or claw, clutches which coupled the appropriate sprocket to the shaft. With this system, used on Frazer-Nash sports cars to 1936, cheapness and lightness were obtained at the sacrifice of the differential.

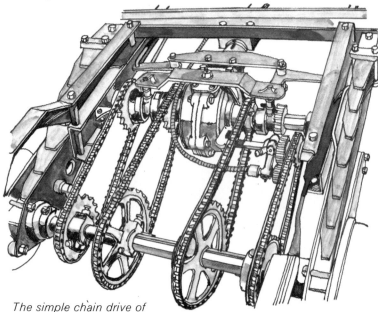

The simple chain drive of
the three-speed Frazer Nash had no differential and used
dog clutches to engage the selected sprocket with the
front drive shaft.

CONVENTIONAL GEARBOXES

The first suggestion that a countershaft change-speed gear could be used on a vehicle is probably that given in the description of a proposed steam vehicle by James Watt in 1784. This vehicle was never built, and it was not until 1894, and the Daimler engined Panhard-Levassor, that the countershaft gear began to come into common use. In this gear there are two parallel shafts – the input and output – or three shafts – the input shaft, the countershaft or layshaft, and the output shaft. In the latter case, the first and third shafts are on the same axis.

Two shafts can be used if it is not necessary to have the input and output shafts in line, as in most cars where the driven axle is near the engine. The drive goes into the

gearbox on the one shaft and comes out on the other at a lower level to drive a differential under the engine.

The three shafts are employed when the input and output are aligned and at opposite ends of the gearbox, as in most cars with front-engines and rear-wheel drive. Of the older cars, a large number had separate gearboxes not secured to the bell housing over the clutch, but secured directly to the chassis.

In the two-shaft (or single stage) gearbox, the input from the engine, via the clutch, is to one shaft on which a number of gears are fixed rigidly. These gears correspond to the number of speeds, or gear ratios, to be used. The other shaft is parallel to the input shaft and carries the

Above: The Frazer-Nash was a brain-child of Captain Archibald Frazer-Nash, later famous for the hydraulically-driven gun turrets of World War II bombers. The Frazer-Nash was a pure sports car with a straight channel steel chassis, quarter elliptic springs front and rear, and, as on this Colmore model of 1935, a change speed gear where dog clutches brought into use chain drives of different ratios.

same number of gears. These are either free to move axially while still in driving connection with the shaft or they can be clutched individually to drive the shaft.

In the first instance, the gears are usually in clusters of two and are so arranged that only one pair on the input and output shafts can be meshed at one time. In the second case, the input and output gears are always in mesh (constant mesh) and the appropriate gear on the output shaft can be coupled, or clutched, to that shaft.

Several types of clutches have been used. One form consisted of a key sliding in a longitudinal slot in the shaft. Another had balls that were moved radially outwards into slots in the gear bore by a tapered plunger inside the output shaft. The most usual form is the dog clutch.

The dog clutch is a sleeve, with axial projections, which can be moved along the shaft to engage its projections with mating projections on the side of a gear. In the more modern gearboxes, the dog clutches have internal teeth which can be slid over external teeth on a boss of the gear.

With this type of dog clutch it is possible to provide a synchronizing mechanism which ensures that the two parts of the clutch are moving at the same speed and that a tooth on one is opposite a gap in the other before engagement can take place. With other types, obtaining a smooth and quiet change was purely a matter of the driver's skill in adjusting the relative speeds of the parts by double declutching. This meant adjusting the driving shaft speed by throttle movement while the transmission was in neutral.

With the three-shaft (or two-stage) gearbox, the input shaft from the clutch (usually the shaft on which the driven plate slides) has a driving gear at its end, formed with dog clutch teeth on its end face. It is bored to provide a bearing for the front end of the output shaft.

The driving gear meshes with a gear on the forward end of a layshaft, parallel to the coaxial input and output shafts, so the layshaft is driven by the input drive gear.

For the typical four-speed gearbox, the layshaft has three more gears which are rigid with it. These mesh with three corresponding gears free to rotate on the output shaft. Double-sided dog clutches slide between the input driving gear and the first gear on the output shaft to provide direct (top) and third gear ratios respectively, and between second and third output gears for second and bottom gears. To obtain reverse, the rear dog clutch member is formed as a gear round its outer edge, and this can be driven through an idler gear from a gear on the layshaft.

SYNCHROMESH

As long ago as 1896, Count Albert de Dion and M. Georges Bouton tried to overcome their dislike of engaging the teeth of rotating gears by axial movement. The French count, whose family was descended from Jean de Dion, a participant in the fifth crusade of 1218, was famed as a duellist and gambler and, in 1881, his attention was caught by a model steam engine.

He traced the builders, Georges Bouton and his brother-in-law Trepardoux, and offered them increased wages to build him a steam carriage. Although his father tried to stop his son squandering money on these new-fangled vehicles, Albert went his headstrong way. A big man, physically and mentally, de Dion nearly always succeeded.

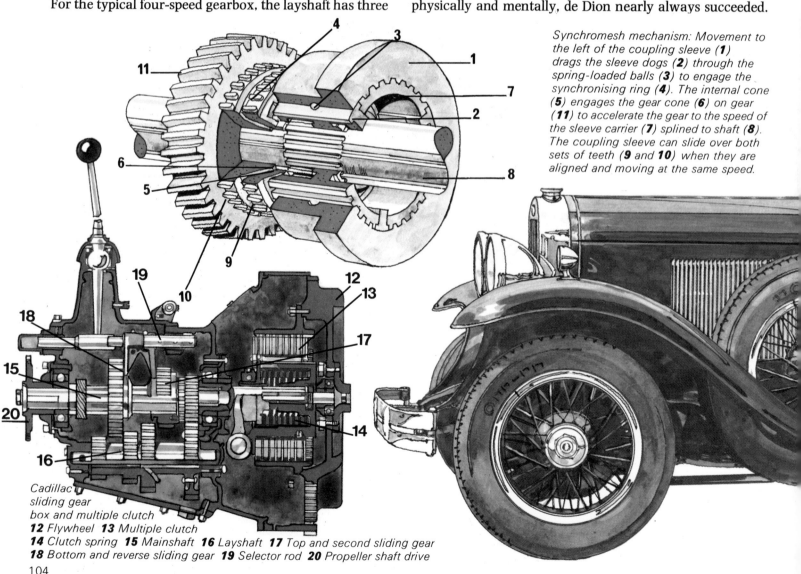

*Synchromesh mechanism: Movement to the left of the coupling sleeve (**1**) drags the sleeve dogs (**2**) through the spring-loaded balls (**3**) to engage the synchronising ring (**4**). The internal cone (**5**) engages the gear cone (**6**) on gear (**11**) to accelerate the gear to the speed of the sleeve carrier (**7**) splined to shaft (**8**). The coupling sleeve can slide over both sets of teeth (**9** and **10**) when they are aligned and moving at the same speed.*

Cadillac sliding gear box and multiple clutch
12 *Flywheel* **13** *Multiple clutch*
14 *Clutch spring* **15** *Mainshaft* **16** *Layshaft* **17** *Top and second sliding gear*
18 *Bottom and reverse sliding gear* **19** *Selector rod* **20** *Propeller shaft drive*

One occasion when he failed was in 1899. For his involvement in a political demonstration he was imprisoned for fifteen days, and the Automobile Club of France, which he had founded in 1895, was closed.

De Dion became fascinated by the petrol engine in 1889. Trepardoux hated it, and eventually his obstinacy and temper made him leave the firm in 1894. The company was reformed as de Dion and Bouton. Georges Bouton was the complete opposite of his partner — small in size and a technically gifted introvert. The firm continued manufacturing until the early 1930s.

The notion that the confident count and the diffident M. Bouton worked on in 1896 was a synchronizing system in which one gear had an extended cylindrical boss of slightly less diameter than the roots of the teeth. The other gear had a ring bolted to it through rubber bushes. When the second gear was slid axially, the ring and the boss engaged so that they nearly equalized the relative gear speeds before the teeth were meshed. This synchronizing device relied on slow relative movement between the teeth to prevent tooth and tooth locking.

In 1927, Piero Salerni designed a dog clutch for use between the gearbox and propeller shaft to allow coasting without engine braking and to facilitate gear changing.

This clutch had a baulking mechanism that prevented its re-engagement until the two sets of teeth were running at the same speed and were aligned tooth to space but it had no means for synchronizing the speeds.

Two years later, Bernard Thompson combined both the synchronizing and the baulking means in one clutch, the two essential features for shockless gear changes. Later the same year, General Motors used Thompson's basic ideas and cone friction synchronizers to develop the first Synchromesh, which was used in Cadillacs and, three years afterwards, by Vauxhall and Rolls-Royce.

There are two main types of synchronizing mechanism, the cone type and the split-ring type.

The cone type uses moving cones to make friction contact between an inner hub and the clutch element of the appropriate gear, so that the cones, hub and clutch element are accelerated to the speed of the input gear as the gear is engaged.

The split-ring type of synchronizer was developed by Ferdinand Porsche from 1947 onwards, although William Wilson of Austin had thought of using such a synchronizer without baulk means in 1932. In this system a split spring ring is used to engage the inside of the axially sliding clutch ring in place of the conical friction surfaces.

The 1929 Cadillac with a transformable town cabriolet body by Fleetwood Body Corporation.

GEAR SELECTION

The Panhard gearbox had a single shift rod with forked selectors engaging in grooves in the gear hubs. Longitudinal movement of the rod moved all the gears and successive positions produced one gear ratio after another. This meant that all the ratios had to be engaged in order for both up and down shifts. It was an inconvenience, but not a particularly serious one – motor cycle gearboxes work under a similar system.

An improvement on this was the use of the gate in the Daimler-Maybach belt-driven car of 1896 and the Cannstatt-Daimler two years later, which had a four-speed single stage gearbox. With a gate shift mechanism, two longitudinal selector rods, each having a single selector fork (or three rods for a four- or five-speed gearbox) are mounted parallel to each other in the gearbox.

Each rod has in it a transverse slot and three smaller grooves, which are acted on by spring-loaded balls, or plungers, to hold the rods in any one of three possible positions. When the gears are in neutral, all the slots are aligned and can be engaged by the end of a short lever inside the gearbox. This lever can pivot about two axes at right angles to each other.

Sideways movement of this short lever, either directly by an upward extension which forms the gear lever handled by the driver, or by linkwork connected to the gear lever, selects which rod is to be moved – the top/third rod, the second/bottom rod or the reverse rod. Movement, in a fore-and-aft direction, shifts the appropriate rod longitudinally to move the selector fork and clutch ring to engage the gear.

In early mechanisms the gear lever moved in an H-shaped gate. This was superseded by a spherically mounted gear lever, constrained only by the two perpendicular pivots. With this mechanism, any gear can be engaged directly from neutral.

To give more floor space at a time when American cars were becoming very wide and three-abreast seating in front was genuinely practicable, the 1938 Cadillac had linkwork from the gearbox which led to a lever mounted on the steering column, bringing back an idea used in the early days. Many postwar European cars (for example, Triumph from 1946) followed suit, although few were wide enough to make three-abreast seating desirable.

However, the arrangement necessary for a four-speed and reverse gearbox was complex. Few arrangements of this type worked well and many became deplorable with wear, so that the idea largely phased itself out. One or two manufacturers pursued the idea, notably Renault with the 16, and with improved techniques the few surviving steering column gearchanges were made to work well.

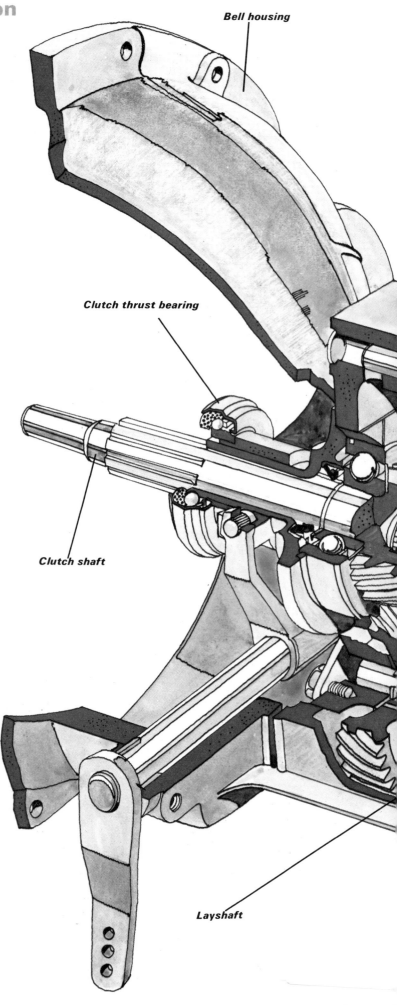

Bell housing

Clutch thrust bearing

Clutch shaft

Layshaft

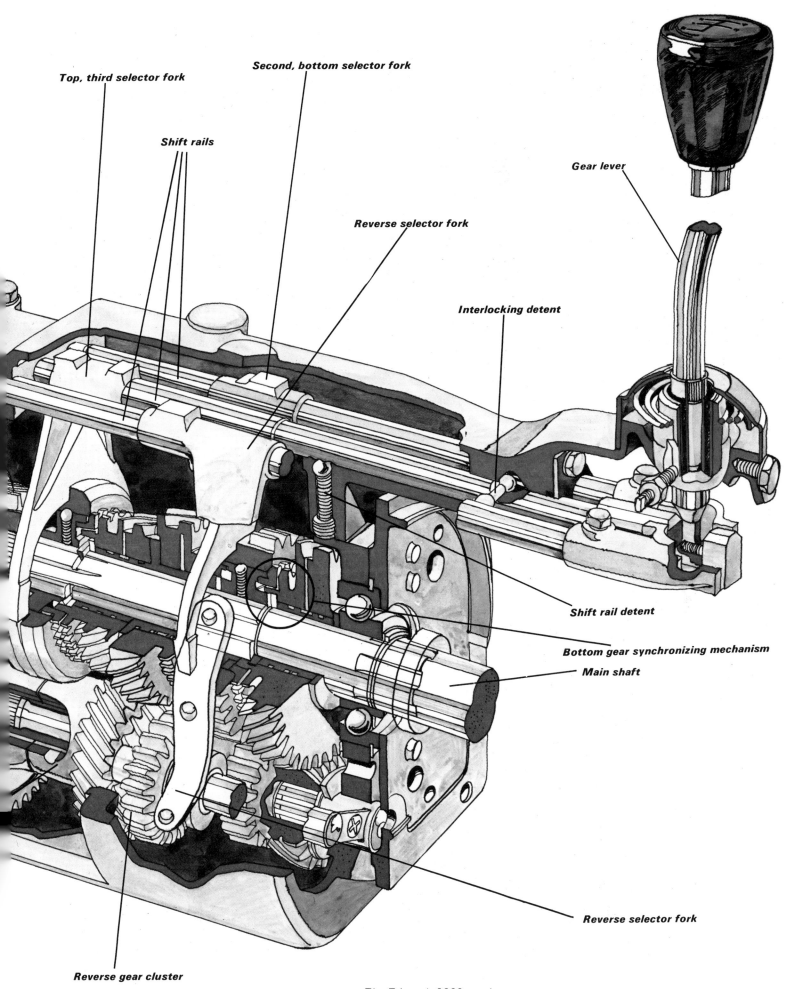

Top, third selector fork

Second, bottom selector fork

Shift rails

Reverse selector fork

Gear lever

Interlocking detent

Shift rail detent

Bottom gear synchronizing mechanism

Main shaft

Reverse selector fork

Reverse gear cluster

The Triumph 2000 gearbox

One of the greatest automobile designs, the Ford Model T. This one was built in 1907.

EPICYCLIC GEARS

The use of trains of epicyclic gears is another popular form of change-speed gear, starting around 1895 with the three-speed Benz Comfortable and the Roots and Venables two-speed Petrocar.

In a simple three-element epicyclic gear train there are three main elements, a central gear called the sun, an outer gear with internal teeth known as the annulus, and one or more planet gears between the sun and the annulus. The planets are held on a planet carrier.

The sun, planet carrier and annulus all have a common axis and, by holding one and using the other two as driving elements, changes can be rung in the ratios produced and the directions of rotation.

If the planet carrier is held, the sun gear will drive the annulus at a slow speed in the reverse direction. If the annulus is held, the sun will drive the planet carrier in the same direction at an even slower speed. If the planet carrier and the annulus are clutched together, then the whole gear train will rotate at the same speed and in the same direction as the sun gear.

The epicyclic gear has the advantage that a change of ratio is not dependent on engaging gears but on braking or clutching. This can be frictional and therefore smooth.

Earlier trains provided either reverse or two speeds, often in conjunction with a belt drive. Later gears used epicyclic trains to provide all the required ratios. Usually, as in the Lancaster of 1900, one train was used for bottom, two trains acting together for second, a direct-drive clutch for top and an additional train for reverse.

One of the most significant cars in the entire history of motoring, Henry Ford's Model T, of which over 15 million were built, used a slightly different form of epicyclic gearing. In the Model T Ford there were no annulus gears but three planet gears, which were fixed together and free to rotate on a spindle fixed to the back of the flywheel.

The planet gears were of different sizes and meshed with sun gears, also of different sizes and on tubular shafts. The front sun gear was connected to the output, or propeller shaft. At the end of its own tubular shaft it carried one side of a direct drive friction clutch. The other side of the clutch was driven by the crankshaft extension, so that, when the clutch was engaged, there was direct drive from the engine to the rear wheels. The other two sun gears were coupled to two separate brake drums having external contracting brakes.

By selectively braking the drums, low, forward and reverse ratios were produced. The Model T had direct and low forward speeds and reverse, all of which were engaged by three pedals. The left pedal, when depressed, engaged the low speed brake band. At mid-travel, it freed both that band and the direct-drive clutch and, when fully released, it engaged the clutch to provide direct drive. The centre pedal engaged the reverse brake band and the right pedal operated the vehicle brake, which was a transmission brake on the outside of the clutch. To save holding

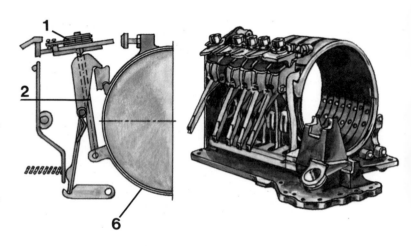

the left pedal in neutral, the clutch was also connected to the handbrake lever and was disengaged at mid-travel.

When working with Beardmores in 1919, Walter Wilson devised the compound epicyclic gear train used later in the Wilson preselector gearbox, fitted to the 1930 Daimler and later cars. This gear system had four sun-planet-annulus trains, four brakes and a direct-drive clutch to give four forward and one reverse ratio.

The Wilson compound train was the first of the "accelerating trains", in which the epicyclic gear sets were used in series to obtain different ratios. It is known as an accelerating train because the first annulus is driven faster for each upward ratio shift.

A preselection mechanism, devised in 1928, allowed a ratio to be selected by a lever mounted on the steering column and engaged some time later, when the driver wanted it, by depression of a pedal. The lever turned a

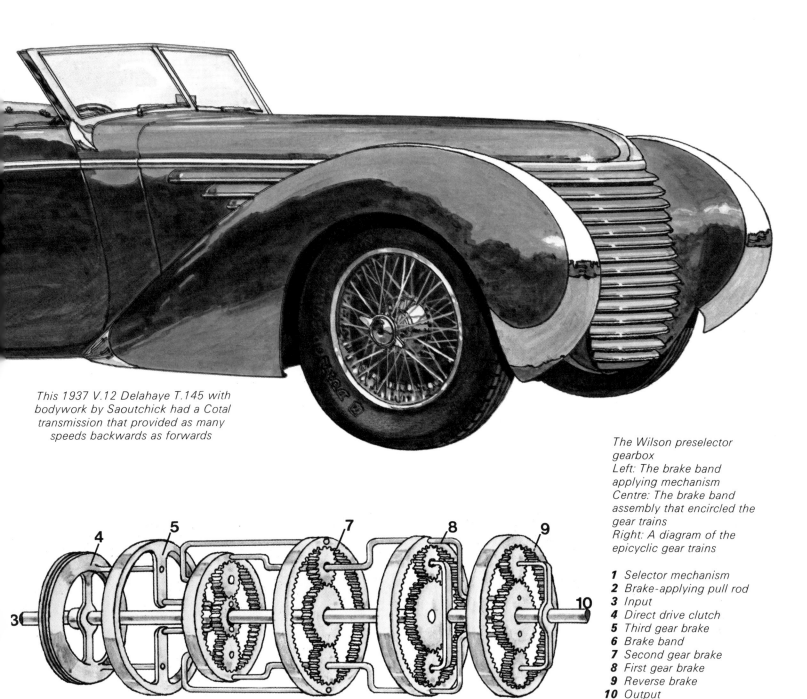

This 1937 V.12 Delahaye T.145 with bodywork by Saoutchick had a Cotal transmission that provided as many speeds backwards as forwards

The Wilson preselector gearbox
Left: The brake band applying mechanism
Centre: The brake band assembly that encircled the gear trains
Right: A diagram of the epicyclic gear trains

1 Selector mechanism
2 Brake-applying pull rod
3 Input
4 Direct drive clutch
5 Third gear brake
6 Brake band
7 Second gear brake
8 First gear brake
9 Reverse brake
10 Output

camshaft in the gearbox and the camshaft selectively operated a row of struts used to engage each of the brake bands which locked the gear trains. When the pedal was depressed, the appropriate strut end moved into a grooved bar and any other strut moved out. Releasing the pedal caused the grooved bar to rock and engage the appropriate brake (and gear train) while at the same time allowing the remaining brakes to be free.

In 1912, George Perret introduced an epicyclic gearbox in which the planet carrier had spindles at right angles to the transmission axis. All the gears were bevel gears, similar to the gearing in the Automotive Products' automatic transmission used in front wheel drive British Leyland cars today. Perret also employed electro-magnetic brakes for obtaining the various ratios, as did George Pollard of the Menco-Elma Syndicate from 1916. Pollard tilted the planet spindles to obtain a better choice of gear ratios.

A parallel spindle location for spur planets, again with electro-magnetic clutches and brakes, was used by Edward Reeve of Wolseley Motors in 1917. Two years later, Jean Cotal employed a similar system with the addition of a pin (turned with a screwdriver) which could lock the gear in the lowest ratio if the electric current failed. An addition to this gearbox was a power take-off shaft which could be used for a dynamo or starter motor.

By 1935 the Cotal gearbox was being driven through a hydraulic coupling. A means of sensing, from the throttle pedal, the precise stage when the coupling was neither driving nor on the over-run was used to inhibit the gear change except in that condition and to provide a smooth and clutchless transition. A facet of the Cotal gearbox was a separate reverse train, with its own control, enabling all four ratios to be obtained in both forward and reverse. This gave the 1935 Delahaye interesting possibilities.

OVERDRIVES

Because of the need to provide good low and middle range acceleration and flexibility, there is a tendency to choose gear ratios suitable for these conditions. A possible result is that the top gear ratio is too low to allow the engine to operate at its greatest power and lowest consumption conditions at higher speeds. To obviate this, a higher fifth gear can be incorporated in the gearbox to give a ratio higher than direct drive, or an additional overdrive unit can be bolted to the rear of the gearbox between the output shaft and the propeller shaft.

Additional two-speed gears have been in use for commercial vehicles for many years, and in the early 1930s Edgar de Normanville devised a simple single-train epicyclic gear for passenger car use. The gear train had the input to the planet gear carrier and the output from an annulus gear with a conical exterior. The sun gear was coupled to a clutch-brake member with conical inner and outer surfaces.

This was lined with friction material and, in one position, engaged the annulus to lock the gear in direct drive. In the other position, the brake exterior cone engaged a complementary cone in the casing to hold the sun gear and provide the overdrive ratio.

A one-way, or freewheel, clutch between the carrier and the annulus maintained the drive while the clutch brake was moving, and prevented engine overspeed during changes. The clutch was shifted into engagement by spring means and moved to the braking condition by hydraulic pressure. This pressure was under the control of an electro-magnetic valve.

A relay in the electrical circuit between the driver's switch and the hydraulic valve prevented the use of the overdrive under high torque conditions in the lower gears and, also in reverse, at the moment when the one-way clutch would otherwise engage.

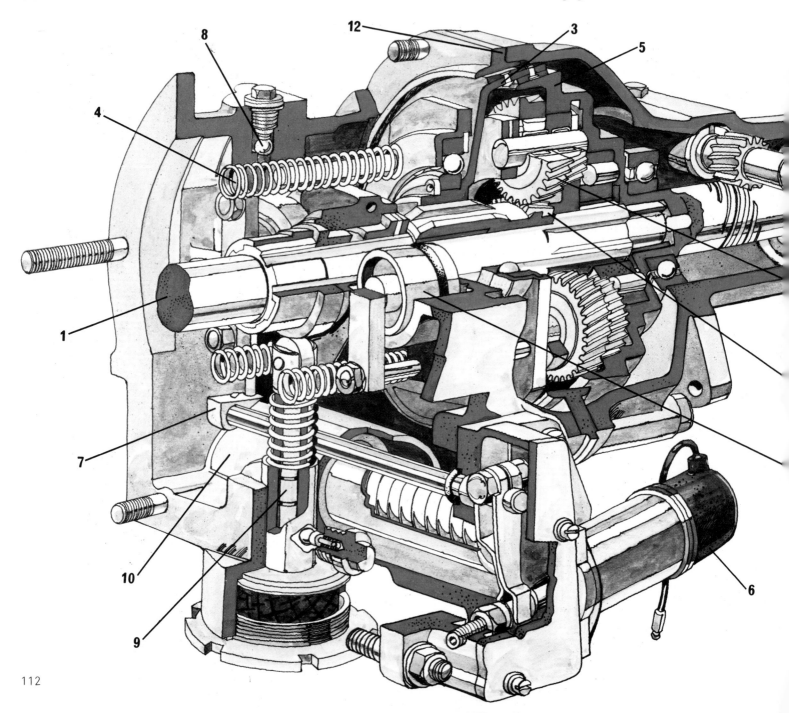

AUTOMATIC TRANSMISSION

From the beginning, engineers, naturally enough, have striven to make cars easier to drive. No single facet of driving has been consistently less popular than changing gear. Over the years it has steadily become easier.

A degree of expertise was formerly required to synchronize the speeds of the engine and road wheels and then effect a smooth engagement of rotating gears or dog teeth. Synchromesh got over that problem. But, although smooth engagement was assured, gear changing became an increasing chore as traffic became heavier.

There was a growing desire for a fully automatic transmission. Early examples, particularly in America, used pneumatic, hydraulic or electric "hands" to move the gear lever in its two planes, and to release and engage the clutch simultaneously. All this was controlled by devices which sensed operating conditions, such as engine speed, road speed, engine torque, the driver's throttle demand and

The 1965 Vauxhall Cresta had a Powerglide automatic transmission.

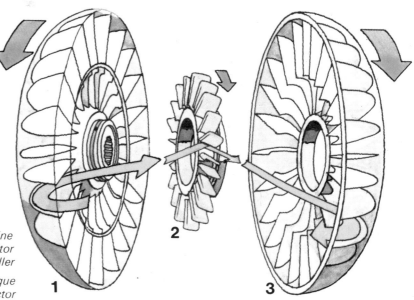

1 Turbine
2 Reactor
3 Impeller

The hydraulic torque converter has a reactor mounted for rotation in one direction only to increase the torque from the impeller to the turbine below coupling speeds

*Left: The overdrive unit has direct drive from gearbox shaft (**1**) occurring when conical clutch/brake member (**3**) is urged to the right by springs (**4**) to clutch with a cone (**5**) rigid with the output shaft (**2**). For overdrive, solenoid (**6**) rocks a lever (**7**) to open a valve (**8**) that passes pressure oil from pump (**9**) and accumulator (**10**) to pistons (**11**). The pistons pull the member (**3**) to the right to hold it against brake cone (**12**). The drive then goes through the epicyclic gear (**13** and **14**) to rotate cone (**5**) at higher speed.*

vehicle acceleration. Such a system was devised by Gaston Fleischel of France in 1933.

Other designers took the idea of the epicyclic gearbox, where smooth changes were obtained by the engagement of brakes or clutches, and combined it with a fluid coupling or a hydraulic torque converter. Whereas in the coupling there can be no change in torque between the input and output shafts, a third stage of stationary blades turns the hydraulic coupling into a hydraulic torque converter.

The third stage of blades (the reactor) deflects the fluid flow from the turbine so that it re-enters the pump (or impeller) vanes in the direction in which they are rotating and thus increases the forward momentum of the fluid. Being in a closed circuit, the forward momentum of the fluid which meets the turbine blades is also increased and results in an increase in output torque. This increase, usually of the order of two and a half to three and a half times, is greatest at stall (i.e. when the turbine is stationary) and falls as the turbine speed rises until, when the turbine speed is equal to that of the impeller, there is no torque increase, since the reactor becomes inoperative. This is a

113

situation suited to all the needs of a motorcar transmission.

In 1924, Allan Coats suggested mounting the reactor on a free wheel, so that at the equal speed (converter lock-up) the reactor could rotate with the other two elements and the torque converter would run as an efficient hydraulic coupling.

Hermann Rieseler, of the Vulcan Works, where so much original development on hydrokinetic couplings was carried out, designed a transmission in 1927 with a torque converter, which could be locked for solid drive by a friction clutch. This drove a two-speed and reverse epicyclic gear controlled automatically by a speed responsive governor. Although nothing more was heard of this transmission, it reappeared in a similar form in 1949 as the Packard Ultramatic.

Meanwhile, in 1940, General Motors had introduced the Hydramatic transmission on Oldsmobile. It was probably this unit, more than any other, which popularized fully automatic transmission and caused it to be regarded in North America, first, as a highly desirable optional extra, and soon, as the normal type of transmission.

In its original design, G.M.'s Hydramatic transmission used a fluid coupling and three epicyclic gear trains to give four forward and a reverse speed automatically, under the control of the position of the throttle valve and a double governor valve which was sensitive to two ranges of road speed. A manual selector lever could override the automatic selection when conditions were right for such a change, and a parking transmission lock was provided.

The Hydramatic was modified, mainly in the complex hydraulic circuitry, to give smoother shifts, both up and down and by developments of the timer, governor, selection and sequence valves. In 1956 a second hydraulic coupling replaced the front friction clutch, and gear selection was by filling and emptying the couplings. In 1960 a three-element torque converter was employed instead of the simple hydraulic coupling. The latter transmission, the 61—05, was designed for smaller cars and European use.

Vauxhall made use of the Hydramatic 61—05 from 1960 onwards. This transmission had a torque converter and two sun-planet-annulus epicyclic gear trains. It employed a wholly hydraulic, wholly mechanical and split torque hydraulic and mechanical drives to obtain bottom and reverse, second and top gear ratios respectively. Smooth brake application in the transmission was provided by a three-stage accumulator servo, and by timing, pressure regulator and engine torque compensator valves.

Among recent advances in automatic transmissions is the tendency to replace the complex hydraulic valve systems of control by electronic systems providing greater opportunities for taking into account more conditions to influence the shift pattern. For instance, one system differentiates between throttle demand and the acceleration produced to give a measure of gradient. It moves the automatic shift speed upwards in the road speed range when climbing hills, and downwards when descending

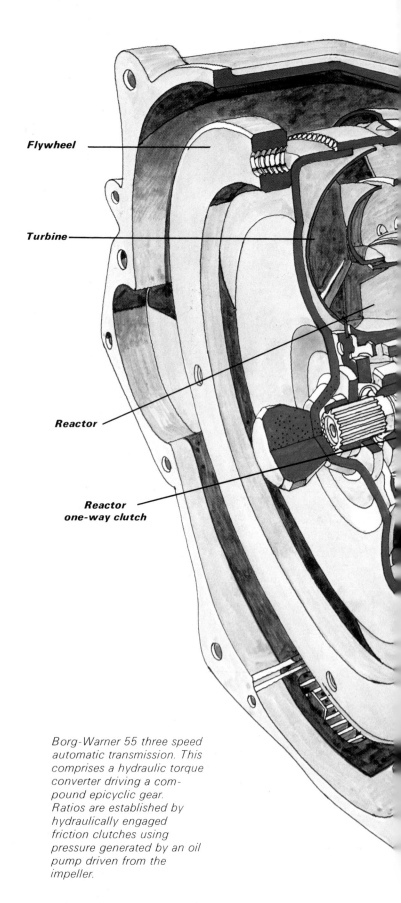

Flywheel —

Turbine —

Reactor

Reactor
one-way clutch

Borg-Warner 55 three speed automatic transmission. This comprises a hydraulic torque converter driving a compound epicyclic gear. Ratios are established by hydraulically engaged friction clutches using pressure generated by an oil pump driven from the impeller.

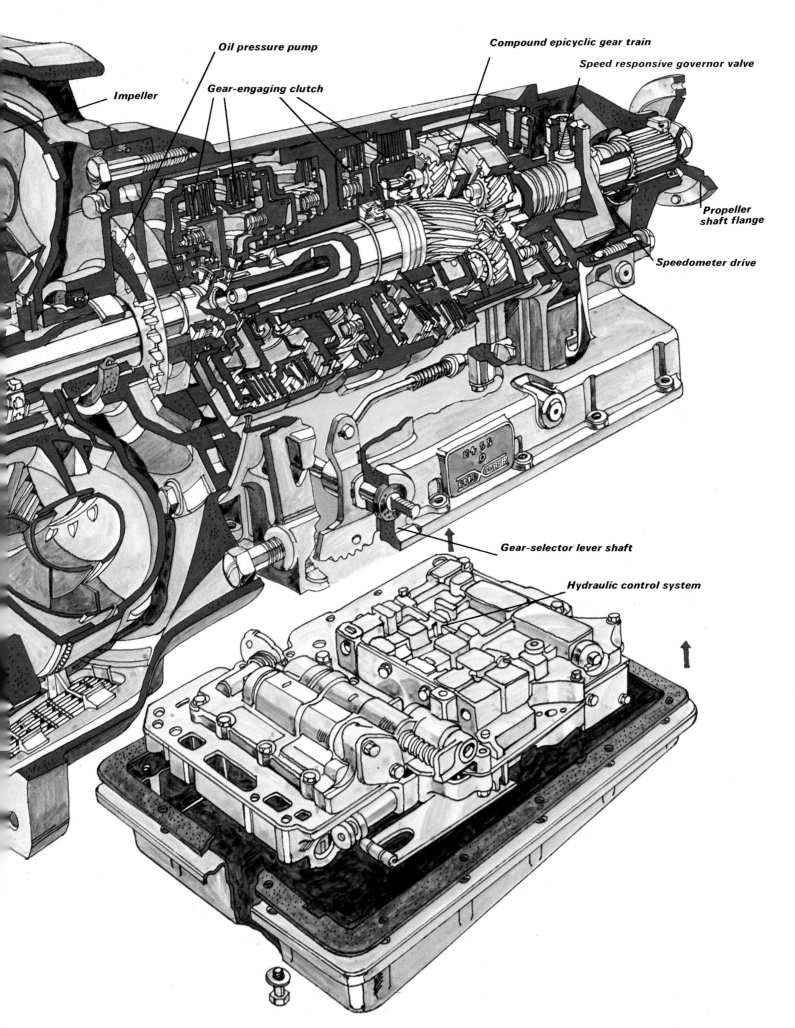

Impeller

Oil pressure pump

Gear-engaging clutch

Compound epicyclic gear train

Speed responsive governor valve

Propeller shaft flange

Speedometer drive

Gear-selector lever shaft

Hydraulic control system

115

them. These electronic "black box" systems still use fluid pressure for the actual engagement of the clutches and brakes of the transmission units.

In 1958 Hubertus van Doorne, whose Dutch company was already well-known for heavy trucks of largely conventional design, developed the expanding pulley and V-belt gearing, as used on some early motor cycles, into a speed and torque controlled automatic transmission for a new product, the DAF car.

The engine drove a transverse countershaft through a dog clutch and bevel reversing gear. The countershaft had the inboard halves of two V-pulleys fixed to it. The outboard pulley flanges were keyed to the shaft, but could move axially under the control of a centrifugal weight system and of inlet manifold suction, the latter providing a measure of engine torque.

The movement of the pulleys altered the gearing by changing their effective diameter. While the centrifugal weights tended to move the pulley flanges to increase the effective diameter on which the belts ran, thereby raising the gearing, a reduction in manifold suction on demand from the accelerator, or through over-run braking, tended to widen the gaps between the flanges and so lower the gear ratio. The two belts from this countershaft drove the rear wheels independently by spring loaded V-pulleys which maintained belt tension.

The DAF 66SL has the Variomatic belt transmission.

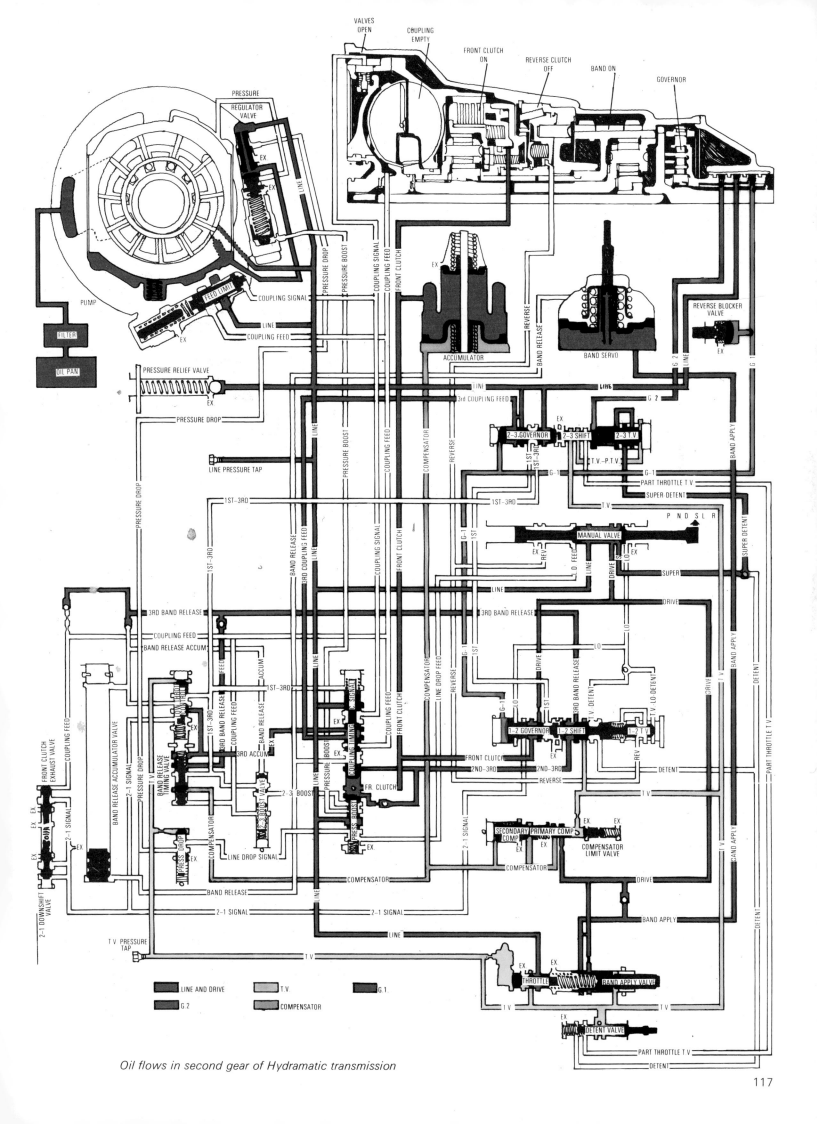

Oil flows in second gear of Hydramatic transmission

FRICTION DRIVES

The DAF belt transmission (called Variomatic) provided a continuously variable gear ratio between the highest and lowest available, corresponding to top and bottom gears of a conventional gearbox. This desirable state of stepless gears was foreseen in a number of friction drive transmissions from the simple knife-grinder type used in the G.W.K. of 1911 and the Cartercar of 1906. In these a flat disc, mounted on the end of an extension to the clutch shaft, was engaged frictionally by a wheel sliding along a transverse shaft.

Movement of the wheel towards the larger diameter of the disc reduced the gear ratio until the wheel was in contact with a path near the edge of the disc which was the equivalent of top gear. With the wheel at the disc centre, a neutral condition was obtained, and movement of the wheel to the other side of the centre gave the same variety of ratios in reverse. The transverse shaft could be either the rear axle or a countershaft driving the axle by chain. The main trouble with this simple transmission system was its tendency for the disc to cause wear on the wheel.

Of other suggested designs of continuously variable friction drives, one used by Austin in 1933 was originated by Frank Hayes of America, who began developing an older idea in the mid-1920s. This was a toric disc transmission in which rollers made contact with toroidal, or saucer-shaped, discs, there being three discs with two sets of three rollers between them.

The input was to the centre disc, and power was transmitted through the rollers to the two outer discs which were coupled to the output. The rollers could be tilted in such a way that they could engage the "saucer" faces of the discs at different diameters in order to give the gear ratio that was required.

Much of the development of the Hayes gear was directed to generating the correct pressure to maintain the friction drive and it is still being continued by General Motors, G.K.N. Transmissions and Citroën.

At the same time, several firms, Renault among them, are experimenting with the Beier friction drive, in which a number of taper section discs on one shaft are engaged by

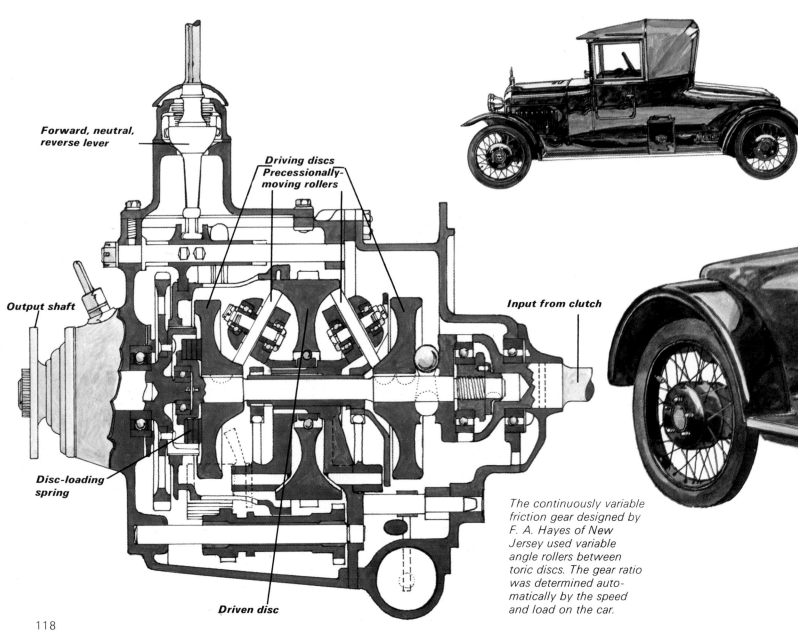

Forward, neutral, reverse lever

Driving discs
Precessionally-moving rollers

Output shaft

Input from clutch

Disc-loading spring

Driven disc

The continuously variable friction gear designed by F. A. Hayes of New Jersey used variable angle rollers between toric discs. The gear ratio was determined automatically by the speed and load on the car.

flanged rims of discs on a parallel shaft. The shafts are moved, together or apart, to change the contact diameter of the rims on the tapered discs, once again providing different gear ratios.

Other forms of stepless ratio drives have been developed from the hydraulic torque converter. To increase the torque multiplication, that is to obtain a wider range of overall gear ratio, a set of variable angle blades is used in the torque converter. This idea was suggested by the Brazilian, Dimitri de Lavaud in 1932 and introduced in the 1956 Buick Dynaflow.

Another development along the same lines was the Variable Kinetic Drive transmission, devised by Howard Hobbs in 1967, in which a centrifugally adjusted row of blades is coupled to the planet carrier of an epicyclic gear train. By using a bevel differential between the sun of this train, the turbine and the output shaft, the system provides a torque ratio of about four to one. This is sufficient to enable ratio-changing gears to be eliminated, only a forward, neutral and reverse gear arrangement being required.

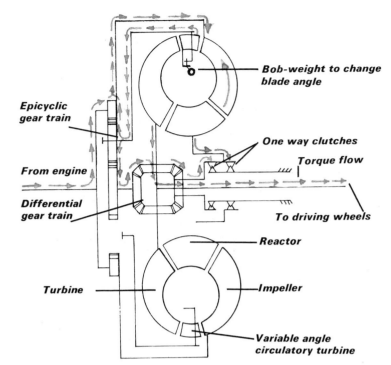

The V.K.D. (Variable Kinetic Drive) transmission has a circulatory turbine with speed responsive variable blades. Torque from this turbine is fed back to the impeller and output shafts to increase the torque multiplication in the transmission.

Built in 1921, this G.W.K. was powered by a four-cylinder 1368 c.c. Coventry-Simplex engine. It was known as a 'knife-grinder' since the continuously variable transmission used two friction discs at right angles to each other.

PROPELLER SHAFTS AND UNIVERSAL JOINTS

With the belt or chain drives of the first cars there was sufficient flexibility to allow the rear axle to move up and down on its springs, while the countershaft remained stationary relative to the chassis. When the differential moved to the rear axle, a propeller shaft with pivoting joints at each end took the drive from the output of the gearbox to the axle unit. The joints, which have to transmit torque and, at the same time, allow relative angular movement of the shafts, are known as universal joints.

They are occasionally called Hooke's joints, after one of the credited inventors of the middle of the 17th century. The shaft with a joint at each end is called a cardan shaft after an even earlier inventor, Jerome Cardan, who devised such a shaft around 1540.

The Hooke's joint comprises a forked member on the end of each shaft to be joined, the two forks being coupled by a cruciform member in which the forks pivot, one on each pair of opposed arms.

The open propeller shaft suffered from the disadvantage that torque reaction on the rear axle tended to bend the long leaf springs into a gentle S shape. Therefore a method of restraining the axle casing was needed. Some manufacturers provided a torque stay bolted to the axle casing and linked to the chassis. Others used a torque tube which was rigid with the axle casing and extended forward, enclosing the propeller shaft, to a big ball joint at the gearbox end. The ball enclosed a single universal joint.

The latter solution brought its own troubles. Owing to the angular movements of the joint parts as they rotate, a single joint does not transmit the rotation uniformly. In extreme conditions, when the shafts are at 30 degrees to each other, there can be a speed fluctuation in the driven shaft of around 30 per cent.

With relatively low engine speeds and with engines mounted behind the front axle, this did not cause a serious problem. However, when engine speeds began to approach 5,000 r.p.m. and shafts became longer, the speed fluctuation and the long whipping shafts made their presence felt.

This led to the adoption of divided shafts with four joints and a centre steady bearing, an arrangement which had the additional advantage of permitting a lower floor line for the car body. By fixing the forks on the two ends of the propeller shaft in line, the speed fluctuation cancels out and the shorter shafts are much more rigid.

In the case of front-wheel drive, the angular deflections of the short cross-shafts and the steering movements of the wheels render the Hooke's type joints unsuitable. In 1925, Carl Weiss invented a constant velocity joint in which the forked members inter-engage and have curved ball trackways in their opposite sides. Balls located in these tracks are retained in the transverse plane which bisects the angle between the shafts. As the force-transmitting elements lie on this plane, the constant velocity joint does not suffer from speed fluctuations, hence its name.

Alfred Rzeppa's design of universal joints, in 1928, replaced the forks by inner and outer spherical surfaces with balls, in shear, between them. Further development of the Rzeppa joint allows not only angular but axial movement, and thus obviates the need for sliding splines on the shaft. Following up the work of earlier engineers, Andrea Bellomo and G.K.N.-Birfield have done much development on this design since 1956.

Similar conditions are found in the drive shafts of cars with independent rear suspension. With swing-axle suspension, a single joint near the differential casing is sufficient. Other forms of suspension have two joints (often of the Hooke's type, as angular deflections are small). A further type of joint providing an acceptable compromise is a rubber "doughnut", through which alternate bolts screw into spiders on the shaft ends.

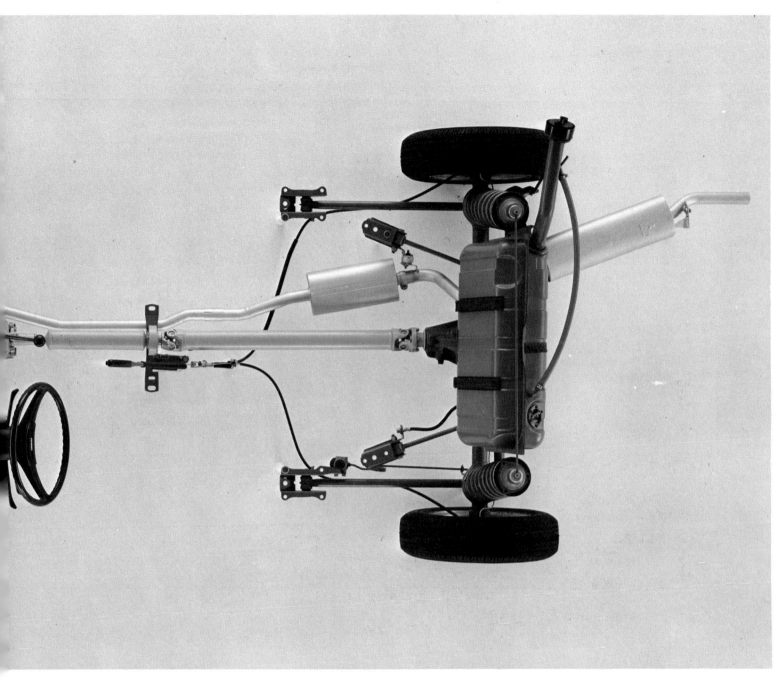

The top view of the bodyless FIAT 131 shows the layout of engine, gearbox, propeller shaft and rear axle.

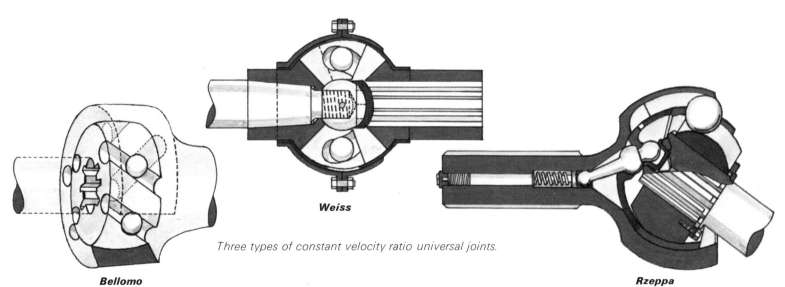

Bellomo

Weiss

Three types of constant velocity ratio universal joints.

Rzeppa

FINAL DRIVES AND DIFFERENTIALS

Bevel gears are used to transfer the drive from a longitudinal propeller shaft to the transverse mounted driving axle, except of course, in cars with transverse engines. The ratio of the bevel gears is the top gear reduction. The simplest types of gear, from the production viewpoint, in the early days of the car had straight radial teeth and could be fairly noisy. Later designs used bevel gears with curved, spiral teeth. Although the younger Bollée used spiral bevel gears as early as 1896, they did not come into general use until much later.

A further development, now almost universal, is the hypoid gear, first fitted by Packard in 1927. This is relatively quiet and, because it is a spiral bevel with the pinion axis below that of the crown wheel, produces high tooth pressures which need special lubricant.

The differential allows the two driven wheels of a car to rotate under power while they go round tracks of different radii on corners, the outer wheel travelling farther than the inner one. It is possible to do without a differential, but the penalties are undue tyre wear and heavy steering. The differential is reputed to have been used first by Pecqueur in a steam carriage in 1828, but it was probably known to the Chinese much earlier.

There are two main types of differential, the bevel gear and the spur gear, and both work on the same principle. In the bevel type, a pair of bevel side gears is rigid with each

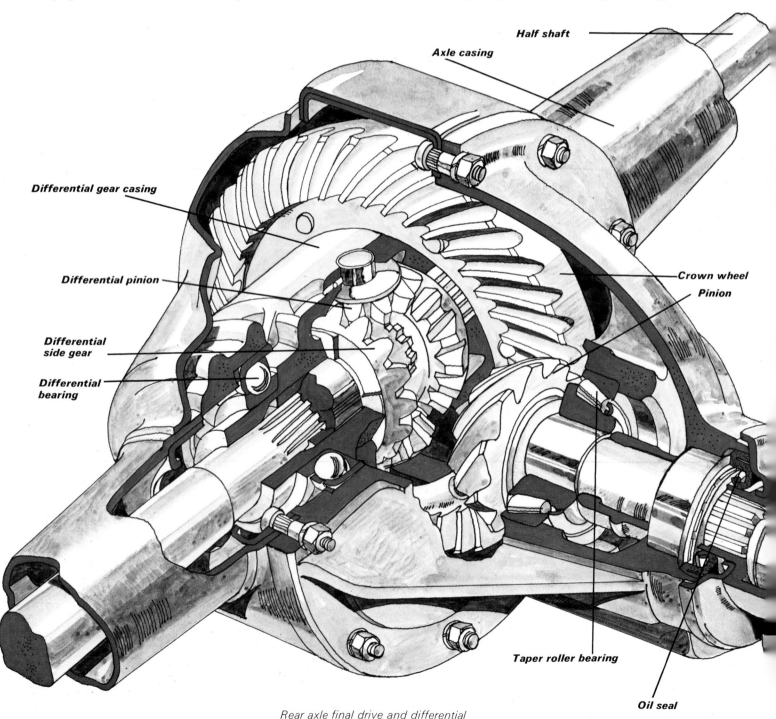

Rear axle final drive and differential

axle half shaft, while a further set of gears is mounted on a radial armed spider and meshed with the side gears. The drive from the crown wheel, itself driven by the pinion on the propeller shaft, is taken to the spider by an outer casing which holds the spider spindles. This outer casing is bolted to the crown wheel.

This is another form of epicyclic gear, in which the spider gears are the planets and the side gears are equal-size sun and annulus gears. With the car running straight, the forces acting on the wheels are the same and the whole gear train revolves as one unit. When one wheel is subjected to more force than the other (for example, the inner wheel when the car begins to turn), that wheel and its

attached side gear in the differential are, in effect, braked. This causes the other side gear to turn faster. Taken to the limit, when one wheel is held stationary, the other moves round at twice the speed of the crown wheel.

In the spur gear differential, spur gears are rigid with the axle shafts and meshed with a planetary gear or gears. These are mounted freely on a spindle, which is carried by the differential housing and driven by the crown wheel. Although such a gear works quite well, it tends, with greater engine power, to become too large in diameter to be accommodated under the rear seats or under the boot floor line of a car.

Once the need for a differential to avoid high rates of tyre wear and heavy steering was realized, the disadvantages of one wheel being able to spin on a low friction surface – and so lose driving force – became apparent. High-powered vehicles in the 1920s demonstrated this problem by spinning their wheels on normal road surfaces. The problem was answered by the limited slip differential, of which one form was devised by Hermann Knab and Gottfried Weidmann in 1925. It consisted of two cam rings, an inner and outer cam ring, which were connected to the two axle shafts.

These cam rings had undulating tracks which were engaged by radially free rollers carried by a cage driven from the crown wheel. While this cam and roller device would allow slow relative rotation between the wheels, it would prevent fast rotation, as for instance when a wheel began to slip.

Other forms of limited slip mechanism have friction facings between the backs of the side bevels and the differential casing. As the tooth loading between the side and spider bevels increases, the side gears are forced outwards to increase friction between the side gear and casing, which are moving relative to one another.

The use of a thixotropic silicone substance, which increases viscosity as it is churned, is a suggested solution.

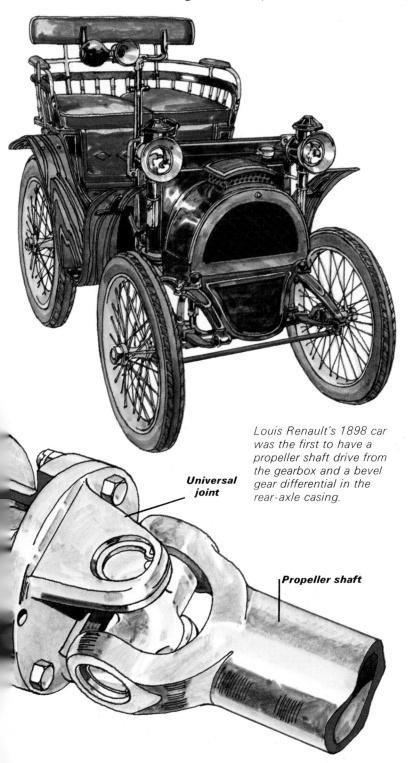

Louis Renault's 1898 car was the first to have a propeller shaft drive from the gearbox and a bevel gear differential in the rear-axle casing.

Universal joint

Propeller shaft

The first FIAT of 1899.

FOUR-WHEEL DRIVE

The desire for greater traction inspired thoughts of driving all four road wheels, thoughts which had been in the minds of Timothy Burstall and James Hill, who made a four-wheel drive steam carriage in 1824. They realized the difficulties of road wheels running on different radii turns and on different surfaces, and drove their axles through free-wheel clutches which could be locked for driving in reverse.

In 1966, Jensen announced a four-wheel drive car, making use of the invention of Claude Hill of Ferguson Research in 1952, for preventing front to rear slip. In this system two oppositely acting free-wheel clutches, and a front to rear differential are paralleled by slightly unequal ratio gears. Under constant drive, the free-wheels slowly overrun. However, when one axle tends to spin and rotate faster, relative free-wheel movement reverses and the free-wheels lock to prevent wheelspin.

REAR ENGINES

While the great majority of cars drove through their rear wheels and had their change speed gears bolted to the crankcase, a few manufacturers took the view that the greater proportion of the weight should be over, or near, the driving wheels, thus providing greater traction. This, of course, happened in some of the earliest cars, but probably more by accident than design. The feature tended to die out as the Panhard set the fashion for many years.

However, engineers like Rumpler in 1921, Sir Dennistoun Burney in 1930, Ledwinka in 1934 and Porsche in the same year, all decided to combine the engine, transmission and final drive over the rear axle. Too little was known at the time about suspension and steering design, so that Rumpler, Burney, Tatra and Volkswagen cars earned a reputation for tail heaviness.

By combining the gearbox and final drive in one unit with the rear axle (that is, by using a transaxle driven by a propeller shaft), more weight could be provided at the rear without moving the engine from the front. Although de Dion had done this in the opening years of the century, it was not popular because of the increase of unsprung weight which occurred when used in conjunction with rigid rear axles. The fact that de Dion had bolted the heavy masses to the chassis and driven the wheels through light, universally jointed shafts, seems to have been overlooked until American makers used the transaxle after the Second World War to provide more interior foot room for the front seats.

FRONT-WHEEL DRIVE

The alternative to these rear drives was front-wheel drive, as suggested by George Sheldon in 1877. Sheldon's patent, which hamstrung the American industry for a number of years until it was eventually revoked, was reputed to be based on a vehicle having a three-cylinder engine

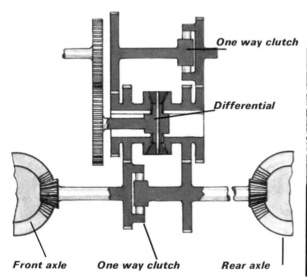

The Ferguson four-wheel drive uses two oppositely acting one-way clutches and a slight difference in driving ratio across a differential to stop wheelspin between the front and rear axles.

Right: The Jensen F.F. 11 that used the Ferguson four-wheel drive system.
Far right: The combined gearbox and rear axle, the transaxle, of the Alfetta.

If it had ever run, the 1877 Sheldon would have been the first transverse-engined front-wheel drive car driven by an internal combustion engine.

mounted crosswise on the axle to drive the front wheels.

In 1904, Walter Christie used a four-cylinder transverse engine, and, four years later, the Front Wheel Drive Auto Co. sold front-wheel drive cars under the name of Badger. In 1926, J. A. Gregoire designed the Tracta with front-wheel drive from an in-line engine and was followed by Alvis in 1928, Audi in 1932, B.S.A. in 1934 and then Citroën in 1936.

Although there were strong adherents to front-wheel drive and much argument raged between those who thought a car should be pushed along by the rear wheels and those who thought it should be pulled by the front wheels, it was not until Alec Issigonis designed the Austin-Morris Mini in 1960 that front-wheel drive became universally accepted. The Mini ranks alongside Henry Ford's Model T and Porsche's Volkswagen as a truly significant car for millions of motorists.

Sir Alec Issigonis, whose outstanding achievements also include the Morris Minor, was born in Smyrna in 1906. His father was a Greek who became a naturalized British subject, and his mother was of Bavarian origin.

The family ran an engineering business in Smyrna for many years, but after mixed fortunes during the First World War, became refugees in Malta. In the early 1920s his mother took him to London where, as a teenager, he studied at Battersea Polytechnic. The fact that mathematics

The 1930 Tracta, built in France to the design of J. A. Gregoire, used a 1½ litre-S.C.A.P. engine to drive the front wheels through a four-speed gearbox.

was always his bad subject apparently never worried or hindered him. In fact, he has been reported as suggesting that mathematics and creativity are bad bedfellows.

When in-line engines are used, transmission layouts for both front-wheel and rear-wheel drive cars are similar. They can be seen with the engines either in front, or behind the driving axle. The usual arrangement is for the final drive and differential casing to be bolted to the clutch casing or bell-housing, and the gearbox to be bolted on the other side of the final drive. A relatively long drive shaft is used between the clutch-driven plate and gearbox input gear, and a single-stage gearbox is used to provide output to the final drive bevel pinion from the input end of the layshaft.

The bevel crown wheel and differential are thus below the drive shaft from engine to gearbox and are mounted between them. Since there is always an indirect drive through a pair of gears within the gearbox, those engines which are mounted behind the driving axle usually rotate in the opposite direction to engines in front of the axle.

An exception to this layout was the 1966 Oldsmobile Toronado, which used a seven-litre V8 engine with a chain drive to a Hydramatic transmission mounted alongside the crankcase. The power output from the automatic transmission was taken forward to a differential driving the front wheels.

When the engine is mounted with its crankshaft transverse to the longitudinal centre line of the car, little room remains for the transmission to be in line with the engine. In some layouts, such as that of the Austin-Morris front-wheel drive cars, the gearbox is moved below and alongside the crankcase.

The clutch is mounted at the end of the crankshaft and drives a gear positioned between the engine and the clutch. This gear is meshed with an idler gear, driving the gearbox mainshaft, and the differential is driven from a spur gear at the other end of the gearbox, more or less at the centre of the power unit. From the differential there are short shafts which terminate in Hooke's joints with rubber

The power unit and front-wheel drive of the FIAT 128 has drive shafts of equal torsional rigidity.

bush bearings. These lead to spline joints on the inboard ends of the wheel drive shafts.

On the other hand, Fiat (as exemplified with the 128) has dispensed with the idler gear to the gearbox mainshaft and the complication of the reversed clutch, by bolting the gearbox to the bell-housing and driving the layshaft.

The gearbox mainshaft, with its gear synchronizing mechanisms, is below and behind the crankshaft centre line and drives a spur reduction gear secured to the differential. As the final drive is not equidistant from the front wheels, the two drive shafts are given the same torsional rigidity by using a solid shaft for the shorter one and a larger diameter tube for the longer shaft.

In the Austin-Morris front-wheel drive cars with automatic transmission, the friction clutch is replaced by a hydraulic torque converter, the output of which drives the idler gear in the case of the smaller cars, or a chain drive on the larger cars. Bevel epicyclic gearing is used to provide the different ratios under the control of a Watt

type centrifugal governor, the spring of which is loaded in accordance with the accelerator pedal position.

Two systems have been tried to eliminate all the complications and frictional losses incurred in gear type transmissions. These are electric and hydrostatic drives.

In an electric drive devised by Ferdinand Porsche, for the Lohner-Porsche of 1900, specially designed electric motors were built into the front wheel hubs. The batteries which had provided the energy source were replaced in 1902 by a petrol engine-driven dynamo. Thus, at this early date, Porsche had produced a front-wheel drive car with an easily controlled transmission, no necessity for a differential and a system allowing high torque at the driving wheels at zero road speed.

The other system uses a hydraulic pump driven by the engine and hydraulic motors in the wheel hubs. Although such a method has yet to be used commercially on a passenger car, the hydrostatic drive has proved its worth on the exacting test-ground of earth-moving equipment.

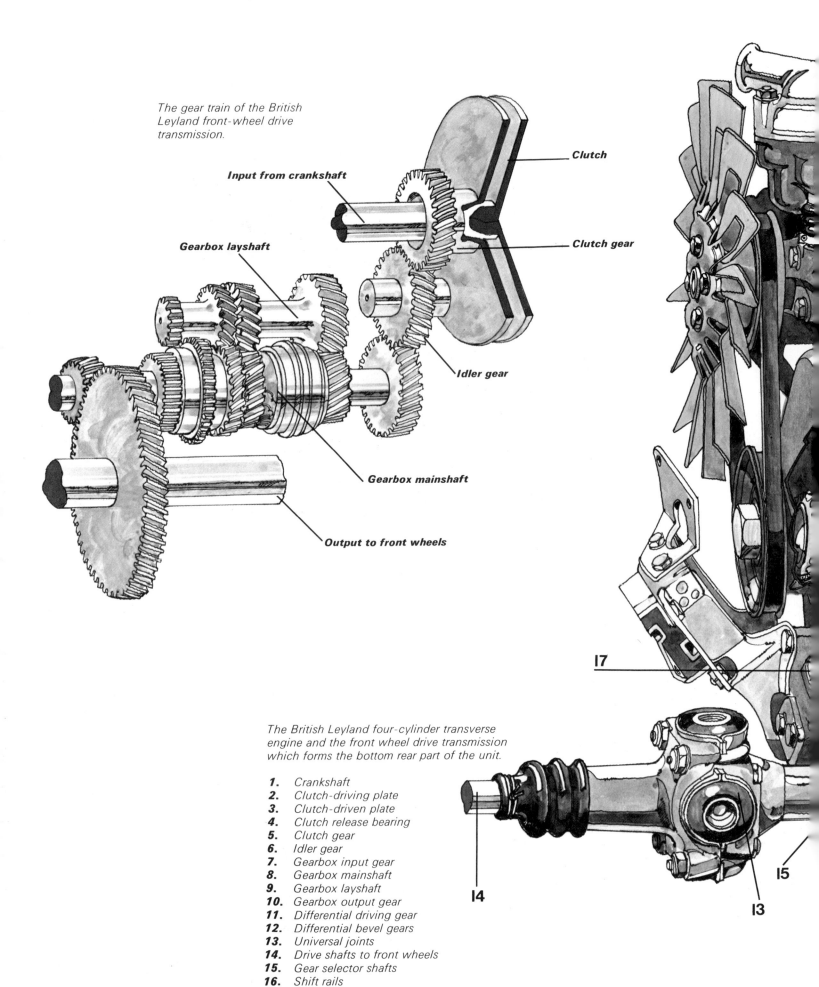

The gear train of the British Leyland front-wheel drive transmission.

Clutch

Input from crankshaft

Clutch gear

Gearbox layshaft

Idler gear

Gearbox mainshaft

Output to front wheels

The British Leyland four-cylinder transverse engine and the front wheel drive transmission which forms the bottom rear part of the unit.

1. Crankshaft
2. Clutch-driving plate
3. Clutch-driven plate
4. Clutch release bearing
5. Clutch gear
6. Idler gear
7. Gearbox input gear
8. Gearbox mainshaft
9. Gearbox layshaft
10. Gearbox output gear
11. Differential driving gear
12. Differential bevel gears
13. Universal joints
14. Drive shafts to front wheels
15. Gear selector shafts
16. Shift rails
17. Speedometer drive

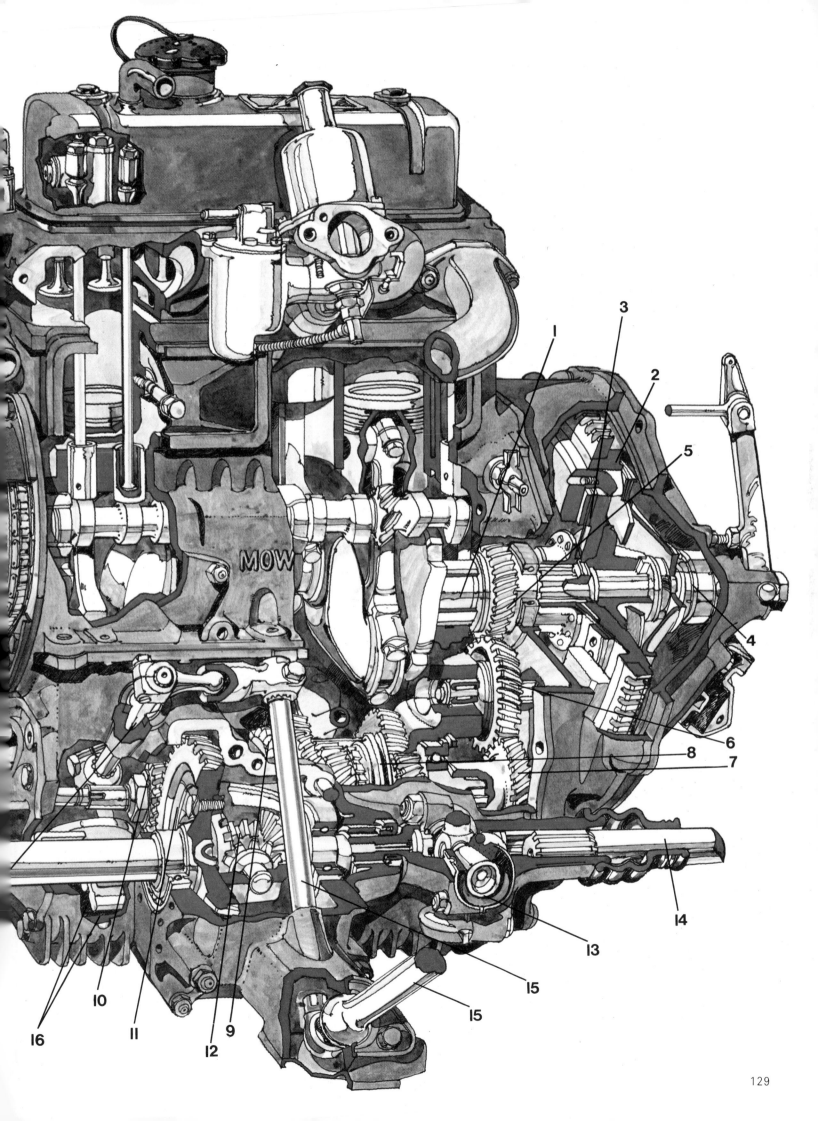

While the heart of the car is the engine, the basic frame or skeleton of the vehicle is the chassis. It is the chassis that keeps the wheels in their proper places and furnishes a mounting for the engine and transmission.

Yet in the car's formative years little attention was given to original chassis design. Perhaps this was due mostly to the inability of designers either to appreciate or to calculate the complex stresses involved. Also, there were already available the relatively successful chassis or frames used for horse-drawn and steam-powered carriages, and even those used for bicycles.

At the beginning there were two main schools of designers. One desired to keep down the weight that the low-powered engines of the time had to move. This school borrowed the relatively small-diameter tubes of the cycling world. The other designers provided larger, heavier engines, and took the steam carriage and heavy cart as their models.

In the Benz of 1885 – which was in fact a tricycle – the chassis comprised a tube about two inches (five centimetres) in diameter and bent into a U shape with the open end at the rear. A cross bracing member at the rear was also used to form the bottom bearing for the vertical crankshaft. Other small cross tubes went between the side members, more to support the mechanism than to strengthen the

structure. At the front, a single swan-necked tube led to the bicycle-type steering head for the front wheel forks. The rear springs were bolted to lugs brazed to the side tubes. Since this vehicle had only three wheels, the twisting, or torsional, stresses produced by uneven road surfaces were much less than for a four-wheeled system. So this frame sufficed for the work it had to do.

Daimler, in 1886, also used a combination of tubes and forged supports for his four-wheel car, copying the design of metal-framed, horse-drawn carriages. No doubt he felt there was enough trouble in the mechanical driving device and was content for the remainder to follow known constructions.

Many pre-1900 chassis were built up from small, thin-walled tubes, often straight, with forged lugs to mount the ends of long leaf springs and other essential components. These chassis were developed from cycle designs, the aim being to build a light vehicle by motorizing a four-wheel manumotive carriage.

Frames of this type were fairly flexible and, indeed, were allowed to flex as part of the suspension system, a trait which contributed to the unreliability of early vehicles. The Orient of 1902 exploited this feature to its full extent. The chassis was made of wooden planks and had no form of springing other than that provided by the frame flexing.

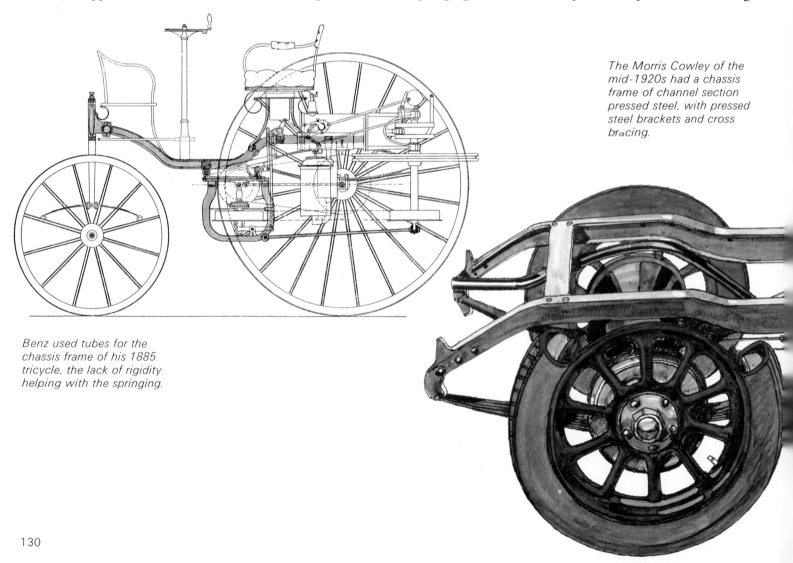

The Morris Cowley of the mid-1920s had a chassis frame of channel section pressed steel, with pressed steel brackets and cross bracing.

Benz used tubes for the chassis frame of his 1885 tricycle, the lack of rigidity helping with the springing.

the skin

The other school of designers, who used horse-drawn vehicles and steam carriages as their models, preferred a wooden framework that required strengthening with steel plates. Such flitched wooden chassis were popular well after the turn of the century and evolved into frames of the kind found on English-built Daimlers from 1888 onwards. These Daimler cars had wooden frame members which were encased in channel-section steel.

When Panhard copied this construction a little later, they discovered that, by using wood of two inches (five centimetres) square section, he could dispense with the channel casing and so gain lightness and flexibility. But this was not to last long.

Around 1900 J. S. Critchley of the English Daimler Motor Company tried a flat light channel steel frame, rectangular in plan, with forged angle brackets to reinforce the front corner joints. The engine was mounted on a pair of three-armed strip-steel supports that could be slid along the top of the chassis to provide belt tensioning.

In the middle of the first decade the main designs still favoured these two ideas. For example, Renault and de Dion-Bouton still used tube frames and the English Daimler used the armoured wood frame. But several firms had begun to make pressed-steel channel-section frames, which slowly changed from being straight-sided to being

swept inwards at the front to provide clearance for the front wheels when on lock. A further change was the sweeping up of the side members at the rear to allow axle movement clearance and at the same time give a lower body and floor line. The centre of gravity of the car was thereby lowered for increased stability.

This type of chassis remained common practice for the following 40 years. Meanwhile it became increasingly evident that a rectangular frame was inherently weak, and stout cross-bracing was used. At first this was done by including a secondary frame for the power unit, but later the engine was provided with widely spaced mounting feet that bolted on to the side members. Thus some of the twisting stresses were transferred to the crankcase and, at times, the gearbox. However, the idea did little to prevent "lozenging", which happened, for example, when a shock at one front wheel tried to force the rectangular frame into a diamond shape.

Gusseted joints between the side and cross members went some way to alleviate the trouble, but much more strength was forthcoming with the advent of diagonal cross bracing in the 1930s. At about this time the channel-section side-members were boxed in by welding on a fourth side. This rectangular tube-section helped rigidity considerably by increasing the torsional strength of the side members.

The FIAT 1500 (Above) had a backbone chassis made from pressed steel members welded together. The V.W. (Right) went further and used both a backbone and a strengthened floor for greater torsional strength.

BACKBONE CHASSIS

Some designers looked upon the chassis as the backbone of the car. In 1904, Rover produced a small single-cylinder car in which the engine, clutch housing and gearbox were all bolted together. A single transverse front spring was held on a front extension of the crankcase, and two cast arms stretched backwards and outwards from the rear of the gearbox to meet up with a wooden body frame. The next model had a gearbox extension going right back to bolt to the final drive. This model was possibly the first tubular backbone chassis.

Twenty years later, in Czechoslovakia, Hans Ledwinka designed the Tatra with a relatively large-diameter central tube backbone. He provided a chassis that had rigidity in both vertical and horizontal bending modes, was largely free from lozenging and was torsionally strong to resist twisting stress when one wheel rose on a bump. Although the design introduced difficulties in providing mountings for the bodywork, it has remained with Tatra for 50 years.

Another backbone idea was that of Edmund Rumpler, a contemporary of Ledwinka at the Nesseldorf works in

Vienna at the beginning of the century. In 1922 he made a car which had a chassis shaped like a streamlined punt. The side members were made of pressed steel, one-thirteenth of an inch (two and a half millimetres) thick, and were 12 inches (30 centimetres) deep through most of their length. They were about three feet (one metre) apart at the widest point and were welded together at the front and rear. Internally eight pressed-steel transverse bracing members were welded to provide a rigid, streamlined tube or box member.

At about the same time, O. D. North produced the North-Lucas car with much the same ideas of a streamlined chassis-body structure. His chassis frame was of light alloy angle-section, covered with 0·05 inch (1·5 millimetres) aluminium sheeting strengthened with light timber. The nose section was an aluminium casting. Although both these designs came to naught, Vincenzo Lancia's monocoque hull, riveted together from deep pressed-steel side members and pressed cross members, formed the basis for over 12,000 Lancia Lambda cars between 1923 and 1931.

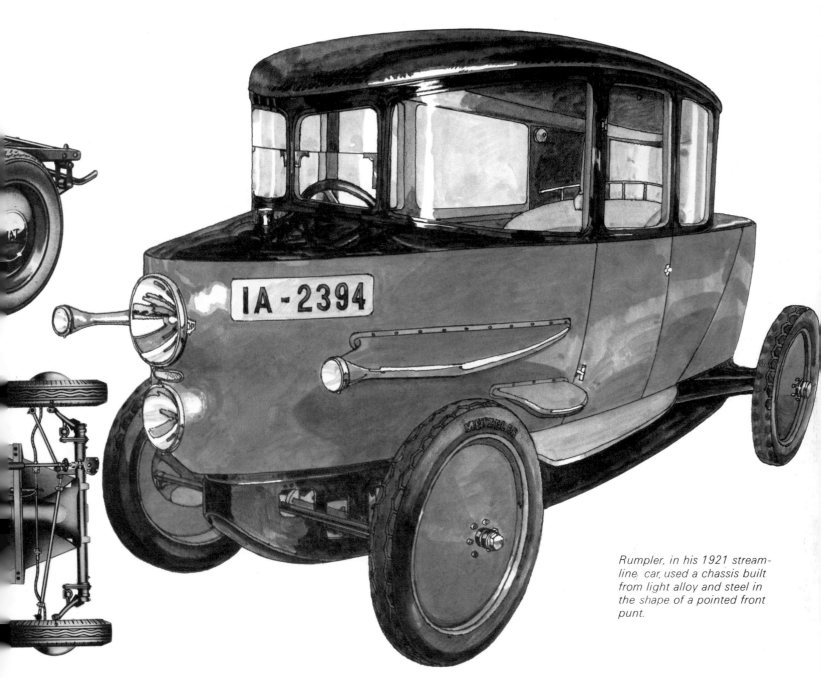

Rumpler, in his 1921 stream-line car, used a chassis built from light alloy and steel in the shape of a pointed front punt.

The Fiat 1500 that appeared in 1935 had a chassis combining both the tubular backbone and the deep pressed-steel channel side members. The side members ran parallel at the front to give a rigid mounting for the engine and independent front suspension. They then swept together at the sides of the gearbox to be welded into a substantially rectangular tubular backbone. In front of the rear axle the side members swept outwards and upwards to support the fuel tank and rear leaf springs in the manner of the more usual chassis. Body mountings were provided by transverse pressed-steel members which were riveted to the backbone.

An extension of this technique was used by Ferdinand Porsche in the designs of the Volkswagen and Porsche cars starting in 1934. A substantially flat central platform was strengthened by one central and two side hollow members, and joined to large box members at the front and rear. The whole of this box platform was built up from steel pressings welded together to provide an extremely rigid structure without excessive weight.

In 1946 Renault introduced the 4CV with a built-up platform-type frame, a design originally conceived some years earlier and owing something to the first monocoque Renault, the Juvaquatre of 1938.

UNITARY CONSTRUCTION

From the middle of the 1940s, the separate chassis faded out for production in large quantities, and the integral chassis/body built from steel pressing became common. Fiat produced, in 1950, the first Italian car with a unit construction body chassis — the 1400. In this, an outer hollow section member swept outwards behind the front wheels to the full body width and continued as far as the front of the rear wheel arches, where it swept in and up to clear the wheels and form rear spring mountings. This was a perimeter frame after the fashion introduced by Amédée Bollée in his steam carriage of 1872, and later used by General Motors in America.

The Rover 2000, which appeared in 1963, had a base unit of pressed sheet-metal parts welded together in a jig and providing a complete steel skeleton to mount not only the mechanical components but also all the body panels. It was perfectly feasible to drive this Rover without any of its outer skin being attached. Another car using a similar idea, but in a different manner, was the 1945 design of J. A. Gregoire that formed the basis of the 1947 Dyna-Panhard. In this the whole of the chassis/body framing was made from Alpax aluminium alloy castings which were bolted together.

The pressed-steel monocoque chassis/body frame structure is well suited to mass production methods where the great cost of the dies used for pressing can be spread over a large number of cars. But smaller manufacturers have had to use other and cheaper methods.

The 1968 fibreglass chassis-cum-body Lotus Elite.

One construction, developed by A.C. from 1954, was the ladder frame. Here two straight parallel tubes of about four inches (10 centimetres) diameter were spaced by tubular and box section cross members. A further tube framework supported the body of the vehicle by forming the framing for aluminium panels.

Aston Martin in 1948 used square section tubes, as did Gordon Keeble in 1960, to produce a space frame that had no major members. This frame approximated to a box platform construction with straight welded tubes outlining the edges of the pressed boxes, the panels between the edges being omitted. Some of the exotic Italian builders, such as Maserati, employed circular section small tubes in great numbers to produce a birdcage framework.

Colin Chapman astonished visitors to the London Motor Show of 1957 with his Lotus Elite, in which a unitary glass fibre platform/body shell provided the whole of the structural strength. This new unit comprised three main elements: a flat floor with raised boxes at the corners to house the road wheels; an intermediate element with vertical sides, boxes fore and aft and a strong tubular shaft

tunnel; and an outer shell that was the visible body. Steel reinforcing plates and strips were moulded into the glass fibre to spread the loads from the engine and suspension mountings. Two square section tubes which were moulded vertically in front of the door openings provided jacking points and door hinge mountings as well as support for a tubular windscreen frame.

The Elite was followed in 1962 by the Elan, which had an open bodywork lacking the rigidity provided by a coupé roof. So it was based on a deep rectangular steel backbone forking at the rear to take the rear suspension cross member and at the front to give a mounting for the engine and front suspension.

Soon after the glass fibre Elite attained full production, Jem Marsh collaborated with an aircraft designer, Frank

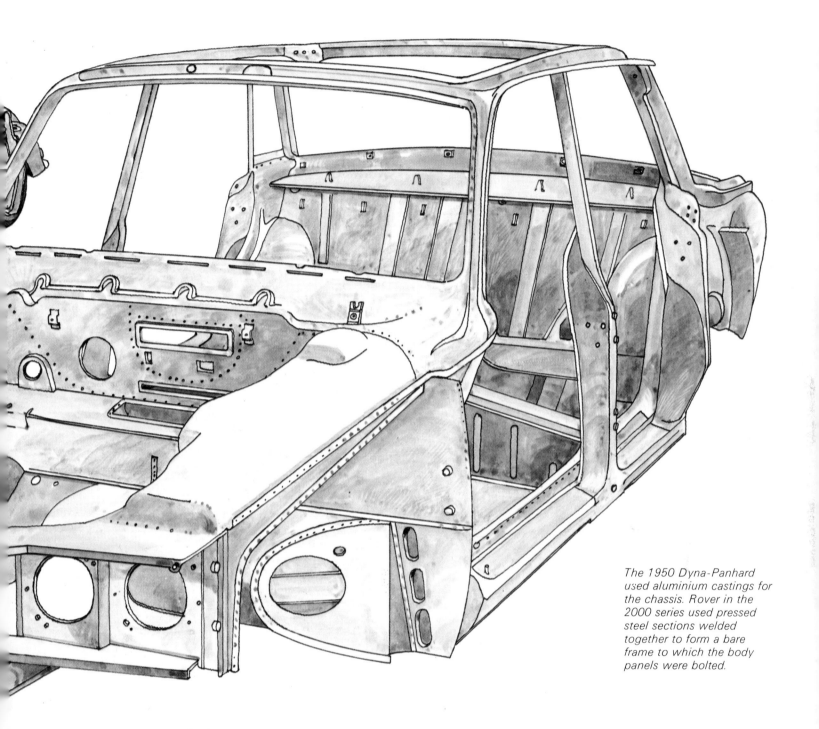

The 1950 Dyna-Panhard used aluminium castings for the chassis. Rover in the 2000 series used pressed steel sections welded together to form a bare frame to which the body panels were bolted.

Costin, to produce the Marcos, a revolutionary design that brought the original wooden chassis up to date by using marine plywood. Advances in adhesives and a sound knowledge of the stresses involved allowed the use of 0·2 inch (three millimetres) mahogany and 0·1 inch (1·5 millimetres) birch laminations bonded with phenol-based adhesives in place of the pressed-steel members of the conventional monocoque body frame.

Again the design was based on a flat floor with three substantial hollow longitudinal members, and boxes at the front and rear. Where double curvatures were unavoidable in the body, glass fibre panels were held in place with Araldite adhesive. The whole structure was given a coat of Cuprinol to ward off attack by wood-boring insects.

The present unitary construction of chassis or frame and body shell is designed to provide an extremely rigid base for relatively soft suspension systems, comfortable protection of the passengers from the elements and a minimal deformable box in case of collision.

In contrast, the motor car pioneers were happy to be able to sit on the contraption while it moved slowly under its own power. They gave little thought to comfort. Such an attitude was, however, a retrogression, for the self-propelled steam vehicles built by such men as Hancock, Maceroni and Gurney around the 1830s had body works displaying the full skill of the contemporary horse-coach builder. Later, as the design of the machinery progressed, the standards of accommodation fell until, by the advent of the internal combustion engine, all that was provided was a thinly upholstered bench with a simple back rest.

BODYWORK STYLES

As soon as the motor car became reliable enough to be used for normal transport, as distinct from driving for fun, thoughts turned to the motorists' comfort and the need to provide for more passengers than just the two people sitting side by side in front. With the front-mounted engine of the Panhard there was space at the rear. But any entrance from the side to the rear seats was obstructed by the rear wheels, which were considerably larger than the front ones.

This problem was overcome by the introduction of the tonneau or rear entrance body, which first appeared on the 6 hp Panhard in 1899. In the tonneau the seats could be arranged facing inwards, facing the rear (back to back with the front seats) or facing forwards with the centre of the seat hinged to allow a small rear door to open. Another idea was a swivelling passenger seat at the front allowing access to the rear seat.

These bodies were designed and built by the carriage makers on chassis supplied by the motor manufacturers. Considerable annoyance was caused to the former by the straight high chassis frames of the time, which gave little scope for good body design and resulted in a lot of high, cumbersome vehicles.

The carriage builders did little at first to design specially for the motor car and merely copied popular types of horse-drawn vehicles. Styles such as the wagonette with transverse rows of seats, the phaeton with a minor seat behind for "the man" and the brougham with a two-seat enclosed body, therefore appeared.

Around the turn of the century designers began to use similar sized wheels all round, allowing the chassis to be lowered. This permitted the use of rear side doors, most of which had to be cut away at the back corners to clear the wheels and mudguards.

Large hoods began to be fitted over the principal seats. They were held on metal-flitched ash frames hinged to the body sides and were kept from ballooning off by leather straps attached to the dash or front wings. The other obvious way to give weather protection was to build a roof over an open body, as was first done on a Panhard in 1896. Next came the enclosure of the rear of the body with a glassed-in superstructure, which at first was so badly made that the rattles precluded conversation.

In the coupé the chauffeur was still without protection, but in 1901 a Parisian coachbuilder extended the roof over the front seats to form a limousine. A large glass windscreen was later fitted between the roof and the dash, and a full-height door added to the front. However, separation of master and servant was still maintained by an interior division.

At that time, when bodies were built by coachmaking techniques, the bodywork and lines owed more to the

The 1905 Lanchester was a most original car.

woodworker than the metalworker. The bodies were built up on a wooden frame, having glued carpenters' joints, and were covered with wood panels. Since it is difficult to bend wood in two directions at the same time – that is, to make a double curvature panel – single curvature panels were used, and impressions of double curves given by sweeping curved edges. Curved panels were produced by clamping them to the required shape after steaming the wood and making a series of parallel sawcuts partially through the panels on the rear side to give the material more flexibility.

The techniques of quality coachbuilding took time and skill, and were therefore expensive. As more less-than-skilled coachbuilders joined the expanding motor industry, the standards of both design and workmanship fell, resulting in ugly, shoddy bodies that failed to stand up to the racking and vibration of faster moving vehicles travelling over rough roads.

To reduce cost and increase production, aluminium panels were used to cover the wooden framework. These had the disadvantage that the cold and damp of winter caused the aluminium to contract and the wood to expand. Conversely, summer heat caused the metal to expand and the wood to dry out and contract. The result was often loose panels and cracking paintwork. Although this form of construction remained with the top-quality

The 1900 curved dash Oldsmobile of which the advertisements said, "Nothing to watch but the road".

specialist coachwork builder for a long time, its success depended on a great deal of expertise and an exceedingly rigid chassis.

Another method was to use aluminium angle for the framing. It allowed much more flexibility in design, and by 1910 more curvaceous shapes began to appear. The radiator ceased to have a purely functional look. It could be any shape and, in turn, determined the shape of the front of the engine cover. As design improved, the bonnet widened out at the rear to mate with the dash.

Leather mudguards, intended only to prevent mud bring thrown up on to the occupants, gave way to curved mudguards preventing the splashing of other people, as required by law. With this change and the lowering of the chassis and floor, the front guard was continued towards the rear as an entrance step or running board. Obeying the natural law that horizontal surfaces attract objects to be put on them, the running board became cluttered with battery boxes, spare wheels, acetylene generators, horns and reserve petrol cans. This often resulted in the driver being unable to leave his seat unless the front passenger got out first, since there was no access on the driving side.

At a time when the car was still regarded in Europe as a luxury and a status symbol, it was already being treated in the vaster lands of America as a necessary replacement for the horse. The different attitude is reflected in the body designs, which were copies of wagons and buggies rather than coaches.

By the early years of the second decade bodywork had settled down to a style of its own, with pressed-steel or aluminium body panels suited to mass production methods. One of the leaders of the pressed panel covering construction was B.S.A. with its open bodied Twelve of 1912. This form of body manufacture was assisted by the development of both gas and electric welding processes enabling the preformed panels to be welded together to produce an apparently seamless body. With the use of steel panels, drumming became a problem that was not present with the dead wood or aluminium panels. So more attention had to be given to sound damping, and the provision of damping blocks between the panels (particularly the large roof area) and the linings.

Another method of sound deadening was devised by Weymann of Paris in 1922, when he stretched a fabric covering over a wire mesh or expanded metal base. These Weymann fabric bodies remained in vogue for about ten years, but eventually fell from favour owing to the difficulty of maintenance and repair.

As the chassis frame itself disappeared, the framing of the body became part of the whole structure and changed from wood to pressed steel. Thus it lost most of its identity, and, except for the hand-built motor car, specialized individual coachwork declined. Meanwhile the covering continued to be fabricated from large sheet steel panels pressed to shape and welded to the chassis framing. This produced a rigid basis and overcame the earlier troubles of flexing in the bodywork. The cost of the tools – the dies – for producing these big panels was so high that body styles remained largely unchanged for several years at a time in an effort to economise.

Although the manufacturing techniques were available in the 1920s, relatively little use was made of their potentialities for most body designs. The bonnet line broadened to full body width and, at the top, swept up to the base of the windscreen. From this point the body was more or less parallel, both in side and top views, as far as the back of the rear seats, where it curved round to a substantially vertical flat panel. To prevent too slab-sided an appearance, some curvature in a vertical plane was used.

The fuel tank was often held between the rear chassis members, extending beyond the back of the body, and the spare wheel (if not on the running board) was clamped vertically above the tank. For luggage, a folding metal grid was provided above and, when extended, beyond the fuel tank. Most of these bodies were open four-seaters, and weather protection was given by a folding hood of rubberized fabric, supported on metal framing and clipped to the top of the windscreen frame.

The hood was supplemented with sidescreens having celluloid panels secured to metal frames covered with fabric. These screens, often stowed in a bag attached to the back of the front seat, were held in place by metal pegs extending from the frames and fitting into tubes built into the body sides and doors. They misted badly in wet weather, the celluloid soon became scratched and yellowed, and they were by no means draught-proof.

Saloon bodies were also available, but were often little more than vertical extensions of the open, torpedo bodies. Some of these closed bodies had two wide doors and a long window at the rear. These were the four-light saloons.

The six-light saloons had four narrower doors and smaller rear windows. Both types had a small window in the rear panel. As an alternative, two-door cars could have the roof and the side area behind the doors, down to the waist, covered with fabric and given a pair of dummy S-shaped hinges to produce what was known as the fixed-head coupé. Another style of body had only two interior seats, and the roof was brought down behind them to meet a curved tail.

The tail was given an opening lid so that it could carry luggage, and protect it from rain and mud. Alternatively the lid opened to reveal a pair of folding seats (dicky seats) for occasional passengers. Sometimes the dicky seat occupants (and those in the back of open four-seaters) were shielded from the wind by supplementary folding windscreens, the most notable of which were made by Auster in the form of a triptych which had small hinged side panels.

Sports cars of the period were similar to the open tourers,

Panelled in tulip wood and copper-plated, this special bodywork on an Hispano Suiza 1924 chassis owed as much to the boat builder as the coach builder.

The Mercer Raceabout was typical of the American sports car of the 1910s.

but were often on shorter wheelbase chassis and consequently had less leg room at the back. Their mudguards, instead of the wide domes of the tourers, were either flat and a long way from the tyres, or small and close fitting. These light guards were often braced across the car in front of the radiator, serving also as a mounting for larger and heavier lamps. The fuel tanks at the rear were made larger and came as high as the back of the body. Later, tanks had wire-mesh stoneguards at the sides.

At the other end of the range, the *haute carrosserie* was built for the rich. Hand-built bodies with individual lines were made to customers' orders. Any extras the customers required were also incorporated. Externally they had neither the line of their horse-drawn forebears,

nor the sophistication that followed in the 1930s and 1940s. Shaped like a large box with doors, with a dog kennel in front for the engine, they were functional passenger carriers, and still retained the old concept that no man should stoop to enter a machine, even if he was wearing a top hat.

The interiors retained an Edwardian appearance with plenty of mahogany, walnut or teak veneers and leather or plush upholstery. With almost an excess of rear leg room, occasional folding-seats were hidden in the base of the division, and in some models, cocktail cabinets were secreted between the folding-seats.

Luggage was still relegated to the rear folding rack, often in a large trunk with fitted suitcases, or strapped to

Another early attempt at streamlining was the 1934 Chrysler Airflow Coupé (Right)

The 1935 Chrysler Croydon Airflow 6 (Above) was an early mass production attempt at streamlining in which bonnet, radiator and wings were combined in a single shape which also incorporated streamlined headlamps. Compare the difference with the 1932 S.S.I. (Below).

the roof, where wood battens saved the paint from scratches and low ornamental railings afforded anchorage for the straps that held the cases in position.

STREAMLINING

By the beginning of the 1930s, motorists, influenced by current taste and fashion, became more concerned with the appearance of their cars. Car body designers regarded the whole of the vehicle as one entity. In America the car became a status symbol as well as a means of transport for its owner. This increased attention to appearance produced great changes in body-styling over a very short period.

In 1934 the Chrysler Airflow and the *traction avant*

Citroën first appeared, with the Fiat 1500 a year later. All these had one idea in common, that of reducing wind resistance to enhance both looks and performance. Streamlining was not new. In 1922, Rumpler produced a car with an aerodynamic body, where the driver sat in front of his two passengers and even the mudguards and lamps were faired with the body. But there was little interest in such strange ideas at that time.

This revolution in styling brought in coverings for the radiator so that a sloping or rounded shape could be given to the front of the car. Some designers produced an air cooling duct that enabled the size of the radiator to be reduced. Others merely cluttered the airway and had to use larger radiators because of this.

Mudguards ceased to be separate entities. They flowed in voluminous curves half-way up the bonnet, from the front of the chassis to the door, and at the same time held the flush-fitting lamps. A downward slope was given to the cover over the engine as designers decided that speed lines were better for sales than the tall prow of power. The windscreen no longer had an upper hinged section which allowed vision in rain and ventilation in summer, but was sloped back into a curved roofline.

The roof was swept backwards and downwards behind the rear seats, its lower part having a lockable panel that guarded luggage in the rear boot. In some models the spare wheel was clamped to the boot lid, in others it was hidden in the floor of the boot space. The windows were made to wind up and down, instead of being raised by straps or moved backwards and forwards, and the front seats could be adjusted to suit the occupants.

But what was gained in style was paid for in comfort. No longer could people enter cars without stooping, no longer could the rear passengers stretch out their legs and no longer could the view be seen — only the hedges at the roadside.

This stage in the development of the automobile body lasted for nearly twenty years, some postwar cars having these smoother, rounder bodies. Even the small, cheap cars were styled in this fashion. The Fiat 500 appeared in 1936 with an obvious family likeness to the earlier 1500.

Sports cars tended to continue in their own way with vertical radiators, separate headlamps, cycle-type mudguards and two-seater bodies with huge fuel-tank tails. Some tanks were an uncompromising slab across the back, behind which were two spare wheels, and other tanks took on a streamlined tail shape.

Hoods in rubberized fabric and celluloid sidescreens gave weather protection for the two-seaters, but the open tourer with four seats was on its way out.

Larger sports cars became part of the specialist coach-building trade and this, together with a growing interest in *concours d'élégance*, resulted in some of the most elegant shapes ever seen as car bodies. The large saloons were influenced by this new elegance, using long horizontal lines to increase the impression of length and, at last, the motor carriage trade separated from the horse carriage.

By the 1950s another pattern began to emerge, that of the three rectangular boxes. One box covered all the front, including the engine, wheels and suspension; the second box provided space for four or, more usually, five seats; and the third box at the back gave a great volume of carrying space for fuel, spare wheel and luggage. The radiator grill went eventually to a full width slot combined with headlamp mountings, and it became just about as difficult to tell one make of car from another as it was to tell which was the front and which the back.

The open tourer disappeared altogether and a new type began to gain popularity — the station wagon, shooting brake or estate car. This was a modification of the standard

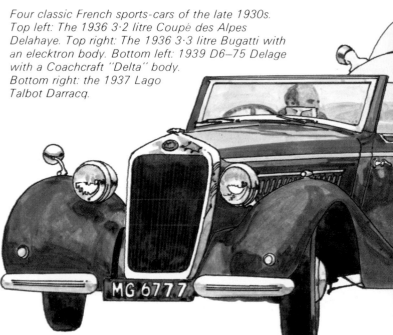

Four classic French sports-cars of the late 1930s. Top left: The 1936 3·2 litre Coupé des Alpes Delahaye. Top right: The 1936 3·3 litre Bugatti with an elecktron body. Bottom left: 1939 D6–75 Delage with a Coachcraft "Delta" body. Bottom right: the 1937 Lago Talbot Darracq.

Below: The 1954 Ford Anglia.

saloon, in which the central box was lengthened to reach the rear of the car and two doors, or a horizontally hinged tail-gate, were provided so that the space behind the rear seats could be used for luggage up to roof height. Provision was also made for the rear seats to be folded out of the way to permit the moving of larger items.

At first these bodies were saloon conversions with external wood-framed bodywork to give an air of stately home status, but the estate car became so popular with a wide range of the public that it progressed to a sheet-steel body that was based on the saloon version of the car.

BODY AERODYNAMICS

The increasing speed potential of cars, together with the roads on which high speeds could be maintained, made a study of the airflow round the bodywork essential by the 1960s. Whereas some manufacturers, such as Bristol, Porsche and Citroën, had seen the need for reduction of

wind drag, and had consequently produced scientifically designed bodies, others merely applied curves with the hope that, if it looked right, it was right. Unfortunately this was not always true, and it soon became evident that body shape could materially affect vehicle stability both from a point of wheel lifting as the car began to take off, and in side winds.

The more streamlined a body becomes, particularly a car that is flat underneath and semi-streamlined on top, then the greater is its tendency to lift as the relative air speed increases.

This may be due to two things: the first is that the front underside forces the air downwards, causing an equal and opposite reaction to lift the front of the car. This effect is increased by high-pressure air being rammed through the radiator and also deflected downwards to find its way out somewhere in the gearbox area.

Secondly, the air moving over the top of the body has a longer path than that going underneath. Therefore the air flows faster, and in consequence reduces its pressure and applies lift to the body top.

Those two unwanted forces are being countered by dams or spoilers running across the body below the radiator grill and across the rear of the tail. The front dam limits the amount of air trying to flow under the car and so tends to inhibit the lifting of the front wheels, while the spoiler across the rear of the car deflects the airflow over the tail upwards to produce a downwards reaction force, increasing the loading on the rear wheels.

Stability, or the ability to remain travelling in a straight line in conditions of cross winds, becomes less as the body shape approaches the ideal streamline. This is dependent upon the relative positions of two imaginary points, the car's centre of gravity and its centre of pressure. The centre of gravity is the point where the whole mass of the car is completely balanced. The centre of pressure is the point where a single force would act to produce the same effect as the wind acting over the whole exposed area of the car, that is the centre of area of the silhouette of the car seen from the direction of the wind.

If the centre of pressure is in front of the centre of gravity, not only will the wind pressure move the car bodily sideways, but it will also push ahead of the mass of the car and tend to move the front away from the straight path. Under such conditions the car becomes very susceptible to side winds and tiring to drive. If, on the other hand, the centre of gravity is in front of the centre of pressure, then sideways movement is accompanied by a force trying to move the front of the car towards the wind. The car is then mainly self-correcting and far less tiring or dangerous in gusty wind.

An attempt to alleviate instability in side winds was made by Bristol, in 1958, and other firms on both sides of the Atlantic through the provision of vertical fins at the rear. The idea was to increase the area affected by the wind behind the centre of gravity and to promote a degree of straight run steering at speed. These fins achieved little, but can still be seen in vestigial form on a number of present-day cars such as Rover and Triumph. It has been found that the real answer lies in steering geometry as well as in the design of the tyres.

PLASTIC BODIES

Some smaller manufacturers have used plastics materials, particularly those reinforced with fine glass fibres. These materials are relatively cheap to use in producing moulds for complex shapes. A further attribute is the ability to use self-colouring, thus obviating the need for multicoat paint-type finishes.

A number of small firms have produced bodies that could be fitted on to existing production chassis, or could take the running gear and power units from cars which are produced by the big manufacturers.

These glass fibre bodies have proved quite successful

Above: the 1975 Ferrari GT4 Dino.

Left: Porsche on the 1975 Turbo fitted a deep dam on the front to prevent air building up pressure under the car and an extended tail wing to help rear wheel adhesion at high speed.

Far left: Renault on the 1974 16 T.S. used a thin blade spoiler across the roof to keep the air flowing down the sloping rear window.

since they were introduced by Jensen in 1954 with the 541. Other examples are the Reliant three-wheeler of 1956, the Chevrolet Corvette for a number of years and the Lotus Elite and Elan. Moulded plastics have also been used to a small extent for unstressed body panels, such as the boot lid on the small Honda.

PAINTING TECHNIQUES

Although these modern materials can have their own colour, the colours of wood, steel fabric and aluminium are not popular with the public. The old coachmakers prided themselves on the deep and mirror-like finishes that they achieved by hand. The wood was primed, undercoated, topcoated and varnished by brush, and smoothed down between each coat with sand and garnet paper, used wet. In a first quality finish there could be as many as twenty-five or more separate coats. These paints were based on white lead, which had two drawbacks. First, the paints were soft, even when thoroughly dried out, and needed constant care when being washed down, to avoid the surface being scratched. It was also necessary to dry the bodywork thoroughly before it was left in the motor house to prevent rain spotting. The other trouble was the chemical reaction which occurred when lead-based paints were used on aluminium panels. To solve these problems, special coatings with other metal oxides as the base were developed.

Oakland, in 1924, and A.C. a year later, introduced nitrocellulose lacquers for body finishing. Cellulose was sprayed on the body panels and force-dried at a relatively low temperature to remove the solvents. It dried to a reasonably hard surface and provided, when sprayed on a fully prepared surface, a deep gloss finish. In the early 1960s cellulose finishes began to be replaced by acrylic resins, which give a much harder and lasting finish, and an extremely deep lustre. The effect of this was very neatly to tie together a material advantage with a superficial but advantageous sales attraction.

At about the same period the system of electrostatic deposition was evolved to prevent uneven application of the finish. In this system the body is negatively charged with electricity and the paint droplets positively charged so that the paint is attracted to all parts of the metal. A further innovation, around the middle 1960s, was electrophoresis. By this means the specially formulated paint is electrically deposited in much the same way as is done in electroplating.

Underbody protection against road moisture became essential once the thick chassis frame was replaced by the thin pressed-steel integral body sections. The application of a coating of zinc phosphate on the alkali-cleaned body shell is carried out with the Rotadip process introduced in 1949. In this the shell is mounted on a spit to be immersed and rotated. Further protection may be given by a sprayed coating of bitumastic or rubber-based compounds.

WINDSCREENS AND WINDOWS

Because early motor cars could only travel at comparatively low speeds, the driver and passengers could protect themselves against the elements simply by wearing thick coats and goggles. Later, vertical glass screens were added to the dashboard. These were sheets of flat plate-glass in wooden frames and they were an obvious source of injury in collisions.

In 1905 a Swindon solicitor, John Crewe Wood, invented a screen made from a sandwich of two sheets of glass cemented with Canada balsam to a central layer of celluloid. Manufacture was difficult and the price high. It was not until 1910 that Edouard Benedictus reinvented Triplex glass in Paris, with the aid of more suitable cements. Manufacture began in England in 1914 with

The Sundym tinted-Triplex windscreen provides safety glass that minimizes the transmission of heat from bright sunlight.

bone gelatine and enamel as the adhesives, but fitting was carried out by local garages, only as a replacement for shattered glass windscreens. In 1928, Hillman fitted laminated safety glass to the windscreen, and the side and rear windows, as standard production.

Laminated glass requires a frame. A cheaper alternative, which can be fitted directly into the bodywork, is toughened glass. This was developed by the French glass-makers, St Gobain, in 1929 from the discoveries of the Corning Glass Company of America in 1922. It consists of a single sheet, which has been heated and rapidly cooled on the surfaces so that, if broken, it is shattered into small blunt particles.

Triplex developed a curved laminated glass, for the fronts of tram-cars, that aroused the interest of motor manufacturers. By 1946, single curvature windscreens had reached an advanced stage in America, and Jowett and Rootes also began fitting curved, toughened glass in windscreens and rear windows. The first Triplex wrap-round windscreen was fitted to the 1956 Vauxhall Victor. In 1959 toughened plate was replaced by toughened float-

An example of the fibreglass bodywork in the Reliant Scimitar.

glass. Differential zoning was introduced to give better vision through crazed windscreens, larger particles being left in front of the driver's eyes.

Tungsten wires, embedded in the laminations to give rear window heating for demisting and de-icing, were first fitted by Rolls-Royce in 1948. Ten years later, silk screen printing with silver ink on to the glass provided the Hotline heated window at a greatly reduced price. To make it easier to drive in bright sunlight, Sundym glass, progressively green-tinted towards the top of the window, first became standard in America and spread to other countries with bright sunlight. Not only does this reduce glare, but it also lessens the build-up of heat inside the car.

As closed bodywork became more popular, the desire to admit sun and air, whenever the weather was suitable, grew in favour. In 1929 W. H. Bishop and T. P. Colledge devised an easily fixed sliding-roof fitment that provided an opening equal to about half the roof area. The rectangular sunroof was operated from inside the car by lifting the sliding panel clear of a water seal and sliding it

rearwards to the desired opening, where it could be clamped. Early versions slid over the top of the existing roof and later ones between the roof and the interior head lining. In the roof introduced on the 1972 Ford Granada, initial movement pivoted the panel about its edge to give increased fresh air flow and further movement produced the roof opening. The first action was an advantage if only a limited amount of air was required.

As a corollary to the sunroof, open sports car owners wanted something more stable and draught-free than the fabric hood. Their requirements were met by the introduction of hard-tops usually made in glass fibre which, as on the Triumph TR2 of 1953, enabled the open bodywork to be converted to a coupé-type body by merely bolting on the rigid roof. These roofs were fixed easily and could be fitted or removed as the season required. Not that the idea was particularly novel, as a number of cars of the early 1900s were available with interchangeable bodywork that could turn a saloon into an open shooting brake. Hardtops were also listed by Lanchester in 1901 and Cadillac in 1903.

147

UPHOLSTERY AND SEATING

Leather has been the favourite material for upholstery, even before the coming of the motor car. It was thus inevitable that leather, stuffed with horsehair, and buttoned at intervals to prevent movement of the filling, should be the choice for early car seats. With the coming of the closed passenger compartment in the quality trade, leather was gradually replaced by the woven fabrics traditionally used for horse-carriage interiors.

Real leather was too expensive to be used when mass production was seeking lower and lower selling prices in the 1920s. Leatherette, or American cloth, was substituted. Also known as Rexine, this consisted of a woven cloth backing, flexibly coated on one side to give an impression of leather. The horsehair padding became thinner and was supplemented by pneumatic springing (air-filled rubber bladders) or "hour-glass" soft steel springs. The first air cushion upholstery had appeared around 1901.

With the growth of the plastics industry, the quality, comfort and appearance of the leather imitations improved greatly, particularly when they were made porous and gave a measure of ventilation in humid conditions. The air bags and cylindrical springs gave way to a form of interwoven strip suspension, either by Pirelli rubber webbing or by strips of zigzag spring wire. Both these systems allowed the seats to be made shallower without any loss of comfort. The springs or webbing were often covered with plastic foam padding.

In the early 1920s several people, such as J. J. McGuire of America and J. Y. Sangster of England, had the idea of providing angular adjustments of the seat backs by the use of either notched stays or leather straps.

G. H. Robinson of Rubery Owen introduced, in 1936, a transverse linear cam acting on vertical rods to adjust the back hinge, which allowed movement while the

The ultimate in 1975 from Germany,
the Mercedes-Benz 600.

passengers were still in their seats. It was not, however, until 1951 that Reutter of Stuttgart went into production with the spiral-spring-loaded multi-position hinge, released by a small side lever. After that the adoption of adjustable seat backs became almost universal, first on the European continent and later in England. Most of these backs allow full folding for sleeping, an interesting flash-back to the ambulance conversion vehicles of the First World War.

The first movable windows followed the coach and railway practice of having a leather strap or cloth strap fixed to the bottom of a vertically sliding frame. The strap had holes that slipped over a peg to keep the window in the desired position.

It was replaced by a gear and linkage system that balanced the window weight and gave finer and faster movement. In 1946 Daimler took all the effort from window raising by operating the gears electrically.

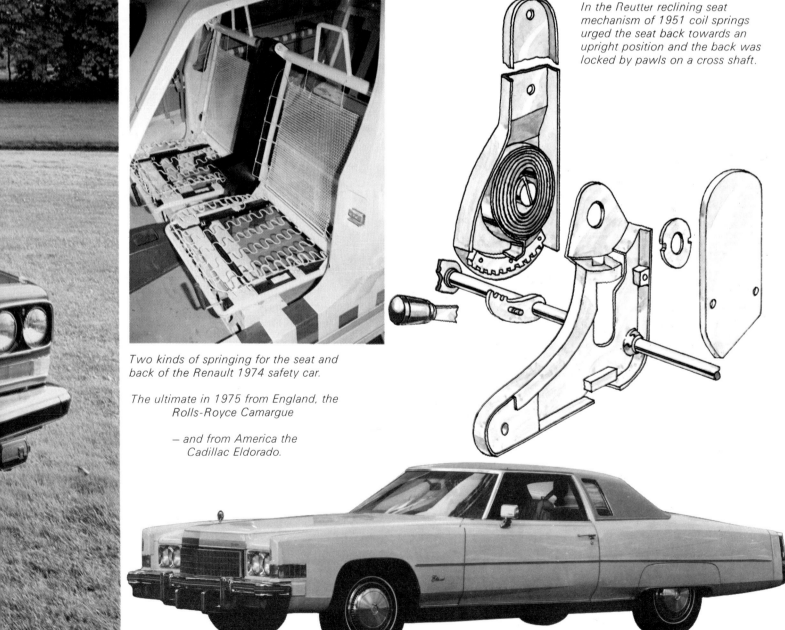

In the Reutter reclining seat mechanism of 1951 coil springs urged the seat back towards an upright position and the back was locked by pawls on a cross shaft.

Two kinds of springing for the seat and back of the Renault 1974 safety car.

The ultimate in 1975 from England, the Rolls-Royce Camargue

– and from America the Cadillac Eldorado.

Although wheeled transport was probably introduced around 3500 B.C., the vehicles were mostly load carriers. Passenger vehicles were restricted to two-wheel chariots with leather-thong floors. When people wanted to reduce the shaking and jolting, they thought in terms of smoothing the road surface, rather than using springs.

About the middle of the 16th century ideas developed for insulating the bodywork from the road wheels. The first known system involved a chassis that resembled an upturned table with the carriage body slung by leather straps from the tops of the legs. This was not a springing system as it only allowed the wheels and body to move their separate ways. This formed the basis for springing being called the suspension.

The first springing development was the replacement, in about 1665, of the table legs by big C-shaped springs, a form of road insulation that can still be seen on children's perambulators. The carriage makers eventually realized that C springs had disadvantages in allowing a degree of fore-and-aft sway, and giving a high centre of gravity and a high roll axis. They also served to spring only the body, leaving the relatively heavy chassis unsprung.

By the time powered vehicles were developing, the springs had changed to an elliptical shape and were bolted between the axles and the chassis or chassis-body. The primary function of suspension at this time was to allow all four wheels to maintain contact with uneven road surfaces. Any increase in passenger comfort was a bonus. Three-wheel vehicles, being tripods, could stand on any uneven-ness and often had no springing at all.

The compromise needed between a suspension system keeping the wheels on the road, where they can drive or steer, and one that provides maximum insulation from road shocks for the occupants has always been a problem, and remains so to this day. The strength, or rate, of the springs between the wheels and the body cannot be altered according to the kind of bump about to be met by the wheel.

When a wheel hits a bump it is moved upwards at right angles to the surface and gains momentum in that direction. With an unsprung wheel this movement is opposed only by gravity, which will eventually bring it sharply back to the ground. By putting a spring between the wheel and the chassis, much of the energy in the bounding wheel is stored in the spring and not transferred to the chassis, which therefore moves upwards through a smaller distance than the wheel.

The lighter the wheel and the other pieces connected to it, such as the axle, brakes, drive shafts or steering gear, the smaller is the total energy involved. That is the reason for designing cars with the least possible unsprung weight.

A soft, or low rate, spring can permit a large wheel movement for a given bump, but the spring must be strong enough to bear the chassis weight properly. So, although soft springs should give the greatest comfort, they cannot do much good if the chassis weight squashes them. On the

comfort

The horse-drawn carriage maker's influence is well shown in the 1899 Canstatt-Daimler

other hand, a stiff spring that does not deflect much under chassis weight gives a hard ride.

The energy absorbed by the spring is not dissipated but merely stored. When the spring load begins to be released, by the wheel moving downwards, energy is returned to the wheel system. This non-destructibility of energy is responsible for the characteristic vibration of a spring.

Every spring has a natural frequency of vibration like the strings of a piano. As with the vibrating blocks of a xylophone, the shorter and stiffer the spring is, the higher is the frequency. It is possible for the vertical accelerations of the bouncing wheel to coincide with the natural bounce frequency of the sprung chassis. In this condition the chassis movement can become large enough to lift the wheel off the road.

To limit this large chassis movement near the natural sprung mass frequency, a damping device known as a shock absorber is fitted between the wheel and the chassis, parallel to the spring. It does not, in fact, absorb any shock, but provides an inhibitor, its action being related to the relative velocity between the two moving systems.

A wheel with a pneumatic tyre has a double springing system in which the tyre acts as a virtually undamped low-rate spring between the road and the wheel itself. When the natural frequency of the tyre spring system and the vibration due to road roughness, or to the vibration of an untrue or out-of-balance wheel, coincide, the resonant forces generated are sufficient to lift the wheel out of road contact against the force of the suspension spring. This phenomenon is known as wheel hop or, in small movements, as wheel patter.

Besides making the compromise in spring rates – helped considerably by acceleration proportioned damping – designers had to consider the effect of the four wheels working together or, more correctly, the front wheels moving just before the rear wheels. If the front and rear springs have the same vibration frequency, there is a tendency for the body to begin to bounce.

It would at first seem an easy solution to vary the two natural frequencies (as has been done in phased suspensions where the spring lengths are arranged to have the lower frequency at the rear). But it must be realized that the frequencies have upper and lower limits. These limits are imposed by the human body being designed for vertical motion frequencies that lie between slow walking, around one to one and a half cycles per second, and fast running.

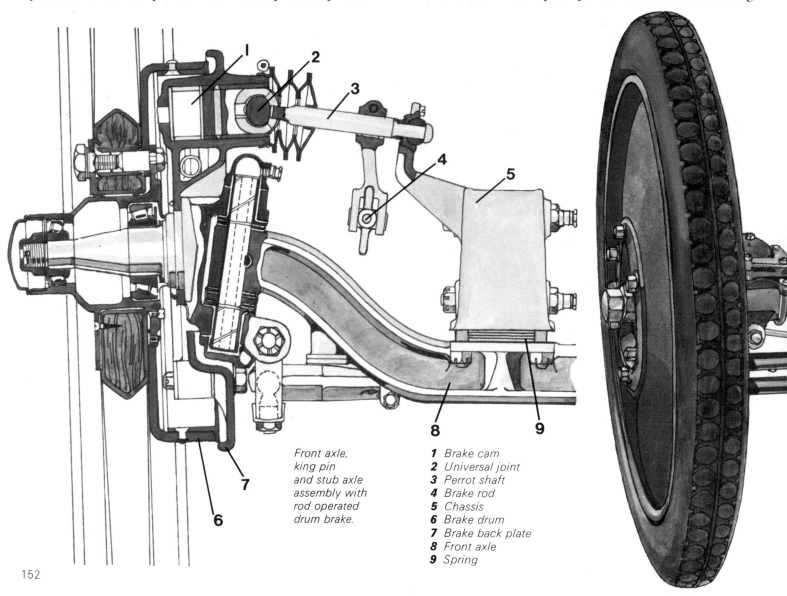

Front axle, king pin and stub axle assembly with rod operated drum brake.

1 Brake cam
2 Universal joint
3 Perrot shaft
4 Brake rod
5 Chassis
6 Brake drum
7 Brake back plate
8 Front axle
9 Spring

about three cps. Frequencies below one and a half cps lead to travel sickness and those above three cps to unpleasant vibrations.

AXLES

Before the common use of independent suspension of the wheels, the front axle generally comprised a tube or an H-sectioned forging, both sections giving the most torsional rigidity and resistance to bending for the minimum weight of metal. Tubular front axles were easy to manufacture, being at first straight tubes and, later, tubes curved downwards at the centre for engine or chassis clearance.

Spring mountings were brazed or, later, welded to the tubes. End fittings to hold a substantially vertical king-pin, or steering swivel pin, were similarly secured. The forged axles had their flat spring-mountings and king-pin bosses forged integrally. Some had forked ends, in which the stub axle carrying the wheel could swivel about a king-pin. Bugatti, in the mid-1920s, combined the two types of axle by forging a hollow axle tube with transverse rectangular openings for the springs and hollow tapered ends from the spring-mountings outwards.

For the belt- and chain-driven rear wheels, the rear axle was again tubular. But when the differential moved back to the axle, the tubes increased in diameter to house the driving shafts. The rear axle then developed into several axle components — one to support a wheel, one to drive the wheel and one to encase the driving shaft.

In early designs the wheels were both driven and supported by the driving shaft which, in turn, was carried in bearings on, or in, the axle proper, to which the springs were attached. The inboard ends of the driving (or half) shafts were rigid with the differential side gears. As the wheel was fixed to the shaft outboard of the shaft bearing, this device was known as a live or semi-floating axle.

With a three-quarter floating axle the wheel hub is supported by a bearing on the casing, in line with the central plane of the wheel, and the half-shaft is rigid with the hub. So any tendency of the wheel to tilt on the bearing is resisted by the half-shaft in bending.

When the wheel is completely supported by the axle casing and the half-shaft has only a torsion load, through being splined to both the differential and the hub, a fully-floating axle is formed. By 1904 F. Pilain was using such an axle to allow the rear wheels to have positive camber.

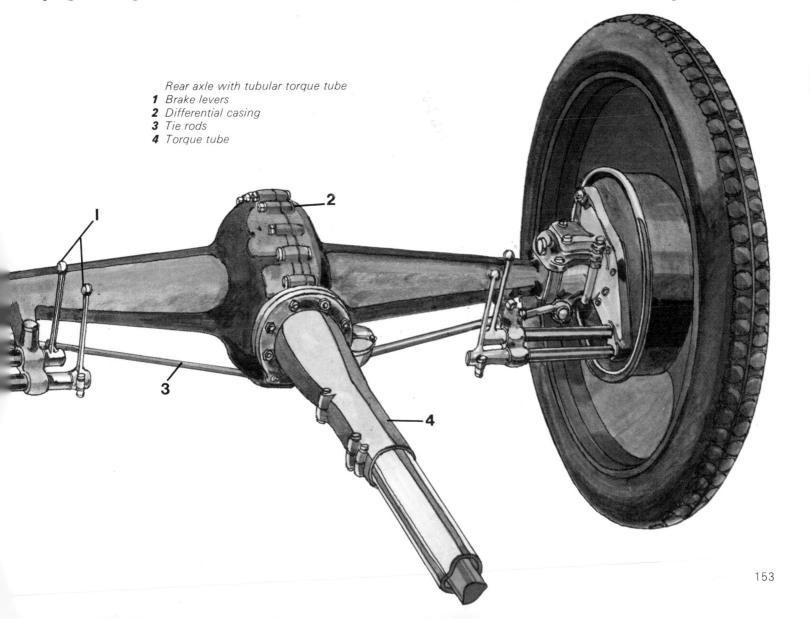

Rear axle with tubular torque tube
1 Brake levers
2 Differential casing
3 Tie rods
4 Torque tube

153

WHEEL BEARINGS

One of the oldest four-wheeled vehicles in the world – the 1st century B.C. wagon found at Dejbjerg, Jutland – had hubs running on the axles through needle-roller bearings. But, cycles apart, it was not until the coming of the motor car that vehicle builders turned to using ball or roller bearings with their wheel hubs.

Although parallel roller bearings have been tried, the tendency has been for earlier ball bearings to be supplanted by taper roller bearings, which are more suited to taking axial loads imposed by cornering. This is particularly the case for front wheels, which rely on relatively closely spaced bearings on the stub axle for lateral rigidity, and, for the same reasons, for independent rear suspensions.

A recent development is the use of a pair of angular contact ball bearings, in which the contact lines of the balls and their inner and outer races are sloped to provide for both radial and thrust loadings.

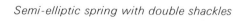

Semi-elliptic spring with double shackles

Transverse leaf spring

SPRINGS

Carried on from the horse carriage, the leaf spring in various configurations has had the greatest usage in automobile suspensions. The original C spring was strengthened by the addition of more steel strips tapering in length from the fixed end. When flattened, it retained the plurality of leaves.

At first the elliptical leaf spring was employed. This comprised two long, curved leaves or blades pivoted together at their ends to form an ellipse – in fact, four flattened C springs. They were strengthened at their mid-points, where they were bolted to chassis and axle respectively, by additional leaves whose lengths decreased as they were located farther from the main blade. Such an arrangement of leaves provides the maximum strength with adequate deflection for given loads.

As the loads increased, the elliptic spring was replaced

by the semi-elliptic. This was a spring that could have its ends secured to the chassis frame and its centre to the appropriate axle. But it had the disadvantage that an increase in deflection produced an increase in length. In other words, the spring became longer as it flattened. To overcome the trouble, one end was pivoted directly to the chassis, while the other was allowed to slide on the frame or, more satisfactorily, was pivoted to a link. Known as a shackle, this link was itself pivoted to the chassis.

Two further forms of leaf springs were designed, the quarter elliptic and the three-quarter. The quarter elliptic spring was half of a semi-elliptic spring with the thick multileaf end bolted to the chassis and the single main leaf forged to a loop at the other end to hold a bearing for the pivot pin connecting the spring to the axle. Shackles were not used with quarter elliptic springs. In consequence the

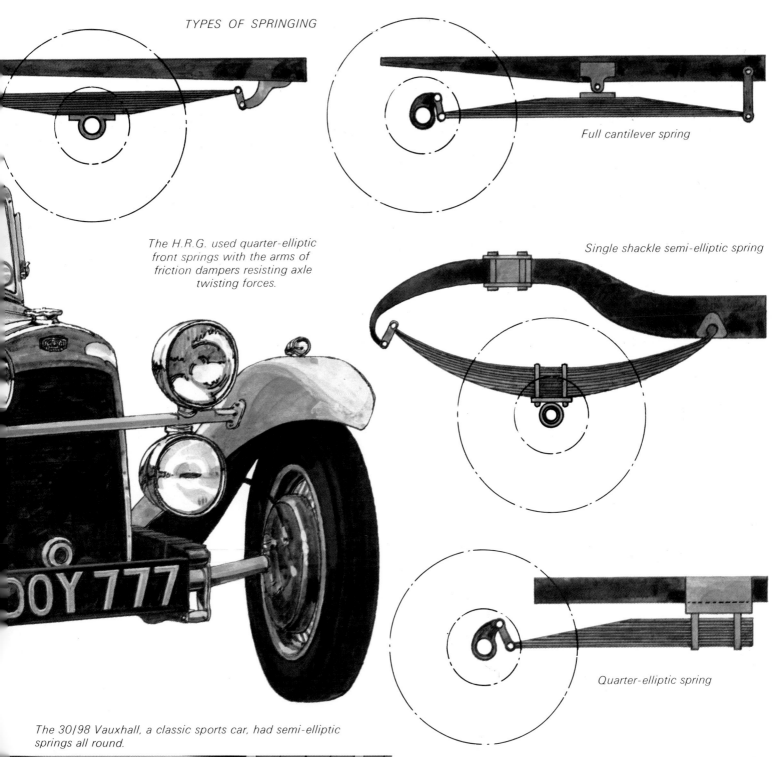

Full cantilever spring

The H.R.G. used quarter-elliptic front springs with the arms of friction dampers resisting axle twisting forces.

Single shackle semi-elliptic spring

Quarter-elliptic spring

The 30/98 Vauxhall, a classic sports car, had semi-elliptic springs all round.

axle was able to move either backwards or forwards as the spring deflected.

The three-quarter elliptic, a semi and a quarter joined at their end pivots, came with a new line of development, that of using multi-rate springs. If the quarter spring was much stiffer than the semi spring, it could deal with heavy shocks, leaving the weaker to deal with small irregularities in road surface. A further form of this two-rate suspension was the subsequent use of coil springs, or even C springs, in place of the shackle.

Later, variable rate springs were made with the shortest, or some of the shorter, leaves initially curved to a greater radius than the remaining leaves. This provided a spring in which the number of leaves in stress increased with the deflection. Over the years the design of these springs has tended to the use of fewer and wider leaves.

In 1962, Chevrolet produced a single chrome-carbon alloy steel leaf, manufactured to close dimensions with a maximum thickness at the centre; a leaf having the properties of a beam of uniform strength along its length.

While the leaf spring reacts to loads by bending, other automobile springs, such as the helical coil and the straight torsion bar, react by twisting. When a coil spring deflects along its axis, the angle between the coils increases or decreases by twisting, or torsion, of the coil material. A torsion bar is no more than a helical spring straightened out. These springs were used in the early days, for example by C. de Kando, who housed his torsion bars in the chassis tubes. But they came into much greater use with the independent suspension systems, because with such systems axle location ceased to be a spring function.

Other elastic media for springs are rubber and gas, usually air. A number of vehicles have been said to have hydraulic suspension. This is not correct as fluids are relatively incompressible and not elastic, their function being as force transmitters between a moving part and an elastic medium. The use of rubber goes back at least to 1847, when de Bergue fitted a cart with springs comprising alternate discs of rubber and steel. Springs of this type have a desirable increase of rate with deflection, but require mechanical location for the moving elements.

Development by A. E. Moulton of Spencer-Moulton and Dr A. Boschi of S.A.G.A. has resulted in a spring where, by virtue of a hollow conical shape, the rubber is in both compression and shear. Such springs are stable without external locating means and can be designed to give a low rate at mid-range with an increasing rate on compression or expansion.

Another form of rubber spring is Torsilastic, pioneered by Alvin Krotz of America, in which the rubber is bonded to inner and outer tubular metal shells. Since 1948, this has been used for vehicles in the shape of the Flexitor. The cone spring came to prominence with the B.M.C. Mini.

PNEUMATIC SPRINGS

George Stephenson fitted a form of gas springing (actually steam) on the locomotives he built for the Kilmarnock and Troon railway in 1817. But pneumatic springing for motor vehicles was not suggested until 1896. In that year J. R. Heath placed annular air bags round the axle ends and held the bags in metal loops on the chassis, the axle being located by swing links.

Five years later M. A. Yeakley devised a vehicle on which all four wheels were driven and were independently sprung by air acting on pistons connected to the axles. This idea was further notable for the provision of an engine-driven compressor and manual control to adjust the suspension height in relation to the load. Automatic levelling was devised in 1910 by P. H. de Saint-Senoch, but such systems lay largely in abeyance until the advent of the Citroën DS 19 in 1955, when Ford and General Motors were also offering low-pressure pneumatic springing.

Both the low- and high-pressure air springs depend on the natural law that as the volume of a mass of gas is decreased so the pressure increases. With the low pressure system

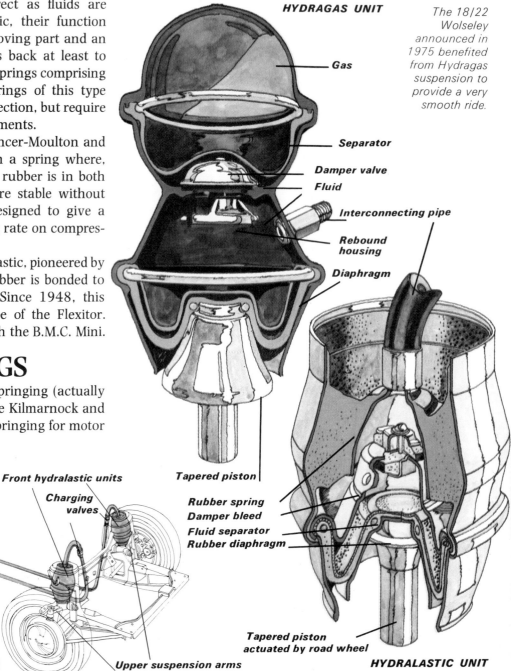

HYDRAGAS UNIT

The 18/22 Wolseley announced in 1975 benefited from Hydragas suspension to provide a very smooth ride.

Gas

Separator

Damper valve

Fluid

Interconnecting pipe

Rebound housing

Diaphragm

Tapered piston

Rubber spring
Damper bleed
Fluid separator
Rubber diaphragm

Rear hydralastic units

Front hydralastic units

Charging valves

Anti-roll bar
Rear swing arms

Interconnecting pipes

Upper suspension arms

Tapered piston actuated by road wheel

HYDRALASTIC UNIT

the gas, usually air, is contained by either a convoluted reinforced rubber cylinder or a diaphragm of similar material. The diaphragm is usually of the rolling type in which a beaded periphery is secured to the rim of a hollow container as a pistonlike member presses on the diaphragm centre. As the piston moves into the container to compress the gas, the diaphragm bulges into the clearance between piston and container and, in fact, rolls on both members. This low-pressure system had a disadvantage of size for private vehicle use.

With the high-pressure system, such as provided by Citroën in 1954, a diaphragm is held between the halves of a metal sphere, and the gas, usually nitrogen, is charged at high pressure into one side of the sphere. The other side of the sphere is connected through a damping valve to a cylinder containing hydraulic oil, a piston in this cylinder being coupled to the suspension links. Thus suspension movement is communicated to one side of the diaphragm by the oil and the nitrogen acts on the other side as a spring. One benefit of gas springing is the increase of spring rate with suspension movement.

In the B.L.M.C. Hydrolastic system the suspension movement acts directly on one side of a rolling diaphragm, the other side being in contact with a fairly low viscosity fluid that can pass through a damper valve to act against one face of a hollow conical rubber spring.

The Hydragas system, emanating from the same company in 1973 and used on the Austin Allegro, is similar to the Hydrolastic, but the rubber spring is replaced by a second diaphragm across the centre of a spherical container. One side of the diaphragm is acted on by fluid displaced through the central damper valve and the other by nitrogen at 330 pounds per square inch which constitutes, in fact, the actual spring itself.

AXLE LOCATION

Independent suspension systems showed that some form of axle location was essential. However, the need was not at first so apparent when leaf springs were used. A little consideration will show that a leaf will bend into a flat S-shape when the axle is subjected either to driving or braking torques.

This undesirable movement was prevented by Lanchester in 1900 and Maybach in 1901, when they added links between the spring centre and the axle mountings to resist twisting of the axle. These were known as torque stays. Rear-axle torque was taken, in many cases, by the tube enclosing the propeller shaft. Links or cables were fitted as front axle torque stays, though a number of designers used the rotation of the axle as a self-servo action to increase the tension in front-brake cables, which occurred when the cables were above the axle centre.

For a long period the leaf spring ends were formed to a loop or eye, bushed with bronze, to rock about a fixed pin on the chassis or in the shackle. By the second half of the century the bronze bushes were being replaced by rubber bushes that did not require regular greasing, would last longer and provided a small vibration damper between the axle and chassis. The rubber allowed a sideways rolling float of the chassis relative to the axle. Sometimes this float was controlled by a diagonal stay between one side of the rear axle and the other side of the chassis. This is known as a Panhard rod.

Body roll, due to centrifugal force produced by driving round corners, was aggravated on early vehicles by the great height of the centre of gravity. In 1904 J. F. Murphy used a mechanical linkage that tilted the body inwards to the curve when the steering wheel was turned. Other people tried to obtain this effect by using screw-threaded king-pins, and in 1909 F. de Lostalot and M. Guerpillion connected the steering column movement to valves adjusting the height of a trailing link pneumatic suspension.

By 1972 Automotive Products had returned to the idea of no-roll cornering and had produced a system in which a hydraulic strut between the suspension arm and a gas spring was adjusted in length according to the suspension movement and the movement of a pendulum.

Meanwhile, the compromise, between the low-rate springing for maximum comfort and high-rate for minimum roll, was achieved by spring systems stiffer across, and softer in line with, the chassis. A. A. Remmington of the Wolseley Tool and Motor Company, as it was called in 1911, produced semi-elliptic rear springs connected at their respective ends to the axle and chassis shackles and joined across the car at mid-point by a torsion bar. Thus the axle ends of the springs could both move vertically at the rate appropriate to their length, but relative vertical movement was resisted by the stiffness of the torsion bar.

Later designers introduced separate torsion bars, and sometimes leaf springs, until, with the acceptance of independent suspensions, the anti-roll bar became a transverse torsion bar held in rubber bushes mounted to

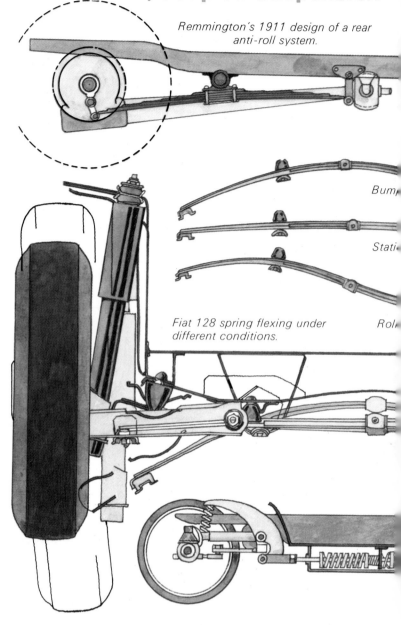

Remmington's 1911 design of a rear anti-roll system.

Bum...

Stati...

Fiat 128 spring flexing under different conditions.

Rol...

the body frame. Longitudinal lever arms were connected to the suspension arms, as on the 1935 Fiat 1500.

Another system, used by Vauxhall and Fiat, was to fit a transverse leaf as the main spring and, by having two chassis mounting points about which it could flex, allow a bump to deflect the spring in a semi-elliptic fashion and a roll to deflect the spring into an S-shape of much higher stiffness.

COUPLED SUSPENSION

As well as bumps and rolling, another undesirable motion for passengers is pitching or rocking in a fore-and-aft mode. This becomes more noticeable with shorter wheelbases. By 1910 designers had the idea of coupling the front and rear springing, so that the chassis remained level when the wheels met a bump.

Although W. Kootz and K. I. Crossley were working independently on this scheme in 1910, it was J. J. Charley who achieved design success and evolved the idea that was popularized by Citroën 38 years later in the 2CV of 1949.

In this system the wheels were carried independently at

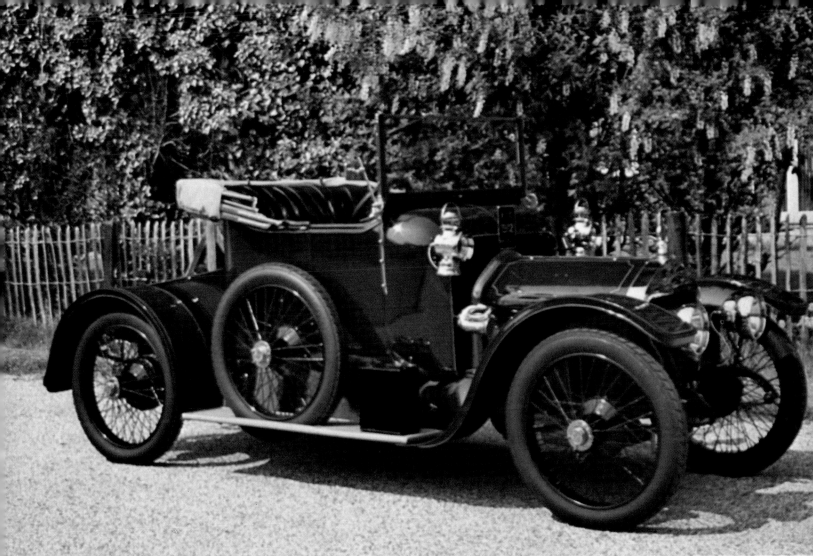

A 1911 Wolseley which had a chassis and suspension designed by A. A. Remmington.

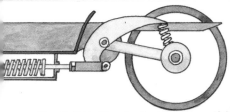

J. J. Charley's coupled suspension with wheels on bell cranks and centre springs.

The 2 C.V. Citroën that used a self-levelling suspension similar to that of J. J. Charley of 1911.

the end of one arm of a two-armed, bell-crank lever pivoted on the chassis. Tension coil springs positioned in the middle of each side of the chassis were coupled to the other arms of the front and back wheel levers of that side. When a front wheel rose on a bump, the spring was tensioned, and the reaction to this tension produced a pull in the connection to the other arm of the rear wheel. As this wheel was still on the ground, the bell-crank pivoted about the wheel axle and raised the bell-crank pivot on the chassis, thus tending to keep the chassis parallel with the road.

In the Citroën system additional springs compensated for uneven chassis loading and kept the main springs central under non-bump conditions.

The same effect is produced in the Hydrolastic system by interconnecting the fluid spaces between the diaphragms and rubber springs above the damper valve on the two sides of the car. As a front wheel lifts, the communicated fluid pressure jacks up the rear of the car on the same side. The later development of the Hydragas suspension has a similar front to rear interconnection, but the pipes connect the fluid spaces below the damper, so that the dampers affect only the individual units, not the pitching movement.

DAMPING

When a wheel meets an obstruction, it tends to move backwards, owing to the blow, and upwards to roll over the bump. With a leaf spring system the horizontal blow is absorbed by the axle tending to twist the spring up at the rear and down at the front and is further absorbed by rubber bushes in the spring or shackle eyes.

The horizontal rigidity of metal to metal bearings which followed with independent suspension, did not allow the small backward movement of the wheel (called compliance) to meet these shocks, and it was later found necessary to introduce compliance into such systems by rubber blocks or bushes. This had, in fact, been realized as long ago as 1897 by A. Gimmig, who put rubber and felt between the springs and the chassis, and by R. H. Hassler, who connected his torque stays through volute springs.

The relative rubbing of the blades of a leaf spring along each other as the spring flexes was a mixed blessing. On one hand, water and grit could get between the blades and cause rusting and squeaking, and on the other hand the rubbing provided a degree of spring damping.

To keep springs in the best condition, they were encased in lace-up leather gaiters or, later, bound with bitumastic-soaked tapes. Another binding was stout whipcord, which not only protected the spring, but held the blades together to increase the damping friction. Constant damping was also provided by interleaving the blades with strips of zinc, or other soft metal, or inserting rubber, lead or Ferodo blocks in recesses at the spring ends.

Shock absorbers are really dampers that have an increasing resistance to movement as that movement gets faster. They are fitted to practically all spring systems. They inhibit or damp out the higher frequency vibrations imparted to the lower frequency action of the main spring and also resist the too-rapid return of the spring (and the wheel and axle) to normal condition after the bump.

The need for some form of spring damping on motor vehicles is reputed to have been first realized by Emile Mors in 1899, when he used a friction-type shock absorber. The simple friction type pioneered by J. M. M. Truffault in 1902 comprised two flat arms, each having a disc shape at one end and being pivoted to the chassis and axle respectively at their other ends. A leather washer was clamped between the discs by a single central bolt, which could be tightened to produce friction damping between the arms.

In 1906, E. V. Hartford used a friction material, eventually Ferodo, between a number of arm discs and employed a star-shaped spring washer to clamp the discs together. Later designs had Bowden cables or hydraulic devices to allow shock absorber adjustment from the driving seat to suit the road surface and vehicle speed. Although these dampers were in vogue for over 30 years, they were by no means ideal because the force required to start movement, "sticktion", was greater than the force produced once movement had started. Moreover, too-enthusiastic tightening could result in the damper friction being greater than the spring force trying to move the axle downwards after

the vehicle had passed over a bump in the road.

While the Hartford was relatively insensitive to the amount of spring movement, Harvey du Cros of Panhard proposed, in 1905, a cam action to increase the clamping force with increases in spring travel. The same year, A. Hertz used a one-way ratchet so that the initial spring movement was undamped and the return movement was retarded. This type of damper was known as a snubber. Probably the most popular was the Gabriel snubber, designed by C. H. Foster in 1925. His device had a flexible strap wrapped several times round two relatively movable members with a compression spring between them. As the axle went up the strap was slack, but in the opposite direction the strap tightened round the sprung core.

It had long been known in other engineering fields that, if a piston, or vane, with a hole in it, was immersed in a fluid, the resistance to movement of the piston would be related to the speed at which it was moving. This was owing to the throttling effect of the hole on the fluid trying to get to the other side of the piston.

In 1901 C. L. Horock devised a telescopic type of damper using a piston and cylinder with an adjustable escape, or bleed, hole between one end of the cylinder and the other, as well as a one-way, or non-return, valve in the piston.

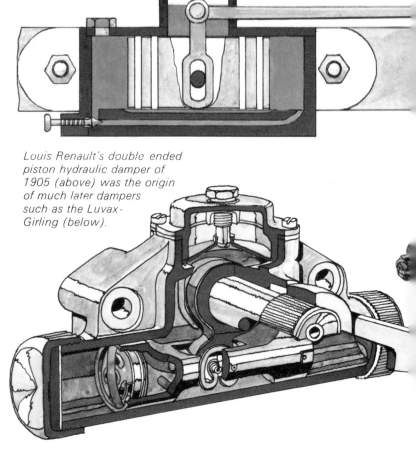

Louis Renault's double ended piston hydraulic damper of 1905 (above) was the origin of much later dampers such as the Luvax-Girling (below).

In one direction of movement the piston could travel relatively freely as the air or oil filling the cylinder flowed through the non-return valve. In the other direction the valve closed and the fluid had a more difficult journey through the bleed passage.

Three years later A. T. Christophe and P. M. Menteyne patented a telescopic damper, in which the bleed passage was in the piston and varied in area, as the piston moved, to give a progressive damping force. They also applied their principle to damping angular movement by using a segmental piston swinging through an arc within a cylindrical casing. Their design was improved from 1908 onwards by M. Houdaille who designed a shock absorber which had a cylindrical chamber divided into two compartments by segmental blocks. The working arm was connected to a spindle, through the centre of the chamber, carrying a vane that extended across the chamber diameter. Passages in the vane and blocks provided for a restricted flow of liquid when the arm moved the vane in one direction. By the mid-1920s Houdaille shock absorbers were available for fitment to most cars. Later came the Luvax, which worked in much the same way.

In 1905 Louis Renault designed a damper that provided increasing resistance to motion with increasing travel in both directions of movement. This used a double-ended piston reciprocating in a cylinder having its extremities connected by a groove diminishing in depth towards the cylinder ends.

Luvax also marketed a shock absorber of this type many years later, though in this case the piston had pressure-regulating valves at each end to control the fluid flow through the piston. The piston was reciprocated by a rocker, engaging a slot mid-length of the piston, on a spindle angularly rotated by an arm connected to the vehicle suspension.

Another form of double acting shock absorber was the Armstrong, which had two cylinders in a narrow V formation. These were single acting in opposed directions, their pistons being connected at opposite ends of a rocking lever pivoted at its centre on the shock absorber arm shaft. Later versions of this damper, which was somewhat similar in action to the Delco of the late 1920s, reverted to the parallel piston design of 1907 by C. Caille.

With the universal acceptance of independent wheel suspension, the telescopic shock absorber became equally universal except for the fluid springing systems, such as Citroën and British Leyland. In these cases damping valves are used to regulate the fluid in much the same way.

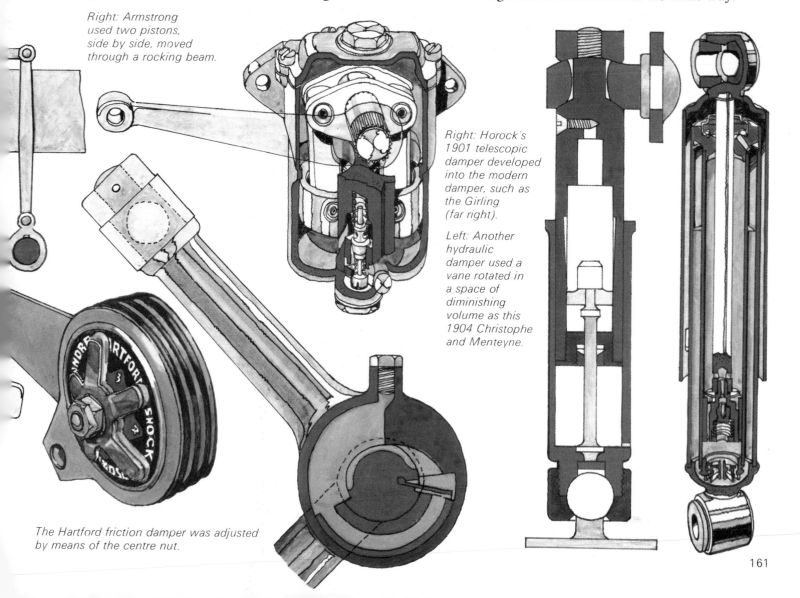

Right: Armstrong used two pistons, side by side, moved through a rocking beam.

Right: Horock's 1901 telescopic damper developed into the modern damper, such as the Girling (far right).

Left: Another hydraulic damper used a vane rotated in a space of diminishing volume as this 1904 Christophe and Menteyne.

The Hartford friction damper was adjusted by means of the centre nut.

One of the earliest cars built in England, the 1895 Knight, had independent front suspension by coil springs on the wheel spindles.

The Fiat 128 also has independent suspension but the coil springs act on links between body and axles.

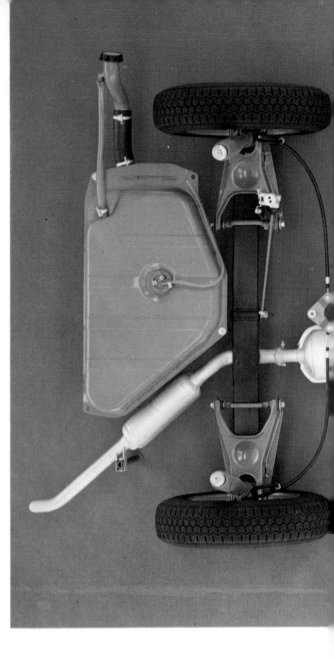

FRONT SUSPENSION

The rigid front axle of the horse-drawn carriage, steered by being pivoted about its centre, more or less enforced the design of a suspension system that sprung both wheels and the axle together. Axle steering had great disadvantages for the higher speeds of powered vehicles. Soon the wheels were steered by pivoting on the axle ends, and designers concluded that it might be better to spring the front wheels independently, so that when one wheel met an obstruction it did not affect the other wheel.

The idea was a good one in many ways, but unfortunately nobody at that time realized the side effects of wheel movements. Little by little knowledge was gained of the movements and forces involved, often more by trial and intuition than by mathematical deduction. It was probably not until the publication of the work of Maurice Olley, after he had left Rolls-Royce for General Motors, and Donald Bastow of Rolls-Royce and Lagonda in the mid-1940s, that the mechanism of independent front suspension and steering began to be understood fully.

A car cornering with an old-type beam front axle and leaf springs would have an equivalent transverse spring length of about two feet (60 centimetres) — that is, the distance between the springs — and would roll about an axis midway between, and at the height of, the springs.

With a change to a transverse leaf spring system which allows the front wheels to rise or fall independently, the transverse spring length was doubled. Consequently the resistance to rolling was greatly increased. But, because the spring allowed the body to tilt while the spring ends remained at an equal height, the centre about which the body rolled moved down to ground level. This increased the distance between the centre of roll and the centre of gravity, through which the rolling force acted. Thus the tendency to roll also increased.

With the transverse leaf spring, or the equivalent of equal-length, parallel links and coil or torsion bar springs, any vertical movement of a wheel relative to the chassis results in a reduction of wheel track, as the spring deflects to move the wheel closer to the chassis. The result is a sideways tyre scrub that can damage the tyre tread.

To obviate this track change, which also has a steering effect on the car, the links were made of unequal length, longer on the bottom, so that the wheel tilted inwards at the top as it rose. This kept the track more or less constant and had produced a bonus by raising the roll centre. It also allowed the wheel to remain more nearly perpendicular to

the road when the car rolled and as a consequence have less effect on tyre grip.

If a wheel is tilted, it has a tendency to move in the direction to which it is leaning as it rolls. Preventing this sideways movement generates a sideways force on the wheel, known as the camber thrust. During cornering there must be a sideways weight transfer as the centrifugal forces on the entire car tend to roll the vehicle, increasing the sideways load on the outer wheel at the expense of the inner wheel.

The addition of the weight transfer and camber forces on the front wheel is likely to produce a situation where the front wheels have less sideways grip, for a particular steering deflection, than the rear wheels. Thus the car is inclined to run wide, or understeer, on a corner. This tendency, providing the degree of understeer is small, is the more desirable because the driver automatically allows for it by increasing the steering angle. It also produces more cross wind stability.

Amédée Bollée's first steam carriage of 1875 had both of its front wheels carried in vertical pivoted forks with full elliptic springs on each side of each wheel between the lower fork ends and the wheel axles. Fortunately for

Bollée he decided to employ a complicated cam and strap mechanism to obtain the proper steering angles on the wheels, and so was not bothered by the change in track affecting the steering as the wheels moved over bumps. Another great advantage was that the leaf springs did not have the nasty tendency to stick because of side loads on the wheels.

A development of vertical movement suspension was made in 1898 by R. Stephens, whereby the wheel axles were supported in cycle-type forks. Outer forks were cross connected for steering and allowed vertical movement of inner forks against the action of a transverse leaf spring. However, a simplified version had already been used by the French constructors, Société Nouvelle des Etablissements Decauville Aine. The wheels were carried on short stub axles on the lower ends of vertical steering spindles, which were able to slide vertically in tubes attached to the frame front cross member. A transverse leaf spring was again used for the suspension.

This vertical post system was later featured in a number of cars such as Lancia, from 1921 onwards, and Morgan, which used it first for the three-wheel vehicle in 1910 and has remained faithful to it ever since.

163

In the Lancia system a square section helical spring was enclosed in vertical tubes forming part of the front framework. A cylindrical member carrying the stub axle moved up and down in the tubes against the spring. A hydraulic damping cylinder was located inside the spring and the axle pivoted, for steering, with the cylindrical member. This neat device maintained the wheels substantially perpendicular to the road surface and had a minimum of unsprung weight, but it suffered from track changing with wheel movement and could tend to stick with heavy side loads.

As an alternative to the conventional full-elliptic front springs and beam axle, J. Roots and C. E. Venables suggested in 1898 that their vehicle should be supported on parallel transverse leaf springs, separated by a block at the centre and coupled to swivelling axles at the outer ends. By putting another pair of parallel springs behind the original pair (as was done by B.S.A. in 1932), the four quarter elliptic springs provided a linkwork system that was able to resist the torsion loads of braking and driving.

In 1908 L. Granieri thought of using short parallel links of equal length between the vertical ends of the axle beam and vertical posts carrying the wheels, the upper links being cross connected by the suspension spring. His design not only resulted in one wheel being able to rise relative to the other, but also provided a kind of transverse levelling, or anti-roll, system similar to that thought up for longitudinal levelling by J. J. Charley.

A. A. Remmington and A. J. Rowledge of the Wolseley Tool and Motor Company who had earlier devised the rear anti-roll bar system, devised two forms of independent front suspension in 1911. The first used equal-length parallel links between the chassis side members and the steering swivel mountings. A transverse leaf spring was pivoted below the chassis centre and coupled by further pivoted links to the outer ends of the lower suspension links.

The other form was a modification, in which the leaf spring formed the lower linkage of the pair and thus produced unequal length links which tilted the wheel, as it rose, to keep the track more constant. This latter system was produced in an inverted form by Leslie Ballamy, as a modification for transverse spring Austin 7s, and Ford 8s and 10s. The front axle beam was cut in the centre and two bosses welded on to the ends, so that the half axle beams could swing independently.

Greater rigidity was given to the links between the chassis and steering swivel by bringing the wheel ends closer together and joining them to prevent interference between the pivot pin and the brake drum on full lock. This wishbone link became the basis of a large number of independent front suspension systems, particularly after the introduction of ball joints between the narrow end of the wishbone and the stub axle by Citroën in the early 1930s. Charles Hayermans and Georges Roesch had this idea some ten years earlier. It allowed the same bearing to act both as the outer suspension pivot and the steering pivot.

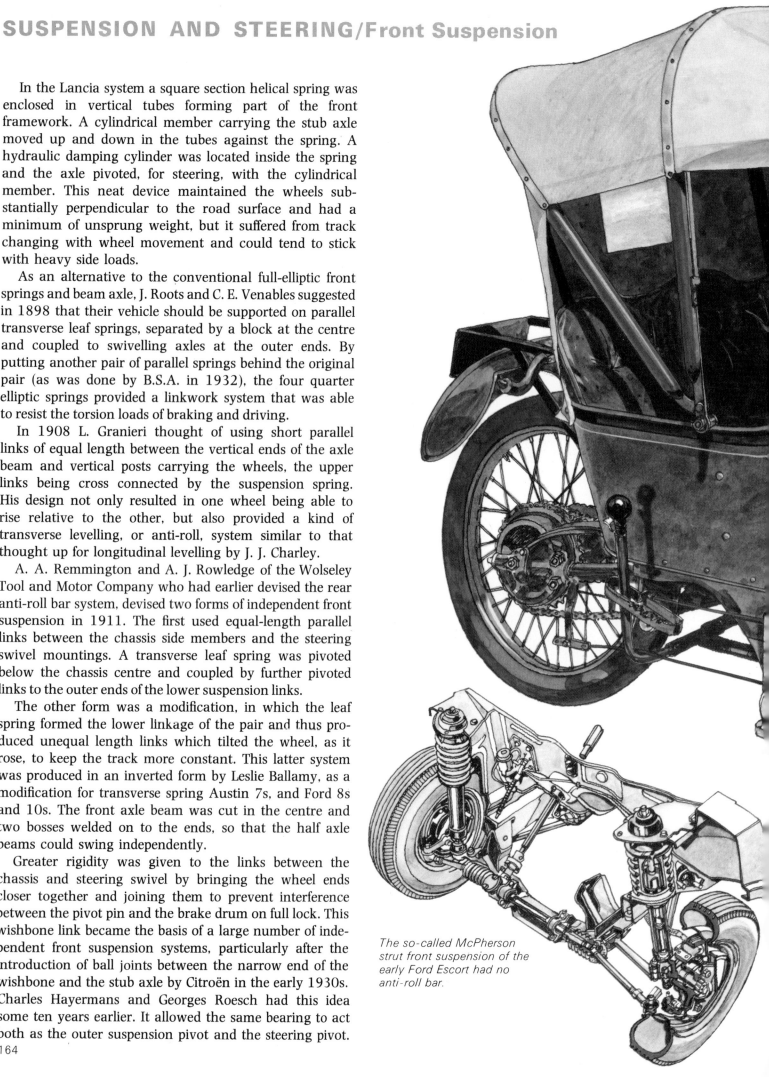

The so-called McPherson strut front suspension of the early Ford Escort had no anti-roll bar.

In the 1913 Morgan three-wheeler independent front suspension was provided by the stub axles sliding on vertical post members.

Other developments led to a double wishbone system, often called "knee action", in which a large helical spring was substituted for the leaf spring. It was mounted between the lower wishbone and an outward extension of the chassis or floor frame. In such systems the damper, if it was of the army type, was used for the upper wishbone. If telescopic, it was concentric and within the helical spring.

Some designs, such as those of Chrysler, Morris and Armstrong-Siddeley, replaced the coil spring with a long torsion-bar spring, rigidly coupled to the lower wishbone at its chassis pivot and to a fixed point about midway of the chassis length. Usually some form of adjustment was provided at the static end of the torsion bar by which it could be partially rotated to provide means of equalizing and prestressing between the two torsion bars.

An interesting combination of the wishbones and the Ballamy-type divided axle was fitted in the Hillman Imp of 1963. Two large pressed-steel wishbones, or A frames,

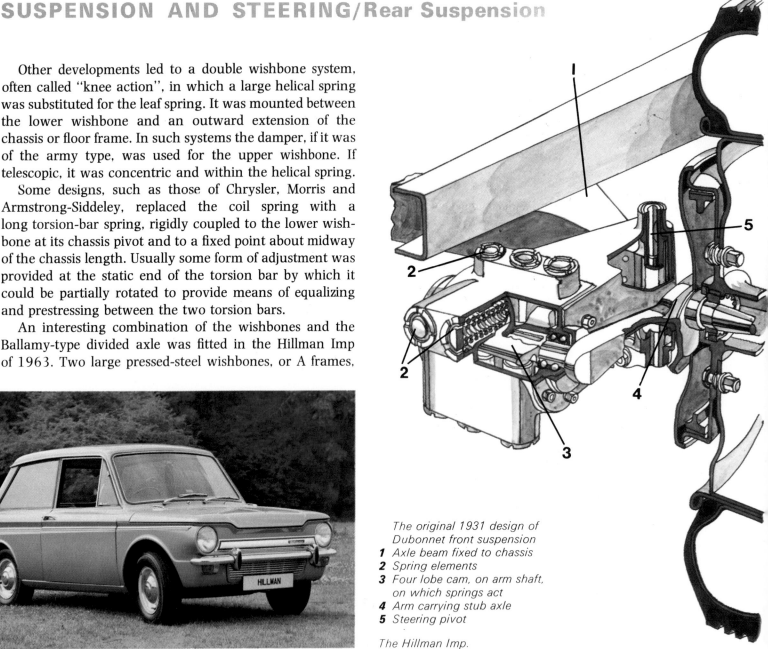

The original 1931 design of Dubonnet front suspension
1 Axle beam fixed to chassis
2 Spring elements
3 Four lobe cam, on arm shaft, on which springs act
4 Arm carrying stub axle
5 Steering pivot

The Hillman Imp.

were rigid with the swivel pin mountings at their smaller ends and were pivoted, through rubber bushes, parallel to and almost on the centre line of the car. The springing was provided by coil springs bearing near the outer ends of the frames, with telescopic shock absorbers mounted inside.

After a design of Guido Fornaca of Fiat in 1926, a simplification of a combination of two systems was designed for General Motors by Earle S. MacPherson in 1947. This was used in a later development on British Fords for a number of years, as well as on numerous other makes.

In the MacPherson strut the wheel stub axle is rigid with the outer cylinder of a telescopic hydraulic damper, the piston rod of which acts as a steering pivot. The top of the piston rod is secured to the car frame within the wheel arch. The same mounting provides a shallow cup to locate the upper end of a helical spring, bearing at its lower end on a flange secured to the damper cylinder.

Single track-control arms, which are pivoted to the chassis frame, extend transversely to ball joints below the stub axle mountings. Longitudinal location is provided by a transverse stabilizer or anti-roll bar that extends

forwards and inwards from the outboard ends of the track-control arms and has a transverse portion pivoted on the chassis. This anti-roll bar is the front link of a triangular wishbone and ensures that the wheel moves in an arc that is centred on the axis of the transverse section of the anti-roll bar.

In all the wishbone types of suspension, the linkwork has to be designed to tilt the wheel inwards as it is allowed to rise. This keeps the wheel tracking constant and prevents the wheel springing movement from interfering with the steering. To achieve these aims, other designers have provided arms, swinging in planes, parallel to the chassis. The idea was suggested by J. F. Murphy in 1904 as part of an anti-roll system, and used by W. G. Charley in 1914 as a longitudinally levelling system.

In the system invented by Dubonnet in 1931 and used later by Vauxhall, the front wheels were mounted on longitudinal arms carried on the ends of relatively short transverse torsion springs. The inner ends of these springs were rigid with containing tubes, themselves resilient, secured to members pivoted to the chassis for steering

Above: The Vauxhall Cadet of 1930 had independent front suspension by the Dubonnet system.
Below: The Porsche 356A had torsion bar springs controlling fore and aft swinging arms for all four wheels, much the same as the V.W.

movement. A toggle system using a coil spring was arranged to lessen the rate of the torsion system for small wheel deflections, and thus give a variable rate system.

With a single arm, vertical movement of the wheel could have resulted in an angular movement of the steering axis that would have changed the degree of castor action. To overcome this, Ferdinand Porsche, in 1931, fitted parallel trailing arms that pivoted in tubular chassis-frame cross members containing multi-leaf springs in torsion. His system was used for many years in both Porsche and Volkswagen cars.

REAR SUSPENSION

It would seem that the difficulty of providing drive to rear wheels having independent suspension is the reason for relatively few cars being given such springing. So it is interesting that practically all the front-wheel drive vehicles have been independently sprung in spite of the added difficulty of providing for steering.

M. E. Hertel had little difficulty in 1897 in providing drive to the rear wheels. The wheels were supported on trailing arms pivoted on a chassis cross-member and sprung by longitudinal leaf springs and they were individually driven by expanding pulley gearing. J. F. Murphy features the same form of swing-arm suspension for the rear wheels as he had used for his front wheels in 1904, and M. A. Yeakley contributed his vertically sliding post and double universally jointed drive shafts from a chassis-mounted bevel gearing.

This trailing link, working in a substantially longitudinal plane, formed the basis of a number of successful rear suspension systems such as the Renault Frégate of 1951, which was equipped with pressed-steel wishbones on transverse pivots, inclined downwards towards the chassis centre line for better geometry, and with coil springing. The Hillman Imp had pressed-steel A frames of the same form as on the front, but pivoted on axes inclined slightly to the transverse. Radius arm suspension of this type results in a change in length of the drive shafts with wheel movement. To allow for it, a sliding spline or rubber

doughnut joint is used. The adoption of the MacPherson system to the rear also involved the substitution of a trailing radius locating member for the anti-roll bar, and the provision of drive shaft plunging joints. Since this system was evolved by Colin Chapman for Lotus, it became known as the Chapman strut.

An independent rear suspension system that did not have need of sliding-type joints in the two drive shafts was devised by Edmund Rumpler in 1915, and later used in his postwar streamlined rear-engined car. In this system (the swing axle), the half axle tubes pivot about the differential casing, the drive shafts being universally jointed to the sides of the differential and carried in bearings at the outboard ends of the swinging tubes.

In the Volkswagen the outer ends of the axle tubes were located by flexible radius arms carried on bearings in front of the axle and coupled to transverse torsion bars to provide the springing. A more complex swing-axle suspension is that of the 1968 Mercedes, where the final

The E-Type Jaguar of 1961: independent rear suspension used the axle shaft as the upper hub bearing locating link.

The Renault Fregate had a successful rear-suspension system.

drive and differential are housed in one half axle casing, and the two casings are hinged together below the wheel centre height. The half casings are located by longitudinal pressed-steel arms, on which the suspension coil springs bear, and have a compensating compression spring mounted between them, over the top of the differential casing, to assist with the roll problems that arise with swing-axle geometry.

A combination of the trailing link and swing-axle suspensions is found in the use of a relatively large A frame member of pressed steel. The two legs are arranged longitudinally and transversely with the apex carrying the wheel bearing and the leg ends pivoted, through rubber bushes, to the body pan on a diagonal axis. The cross bar of the A is the lower support for the coil spring and damper. Such a system has been used on the smaller Fiats from the 600 to the 126.

A somewhat similar geometry is achieved by fitting a trailing arm in a diagonal plane between the body floor pan mounting and the hub bearing, and using the drive shaft as the other side of the triangle. As there is no cross member, the spring and damper are carried on an extension of the hub bearing. The movement of the wheel in this system, as on the Fiat 130 of 1970, is such that, though each drive shaft needs two universal joints, there is no endwise movement in the shaft and thus no need for plunging joints or splines.

Moving the plane of the arm nearer to the transverse and employing a second arm behind the drive shaft have the effect of producing a wishbone type of suspension link, as on the Jaguar E-type of 1961, where the drive shaft acts as the upper wishbone. If the hub-bearing carrier is then also linked to the chassis, as by a transverse leaf spring in exactly the same manner as the 1954 A.C. Ace, the system is then very much the same as that proposed by Remmington and Rowledge for the front wheels and, of course, needs provision for length changes in the drive shafts, as the wheels move vertically over bumps.

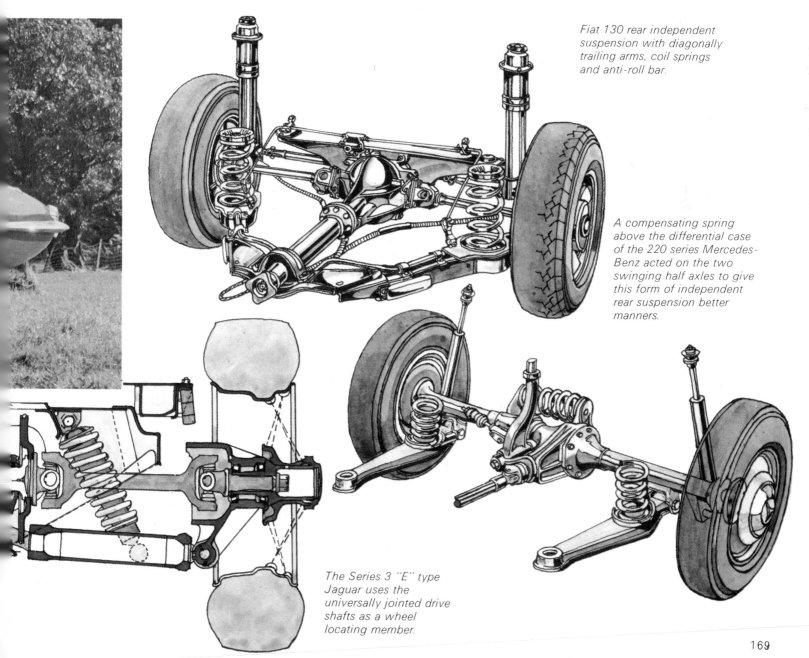

Fiat 130 rear independent suspension with diagonally trailing arms, coil springs and anti-roll bar.

A compensating spring above the differential case of the 220 series Mercedes-Benz acted on the two swinging half axles to give this form of independent rear suspension better manners.

The Series 3 "E" type Jaguar uses the universally jointed drive shafts as a wheel locating member.

STEERING GEOMETRY

For a vehicle to travel on any path other than a straight line without sideways slip of the wheels, all the wheels must roll along arcs of circles which, though they may be of different diameters, must at any instant have the same centre. With horse-drawn vehicles, traction engines and very early cars having a front axle turning on a vertical pin at its centre, this was achieved automatically. Lines drawn through the axes of the steering front and fixed rear axles will meet, and this point is the instantaneous centre about which the vehicle is turning.

Such a method of steering soon proved unsuitable for motor vehicles as it was far too susceptible to bumps in the road moving the axle against the wishes of the driver. Further, it had limitations of steering lock through the wheels trying to get under the chassis for the purpose of smaller radius curves.

In an attempt to overcome these disadvantages, the front axle was kept rigidly in a transverse plane and each front wheel was provided with its own steering pivot, or king-pin. As far back as 1818, George Lenkensperger of Munich devised a linkage that swivelled the front wheels through different angles. At the same time, he ensured that the wheels followed paths which were tangents of circles with the same centre, although of different diameters, the outer wheel describing the larger arc.

The steering arms were made rigid with the stub axle mountings and set at an angle so that, when the front wheels were straight, lines drawn through the king-pins and the ends of the steering arms would meet at the centre of the rear axle. The steering arms were pivoted to a transverse bar, or track rod, which was of a length different from the distance between the king-pins, being shorter if behind the axle or longer if in front. It was this factor that made the outer wheel describe a larger arc than the inner wheel.

Such a system is known as Ackermann steering, because Lenkensperger arranged for Rudolph Ackermann, a London bookseller and publisher, to have sole rights to benefit from the invention in England and Wales.

With both the wheel and the king-pin axis vertical, as was used in early car construction, a blow to the front wheel caused by hitting a bump in the road made the wheel and stub axle turn about the king-pin. This force was transmitted back to the steering tiller and considerably reduced the driver's steering control. Remedies were provided by several people, who, like H. Lemp in 1900, devised means for locking the steering to straight ahead. The lock could be released when it was desired to go round a bend.

In 1895 C. E. Duryea had the idea of inclining the king-pin axis outwards at the bottom so that the wheel rotated about this axis where it touched the road. Shock and drag produced by the road surface on the wheel could be reduced by tilting the king-pin or the wheel, or both, and later became known as king-pin angle and camber angle respectively.

True centre-point steering is rendered difficult unless the

wheels are deeply dished to provide room for the king-pin, or steering swivels, or unless excessive king-pin and camber angles are used. So a compromise was achieved by lessening the distance between the tyre contact centre and the point about which the wheel was steered, and using a steering mechanism with more or less irreversible gearing, such as a screw and nut or a worm and wheel.

By inclining the steering swivel axis, the weight of the vehicle produces a force tending to move the wheels to the straight ahead position. Duryea realized seven years later that this action would provide a degree of self-centring or castor action that would make steering less tiring and more predictable.

Meanwhile, in 1898, the Decauville, with its independent front suspension, had stub axles behind the pivot axes of the steering swivels so that the wheels trailed in the manner of chair castors to return automatically to the straight position. Two years later E. H. Gordon sloped the king-pins' axes rearwards at the top so that their pivoting line was ahead of the centre of wheel and road contact, and thus produced an equivalent castor effect. This sloping

Steering geometry angles are the important angular dimensions that determine the handling capabilities of a car.

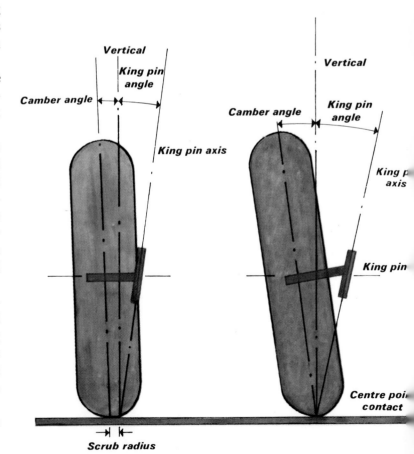

of the steering axis through a castor angle has long been standard practice.

Particularly with the single beam axles, the rearward forces on the wheels, produced by pushing them along the road surface, tended to splay the wheels outwards. The lack of true running caused a scrubbing action on the tyres and increased the effort required for steering. To offset this, the wheels were given a small "toe-in". The fronts of the wheels were set slightly closer together than the rears of the wheels.

Apart from the geometry of the steering mechanism, directional stability, both in straight and curved running, depends a lot on the tyres, a fact little appreciated until half way through the century. Except when a car is moving in a straight line in still air, sideways force is always being applied to the contact patch between tyre and road. This force causes a distortion so that the tyre is no longer rolling in the true direction of the car, but at an angle to that direction. The angle is known as the slip angle. Tyre distortion is greater in the front part of the contact patch and produced a turning force on the wheel, the

cornering force, which tends to move it towards its true running position. This force depends on such factors as the slip angle, the load carried by the tyre, the inflation pressure, the wheel diameter and, of course, the characteristics of the tyre itself. Slip angles for the front and rear wheels are seldom exactly the same.

When a car goes round a corner, there is a centrifugal force acting through the centre of gravity of the vehicle. A side wind has much the same effect, except that the force is acting at the centre of pressure, which is not in the same place as the centre of gravity of the car. If the centre of pressure is behind the centre of gravity, the car will tend to head into the wind like a weathervane, and if the centre of pressure is ahead of the centre of gravity the car will tend to swing away with the wind.

Under such conditions the slip angles of the four wheels have a bearing on the ultimate tendency for the car to steer one way or the other. If the slip angle, and therefore the cornering force, generated at the front wheels is smaller than that at the rear then the front of the car will nose into the corner, or the wind, and is said to oversteer.

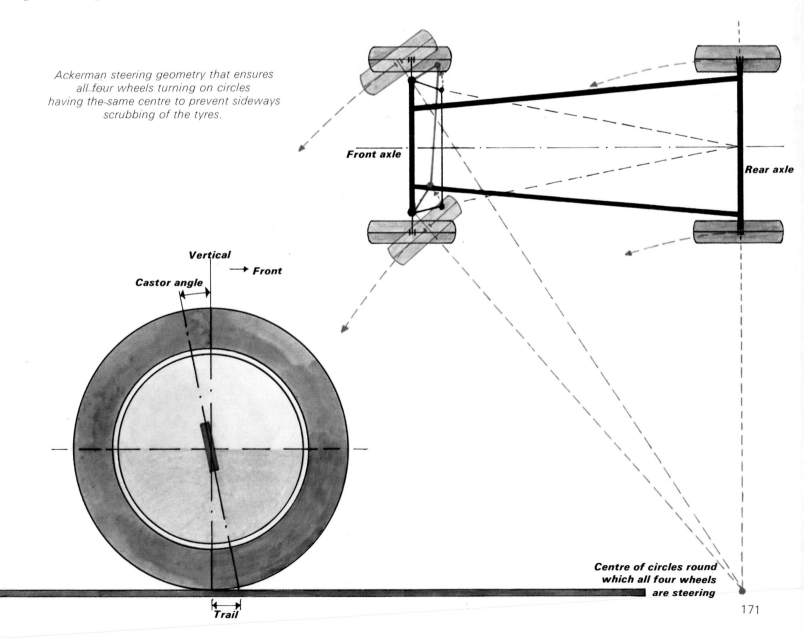

Ackerman steering geometry that ensures all four wheels turning on circles having the same centre to prevent sideways scrubbing of the tyres.

Front axle

Rear axle

Vertical

→ **Front**

Castor angle

Centre of circles round which all four wheels are steering

Trail

Conversely, if the slip angle at the front is greater than the rear the car will understeer and tend to run wide.

The distance between the centre of the tyre contact patch and the point where the steering axis meets the road is called the scrub radius. If, as in most cars made until recently, this distance is on the chassis side of the wheel, the result is an inboard scrub radius. When a car with an inboard radius has braking forces on its front wheels and one wheel meets a slippery patch, the braking force on that side decreases. This unbalances the forces on the car so that the side having the weaker braking tries to overtake the other side, and consequently the car begins to slew out of the straight ahead.

At the same time the force on the well-braked wheel tends to turn that wheel on its steering axis. Since the force acts in a rearwards direction, the wheel tries to steer the car in the same direction as it has begun to slew. This makes things worse and has to be corrected by turning the steering wheel in the opposite direction to keep the car on a straight course.

In 1973, Audi-N.S.U. introduced the Audi 80, which by clever mechanical design, had an outboard scrub

Audi 80

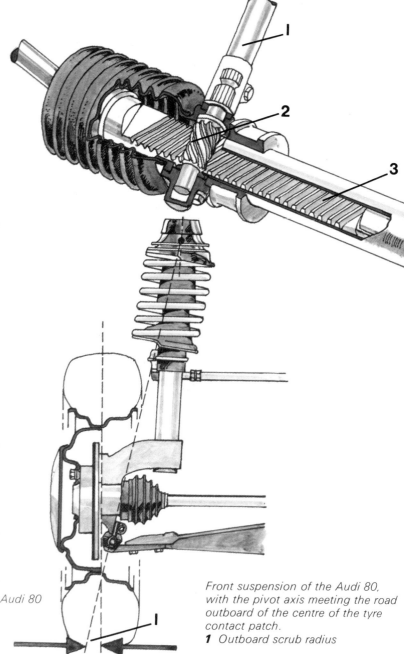

Front suspension of the Audi 80, with the pivot axis meeting the road outboard of the centre of the tyre contact patch.
1 Outboard scrub radius

radius. This was obtained, to some extent, by raising steering pivots and so allowing the steering axis to be sloped enough to move the road contact point without the axis being too far from the vertical. With outboard scrub radius, unequal longitudinal forces on the wheels during braking produce a self-correcting movement of the wheels, so that the car steers itself against the slewing direction.

STEERING MECHANISM

Steering with a centre pivoted axle was easy to design but difficult to use at more than walking speeds. Merely connecting a tiller to the steering pivot meant that the driver was liable to be thrown overboard when a wheel met an obstruction. The next idea was to fit either a gear or a chain drive between the tiller and the axle so that more force could be brought to stop the wheels going their own way.

This crude system lasted into the early 1920s for some of the very light cycle cars. In them the steering column

had a bobbin at its lower end with cables connecting the axle ends to the bobbin. Turning the steering wheel took in one side of the cable and let out the other.

With the Ackermann steering linkwork, there were direct connections between the track rod or steering arms, similar to those of a simple tiller. It was soon realized that a degree of irreversibility was necessary to stop the wheels reacting on the driver's arm. The need was supplied by means of a screw thread on the lower end of the steering column and a nut, limited to axial movement, connected to a drop arm. This arm was, in turn, joined by a drag link to a steering arm. A steering wheel was also needed because several turns were required for a relatively small angular movement of the road wheels.

One of the earliest screw-and-nut devices was invented by the Lamplough brothers for the Albany Manufacturing Company in 1901. It had right and left hand threads cut on the steering column and two corresponding half nuts connected by a rocking link to the drop arm.

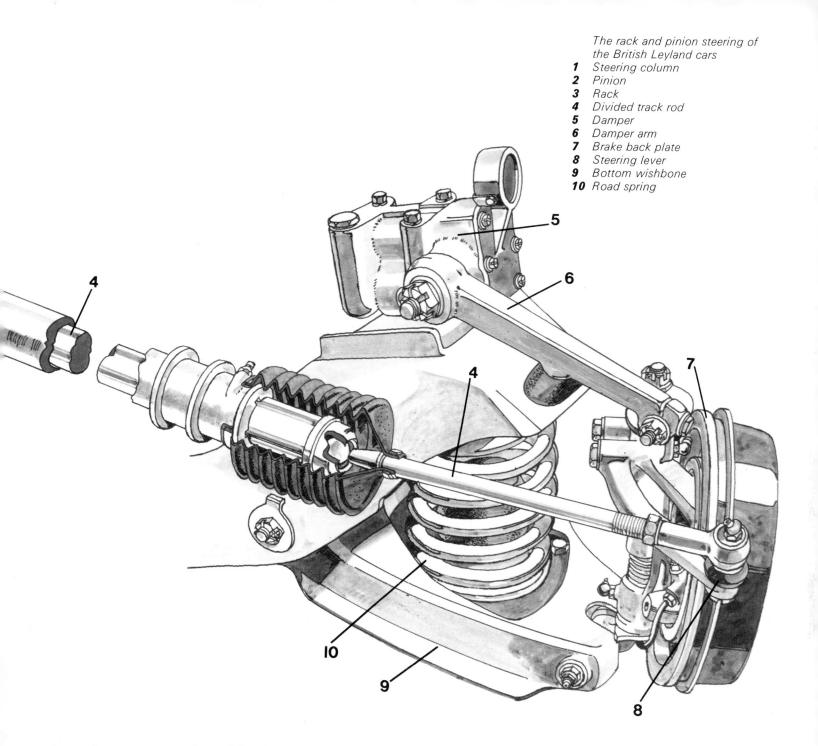

A year later, P. W. Northey of the Electric Motive Power Company used worm gearing with the worm on the steering column and a lever on the shaft of the worm wheel connected to the steering arms. In a modification of this, he engaged the worm wheel teeth with a rack, the to-and-fro motion of which was transmitted to the steering arms. This early rack-and-pinion steering had already been thought of by Léon Bollée in 1896 in his well-known early tricycle.

L. Megy, also in 1902, went a stage further and used a pinion on the steering column and the rack as the track rod. This rack-and-pinion steering slowly faded from the scene as it did not provide enough irreversibility and suffered from backlash in the gearing.

Over the last ten or twenty years this gearing has come back into favour. The rack is used as the centre section of a three-part trackrod, which has joints in line with the inboard pivots of the independent front suspension. The modern racks have spring-loaded metal or plastics inserts

pressing on the back of the rack to provide some damping and maintain the tooth backlash at a minimum.

To obtain some feedback of feel from the wheels to the driver, the friction in the screw-and-nut system has to be reduced. This is done by making the thread much coarser, until it becomes more of a helical groove engaged by a single peg. The idea was introduced in 1902 by E. L. N. Denis, who also designed the angle of the helical groove to give more steering movement per turn of the steering wheel around full lock than in the straight ahead position.

This form of gear, known as the worm-and-peg and, later, as the cam-and-roller was reintroduced by H. Marles in 1913. His gearing used an hour-glass shaped cam looking like a pair of right and left handed snails side by side. Two rollers engaged the snail cams so that, as one cam diameter increased and the other decreased, the roller spindle rocked.

In 1920 Marles was joined by H. W. Egerton and R. Bishop, who devised his own cam and roller gear in 1923, to form the Marles Steering Company. Next year the two rollers were replaced by a single disc with an axis at right angles to the cam axis. In 1922, the Marles design changed to a helical globoidal cam – looking like an hour-glass with a groove cut in it – and a roller whose edge engaged the cam groove. The roller, later a double roller, was held in a forked rocker to whose spindle the drop arm was fixed.

In the Bishop gear the rocker was lengthened to reduce the pressure on the cam or worm, and a conical roller engaged the groove of the worm. The Marles and Bishop gears, together with the screw-and-nut design, remained until the rack-and-pinion system began to supplant them in the 1950s.

The screw-and-nut idea was brought up to date by using a string of balls to reduce the thread friction and provide more feel. Both the screw and the nut were formed with semi-circular section thread grooves, and balls were used in these grooves as the connecting members. As the balls moved along the nut groove, they were fed back from one end of the nut to the other by an external tube, giving the gear the name of recirculating ball. The outside of the nut

was formed as a rack, or pivoted to an arm on the drop arm shaft to give the steering movement.

POWER STEERING

Power-assisted steering is a relatively modern form of equipment, made desirable by the muscular effort required to turn the steering wheel of heavy cars with large, soft tyres and the advent of front-wheel drive. Like so many other automobile developments, the original idea is not entirely new.

Some early steam vehicles had a form of steering-servo mechanism in which a small pilot wheel guided the main, centre-pivoted, steering wheels. The system was first suggested by F. Andrews in 1826 and introduced by Sir Goldsworthy Gurney in his steam bus two years later. More lasting memorials to Gurney were the heating stoves in British cathedrals.

In 1899 W. P. Schuyler thought of engine power, through a reversing gear, for moving the front axle for steering. Both these ideas were smothered by poor road

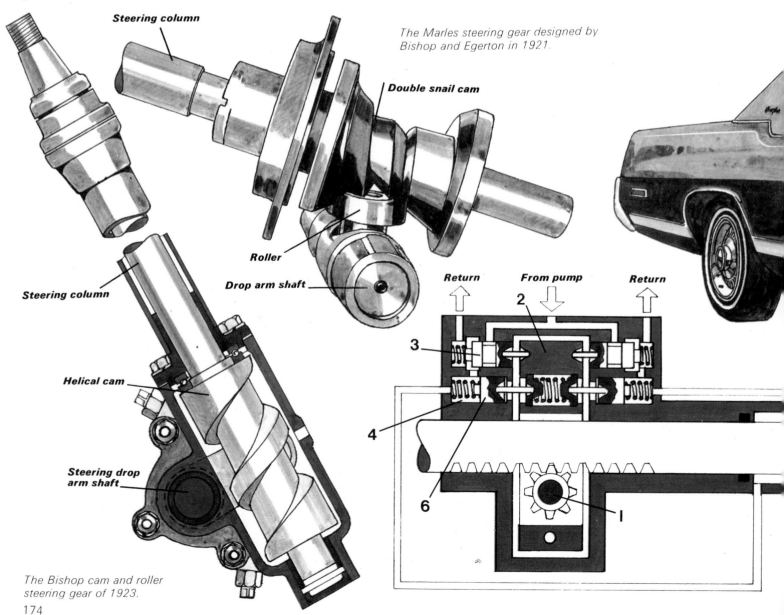

The Marles steering gear designed by Bishop and Egerton in 1921.

The Bishop cam and roller steering gear of 1923.

surfaces and the need for irreversible steering. The conception of power-assisted steering lay fairly dormant, except for an essay by Stutz in 1927, until the 1950s. Its need then became apparent for large cars when full lock was required at parking speeds.

The aircraft industry had by then carried out a lot of development work on hydraulic jacks for servo-systems. So the field was set for the introduction of power steering to the passenger car by Chrysler in 1951.

Since it is essential for any power steering system to fail safe, the assistance is provided by a hydraulic power cylinder and piston, or jack, connected in parallel to the track rod between the chassis and a steering arm. A double-acting valve, extremely sensitive to the force in steering gear or the drop arm, supplies pressure fluid from an engine-driven pump to the appropriate end of the jack cylinder. As the car wheels begin to move, the steering assisting force decreases and the fluid supply is reduced. Return of the steering wheel to the straight ahead position reverses the direction of the steering force and the jack then assists the road wheels to the desired position.

In the American Ford system the control valve is connected to the end of the track rod. The valve is, therefore, sensitive to any track rod movement strong enough to overcome the loading of a spring that centralizes the control valve.

A somewhat different system is offered by Lincoln. In this the exterior of the recirculating ball nut cooperates with the interior of the steering gear casing to form the piston and cylinder of the hydraulic jack. Steering movements are sensed by small axial motions of the steering column thrust bearing as the column tries to screw itself in or out of the nut. These movements actuate a spool valve to pass pressure fluid either to one side or the other of the steering nut piston.

In 1970, Citroën gave recognition to the fact that power steering is normally necessary only at slow speeds. The Citroën S.M. has a refinement in the hydraulic system that reduces the degree of power assistance as the road speed rises, but at the same time continues to provide assistance to keep the wheels straight in the event that they should encounter a sudden shock or a rapid tyre deflation.

The 1975 Dodge Royal Monaco Brougham two-door hard-top with power-steering.

In the Bosch power-steering system, clockwise torque on the pinion (1), for a right turn, rocks a carrier (2) to open a valve (3) and pass pressure oil through chamber (4) to the

The 1951 Chrysler introduced power steering to the passenger car.

5

left hand side of track rod piston (5) Piston (6) acts on the carrier (2) to provide feel and to return the carrier to the centre when the torque decreases.

WHEELS, TYRES AND BRAKES - Safe

No one knows when the wheel was invented but one of the earliest records of it in action dates back to about 3,500 B.C. This is a drawing of a wheeled sledge from Mesopotamia.

The earliest wheels were probably made from three flat pieces of wood clamped together by cross pieces and shaped to a circle round the rim. They were unlikely to have been made by slicing through tree trunks. Such a disc would need a large tree, difficult to cut across with a primitive saw. Also, the direction of the grain would cause the wheel to split and fall apart.

A thousand years or so later, the wheel had been given a tyre consisting of pieces of curved wood, or felloes, round the rim. Metal nails were driven into the felloes to give them longer life.

Spoked wheels developed around 2,000 B.C. in Asia and later in Egypt for use with lighter and faster vehicles such as war chariots. Later came the cart wheel in which the spokes were socketed into a hub and into a rim of felloes, the whole being held together by shrinking an iron tyre round the outside.

WOODEN WHEELS

These wheels were not well suited to taking driving or braking torque. In 1830 Walter Hancock of London invented a wooden spoked wheel in which the inner ends of the spokes were tapered so that they all fitted together.

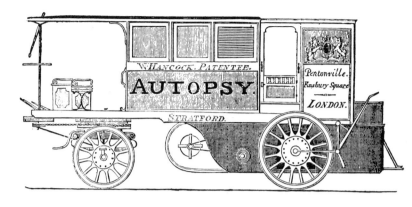

Hancock's Autopsy steam bus had wooden wheels that could transmit driving torque from the engine crankshaft cum axle to the road.

The spokes were set round a flanged iron hub and were clamped by a second flange and by bolts passing through the tapered ends. An iron tyre was bolted to the outside of the felloes. Hancock was the most successful of the steam carriage builders. He built sixteen, mostly omnibuses that plied for hire in London, and he exported at least one to Vienna. His wheel was the prototype of the wooden wheels, known as artillery wheels, used on many of the early cars.

Wooden spoked wheels began to show their short-

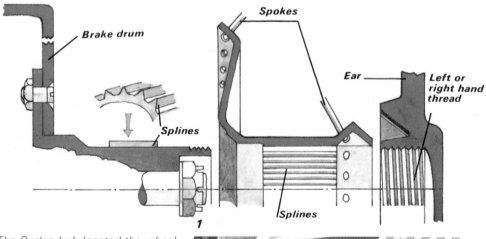

The Rudge hub located the wheel by two conical surfaces and drove through splines. The central nut had ears for tightening with a hammer.

1. *A wire-spoked wheel on a Rudge hub*

2. *A pressed-steel wheel with plated nave plate to cover the wheel nuts*

3. *A wooden rear wheel with bolted-on brake rim*

4. *A hollow pressed steel artillery wheel*

contact with the road

comings when they were run at higher speeds. As they became hot, the wood shrank and the joints loosened so that buckets of water were needed to cool them down. Also, the spokes were liable to splinter if the wheel hit a pothole, with the possible collapse of the whole cart.

STEEL WHEELS

In 1908 Joseph Sankey of England produced a ten-spoke wheel that looked like the artillery wheel but which was made of two steel pressings welded together for strength. The hollow interior was protected against rust by being filled with paint and then drained.

Another form of steel wheel arrived a few years later with the spring-steel disc wheel of C. E. Goodyear of Dunlop. This had no spokes and was easier to keep clean. As there were no front wheel brakes at this time, there were no problems about brake cooling. Actually, pressed-steel wheels had become quite common in the 1860s mainly for railway use.

WIRE WHEELS

With the wooden artillery wheel and, to some extent, the pressed-steel wheel, the weight of the car was carried by compression in the spoke which happened to be more or less vertically under the hub at the time. But the bicycle designers, in their search for lightness and strength,

used wheels in which the hub was suspended by wire spokes from the top of the wheel. Since steel wire is very strong in tension, the spokes could be made extremely thin in relation to their length.

As far back as 1490, Leonardo da Vinci designed a wheel having a hub suspended from the rim by thin spokes. This kind of wheel was used on most of the very early cars, particularly those having a bicycle tube type of chassis.

Wire wheels with radial spokes proved unsatisfactory when too much torque was applied between hub and rim, as the load tried to bend the spokes. In 1870, J. Starley and W. Hillman had the idea of fitting the wire spokes at a tangent to the hub so that, under all load conditions, the spokes were only in tension and never in bending. The result was the well-known bicycle wheel.

Sideways strength was given to the wire wheel by fixing the inner ends of the spokes to hub flanges. These were spaced to form with the spokes a triangular pattern, in section, that was rigid.

J. V. Pugh of the British Rudge-Whitworth Company, well known at the time for their bicycles that used ball bearings, designed a detachable wire wheel in 1905. The Rudge hub became popular — indeed essential wear for sports and racing cars — and was in common use for over 60 years.

Another wheel often used was the Magna, devised for Dunlop by C. E. Goodyear and J. Wright towards the end of the 1920s. In this a large, hollow pressed-steel conical hub had an inward flange that bolted to studs on the brake drum. A cover was clipped or bolted into the outer open end to hide the wheel nuts and hub. Short stiff wire spokes supported the rim from the conical hub.

The Magna was similar to the earlier type of wheel, such as that used on the original Austins, where the pressed-steel hub was a substantially top-hat section, fitted over the brake drum with its securing bolts poking between the spokes.

In the 1930s, Ford modified the Magna wheel by using thicker wire spokes welded to both the hub shell and the rim. Few people realized that this Ford wheel no longer had screwed nipples for tensioning and trueing the wheel. The threaded spoke and its flange headed nut, or nipple, was the invention of W. H. J. Grout in 1870.

DISC WHEELS

Detachable wheels continued to develop from a combination of the disc wheel and the Magna wheel. Spokes, particularly the 40 or 52 of the wire wheel, became more troublesome to clean. So the Magna lost its spokes and became a deeply-dished pressed-steel wheel with flanged holes between hub-mounting and rim. These holes provided vestigial spokes for styling purposes and allowed a flow of cooling air over brakes buried deep in the wheels. The four or five stud fittings were hidden by a sprung-on nave plate, often carrying the badge of the maker.

The further quest for strength and lightness to reduce the unsprung weight led to wheels cast or forged in the light alloys. They look similar to the contemporary pressed-steel wheel, but the spoke of the artillery wheel appears in a stylized form to add thickness and therefore lateral strength. Alloy wheels have the added advantage of being easily machined to accurate dimensions and so give a more accurately running tyre for high speed use.

The introduction of pressed-steel wheels, together with the Rudge-Whitworth wheel, brought about the use of spare wheels. Loose surfaced roads and horseshoe nails caused frequent punctures in the thin, weak tyres of the time. It was far easier to change a wheel by bolting the spare in place of the one with the punctured tyre than to mend an inner tube with the wheel still on the car.

DETACHABLE RIMS

An early attempt to make puncture mending less troublesome was the Stepney spare wheel of T. M. and W. Davies in 1904. A rim, fitted with a ready inflated tyre, had claws that hooked into the bead of the punctured tyre rim and wing nuts to tighten the claws. A leather strap was provided to hold the Stepney rim to the wheel spokes and prevent it slipping round. The Stepney design was used with wire wheels and had a forked piece that engaged a clip riveted to the wheel rim.

Another idea, particularly for wooden wheels, was the Captain wheel, in which the rim, complete with the tyre, was bolted to the felloes. Six bolts, passing through a flange on the rim and through the wheel rim, screwed into a steel ring on the other side of the felloes. A hole was provided in one felloe for the tyre valve.

The natural follow-up to the Captain wheel, with pressed-steel wheels, was the split rim. One side of the rim was made detachable by bolts or a big spring ring. This enabled the tyre to be slid off sideways, an idea that found favour in America and is still in use on large commercial wheels.

An alternative to the split rim was the Michelin system, where the tyre was mounted on one rim that was itself fitted on to a split rim.

WHEEL TRIMS

Dislike of cleaning spokes led, after the First World War, to the fitting of wheel discs. These were copied from aircraft streamlining. The discs were clipped or bolted outside the spokes and gave the appearance of a disc wheel. But they took no load and were only for show and convenience. For the benefit of people who liked the look of wire spokes, some discs were even made with dummy spokes embossed into the surface.

Modern pressed-steel wheels still use a similar trim. The cover disc that hid the hollow centre and the securing studs of the Magna wheel has grown in diameter, and now clips inside the rim to hide the whole of the actual wheel and provide a pleasing appearance.

178

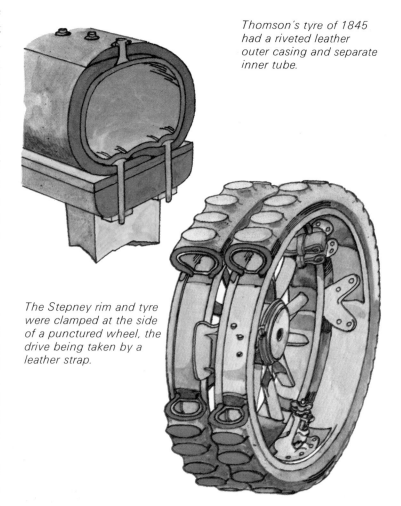

Thomson's tyre of 1845 had a riveted leather outer casing and separate inner tube.

The Stepney rim and tyre were clamped at the side of a punctured wheel, the drive being taken by a leather strap.

TYRES

Wheels of 5,000 years ago soon wore their wooden rims away on the rough roads. So metal nails with large heads, first of copper and later of iron, were hammered into the wood to take the wear and give more grip.

With the coming of the spoked wheel, iron rims were shrunk round the felloes to keep the wheel together and to give a wearing surface. Many early cars had wooden artillery wheels and plain iron tyres. But even before the coming of the car, many makers of wheels for horse-drawn or steam-powered road vehicles looked to rubber to absorb the shocks from loose-metalled roads.

One of those who used thick rubber tyres for wheels was a Scotsman, Robert William Thomson. He was brought up to be a clergyman but, not liking the idea, ran away to Charleston in America, where he apprenticed himself to a blacksmith. At the age of 22 he was back in England as a railway engineer and two years later, in 1845, he applied for a patent for a pneumatic tyre. However, this tyre was before its time and suffered from the lack of suitable material. So Thomson used solid rubber blocks again.

Solid tyres, including rubber tyres having circumferential or axial holes to increase the resiliency with harder wearing rubber compounds, remained in use, in small numbers, for a long time. Among the last to be seen were on the pressed-steel disc wheels of Trojans well over 40 years after

The solid-tyred 1899 Bassett had radial spokes. The engine was a 4 h.p. Schwanemeyer.

Mackintosh and Company had thought of the hollow or porous solid tyre in 1884.

PNEUMATIC TYRES

Thomson's Aerial Wheel, as he called it, had an inner tube of several thicknesses of canvas, saturated with a solution of rubber, laid one over the other. The built-up tube was covered with more solution and then vulcanized. Vulcanization, the process of heating raw rubber and sulphur together to give a stable and harder material, was discovered by Charles Goodyear of Massachusetts in 1839. A leather cover was riveted over the inner tube and the tyre inflated with an air pump. Thomson's tyres were said to have been run for 1,200 miles (2,000 kilometres) without "deterioration or decay", but they were regarded merely as a curiosity.

In 1870, three more inventors thought of pneumatic tyres, but the idea lay dormant until 1888. In that year, John Boyd Dunlop, a Scottish veterinary surgeon, practising in Belfast, thought of a way to make his young son's bicycle travel faster. He bound an inflated rubber tube round each rim with tape and, in so doing, restarted the pneumatic tyre industry, originally under the name of The Pneumatic Tyre Company. Within a few years J. B. Dunlop sold his tyre interests to Harvey du Cros and left the

company that still bears his name and uses his portrait.

The following year J. B. Dunlop improved his bicycle tyre by using a separate inner tube reinforced with linen or canvas and an outer cover of rubber with a thickened tread portion. This cover fitted outside the rim sides.

At the same time, A. T. Thomas thought of a pneumatic tyre for use with carriage wheels. This tyre was U-sectioned and the legs were provided with thickened ends clamped on the sides of the rim by metal rings.

A self-inflating tyre was suggested by A. S. Bowley in 1890. This had a small pump built into the rim, the pump plunger being operated each time the part of the tyre opposite the plunger met the road.

The year 1890 was an important one in the development of securing tyres to rims. In August, R. C. Wilson designed a U-section tyre in which the side walls sloped outwards to be wedged against inwardly sloping walls on the edges of the rim by the air pressure in a separate inner tube. This was similar to the clincher form of securing a solid tyre, devised by W. H. Carmont in 1881. Wilson also thought of strengthening the outer cover by the insertion of canvas or wire gauze within the rubber, a layer which became known as the breaker strip.

In the same month, H. Faulkner used canvas with the warp and weft inclined to the length of the tyre for strengthening. This cross-ply tyre also had an integral inner tube. Shortly afterwards, W. F. Hill cemented strips of material to the outside of the tyre in order to provide a non-skid tread.

TYRES AND RIMS

September, 1890, saw the birth of the wired bead tyre invented by Charles Kingston Welch. Wires were moulded inside the beads at the inner ends of the tyre walls. These bead wires were enclosed in loops of canvas that reinforced the tyre walls. The shallow trough-shaped rim had shoulders towards its outer edges, against which the inextensible wire-reinforced beads were pressed by the inflation of the inner tube.

Two years later, Dunlop bought the rights to an almost identical invention by A. T. Brown and G. F. Stillman of New York. On this was based the American Dunlop Company under whom the Hartford Rubber Company evolved the Dunlop wire bead tyre, later manufactured by the United States Rubber Company.

But back in October 1890, William Erskine Bartlett of the North British Rubber Company had also thought of the clincher tyre. For this North British received £200,000 from Dunlop, even though the idea was substantially the same as that of R. C. Wilson, two months earlier. From this grew the beaded-edge tyre that remained in use until the middle 1920s.

Rims for beaded-edge tyres turned inwards at their edges, the beads curving outwards to clinch under the rims when the tyres were inflated. Since the beads had no inextensible wire reinforcement, the tyres were fitted to the rims using long levers to force the beads over the edges of the rims.

Winton, Apperson, Hayes and other pioneer American manufacturers used a tyre built as a straight tube, with the ends brought together and spliced. This "hose pipe" tyre was cured in a circular mould. It soon proved unsuitable for automobile use, and the clincher type of tyre became the standard fitting.

In 1891, Dunlop produced a rim that allowed the wire bead tyre to be fitted more easily. This well-base rim, as it is known, had a deep central recess, flanked by flat portions with upturned edges. In fitting a tyre, one side of the bead was placed down in the well to give clearance for the diametrically opposite portion of the bead to pass over the upturned edge. Once a bead was over the edge, it rested on a flat portion against an edge and was held there by the resilience of the tyre carcass and the inflation pressure.

The well-base rim and the wire bead tyre are still in use, though they did not come into prominence until the mid-1920s when the beaded-edge tyre faded from the scene.

J. B. Dunlop, as he was living in Ireland, used linen to reinforce the rubber of his tyre. When these tyres were subjected to the higher speeds and heavier loadings of the automobile – all the original development having come from the bicycle tyre – the linen threads chafed badly where they crossed. The American manufacturers tried cotton fabrics, which gave some improvement, but it was left to John F. Palmer and the G. and J. Tire Company of Indianapolis, to introduce the cord tyre.

CORD TYRES

The cord tyre was invented in 1893 and was first used for motor cars in 1900, when it was made by the Palmer Cord Tire Company in England and the B. F. Goodrich Company

Wooden wheels and pneumatic tyres were fitted to the 1903 Fiat 16/20 h.p. car.

in America. In this tyre the reinforcing was provided by two or more layers of parallel cords crossing each other at such an angle that they were approximately tangential to the rim and nearly in the line of strain on the tyre. Each cord was made up of several rubberized warp threads in the form of a flat ribbon with little or no weft thread to hold them together.

In 1903 Christian H. Gray and Thomas Sloper improved the Palmer cord tyre by using complete plies of diagonal cords rather than strips. Their design became known as the cross-ply tyre. Ten years later the same two inventors suggested using inextensible cords of fabric set radially to the tyre with circumferential belts of fabric or wire. This idea, which was the radial-ply tyre, lay dormant until revived by Michelin of France in the late 1940s with steel belts, and Pirelli of Italy in 1953 using textile belts.

Pneumatic tyres up to 1904, had, in general, a round tread section, usually smooth. In that year the Continental Caoutchouc Company and Michelin et Cie brought out tyres with a raised flat tread. These lasted longer, were less liable to skid and gave more road grip. Soon Palmer and Imperial tyres of this section were made with bold corrugated ribs to add to the anti-skid properties.

André and Edouard Michelin were distantly related to Charles Macintosh who in 1823 dissolved rubber in benzene, thus starting the rainwear industry. Both Michelins showed a singlemindedness towards the advance of motoring, particularly in the adoption and development of the pneumatic tyre. In 1896 half a year's production of de Dions were bought and fitted with their tyres before resale. This, and continual racing, eventually achieved public acceptance of the pneumatic tyre.

The "dreaded side-slip" of those days posed serious problems. Attempts to solve them included steel studs embedded in the tread and steel-studded leather bands cemented to the outside of the tyres. Another device was a rubber or leather clip-on protector that was fitted over the tyre in the manner of an overshoe. Chains were often wrapped round the tyres in slippery conditions.

A pioneer of the all-rubber anti-skid tyre was the Bailey "Won't-Slip", which had lozenge-shaped studs moulded into the tread. It was followed by a spate of tread designs using all known geometrical patterns and even the tyre makers' names. Most of these were more ornamental than useful, and it was to be many years before the mechanics of tread design were understood.

Firestone moulded the words "non-skid" in capital letters diagonally across the tread area. Odell of Indiana designed a tread of rubber anchors facing sideways. Lucky horseshoes formed the patterns of the Racine tyre, and Goodyear used crossed diagonal grooves to give the diamond stud for which they were well known for years.

INNER TUBES

Use of a separate rubber tube to hold the compressed air inside the tyre casing is as old as the original idea of

The beaded-edge tyre was held by outwardly projecting beads engaging under the rim edges.

A well in the rim allowed the inextensible wired beads of the 1890 Welch design to clear the rim.

Thomson. Welch also needed an inner tube for his wire bead tyres, but several firms made beaded-edge tyres with an inner tube vulcanized inside the tyre.

To ease the lot of motorists with punctured tyres, a butt-ended tube was originated in 1893 by Morgan and Wright of America. This tube was straight with blank ends so that it could be more easily threaded into place. There were a number of different ideas for holding the ends together such as hooks and eyes, buttons and expanding ball-and-socket joints such as the Hannover Gummi-Kamm tube. A better scheme was the male and female connection that relied on the air pressure for tightness and allowed a flow of air right round the tube.

Puncture proof tubes became popular in the early years of the century. Some designers used armouring canvas within the tube thickness and some put felt between the tube and the outer cover. Others used multiple inner tubes mounted one within the other. The Magowan had three concentric tubes, each with its own inflation valve.

Another idea for tackling punctures was the self-healing tube. Early forms had a quantity of viscous material inside, which flowed out to seal the hole as a nail or stone was withdrawn. Later C. E. Miller of America used a double tube with a filling of plastic tacky rubber between. Dow had a similar device, but used paste, feathers and fibres for the purpose.

INFLATION VALVES

The outward appearance of the valve used by Thomson for inflating his tyre was like most that have been made since. Dunlop, in 1889, used a plug within a rubber tube, rather like that used for air cushions. Two years later C. H. Woods invented a valve that was to be used for a long time, particularly for bicycle wheels.

Like all other valves up to the mid 1930's the Woods

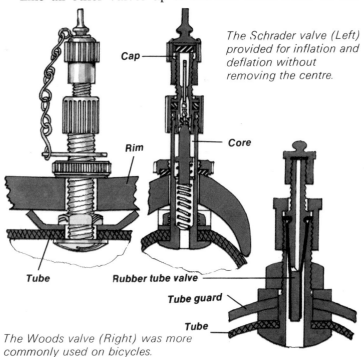

The Schrader valve (Left) provided for inflation and deflation without removing the centre.

Cap — Core — Rim — Tube — Rubber tube valve — Tube guard — Tube

The Woods valve (Right) was more commonly used on bicycles.

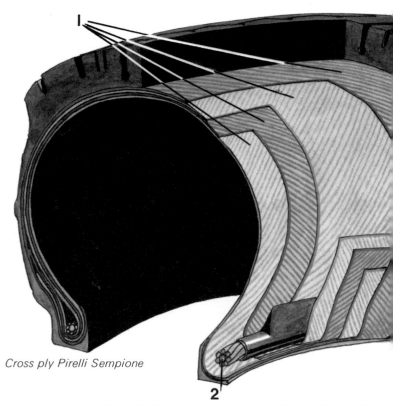

Cross ply Pirelli Sempione

valve body was threaded along its length and had a flanged head that went inside the tube. A washer and nut on the body clamped the tube against the head with an air-tight seal. The washer usually had two bent-up ears to protect the tube from the nut. Another nut clamped the valve into a hole in the wheel rim, and had an external thread for a cap that protected the valve from dust.

The core of this valve had a central hole ending in a transverse hole in a small diameter end of the core. The other end had a screw thread for the pump. A finger nut engaged a collar on the core to hold it in position, and below the collar was a tapered portion. A piece of thin rubber tube was slipped over the thin end of the core and was held between the taper and the inside of the valve body. The valve rubber was blown away from the core when the tube was pumped up and was held by tyre pressure over the transverse hole at other times.

Although there were dozens of other designs, the valve that stood the test of time and became the standard valve was the Schrader. George H. F. Schrader, who designed the valve in 1898, was the son of August Schrader a maker of Daguerreotype photographic plates. August opened a workshop in New York in 1844, and later turned to making brass parts for diving equipment and valves for rubber mattresses. George joined his father in 1890, and in 1904 formed the firm known as A. Schrader's Son. This valve, particularly its core, is the only part of a motor car that is interchangeable with any other car throughout the world, and a modern core will screw into an 1898 valve body.

The body of the Schrader valve is similar to the Woods but has an internal screw thread to receive a core. The core has a conical rubber seal to mate with a conical bore

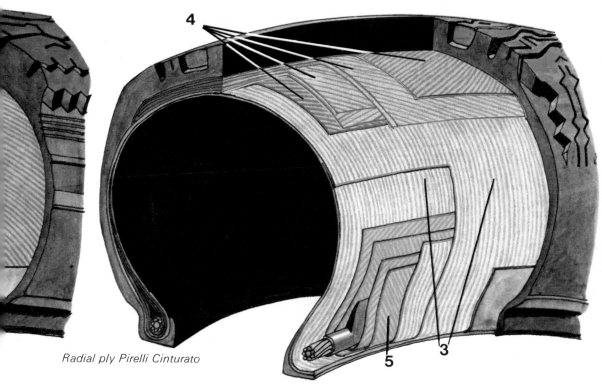

1 Cross plies at about 40 degrees to the tyre centre line and 100 degrees to each other
2 Steel bead wires
3 Radial carcass plies at 90 degrees to the bead
4 Belt plies at relatively narrow angles to centre line
5 Bead reinforcing flippers

Radial ply Pirelli Cinturato

André Michelin 1853–1931

Edouard Michelin 1859–1940

in the body and a circular knife edge at its inner end. A small rod passes through the core and has a fixed flange containing a rubber ring that normally seats against the knife edge. A spring below the flange rests on a light bridge piece that rests on a ledge within the valve body.

The spring holds the rubber faced flange against the knife edge for sealing, augmented by the air pressure in the tube. Inflation moves the flange away from the core body and allows air to enter. The air can be released, or the pressure measured, by depressing the small rod to unseat the valve.

In 1933, A. Schrader's Son modified the valve mounting by vulcanizing the threaded body into a flanged rubber core that was, in turn, vulcanized to the inner tube.

MODERN TYRES

By the early 1920s there was a demand for more comfort and more resistance to skidding. The high-pressure, straight-wall, beaded-edge tyre gave way to the balloon tyre pioneered by Firestone in 1923. The balloon tyre had around double the tread width, bulging side walls and was inflated to half or a third of the pressure.

These balloon tyres had a width and height that were approximately equal, dimensions which remained common until about 1950 when the ratio of height to width began to drop. This profile is expressed as a percentage that by 1965 had dropped to 80 per cent and is now around 70 per cent or lower.

The change gives more sideways stability to the tyre through the use of wider rim sections and lower side walls. The lower walls tend to reduce the tyre's suspension function, which has been taken over by more advanced suspension design.

Tyres have two opposing functions. First, to provide flexibility in a vertical direction to deal with road surface unevenness. Second, to have horizontal rigidity to maintain stable steering and wheelgrip. With the Palmer cord and later tyres, a compromise was reached by using alternate layers of reinforcing cords at 45 degrees to the centre plane of the tyre. This was a cross-ply tyre and the cords crossed each other at about a right angle.

Although Gray and Sloper had long before suggested the use of two different types of plies for the tyre walls and the tread reinforcement, there was no change in design until Michelin, in the late 1940s, and Pirelli, in 1953, produced tyres with radial wall plies.

Both Michelin and Pirelli used cords that ran radially to the tyre from one bead to the other. This gave a tyre that had much greater vertical flexibility. To keep the tread horizontally rigid under the longitudinal braking and accelerating forces and lateral steering forces, further belts of bracing plies were added under the tread. These bracing plies, or breakers, were of inextensible fabric, steel cords in the Michelin and textile fibres in the Pirelli. They were again very lightly woven with all warp and only a little weft just to hold the cords together. By placing the cords at a small angle to the circumference and using at least two plies of opposite angle, a rigid structure was formed under the tread.

By these means the tyre was able to deal vertically with bumps, and at the same time there was little tread distortion under horizontal forces.

The rigid-breaker tyre, as the radial-ply is sometimes known, has the advantage of lower rolling resistance, better wearing qualities and a decrease in slip angle compared to the cross-ply tyre. These benefits are largely due to the greatly reduced tread deformation when the tyre is rolling.

On the other hand this rigidity gives a harsher ride on small bumps at lower speeds, heavier steering at parking speeds and a tendency to a rapid increase in slip angle as cornering forces increase. Thus the radial tyre has higher cornering ability but loses adhesion more quickly once the higher limit is reached.

MATERIALS

Although natural rubber vulcanized with sulphur was used for a long time in the production of tyres, it was not a wholly ideal material. Rubber is susceptible to extremes of heat and cold. A tyre that is rolling under load is being continually bent where the tread flattens on the road surface. The continual bending produces friction within

The Dunlop Denovo tyre has lubricant cans clipped to the rim.

the tyre, both in the rubber itself and between the cords of the plies, and the heat build-up causes the rubber to deteriorate and lose its strength.

In contrast, low temperatures may cause the rubber to harden, almost to the point of becoming inelastic. The rubber will then crack and break like a brittle material. Similar effects are produced by atmospheric oxygen and ultra-violet light from bright sunshine.

Synthetic rubbers that could be chemically designed to meet particular conditions have long been a subject of research. Faraday stated the equivalent chemical formula for rubber in 1826. Twenty years after Greville Williams, a British chemist, produced isoprene in 1860, rubber-like articles began to be made in a small way. By the 1930s Germany had progressed far enough to produce Buna tyres of artificial rubbers, the forerunners of styrene butadiene rubber (SBR).

At about the same time the Du Pont company developed polychloroprene, more familiarly known by its trade name of Neoprene. Neoprene was used for tyre walls, often blended with natural rubber, until it was supplanted by SBR, which had good wear resistance and a better wet-grip than rubber. Unfortunately SBR was not springy, and

tended to absorb energy so that more power was needed to move the wheels.

By adding polybutadiene to SBR the wet-grip was reduced a little, but the wear and tear properties were increased. The composition giving the best wet-grip does not give the best grip on snow or dry roads. So a compromise has to be struck.

Since the tyre walls and treads deal with different conditions, it has become the usual practice for different compositions to be used. This method was first used by Avon around 1961.

To save the use of too much expensive rubber, a filler is added to the mix. The best of the fillers is carbon black because this not only fills but adds strength and wear resistance. The blackness of tyres caused by this addition acts as a filter for ultraviolet light.

TREAD PATTERNS

A tyre running on a perfectly dry smooth surface would have the greatest grip if it were bald. But roads are often wet and seldom smooth, and a tyre needs a tread to clear water away and to bite on rough surfaces.

To get a mechanical grip against the surface texture of a road, the tread pattern has to have edges at the maximum angle to the direction of the needed grip. For braking and driving this is across the tyre, but for steering the edges should be in line with the tyre. As these needs are at right angles and tyres are usually doing both things at the same time, the tread pattern is generally given a diagonal edge, with a bias towards directional stability forces.

When tyres are produced for cross-country or snow use, deep separate tread blocks are used to bite through the slushy surface and get traction from the more rigid subsurface of the track.

Wet roads give an extra problem. Surface water has to be removed because no tyre will grip a surface of water. The tyre edges can sweep the water aside, but the water at the centre of the tread has to be piped away. This is done by designing the diagonal wavy grooves in such a way that they give a continuous channel for water to flow and do not close up under the distortion of the tread on the road. In the Dunlop SP Sport tread small transverse tunnels connected the outer wavy channels to the open sides of the tyre so that the water was squirted out sideways.

If the water is not led away fast enough and builds up a film under the whole contact patch, the grip decreases to nil and the tyre is said to be aquaplaning.

The front third of the contact area is concerned with getting the water out of the way, the second third in mopping up and drying the road and the last third in providing grip. This is the main reason for loss of grip on wet roads — and for the small cuts or sipes in the tread blocks. The sipes provide more wiping edges, like squeegees, to dry the road and the cuts temporarily hold the water that the sipes mop up.

Ideally, different treads are needed for dry, wet, mud,

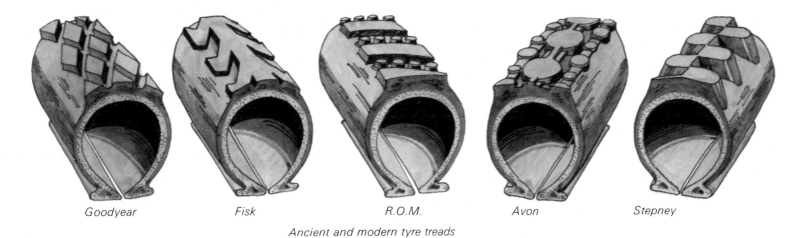

Goodyear   Fisk   R.O.M.   Avon   Stepney

Ancient and modern tyre treads

Michelin XAS radial tyre with asymmetric tread

Pirelli Cinturato CN54 radial ply tyre

Pirelli BS3 tyre with three removable tread bands

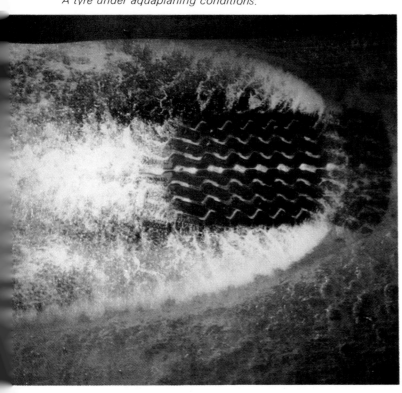

A tyre under aquaplaning conditions.

snow and ice surfaces. Either a compromise must be reached or different tyres fitted to suit the conditions. The Pirelli BS3 introduced in 1959 had three tread bands that could be removed when the tyre was deflated. These tread bands were replaceable either by new bands or bands of a different tread pattern.

RIM DESIGN

After the adoption of the wire edge tyre and well base rim, design remained static for a long period. Although tyres without tubes had been tried many years before, Dunlop reintroduced the tubeless tyre in 1953. Tyre and rim design were more or less normal. But the pressed-steel rim was more accurate, had no spoke holes from which air could leak and the valve was rubber mounted directly into the rim. The soft rubber of the tyre beads was held in sealing engagement with the rim shoulders by the internal air pressure and carcass rigidity.

These tyres were less prone to sudden deflation than tubed tyres, but tended to roll off the edge of the rim when deflated. To meet this defect, a rim was designed with a safety ledge to prevent the bead moving into the well and allowing the opposite side to climb over the rim.

In 1973, both Rubery Owen and Avon looked back to motor cycle racing tyres of the 1930s that had stout rubber bands, known as well-fillers, fitted with difficulty into the central well. In the Avon design a special section rim with a small well is used. The Rubery Owen design employs a number of polyurethane blocks held in the well by a metal band. These can be used with existing rims.

In the same year Rover began to fit the Denovo tyre, Dunlop's solution to the high speed deflation problem. This adopted two earlier ideas of dispensing with the well and using puncture-sealing fluid. To these was added the idea of lubrication between the inner wall surfaces when the tyre was running flat. The original rim was pressed axially, once the tyre had been fitted, to close up the well. Later production designs went to earlier ideas, as used on large commercial wheels, of having the rim in two pieces bolted together.

The lubricant was held in metal containers, secured to a band round the rim, that fractured when the tyre flattened. The liquid performed three duties: it acted as a lubricant to reduce the high friction and heat generated when the walls bulged outwards and rubbed on their folded selves; it conducted heat away from the contact area; and it

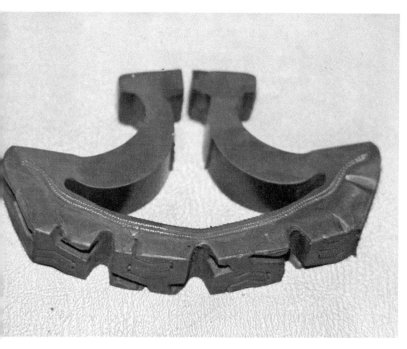

Pirelli's triangular section tyre in which the rubber is only in compression even when deflated. This development tyre has a steel reinforcement under the tread.

Inflated   **Punctured**

provided a seal for punctures up to a few millimetres in diameter. At the same time some of the fluid evaporated and, together with any air remaining, gave a low inflation pressure to help keep the walls from touching.

The approach of Tangora, chief engineer of Pirelli, to the deflation problem was similar to that of Philip Henry Johnson of Roadless Traction Ltd in 1928. The Pirelli rim is made so narrow that the tyre beads almost touch, and the tyre is triangular in section. Fundamentally, the idea is to keep the side walls always in compression so that they act as struts between the tread and the rim. Since rubber is best when compressed, there is no need for internal reinforcing, and the tyre can be moulded purely of rubber with no internal plies.

With the rubber always in compression, there is no force reversal in the material and so far less heat is produced. Also, the tyres will run with little or no inflation. They have even been used when cut into two right round the centre of the tread.

BRAKES

The ancient potter stopped his rotating wheel with his foot. A few thousand years later the bicycle was slowed in the same way. But in 1838 a Scottish blacksmith, Kirkpatrick Macmillan, decided that pressing a boot sole on a bicycle wheel produced too much instability. He designed a brake in which a block of wood was pressed on the iron tyre by a lever.

This kind of brake, called a spoon brake after the shape worn in the block by the wheel, was used on most of the early motor vehicles. Some had spoon brakes pressing on the wheels and others, like the 1885 Benz, used a brake block pressing on one of the countershaft belt pulleys. The latter type is known as a transmission brake, and it remained in use, in various forms, for a long time.

Another form of transmission brake was used by Frederick Lanchester in 1895. The central cone of the clutch moved rearwards to disengage the power, and the back of the cone pressed against a fixed block.

When the spoon brake revealed its weaknesses, motor designers followed the example of the millwrights and began to use an external contracting brake. A number of wooden blocks were secured to a steel strap encircling an enlarged hub or a ring on the wheel. One end of the strap was fixed and the other pulled by a lever or screw mechanism. This method greatly increased the frictional area and improved cooling. But the brake was useful only when the wheel was turning in one direction. If the direction helped the movement of the lever, the band would try to tighten round the brake rim in a self-servo action. When the wheel went the other way, the band tried to unwrap and release the brake. To stop cars running backwards down hill, the back of the chassis was fitted with a hinged and pointed sprag which could be let down to stick into the road.

Amédée Bollée equipped his early vehicles with band

brakes that worked in both directions. This was done, at the expense of some servo action, by pulling on both ends of the band.

Other forms of external contracting brakes were used both on rims attached to the hubs and on drums on the propeller shaft. These had two curved shoes pivoted to the axle casing or chassis and drawn together by a lever system at their other ends to clamp the shoes round the drum. Most cars at the beginning of this century had band brakes on the rear hubs and a transmission brake behind the gearbox. Although front wheel brakes had been tried, they were thought to be too complicated and they were also considered too dangerous.

DRUM BRAKES

In 1901, Maybach designed an internal expanding brake that was used on the rear wheels on the 40 hp Mercedes of 1903. It had an expanding ring, carried on internal supporting rollers, opening against the inside of a drum forming the hub of the chain drive sprocket. The split expanding ring was moved into drum contact by a double-armed lever system pivoted on the wheel axle support.

Louis Renault produced in 1902 an internal expanding drum brake with features that typified this kind of brake for over half a century. Two curved shoes were pivoted together at their ends on a pin fixed to a back plate rigid with the axle casing. A flat cam was positioned between flat radial surfaces at the other shoe ends. When this cam was turned, it forced the shoe ends apart and the curved peripheries of the shoes against the inside of a drum attached to the wheel. When the cam was turned in the opposite direction to release the brake, the shoes were pulled away from the drum by springs stretched between the shoes.

This brake slowly overtook others in popularity and became universal. It was eclipsed only by the disc brake. The drum brake was neat, uncomplicated in its earlier forms and easily adapted to front or rear wheels. In theory, at least, it kept the friction surfaces clear of oil, water and even from dust.

SHOE ACTION

The shoes in a drum brake have a self-servo action. The shoe that is arranged so that the brake drum surface travels from the cam end towards the pivot will tend to

In 1902 Louis Renault produced this internal expanding brake that formed the basis of drum brakes for 50 years.

A steel wire wrapped round a rim on the rear wheel formed a band brake on the 1899 Daimler.

187

follow the drum. This tries to turn the shoe round the pivot and increases the force applied by the cam. The other shoe also tries to turn about its pivot under the action of the rubbing forces, but that tends to move the shoe away from the drum and reduce the braking. The first shoe is called the leading shoe and the other the trailing shoe. With a fixed pivot most of the work is done by the first half of the leading shoe – the part nearest the cam.

When this was realized by the brothers Henri and Maurice Farman in 1920, the knowledge was used to provide a self-servo. The cam, or some other type of expander, only worked on one end of the leading shoe. The other end of the shoe was pivoted, or linked, to the adjacent end of the trailing shoe and the only fixed pivot was at the other end of the trailing shoe near the cam. As the brake was applied, the leading shoe began to move round slightly and applied a force to move the trailing shoe outwards. Thus both shoes became leading shoes in what became known as a two-leading-shoe brake. The idea does not work so well in reverse when both shoes become trailing, but then drivers do not tend to drive backwards rapidly!

To balance the braking forces between the shoes the

true leading shoe was made shorter than its companion. Instead of just pivoting one shoe on the other, an adjuster was fitted between the shoe ends, as suggested by W. A. Cocking and W. E. Hean in 1922. Usually this adjuster was of the jacking screw type and could be operated through a hole in the back plate.

A further systm, developed by A. H. G. Girling, used two bellcrank, or double-armed, levers, one at each end of the trailing shoe. As the expander forced the shoes apart, it transmitted a force to the nearest bellcrank, which relayed it through a strut to the other crank. The second crank pressed against the end of the adjuster, which also transmitted the force produced by the self-servo of the leading shoe. The result was that the trailing shoe moved out into drum contact at both ends, adding considerably to the stopping effort.

Early shoes were forced apart by rotation of a flat cam, but later brakes had pivoted levers acting only on the leading shoe end. Girling, in 1928, used a floating housing having two opposed slanting-ended plungers. These were acted on by a wedge, moving at right angles to the shoes, through rollers to reduce friction. The adjuster for this

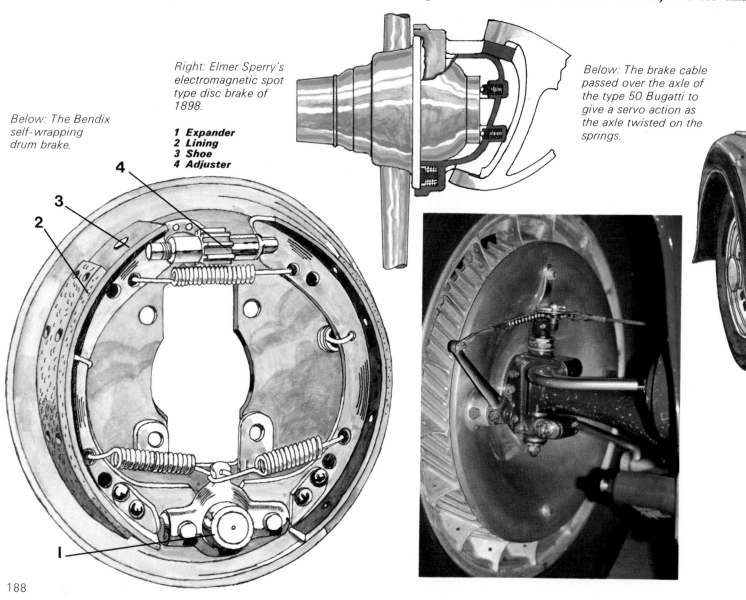

Right: Elmer Sperry's electromagnetic spot type disc brake of 1898.

Below: The Bendix self-wrapping drum brake.

1 Expander
2 Lining
3 Shoe
4 Adjuster

Below: The brake cable passed over the axle of the type 50 Bugatti to give a servo action as the axle twisted on the springs.

system was a screw with a conical end moving similar plungers apart to spread the shoes.

DRUMS

Early brake drums were pressed out of sheet steel. These had several disadvantages. They tended to score if dirt got between the lining and drum surface; they were resonant and squealed badly; and they did not conduct away the heat generated by braking. Another failure of pressed steel was that, being relatively thin, it had not enough rigidity to resist belling open under the shoe forces. This was countered by a flange outside the open end.

Rigidity was later obtained by casting the drums in a nickel-iron alloy that provided a better friction surface. These cast drums also had ribs or fins on the outside to help get rid of the heat.

A later advance, particularly in larger and faster cars, was the use of cast aluminium drums with cast iron liners cast in place – an idea pioneered by Marc Birkigt, the designer of the Hispano-Suiza in 1919. These Al-Fin drums, as they were known when made by Wellworthy in the 1930s, were lighter and had better heat-dissipating qualities.

An interesting drum of this kind was used by Bugatti in 1924. The entire wheel and rim was cast in aluminium with an iron liner for an integral brake drum cast inside the wheel.

DISC BRAKES

Since the main function of a brake is to turn the energy of a moving car into heat and then to get rid of the heat, the drum brake began to have two serious limitations as cars became heavier and faster. To obtain more efficient braking, the drums were made larger although the wheels grew smaller and, as well as the physical limitation, there was no room for cooling air to get to the drum. Further, the heat expanded the drum radially away from the shoes and also reduced the friction characteristics of the linings. The result was brake fade, and, ultimately, no retardation.

These drum brake drawbacks were eliminated by using a disc, with friction pads moved axially to grip the disc sides. This idea was similar to the bicycle caliper brake invented by James Starley when he was foreman of the Coventry Machinists Company.

The first of the motor vehicle disc brakes was devised by

The Type 50 Bugatti had cable operated brakes on all four wheels.

189

the German firm Union Elektricitats-Gesellschaft in 1896. An electromagnet clamped a circular brake friction plate against a disc on the wheel, the device being the forerunner of the clutch-type brake.

The spot-type brake, the type used on cars, was devised by Elmer Ambrose Sperry, a civil engineer of Cleveland, Ohio, far better remembered for his development of the gyro compass. Sperry designed an electric car in 1898 which had disc brakes on the front wheels. A disc was cast integral with the hub and a part-circular electromagnet pressed a friction member against one side of the disc. A dust-excluding rim was fitted over the disc edge and springs moved the disc and friction members apart when the current was switched off.

Four-cylinder disc brake of the Jaguar XJ6.

In 1902, Frederick Lanchester produced an idea for a spot-type of disc brake, in which the disc was clamped between two friction pads. This was a caliper brake using both sides of the disc. Thereafter the disc brake appeared occasionally, often as a transmission brake, like the disc behind the rear axle gearbox of the 1919 A.C. In 1940, Girling fitted a clutch-type brake to a military vehicle and ten years later Chrysler used twin discs forced apart into contact with the interior of a finned drum.

In 1949 Crosley of America provided a swing caliper spot-brake for the front wheels of their 722cc car. This brake was derived from aircraft and was a clean design, but the firm stopped production after three years.

Again following the aircraft lead, both Dunlop and Girling developed disc brakes for production cars. In 1956, the Triumph TR3 was offered as standard with Girling and the Jensen 541 saloon with Dunlop brakes. Dunlop brakes were also available as optional fitments on Jaguars. The same year, Citroën fitted their own design of disc brake to the DS19.

The two kinds of spot-type brakes are the swing caliper and the fixed caliper. In the swing caliper a rigid casting, or caliper, is free to pivot and thus provide equal pad-engaging

pressures on the two sides of the disc when an applying force is acting on the pad on one side only. The rigid caliper has separate applying means for each of the pads on the two disc sides.

Although in some designs a measure of self-servo has been attempted with disc brakes, in general there is no servo action. Therefore, the brakes work equally well in both directions, but need a heavier application pressure – a necessity that led to the main brakes being hydraulically applied. The fixed caliper, for example, is bored to form cylinders on each side of the disc. In these cylinders pistons press on plates to which the friction pads are bonded. Since the pads are relatively thick, to allow for greater wear rates caused by higher pressure and smaller areas, a linear free-wheel device working in conjunction with retractor springs gives automatic adjustment.

With the heavier duty brakes more than one cylinder and pad assembly is used in each side of the caliper. Additional cooling can be provided by radial passageways in the disc thickness, allowing air to flow outwards through the disc.

BRAKE SYSTEMS

Since the four-wheel brake system, in which all four were operated at the same time from one control, was not suggested until after the turn of the century, the early operating systems were primitive and easy to design. They were either rods or wires worked by levers to pull the brakes on to the wheel or drum.

It was soon found necessary to equalize the braking on the two rear wheels. So an idea was borrowed from the horse-drawn carriage. This was the whippletree, where the brake rods were connected to the respective ends, and the pedal applying the pull to the centre, of a transverse beam. Any force applied to the centre was equally divided between the two brakes.

With the introduction of brakes on all wheels, an optional extra on the 1903 Mercedes and a standard fitting in the 1909 Arrol-Johnson for eighteen months, it became necessary to balance the four brakes. To this end the whippletree system was joined by pulley systems, for wire cable operated brakes, linkwork systems and even differential type gears.

The original ideas for four-wheel braking did not last long as they were thought to be too dangerous, probably because nobody at that time realized the need for proportioning the braking between the front and rear wheels. Around the 1920s the need for greater stopping power compelled the use of front wheel brakes. Cars of that time had red triangles on their mudguards to give a warning to following traffic.

One difficulty with front brakes was to provide a mechanism that would rotate the brake cam and, at the same time, allow the wheels to steer. In 1910, when he was working for Argylls of Scotland, Henri Perrot designed a system that was to bear his name, though he was partnered by John Meredith Rubury. The Perrot actuator was a shaft having a universal joint on the outboard end and carried in a spherical bearing on the chassis at the other end. The centre of the joint was on the centre line of the steering pivot and the joint was coupled to the brake cam. At the chassis end of the shaft a lever was connected to either the rod or cable braking system.

Another solution to the problem was the mounting of a guide pulley on the top of the steering pivot. The brake cable was led round the pulley from the chassis to a lever clamped to the cam spindle.

The Bowden cable, invented by E. M. Bowden in 1896, in which use is made of the relative movements of the ends of a flexible tube and a cable passing through the tube, was employed in a large number of brake systems. The inner cable was connected to the brake cam lever and the applying device (pedal shaft or whippletree), and the outer casing to the brake plate and the chassis. With the great flexibility of the cable allowing free wheel movement, even with independent suspension systems, the Bowden cable became almost universal until the coming of hydraulic actuation.

HYDRAULIC BRAKES

Although most modern cars are said to have hydraulic brakes, this is not really true. They have, in fact, hydraulically-operated brakes, where use is made of a virtually incompressible fluid to act as the link between pedal or

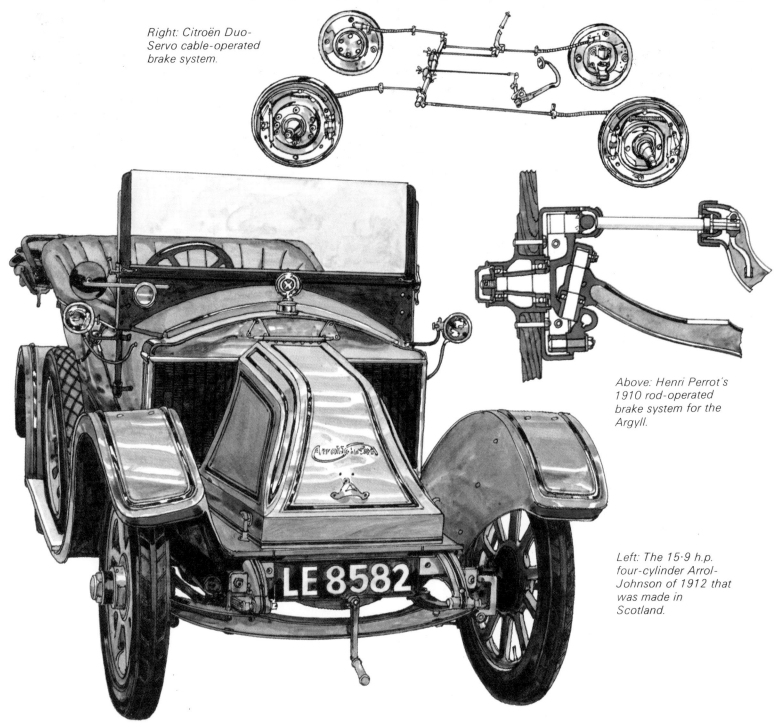

Right: Citroën Duo-Servo cable-operated brake system.

Above: Henri Perrot's 1910 rod-operated brake system for the Argyll.

Left: The 15·9 h.p. four-cylinder Arrol-Johnson of 1912 that was made in Scotland.

LE 8582

191

The 1926 Chrysler 3-litre 4-cylinder '58' had hydraulic brakes.

lever and the mechanism that actually applies the brake.

In 1897, H. Heathly applied fluid-pressure operation to bicycle brakes. Pressure was produced in the handlebar by a hand grip that screwed on to the end. Flexible tubes led to cylinders fixed to the wheel forks and containing pistons that moved under the pressure to apply the brake blocks to the wheel rim.

J. C. Bayley and A. Rigg reversed the system when they applied fluid pressure to four-wheel vehicles in 1897. They used springs to apply the brakes and pressure to release them.

The fundamentals of the modern system were devised by E. W. Weight in 1908. He coupled the piston of a main hydraulic cylinder to a brake pedal and led the pressure by flexible pipes to cylinders and pistons within the brake drums. These slave cylinders expanded the two pivoted shoes into contact with the drum. A fluid tank above the main, or master cylinder, led make-up fluid to a point just in front of the piston, when the brake was off, to keep the system full.

In 1911, Rolland and Pilain of France produced four-wheel brakes where the slave cylinders for hydraulic front wheel brakes were contained in the steering pivots and the rear brakes were mechanically operated.

Dusenberg and Chrysler offered hydraulic four-wheel

brakes in America in 1921 and 1924 respectively. Triumph and Horstman both fitted similar brakes in England in 1925.

SERVO SYSTEMS

While the two leading shoe and similar self-servo systems will supplement the effort of the driver, they can do so only up to a point. Eventually the self-generating force increases too rapidly, since in such mechanisms force begets force, and the brakes suddenly snatch full on.

To obtain higher friction shoe or pad pressures, it is necessary to have additional outside assistance that can be controlled. An obvious source is engine power or, better, the output end of the gearbox, because this rotates as long as the car is moving.

Among users of mechanical power servo in the 1920s were Hispano-Suiza and Rolls-Royce. In both cases depression of the brake pedal engaged a friction member with a rotating drum or disc driven by the gearbox output shaft. The friction member started to rotate in the manner of a driven clutch member and pulled the rods actuating the front and rear brakes. The higher the pedal pressure, the greater the clutch engagement and the greater the braking force.

Citroën, having a fluid pressure main for their self-levelling suspension of the DS19, used engine-pumped

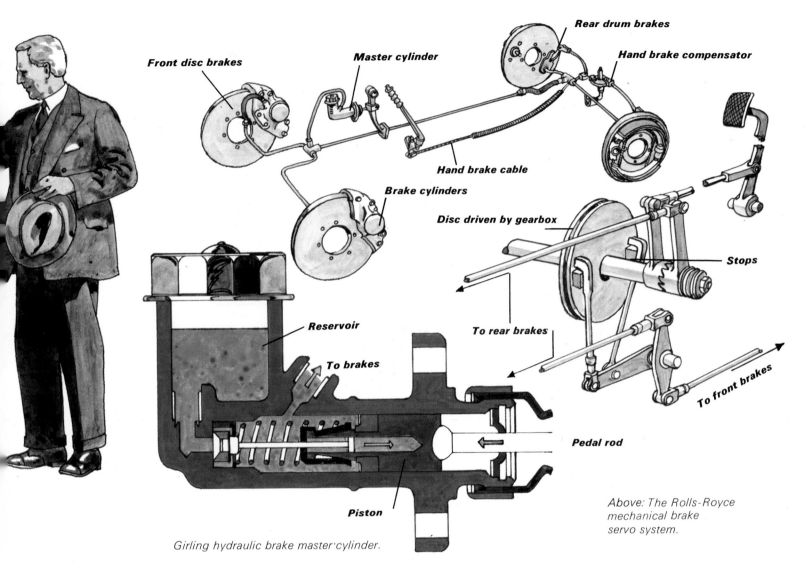

Girling hydraulic brake master·cylinder.

Above: The Rolls-Royce mechanical brake servo system.

hydraulic pressure for brake actuation. The brake pedal acted as a throttle in the pressure line and an accumulator provided a reserve of pressure when the engine was stopped.

The most common servo system uses atmospheric pressure acting on one side of a piston, the other side of which can be subjected to the depression, or vacuum, in the engine inlet manifold. The force from the piston is used to augment the pedal force on the master cylinder piston and increase the fluid pressure in the system. This possibility was suggested by J. G. Parry Thomas of Leylands in 1919 and it was then developed by Albert Dewandre from 1923 onwards.

In all these servo systems the additional force is added in parallel to the driver-produced force, so that servo failure does not result in loss of brakes. A further safety measure which is of more recent origin is the use of tandem master cylinders.

By using two master cylinders, where one can take over the double duty at the expense of increased pedal travel, it becomes possible to isolate one pair of brakes from the other. This gives a further insurance against total failure by arranging for the two separate circuits to operate on diagonal wheels as done by Saab, Audi-N.S.U. and others.

PROPORTIONING SYSTEMS

When a car is braked, the force acts on the tyres at road level, but the forward momentum of the car's weight acts through the centre of gravity, which is above that level. So the car tries to go rear axle over radiator, increasing the weight on the front wheels and decreasing that on the rear wheels.

In the early days of four-wheel brakes there was great fear of front wheel locking and loss of steering control. Rolls-Royce, in fact, designed its mechanical servo to give more force to the rear brakes. This was the wrong way round because the rear wheels, being more lightly loaded, would lock easily.

Later, Bendix produced a proportioning device for mechanically-operated brakes. A spring allowed relative movement between the front and rear sections of the rear brake rod, proportional to the force in the rod. When that force produced a predetermined movement in the spring, a wedge on the end of the front rod expanded balls into jamming engagement with a fixed member and so limited the force applied to the rear brakes.

The same effect was produced in the hydraulics systems by spring-loaded valves that limited the rear application pressure as in the B.L.M.C. Mini. This followed a 1931 idea of Bendix-Perrot Ltd.

PARKING BRAKES

At first it was prudent to have two independent braking systems. Later it became a legal necessity. In the "prudent" days both systems, one hand and one foot, worked on the rear wheels.

With the coming of four-wheel brakes and the mistrust of those at the front, the handbrake was regarded as an emergency and parking device. It was relegated to work on the front wheels, as in the Austin 7.

Later, when it was realized that most of the retardation was produced by the front wheels, the parking brake was moved to the rear wheels where it was simpler to arrange for its action.

The law has required two main things of the second brake. First, it must be independent of the main brake except for the actual friction members (the shoes and drum). Second, it must be capable of being set to brake at least one wheel when the car is unattended.

The first requirement is met by the use of a secondary rod or cable operation to the rear brake shoes, whether they are mechanically or hydraulically operated. In the case of disc brakes there is usually a secondary mechanically operated caliper with separate pads. Because of the higher applicaion pressures needed with disc pads, an alternative, such as used by Porsche, is a small drum brake within the centre of the disc hub.

The second requirement is provided by a pawl and ratchet mechanism that allows the lever to be pulled for application and then holds it until a release lever or button disengages the ratchet pawl.

As the handbrake became less used in normal driving and more of a parking device, the lever became less accessible. Cadillac, in 1934, used a pull-out device like an umbrella handle. Chevrolet moved away from a hand lever in 1916 to the main pedal, on which they merely put a latch. Buick followed with a separate pedal in 1942 and Mercedes a few years later with a pedal and separate dash button for release.

ANTI-LOCK SYSTEMS

Although the "dreaded side-slip", as skidding used to be called, has always been a peril of motoring, higher speeds and higher traffic density have brought wheel locking into greater prominence.

Recent developments by Dunlop, Bosch and Teldix, Lucas and Lockheed have produced anti-locking devices that sense the slowing rate of the wheels. When this rate exceeds a predetermined figure, as occurs when a wheel suddenly stops and begins to slide, an electronic device senses the increased slowing rate and reduces the pressure in the hydraulic pipe system until the wheels once again reach an appropriate speed of rotation.

With these systems full braking capability is maintained and the wheel speed is prevented from falling below gripping speed. At the same time, since the wheels continue to rotate, full steering control is maintained.

FRICTION MATERIALS

The spoon brake, which was a lighter adaptation of the block brake used on the iron tyres of horse-drawn vehicles, had wood, leather or old rope as a friction material.

The external band brake often had a metal to metal contact with the drum, or was lined with the same available materials as the block brake. This was a legacy from the windshaft brake of windmills.

Early internal expanding brakes fared little better. Original designs used metal — usually cast iron — shoes pressed against steel drums. Bugatti was still doing this in the early 1920s. Before them Wolseley had linings

Herbert Frood's first experimental shed with a waterwheel-driven dynamometer, built in 1897 and still preserved.

Left: Spot type disc brake of the Saab 99.

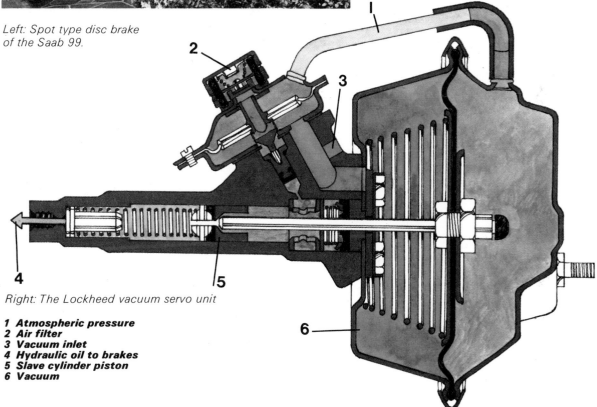

Right: The Lockheed vacuum servo unit

1 **Atmospheric pressure**
2 **Air filter**
3 **Vacuum inlet**
4 **Hydraulic oil to brakes**
5 **Slave cylinder piston**
6 **Vacuum**

which were made of walrus hide on the shoes.

But in 1897, Herbert Frood had seen the wooden block brakes of wagons carrying Derbyshire limestone smoulder on steep downhill journeys. He set his mind to this problem and built the world's first friction-and-wear test machine. Powered by a four foot (1·22 metres) diameter water wheel, the machine was housed in his garden shed.

Frood's first basic material was cotton belting and he searched for bonding agents that would strengthen and improve its frictional properties. He was also a good salesman and within four or five years had developed the foundations of the friction material industry with his firm, Ferodo.

Cotton proved unsuitable for automobile use because it charred at about 150°C. In 1908 Ferodo introduced bonded asbestos lining material. It was made from cloth woven from asbestos yarn and reinforced with brass wire.

The material was impregnated with a resin to add strength and raise the frictional properties.

Four years later, Frood produced linings that were pressed to shape in dies. This reduced the initial need for bedding-in and increased the material's life.

Asbestos has the disadvantage that many of the fibres are too short to be spun into strands for weaving. Also, the initial preparation for weaving increases the cost of the finished material. In 1921, Ferodo introduced friction material that was moulded and used random length fibres.

Considerable development has taken place in the production of the bonding resins. It is now possible to design the friction material for the conditions of heat, pressure and wear under which it has to operate.

Research is being carried out on sintered metals — already used for some applications — and cermets, a combination of metal and ceramic.

ELECTRICAL SYSTEMS - Generating

The earliest of the petrol-driven cars had no electrical systems. A red-hot platinum tube initiated the burning of fuel in the cylinder, and light for driving at night was given by candles or oil lamps.

The present method of producing electricity to ignite the fuel mixture in an engine and provide light and other services owes its origin to the work of two men, Oersted and Faraday, who were experimenting with electric currents nearly 150 years ago.

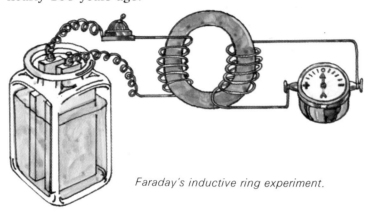

Faraday's inductive ring experiment.

Oersted and Faraday found one basic principle; that when an electric current flows through a wire a magnetic field is created round that wire. Moreover, they discovered that, if the wire is formed into a coil, then the magnetic field is just the same as if an actual magnet were put in the centre of the coil.

If a piece of soft iron is placed in the centre of the wire coil, this soft iron will become magnetized when the current is flowing. The strength of this magnetism will be in direct proportion to the strength of the electric current.

Oersted and Faraday also discovered that the movement of a wire near a magnet (in a magnetic field) produced an electric current in the wire when that wire was part of a circuit. These two discoveries are the basis not only of the ignition coil and the magneto, but of all electrical generators, motors and electro-magnetic relays.

In 1831, Faraday conducted an experiment in which he wound two coils of wire on an iron ring. He connected the second coil to a galvanometer, which showed the presence and direction of any electric current in that coil, and then connected the first coil through a switch to a battery. When he closed the switch, the galvanometer needle swung one way indicating that, as the magnetism was being built up by the current in the first coil, it was being forced round the ring through the second coil and that the movement of the magnetic field in the second coil was producing a current to deflect the galvanometer.

Switching off had exactly the reverse effect of swinging the needle in the opposite direction. These needle movements were, in fact, quick kicks as the phenomenon occurred only during the build up or dying away of the current and field, and not during the steady state which occurred after the magnetism had built up to its maximum. The current in the second coil was, of course, an induced

current, which is why this piece of electrical equipment is called an induction coil.

Another useful capability of the induction coil is its capacity to change voltages, either by increasing or decreasing them. It can do this because the magnetism produced is directly proportional to the voltage per turn of a coil and vice versa. So, if a current at twelve volts is applied at the terminals of a first coil of ten turns, around 1200 volts will be available at the terminals of a 1000 turn secondary coil.

IGNITION SYSTEMS

As engines ceased to be governed to one speed and subsequent speeds increased, the hot tube showed its defects of inflexibility and uncertainty of ignition timing. A few designers looked at the old flint and steel. Others turned to electricity to supply a more consistent spark, whose timing could be varied to regulate power and speed and which would fire a weaker mixture allowing speed determinations by throttle.

Among the early users of flint and steel were Ott and Fanto, who had the simple idea of welding a roughened piece of steel to the piston top. As the piston rose this steel rubbed against a spring-pressed flint in a tube fixed to the cylinder wall. J. G. Newman devised a more complex means that added an overhead camshaft to a side-valve engine. The spindles of rockers operated by this camshaft passed into the cylinder head and carried serrated wheels against

The hot-tube ignition of the 1893 Benz Victoria.

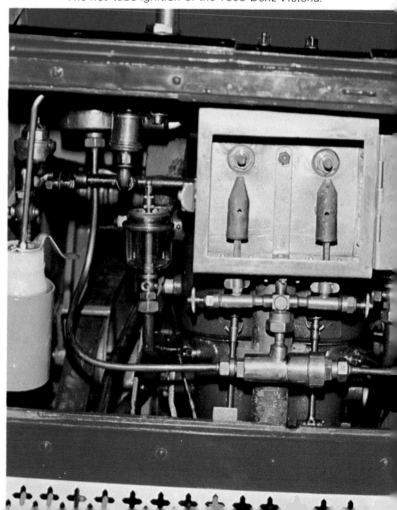

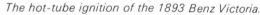

which pencils of lighter-flint were pressed. As late as 1924, M. Gatti suggested a hand-driven wheel and flint for help with starting. But these pyrophoric devices were doomed from the beginning.

Others, who favoured electricity, began by following the ideas of early gas engines that used low voltage/low tension – L.T. – sparking plugs to ignite fuel. This was soon joined by high voltage – H.T. – systems that formed the basis of ignition systems used today.

The H.T. current was produced either by a self-contained engine-driven generator – magneto ignition – or by a battery and induction coil – coil ignition. Since the battery needed charging, a dynamo was fitted to the car. Once there was a source of electricity people began to think of other uses for it, such as lighting, starting and ancillary equipment (Chapter 7).

There were three outstanding men concerned with the development of automobile electrical systems. Robert Bosch of Germany who, with Frederick Simms of England, was responsible for the L.T. and H.T. magneto ignition and Charles F. Kettering of America, who developed the coil ignition system.

ROBERT BOSCH

Robert Bosch was born in September 1861, the eighth child of twelve. His father was the landlord of the "Gasthaus zur Krone", a hotel in the village of Albeck, near Ulm. The secondary school he attended in Ulm reported there were "gaps in his knowledge", which led to his being apprenticed as a precision mechanic at the age of eighteen. Bosch really wanted to be a botanist and zoologist.

During his apprentice days he travelled round Germany, working in Cologne, Stuttgart, Nuremberg and Hanau. In 1884, regarding America as "a land of boundless possibilities" he crossed the Atlantic to seek work as a mechanic. Although he secretly feared he would have to begin as a waiter or dishwasher, he found employment with Bergmann in New York. Working on various electrical devices brought him eight dollars a week.

He became interested in the rights of workers and joined the "Knights of Labor" trade union. The following year he returned to Europe and, after a short period with Siemens in England, resettled in Stuttgart.

In 1886, he opened his own workshop with a capital of 10,000 marks, partly from his savings and the remainder from an inheritance from his father. His only staff was a skilled mechanic and an apprentice. To those who thought him foolish he replied "Big firms cannot make everything, there are definitely things where personal trust plays a part." He would tolerate no second rate work and built a sound reputation for quality.

The firm outgrew its capital, since too much of the money had been invested in machinery to meet increasing trade. In 1892, he reluctantly sacked nearly all of his 24 workers, but kept on Arnold Zähringer (later to become manager), Richard Schyle (who remained for 40 years) and

The 1893 Benz Victoria Vis-a-Vis.

Robert Bosch

an apprentice Gottlieb Honold, who became one of the most important men in the Bosch undertaking. Zähringer and Honold were to be the developers of the L.T. and H.T. magnetos.

By 1896, the setback was passed and the employees celebrated the completion of the first thousand orders for magnetos by going on an outing to Remstal.

Robert Bosch was always concerned with his workers' conditions. In 1894, he introduced a nine hour day, two hours less than the then legal limit for women and in 1906 he shortened the working day again, to eight hours. This earned him the nickname of "Red Bosch" for his short hours and high wages. He replied to this by saying "I do not pay good wages because I have a lot of money, I have a lot of money because I pay good wages".

Realizing the need for relaxation, Bosch shortened the working week to five and a half days in 1910, on the grounds that "employer and employee are equally dependent on the fate of the undertaking".

And Robert Bosch meant what he said. In 1910 he contributed a million Deutschmarks to the Stuttgart Technical College. He also paid out substantial sums for general social purposes. He was particularly interested in education and medicine and offered support to poor but talented people. He also contributed to homeopathic medicine. He formed a library to help his workers study and improve themselves, launched a works newspaper "Der Bosch Zünder" in 1919 and promoted needlework and domestic science classes for his women workers.

In the following years, as a memorial to his first son, who died in 1921, Bosch set up the still operative foundation for the orphans of former employees. He also instituted retirement pensions for those over 40, who had served the firm for over ten years. The Robert Bosch Hospital, in Stuttgart, was founded in 1936 as a research and welfare centre for homeopathic medicine, and an honorary degree of Doctor of Medicine was conferred on Bosch by Tübingen University in 1941, a year before his death at the age of 81.

FREDERICK SIMMS

In 1863, when Frederick Simms was born, there were only five English families in the German free city of Hamburg. Simms' father owned an old established firm supplying the Newfoundland fishing fleets. There is no doubt that this cosmopolitan upbringing was later to be responsible for Simms' business foresight and also to have an effect on his wide interests.

Simms was introduced to Daimler in 1888 and soon became a director of the Canstatt engine firm, a position he held until 1892. He secured the patent rights for the Daimler engine in Great Britain and eventually sold them to the Henry Lawson financial group giving the shareholders a 200 per cent bonus.

Simms continued his good relations with Daimler. The 1897 scheme for reorganisation of the works and the

drawings and specification of the first gear driven Daimler car were both his.

By 1899 Simms had spent a number of years experimenting with different forms of electrical ignition and had been introduced to Robert Bosch by the President of the Berlin Automobile Club.

The combination of Bosch's electrical knowledge and Simms' experience with motor cars resulted in the perfection of a reliable magneto.

Among the many things for which Frederick Simms was responsible were the invention of the expression "motorcar" in 1896 and of "petrol" around 1890. Petrol was originally coined as a trade name for petroleums, otherwise known as gasoline, motor-naphtha or essence, refined by the firm of Carless, Capel and Leonard.

Founder of the Automobile Club of Great Britain and Ireland in 1897, later to become the Royal Automobile Club, Simms' non-motoring pursuits included chamois hunting in the Tyrolese Alps.

Frederick R. Simms   *Charles F. Kettering*

In 1907 the Simms Manufacturing Company ceased production of engines and cars and became the Simms Magneto Company Limited. Four years later the American Simms Magneto Company was founded at East Orange, New Jersey.

CHARLES KETTERING

Son of a farmer, Charles Franklin Kettering was born in Ashland County, Ohio in 1876. Determined to work his way through all the educational establishments he could, he did not finally graduate from Ohio State University until he was 28.

After working as a school teacher, he began his electrical career as a telephone installation man. A great believer in efficiency, Kettering was soon telling the Star Telephone Company the right and wrong ways to dig post holes.

Later he installed what was thought to be too large a switchboard and almost bankrupted his firm. Kettering's far sightedness proved, as usual, correct and the company prospered from the increased business.

Moving to the National Cash Register Company in Dayton, he became head of the inventions department. One invention was the electrically operated cash register, which did not come into general use for a number of years.

Colonel E. A. Deeds, general manager of N.C.R., and

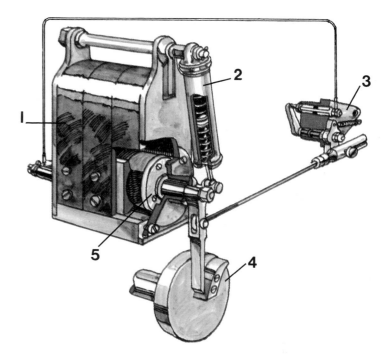

Left: An early high-tension magneto and distributor by Bosch.

The Bosch low-tension magneto of 1897 where the armature was rocked by an engine-driven cam and a pull rod opened the contacts in the cylinder.

1 Magnets
2 Damper
3 Igniter
4 Engine driven cam
5 Armature

other Dayton business men founded the Dayton Engineering Laboratories Company (Delco) in 1911, with Kettering at its head.

Charles "Boss" Kettering had long seen the need for an electrical starting system for the automobile, particularly if women were to drive, and Delco put its mind to this problem.

The automobile industry was not convinced that electric starters could be made to work, but Kettering got his chance through an accident. Henry M. Leland, the founder of Cadillac, sustained serious injury cranking his car on Belle Island Bridge. After this Leland gave Kettering the go-ahead and on February 27th 1911 the first Delco starter was installed on a Cadillac car. The following year Delco starters, lighting and coil ignition systems became standard on all Cadillacs.

In 1916, Delco was taken over by W. C. Durant as part of his United Motors combine. This combine became General Motors in 1918 and two years later Kettering organized General Motors Research Laboratories.

LOW TENSION MAGNETOS

The L.T. ignition systems relied on the desire of an electric current to keep on flowing as long as possible once it has started. When a break occurs in a circuit this desire produces an arc across the ends of the break. The arc continues until the gap is too wide for the voltage to force the electricity from one side to the other. Even a couple of volts are sufficient to produce a small arc. When a coil with an iron core, or an electromagnet, is included in the circuit the arc has the energy to fire the charge in a cylinder.

In 1897, Robert Bosch produced a low-tension magneto, which provided a sparking current without the need for a battery. It was, in fact, a special dynamo.

This magneto had a pair of inverted U-shaped permanent magnets secured to a non-magnetic baseplate. Soft iron pole pieces with part-cylindrical recesses in their facing faces, were bolted to the ends of the magnet arms. A cylindrical iron core carrying a coil was fixed in the tunnel between the pole pieces. The magnetism could thus flow from one pole of the magnet through the pole pieces, across an air gap, through the coil and iron core (the armature) across the other air gap and finally to the other pole of the magnet. But, of course, since nothing was changing, this flow of magnetism produced no current.

However, a current was produced by arranging a movable shield consisting of two soft iron segments, mounted on pivoted bronze discs at each end, in the air gaps and oscillating the shield. The cylindrical core, or armature had two deep grooves cut in its sides to give a central vertical web round which the coil was wound. Each shield segment extended, like the top and bottom of the armature, over about one quarter of a circle. So rocking the shield about its pivots was sufficient to vary the magnetic field passing through the coil and create an intermittent low-tension current.

The L.T. current was used to produce an arc between two contacts inside the cylinder. These contacts were moved mechanically to initiate the arc. A metal disc, secured over an opening leading to the combustion space, carried a metal pin which projected into the space and was insulated from the disc by hollow ceramic cones. These could be tightened to make a gas-tight seal.

A spindle, rotatably supported in the disc, had arms at each end. The inner arm was pressed on the fixed pin by a spring pulling on the outer arm. The fixed pin was wired to one end of the magneto coil and the remainder of the circuit was completed by an earth return from the spindle, disc, engine, magneto frame and armature to the other end of the coil winding. On the end of the engine camshaft was a snail-shaped cam. This cam carried on its face a crankpin which oscillated the shield through a connecting rod, and the cam periphery raised a rod against the force of a spring. When the notch in the cam came opposite the rod end, the rod shot down under the spring action and a hammer head on the rod end hit the outside arm. This flicked the inside arm away from the metal pin at the instant the magneto current was at its maximum. An arc then built up between the pin and the lever.

A year after Robert Bosch's invention, Frederick Simms devised a couple of ingenious mechanisms for varying the position of the ignition cam in relation to the camshaft, thus providing variable ignition timing in what became known as the Simms-Bosch L.T. ignition system. This system ran parallel in use with the trembler coil system until six or seven years later when Robert Bosch produced a high-tension magnet as a commercial proposition.

Meanwhile, the moving contacts within the cylinder saw a certain amount of detailed development. One of the ideas produced by Bosch was the use of an electro-magnetically actuated sparking plug in which the current in the coil pulled an armature away from an earth electrode. As the armature broke contact with the electrode, the ignition circuit was broken and the higher voltage induced by this interruption produced an arc which went across the opening contacts.

HIGH TENSION MAGNETOS

A. Boudeville is said to have produced a high tension magneto before the turn of the century, but this failed because he omitted to put a condenser across the contact breaker points. It was not until 1903 that the H.T. magneto became a reality. It continued to be used on the great majority of European cars until the 1930s.

The H.T. magneto, designed and developed by Bosch, was a logical development of the L.T. magneto combined with the induction coil. The armature was made to rotate and the shields were dispensed with, thus producing a low voltage generator in which current flowed when a contact breaker at the end of the armature was closed. A secondary winding surrounded the primary and was connected through a distributor to the sparking plugs. By rotating the induction coil in a magnetic field the whole system was made self-contained.

After this the basic design of the magneto remained unchanged for a long period, although detail developments

continued. For instance, in the early days the magnets needed re-magnetizing every few years, but the later alloys retained their magnetism for life.

Two or three U-shaped magnets were bolted side by side to a brass plate and soft iron pole pieces formed a circular tunnel, open at the top and bottom. Non-magnetic plates, secured across the ends of the tunnel, supported ball bearings and, at one end, also supported the casing for a contact breaker and an H.T. distributor. The bearings in turn supported a rotatable armature made of thin laminations of soft iron, painted on their sides to prevent heating by eddy currents induced in the armature.

The circular armature had longitudinal and transverse slots so that it was roughly H section, for the reception of two superimposed coils of wire. The inner coil, or primary, was connected at one end to one side of a condenser embedded in a broad endplate forming one armature endshaft.

The other end of the primary coil was connected by an insulated wire to a centre screw that clamped the contact breaker in position through an insulated block. This block held one of the contact breaker points and the other point was carried by the base of the contact breaker, which was clamped to the armature and thus earthed. The other side of the condenser was also earthed. The earthed breaker-point was held on an L-shaped lever, the other end of which was spring-loaded against the inside of a cam ring.

Outside the primary winding there was a secondary winding, consisting of many turns of fine wire. One end of this secondary winding was connected to the live (condenser) end of the primary winding and the other end to a brass slip ring held in the bottom of a circular channel-section insulator.

A spring-loaded carbon brush rubbed on the ring and was connected to another contact leading to the centre of a rotating distributor arm. This was driven by a half-speed gear from the armature. The outer casing of the distributor had four (for a four-cylinder engine) contacts, with terminals leading to the sparking plugs. A brush in the base plate rubbed on one armature endplate for an earth.

A later form of magneto, known as a polar inductor, had the windings stationary and the magnets rotating. This had the advantages that a much stronger one-piece shaft could be provided and, owing to the laminated coil core and poles, a much faster collapse of the magnetic field was achieved. By using more than two rotating magnetic poles, it became possible to provide four or six sparks for each revolution. Scintilla used this feature to make a magneto (called Scintilla vertex magneto) interchangeable with the contact-breaker and distributor unit of a coil ignition system.

When the magneto armature is rotating and the contact-breaker is closed, the movement of the primary winding wires through the magnetic field generates a current in the winding. This current builds up the magnetism in the armature core. This does not happen instantaneously, since as soon as the magnetism starts to grow it induces an opposing voltage in the primary winding. The magnetic field that is growing is, in effect, moving relatively to the wire of that winding and it is this that causes the slow build-up.

Eventually the magnetism is at a maximum and at this point the cam ring rocks the contact-breaker lever to separate the points and break the primary circuit. As the current is switched off, the magnetic field decays rapidly, thus moving the field very rapidly relative to the secondary

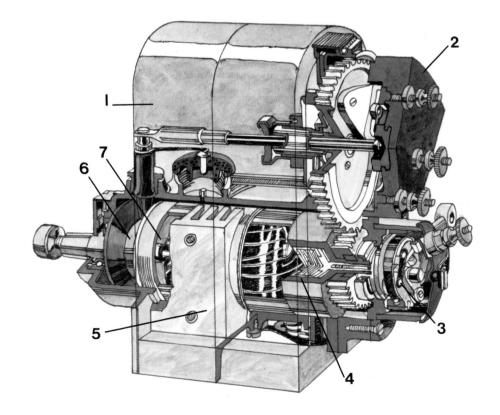

Far left: Low-tension ignition of the 1897 Maurer engine used a piston crown contact breaker.

Centre: Bosch K4 magneto of 1907 with electromagnetic sparking plugs.

Bosch model DU4 high tension magneto of 1908.

1 Magnets
2 Distributor
3 Contact breaker
4 Condenser
5 Magnet poles
6 Slipring
7 Armature

winding. The voltage produced by this relative movement is sufficient to break down the air insulation between the the sparking plug points and so cause a spark to "jump".

No voltage is built up in the secondary winding as the primary current and magnetic field increase, since the rate of increase is insufficient to give a voltage that will jump the gap and complete the secondary circuit.

When the current suddenly flows in the secondary winding, approximately 400 volts is induced in the primary winding. This is sufficient to produce a spark across the narrow gap of the breaker points as they open. This spark would have enough energy to erode, or burn, the points. This was discovered by a Frenchman, Fitzeau, when experimenting with an induction coil for other purposes. Fitzeau solved the problem by connecting a condenser across the breaker points.

The condenser stores electrical energy, rather as a spring stores mechanical energy, and pushes this unwanted voltage back from whence it came – in the reverse direction – when the points close again. This boosts the energy level, or voltage, in the primary winding.

During rotation of the armature through one revolution the magnetic field through the primary winding goes from minimum to maximum strength twice – once in each direction. This produces two peak primary voltages for every revolution and so, with a two-lobe breaker cam, two sparks. For a four-cylinder, four-stroke engine the magneto is driven at engine speed and for a six-cylinder engine at one and a half times engine speed.

TREMBLER COILS

Faraday's discovery of magnetic induction was followed by considerable development on the spark-producing coil. This culminated in 1851 with their production on a commercial basis by a French mechanic Ruhmkorff. Etienne Lenoir used such a coil on his 1860 gas engine when he initiated the electric ignition system and invented the sparking plug.

In the Ruhmkorff coil, the primary and secondary windings were wound on a bundle of soft iron wires in a

1919 Bosch ignition coil for a dual magneto/coil system and a coil for battery ignition only.

similar fashion to the laminated armature of the magneto. The primary coil was connected to a battery through a trembler or interrupter. This consisted of a thin spring-steel blade fixed to the coil casing at one end and having a piece of soft iron at the other. This was positioned opposite, and at a small distance from, the end of the coil core. A contact mid-way along the blade met an adjustable contact fixed to the coil casing.

When the current was switched on, it flowed through the contacts and the primary winding. This magnetized the core, attracted the soft iron to the blade and caused the contacts to open and switch off the current. With the current off, the magnetism ceased, the blade sprung back to close the contacts and the whole cycle started again. The whole thing was much the same as an electric bell and vibrated at the same kind of speed.

The continual change in the magnetism of the core induced a high voltage current in the secondary winding. This was high enough to send a steady stream of sparks across the points of a sparking plug as long as the battery was connected. By putting a camshaft-speed driven switch in the primary circuit the sparks could be timed to flow when, and only, as needed.

Lenoir used a rotary switch in the secondary circuit to time the sparks for his engine. This switch had an insulated arm driven by the engine and carrying a brass pad. The pad swept round a brass ring, connected to the live end of

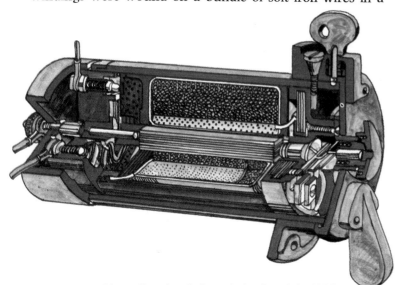

The neat trembler coil and switch made by Bosch in 1908.

the secondary winding, and round the inside of an insulated ring holding two further brass pads connected to the two sparking plugs. As these two pads were spaced at 180 degrees, the plugs fired alternately for each revolution of the arm.

A small gap was left between the moving pad, the ring and the stationary pads. The high voltage caused a spark to jump these gaps; this was a simpler way of switching the current than using rubbing contacts that could wear. This rotary H.T. switch was the first of the distributors which were used later in both H.T. magneto and induction coil ignition systems.

The trembler coil system, first fitted to the single cylinder Benz of 1896, became quite popular. It was used on the Model T Ford, where the four coils were mounted in a box on the dashboard for easy access to the tremblers. An innovation of the T was the production of the primary current from a flywheel generator comprising sixteen horseshoe-shaped permanent magnets. These were secured to the flywheel and radially positioned so that two north poles came together and two south poles came together.

A plate carrying sixteen pole pieces, with coils connected in series and wound in opposite directions to provide the necessary alternation of north and south poles, was fastened to the crank-case. The faces of the pole pieces were near the faces of the magnets. When the flywheel rotated, the lines of force from the magnets cut through the

coils on the plate and produced a low-tension current in the coils. This current was passed by a distributing switch, driven at camshaft speed, to the primary circuits of the four trembler coils.

The distributing switch was a wipe contact switch in which a rotating arm carried a lever, spring-loaded at one end to press a roller at the other end into contact with the interior of a ring of insulating material. This ring had four metal contacts on its inner surface and these were connected to the four coils. A method for adjusting the timing of the sparks in relation to the piston positions was devised by rotating the plate on which the insulated ring was mounted.

COIL IGNITION

While the European motor industry largely relied on the highly efficient magneto pioneered by Robert Bosch, the American industry favoured a battery and coil ignition that was part of a complete electrical system, including lighting and starting. For this C. F. Kettering, one of the founders of Delco, was largely responsible.

The modern coil is fundamentally the same as the early trembler coils (without the trembler contacts) and the H.T. magneto armature. It has a laminated iron core round which is wound the H.T. winding of 15,000 to 30,000 turns of fine wire. Outside this, and insulated from it, are a few hundred turns of much heavier wire which are made use of for the primary winding.

One end of the primary winding is connected to a terminal connected through the ignition switch to the battery. The other end of the primary is joined to one end of the secondary winding and to a terminal connected to the contact-breaker. The remaining wire from the H.T. winding leads to a cable insert in the insulating cap covering the coil and closing the top of the casing, which is filled with a sealing and insulating compound.

The contact-breaker consists of a lever pivoted at one end on an insulating bush and having a contact of tungsten, or other spark erosion resistant metal, at the other. A blade spring does the double duty of passing current from the coil to the contact and of urging an insulating rubbing block, midway of the lever, on to a cam. The cam is driven at engine camshaft speed and has as many lobes as the engine has cylinders. To keep the "dwell" time – the time the contacts are closed – as long as possible, six-cylinder and eight-cylinder engines sometimes use double breakers in a dual circuit.

The lever contact makes and breaks contact with another contact fixed to a plate carrying the breaker assembly. This plate is earthed and can be moved through a small rotational angle by a link attached to a spring-loaded diaphragm. This diaphragm is responsive to the suction in the engine manifold and is thus able to advance and retard the ignition timing. The contact-breaker is covered by an insulated cap that forms part of the H.T. distributor device and the condenser is clipped to the outside of the metal contact-breaker casing. The clip forms the earth connection and a wire from the other side of the condenser connects to the lever springs.

Bosch's first distributor made in 1910.

The drive from the engine ends in a support plate with two vertical pivots about which can swing a pair of flyweights. These weights are spring-loaded towards a yoke that has two pivots which engage slots in the weights. The yoke has an upwardly extending shaft which carries the cam and provides a drive for the rotating distributor arm. The movement of the flyweight under centrifugal force advances the ignition timing with increase of engine speed.

IGNITION TIMING

Since the early days, almost all the ingition systems have had some method of varying the time at which the spark occurs in relation to the position of the camshaft. This is essential for the efficient running of a variable speed engine.

Obviously the spark must begin the fuel burning process at a time in the cycle such that the maximum pressure of the exploding gas happens just as the piston starts down on the power stroke. If it is too early the pressure will resist the piston on the upward stroke and give a braking effect. On the other hand, if the full pressure is produced too late it will not act on the piston long enough for full power.

A short time elapses, about two thousandths of a second between the spark starting burning and the full combustion of the charge. This time is not dependent on engine speed as is the speed of the piston up and down the cylinder. Therefore the faster the engine is running the earlier the spark must begin ignition to allow sufficient time for the pressure build-up.

The early ignition systems were provided with a manual control to adjust the relative positions of the cam and the contact-breaker lever. With the trembler coil systems it was usual to rotate the plate carrying the contact-breaker, though sometimes it was the distributor casing that was moved. Magnetos, on the other hand, had a lever on the contact-breaker casing that rocked the cam ring.

Around 1930, the hand ignition timing control began to be replaced by an automatic system. In this, centrifugal weights were used to rotate the cam in relation to its driving shaft. This rotation changed the timing from around top dead centre at starting and idling, when piston speed was low, to full advance when the engine was approaching maximum speed.

Some H.T. magnetos were fitted with centrifugal advance devices in the drive to the magneto. Since coil ignition was taking the place of the magneto at this period, it was the coil contact-breaker and distributor on which centrifugal advance became universal.

A further refinement that came into common use some ten years later was the vacuum advance mechanism.

When an engine is operating under partial and low-load conditions – when the throttle is not fully open – the combustion chamber receives less mixture. As this charge has to fill the same space, it is rarefied and burns more slowly. Thus it is necessary for the ignition to be advanced under these conditions.

By using a diaphragm sensitive to the manifold suction

to move the contact-breaker base plate, or the whole breaker assembly, relative to the drive shaft the ignition can be advanced for low load conditions. As the load increases, the vacuum device tends to retard the ignition but is overruled and overtaken by the centrifugal advance mechanism.

To reduce atmospheric pollution, a recent innovation is the provision of a suction lead to the other side of the diaphragm to give a retarded ignition at idling and on over-run. This retarded timing causes the engine to run hotter and reduce the noxious emissions.

TRANSISTOR IGNITION

With increasing engine performance, the limits of the conventional coil ignition system were being reached, because the ignition energy and firing voltage are limited by the switching capabilities of the contact-breaker. The rapid development of semiconductor, transistor devices by Bardeen and Bratain of The Bell Telephone Company from 1947 onwards, provided a new means of switching primary currents of up to nine amps, about double that of the mechanical breaker.

A transistor is a solid state device, with no moving parts, which can be made to act as a relay to switch current in one direction by the application of a much smaller control current. By placing a transistor in the main primary circuit of the coil and using the conventional contact-breaker merely to switch the low control current, more electrical energy can be fed through the system. This is particularly so at high speeds. Moreover, wear on the contact-breaker

can be eliminated and the condenser across the points is no longer needed.

The transistor is very sensitive to electrical overloads and the circuit must therefore include resistors to limit the control current. Further transistors, a diode and a Zener diode, to limit the control and main currents to the main transistor must be provided. There must also be a resistor to limit the current when the circuit is switched on and the engine is not running. Finally, there must be a condenser across the primary circuit to protect against voltage fluctuations in the battery-dynamo supply.

In view of the low current needed to trigger the transistor, it becomes possible to exchange the mechanical contact-breaker, which has a tendency to bounce at high speeds, for a magnetic timer, which will produce a small induced current pulse four, six or eight times for each revolution. This small current is fed to an electronic pulse shaper and amplifier, which in turn renders the main transistor conductive at the appropriate time.

Another step in the progress of electronic ignition systems is the use of a condenser, in place of the magnetic core of a coil, in which to store the electrical energy as it builds up. This system uses a similar primary circuit to the transistorized coil, but this is used to trigger a thyristor, which is another form of transistor capable of handling several hundred volts and currents up to 100 amps. In this Capacitor Discharge Ignition system the induction coil is replaced by a transformer, the sole duty of which is to increase the spark voltage to the distributor. The C.D.I. can provide 40,000 sparks per minute without difficulty,

Ford Mk. I Mustang.

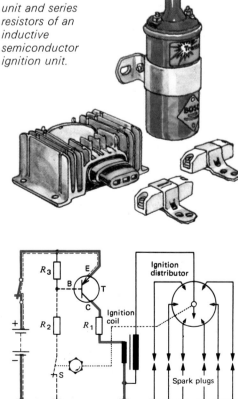

The coil, control unit and series resistors of an inductive semiconductor ignition unit.

about twice the number which begins to be the limit for a conventional contact-breaker and coil system.

SPARKING PLUGS

The first sparking plug made by Lenoir in 1860 had all the main features of a modern sparking plug. A hollow brass bolt, which screwed into the cylinder head, had cemented inside a porcelain core containing two platinum wires. One wire was fixed to the interior of the bolt and the other to a terminal at the top of the porcelain. the two wires projected from the business end with a small gap between them.

After this, scores of inventors battled with the problems of plugs. Insulation able to withstand some 20,000 volts was the major difficulty. Other problems included conducting away the heat generated by combustion from the points and nose, freedom from fouling by carbon and attack from fuel additives.

While porcelain was for long a favourite insulator, other

Only Bosch remains of the makers of these pre-1910 spark plugs.

ceramics, mica rings and even glass had their advocates. The modern insulators are usually from the aluminium-oxide family with silicon additives. Finely ground powder is pressed, then fired in high-temperature furnaces and finally the exterior is glazed.

These materials are much harder than porcelain and have better heat resisting and conducting characteristics. This is obviously necessary because the tip is exposed to, and can be working at, temperatures as high as 850 degrees Centigrade or approximately ryed heat. If the insulator tip and/or the electrodes become incandescent, the engine reverts to the hot-tube type of ignition and the gas is ignited by the plug irrespective of the spark. This is called pre-ignition and can damage the engine.

By increasing the size of the insulator tip to enable more

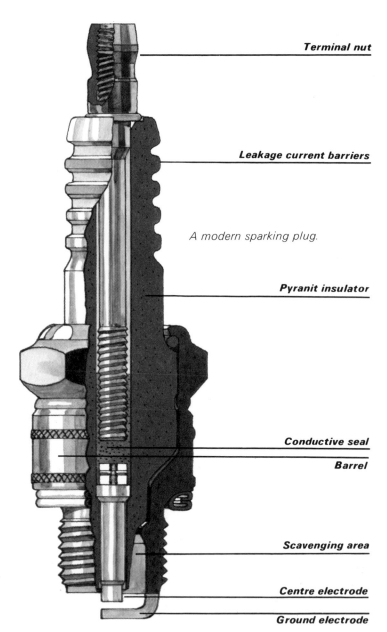

A modern sparking plug.

Terminal nut

Leakage current barriers

Pyranit insulator

Conductive seal

Barrel

Scavenging area

Centre electrode

Ground electrode

heat to be carried away, the area between the tip and the body interior, called the scavenge area, decreases and the plug becomes much more susceptible to carbon and oil fouling. This fouling provides a parallel path for the spark current and, since its resistance is lower, the current takes the easier way out.

Plugs are therefore matched to the engines to reach the best compromise of clean running and heat resistance at full power. Similar problems of conductivity and chemical erosion beset the electrodes. The solution calls for relatively inert precious metals such as silver and platinum, which are expensive. Since they resist chemical attack and have very good heat conducting properties, they can be made much thinner than the nickel-chrome alloys, which are more often used.

The shape of the electrodes at the gap is yet another compromise. Hundreds of different shapes have been tried over the years. The main argument has been between putting the gap up inside the body, where it was shielded

In the lead-acid accumulator the dark brown positive plates are held apart from the blue negative plates by plastics separators.

from the heat and, to some extent, from the mixture, and exposing the gap in the hope that the electrodes could deal with the heat. The standard plug, with modern materials, opts for the latter and has the earthed point at the side of the central electrode.

BATTERIES

With the coil ignition system, a battery is needed as a source of electrical energy. Early batteries generated electricity by chemical means. When the chemicals became exhausted, the battery was useless because the process could not be reversed. The other form of battery was an accumulator. This could be charged with electricity, which it could store until required. When the accumulator was discharged, it could be recharged, originally by a separate dynamo in the garage and later by a dynamo driven by the car engine.

By far the most common batteries are accumulators of the lead acid type. These have interleaved lead grids, alternately connected to the positive and negative terminal

posts, immersed in dilute sulphuric acid. The positive plate of a charged accumulator has its grids filled with lead peroxide and the negative plate with spongy lead.

As the battery discharges, the peroxide changes to lead sulphate, having taken some of the sulphur from the acid, and the same change affects the spongy lead plate. When both plates are the same and all the sulphur has gone from the acid, leaving only water, the battery cannot produce any more current. By applying a charging current across the terminals the chemical action can be reversed.

Recent developments in batteries have been directed to the use of better materials for the plates and the separators between the plates, and also to improvements in the design of the separators. The latter is a mechanical problem, since on heavy charge or discharge the heat generated tends to buckle the plates and could, but for the separators, make them touch and short-circuit. Further, when the sulphate is formed it has a greater volume than the peroxide it replaces and tends to crack, then fall off the plate and short-circuit the plates which are at the bottom of the cell.

The separators are, therefore, made of thin wood or of porous artificial rubber. When an accumulator is fully charged continued charging breaks up the water into hydrogen and oxygen, which bubble off as gas, so that vent plugs must be provided in each cell. This gassing reduces the volume of the electrolyte and the plugs provide access for replenishing the pure water which is lost. Since each cell has a voltage limitation of about 2·2volts, it is necessary to link three or six cells together in series to obtain six or twelve volts respectively.

DYNAMOS

The dynamo which provides the battery-charging current and in most cases now powers the entire electrical system (while the battery exists for starting, stand-by and make-up current) produces its current in the same way as the primary winding of the magneto. A cylindrical armature of thin, soft-iron laminations with longitudinal slots, carries a number of coils of wire in different diameteral planes and is rotated between the poles of a magnet.

As each coil passes through the magnetic field a current is generated in the wire. Since each wire cuts the field in opposite directions each half a revolution, the voltage generated in the wire rises from zero to a maximum then falls past zero to an equal minimum and goes back to zero at the end of the revolution. In other words, an alternating current is produced.

Since a unidirectional, or direct, current is essential for battery charging, a device known as a commutator is included in the circuit. This consists of a metal ring divided into segments and fixed to the armature spindle. The ends of the coils are connected to diametrically opposite segments. Two spring-loaded carbon brushes press on the segments to collect the current and, as these are also diametrically opposed, the current flows alternately to one brush and then to the other.

By this means the positive voltage is always fed to one brush and the negative to the other, and a direct, although fluctuating, current is produced. The use of a number of coils on the armature, all generating one after the other, provides a rippling voltage, of which the average voltage is that required.

Originally, as in the magneto, the magnets for the field were permanent magnets. The use of an electromagnet fed by the dynamo itself provides a much stronger field. This means a smaller dynamo can be used and the current can be governed or controlled. The best way to connect the field winding is in parallel, or shunt, across the brushes.

VOLTAGE REGULATION

As the voltage produced by the dynamo is proportional to the armature speed, and as dynamos are dependent on engine speed, some means must be provided to reduce the field current as the speed increases. This is necessary to stabilize the voltage.

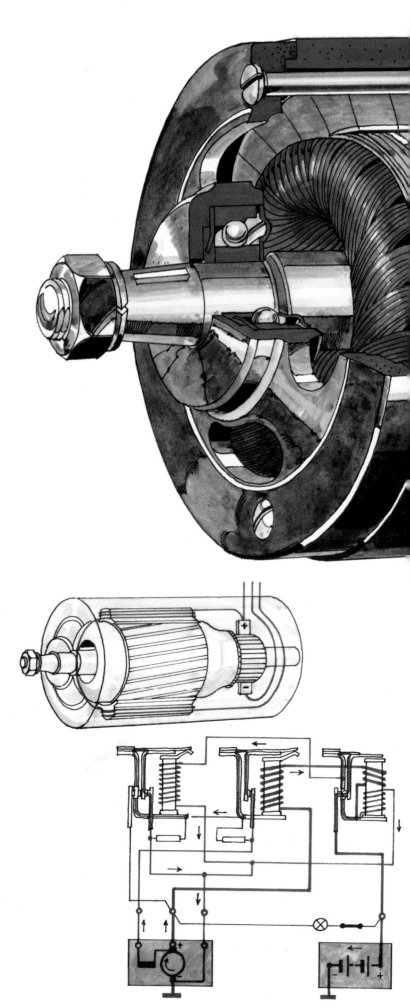

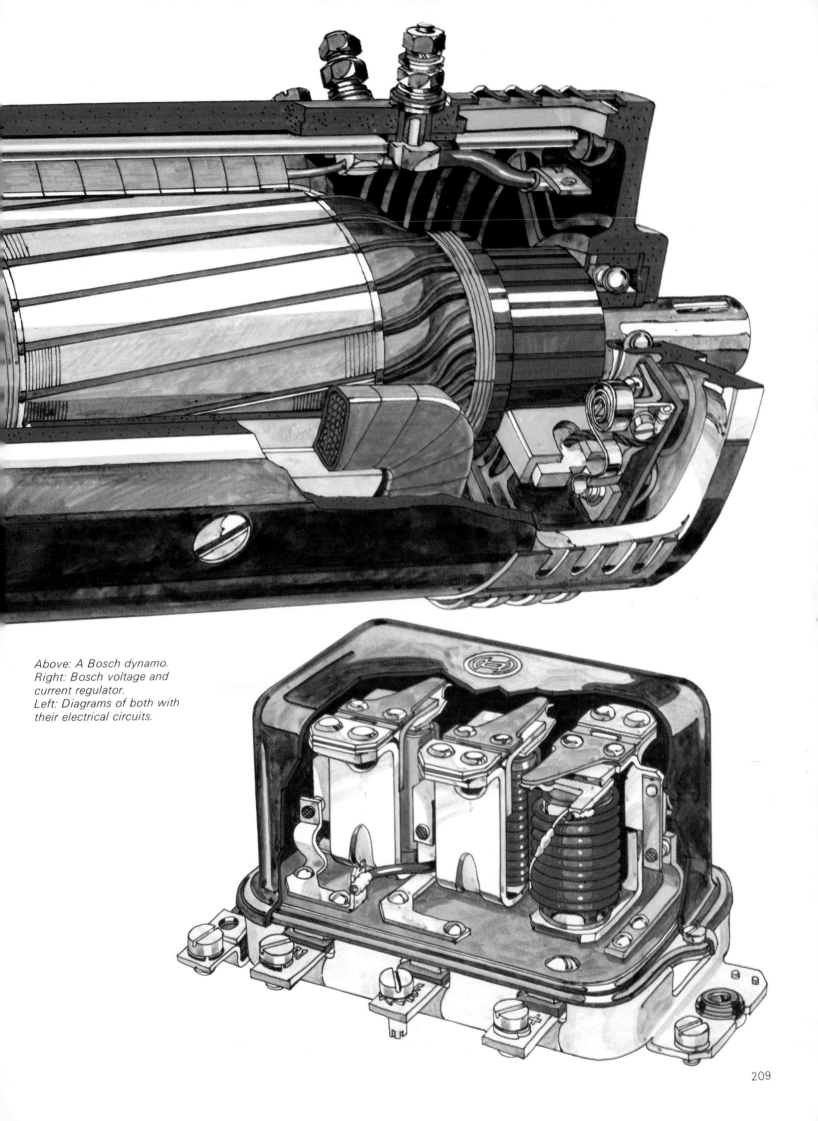

Above: A Bosch dynamo.
Right: Bosch voltage and current regulator.
Left: Diagrams of both with their electrical circuits.

Early dynamo drives tried to provide constant armature speed by mechanical means. Later, an automatic method, the third brush, credited to H. Leitner and R. H. Lucas in 1905, came into favour and was used on the Delco system. This regulating device made use of the tendency of the armature to drag the magnetic field round with it to a degree related to armature speed.

By connecting the field between one main brush and a third brush collecting current from coils passing one side of the magnetic pole, the current collected for the field falls as armature speed drags the field away from that pole. The snag with this third brush system is that, if the battery becomes disconnected, the field current rises high enough to burn out the field winding.

At the lower end of the speed range the problem is reversed, in that the battery voltage is higher than that of the dynamo. If it were not for a low voltage cut-out, the battery would try to make the dynamo rotate the engine. The cut-out is an electro-magnetic switch which has a series winding of thick wire and a shunt winding of thin wire round a soft-iron core.

The shunt winding is connected across the dynamo output. When the voltage generated exceeds a predetermined value – that is just above the battery voltage – the core attracts a movable contact to complete the circuit passing the dynamo output to the battery. Since the series winding is in this circuit, its magnetic force adds to that attracting the contact.

If the dynamo voltage drops below the voltage of the battery, the current in the series coil reverses to destroy the magnetic attraction and the contacts spring open and disconnect the battery. The cut-out was known long before its use in cars. It was essential for the charging plants used in garages and for domestic use before the coming of mains electricity.

From 1912 onwards, Ward-Leonard and Tirrill developed voltage regulation systems for use with power station generators, which in those days were often D.C. generators with great banks of accumulators for ballast and off-peak service. This work led to the constant-voltage regulator, in which a resistance is connected in series with the shunt winding to reduce the field voltage.

The resistance is short-circuited by spring contacts, opened by an electromagnet energized by the voltage across the field winding. As the field voltage (and, therefore, the field strength) rises, the resistance is switched into the circuit to reduce the field strength and so maintain a substantially constant dynamo output voltage. This has no effect on the quantity of current or amps flowing, so the generator output can vary considerably according to the demand of, for example, a flat or a fully charged battery.

Physically, the cut-out and the constant voltage regulator were combined as one control unit, although electrically they were separate. At the same time a second winding was added to the shunt winding of the voltage regulator. The second winding, in series with the battery and the ignition and other services, aided the shunt winding to reduce the dynamo voltage to limit the current output to a safe level. This was known as a compensated voltage control.

Later the function of the current regulator was removed from the voltage regulator, and a separate current regulator, electro-magnet and contact points, were fitted alongside the other two control units.

ALTERNATORS

As cars acquired more ancillary electrical equipment and demanded greater currents to power heaters, radios, and other such extras, two disadvantages of the dynamo became more apparent.

The first is the inability to generate sufficient current at low speeds to deal with equipment in use at slow traffic speeds. The second is that since the whole of the generated current has to flow through the rotating armature

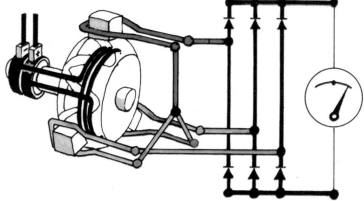

The first Bosch dynamo of 1906 had the commutator inside the permanent magnet and a contact breaker on the shaft end.

windings and the commutator and brushes, there is a mechanical limitation on the conductor sizes large enough to carry the heavier currents.

The use of an alternating current generator — an alternator — enables both of these drawbacks to be overcome providing some device is used to convert the alternating current to direct current. One such device is a rectifier that allows current to go in one direction only.

Selenium rectifiers have been in use for a long time in radios, home battery chargers and motor cycle electrical systems. Rectifiers of this type — capable of dealing with the much heavier currents needed in car electrical systems — would be too large to be easily accommodated.

However, just as the transistor changed the old concepts of ignition, so in its function of passing current in one direction only it has also made a change in the electrical generating circuit.

The transistor used is a semiconductor diode, which consists of a very thin wafer of silicon soldered to a copper plate and pressed into contact with another copper conductor which forms the casing. The whole is sealed into the casing by a glass seal. The entire device is no larger than an average-sized button.

These diodes have further advantages in that they do not begin to conduct, in their one direction, until about 0·6 volts are applied, and they can be manufactured to pass current either from positive to negative or vice versa.

The alternator can be loosely regarded as a dynamo constructed inside out. The driven rotor is the magnet and consists of two discs each having six axial claws that interengage. Between the clawed discs is an exciter winding, fed with direct current through two slip rings on the rotor shaft, which makes the claws alternate north and south magnetic poles.

The stator, or casing, carries three windings on laminated cores. Single ends from each winding are connected to-

A Bosch alternator with interdigitating poles on the rotor and a cooling fan behind the pulley. The diagram on the left shows how the three phases are connected and how D.C. is supplied for rotor excitation.

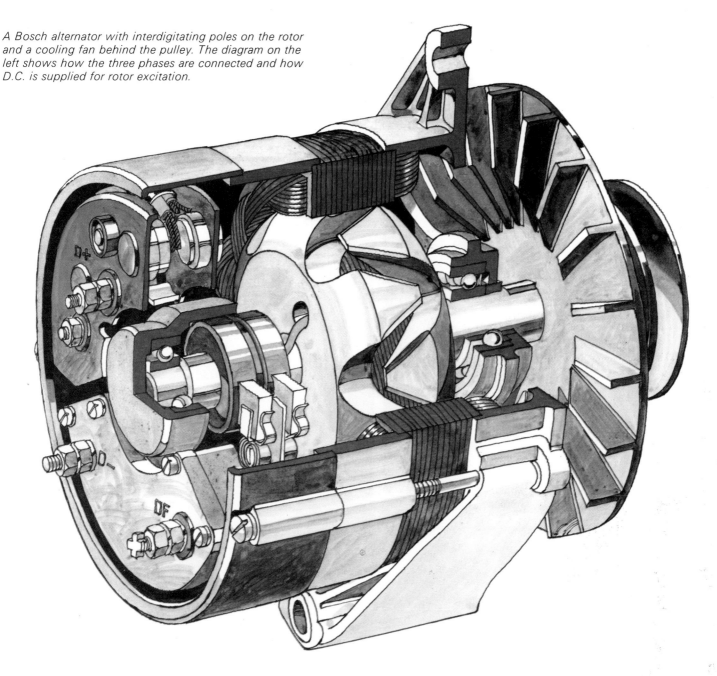

gether and the other three end wires lead to the rectifier circuit. Since the windings are equally spaced, they each produce an alternating voltage current with three peaks separated by 120 degrees or equal one-third time intervals. For example, a three-phase current has 36 half-waves for each revolution of the rotor.

These three outputs are fed to three diodes which have positive flow and are connected to the positive line and three more which have a negative flow connected to the negative line (usually earth). A direct current, which once again has a slight ripple in its voltage is thus provided. This D.C. is fed to the exciter circuit and its regulator, as well as to the main circuit.

The control of an alternator circuit is much simpler than a dynamo. In the first place, the rectifiers will not allow the battery to try to drive the engine, as they will not pass a reversed current flow. Secondly, as the output is dependent solely on the speed and degree of magnetization of the rotor, output can be controlled by varying the current in the exciter winding.

To maintain the generated voltage constant, use is made of a type of transistor known as a Zener diode (suggested by Clarence Zener in a paper to the Royal Society in 1934) which suddenly becomes conductive once a predetermined voltage is reached. This voltage is used as the reference voltage in a transistor circuit which passes pulses of D.C. to the exciter winding.

By altering the duration of the pulses, to increase or decrease the excitation, a constant output voltage is maintained. Excitation at the beginning, when the engine is being started, is partially provided by the residual magnetism in the rotor claws and by the current through the ignition warning light and ignition switch.

When the alternator is stationary the current flows from the battery through the lamp to the winding. As the alternator speeds up, the charging current opposes the battery current and the sum of these two voltages across the lamp becomes too low for it to glow. Because the transistors and their connexions are small and do not have any moving parts, the whole of the control system can be encapsulated and it can then be mounted on, or actually in, the generator.

WIRING

From the pioneer days, when the electrical system had few components, to the present time with its multiplicity of ancillary equipment, the wiring has had to develop to keep pace with these requirements. Originally single wires,

helically coiled to combat vibration, stretched between screw terminals on the electrical devices. This was followed by wires, all separate but side by side, clipped at short intervals in straight lines to the chassis.

On more expensive cars, where a lead was required to pass through the chassis or a body panel, metal armoured leads had spring loaded contacts at the ends to screw into threaded tubes, riveted to the part through which they were required to pass.

As the complexity and production volume grew, a complete loom, or harness, was made by bundling all the pre-cut wires together and holding them in a woven fabric or rubber sleeve. At the same time the screw terminals began to give way to single plug and socket connectors soldered, and later crimped, to the wire ends.

In 1972, the loom, which tended to hide a lot of the colour coding of the wire insulation, was supplanted by welding plastics-insulated wires to a flat plastic strip which could be clipped along the bodywork and each lead separately inspected for faults, if necessary.

The maze of wiring that grew behind the instrument panel was reduced by Ford in the Cortina by the use of a printed circuit board. This board comprises a sheet of copper firmly secured to a sheet of insulation. The required circuit is printed on the copper in acid-resistant ink, and the remainder of the unprotected copper is etched away to give a flat, rigid, ready-wired circuit.

GAS LAMPS

As long as the motor car could travel little faster than a running man, the dim glimmer of horse carriage candle lamps was sufficient for the few journeys made at night.

These lamps gave way to oil lamps using a flat and, later, a circular wick dipping into a container of paraffin. The long use of such oil lamps on railways provided enough knowledge for them to remain alight despite the vibration and the forward speed of the car.

ACETYLENE LAMPS

The need for lights which actually lit the road ahead was next met by using acetylene, a hydrocarbon gas produced by the action of water on calcium carbide. In the earliest of these gas lamps the acetylene was generated by dropping water, drop by drop, on lumps of carbide. The rate of wetting was adjustable. If, as often happened, gas was generated faster than it was being burned, it bubbled through the water and escaped through a small hole in the generator top.

These generators were either mounted in the rear of the lamp body, as in the Blériot design of 1896, or clamped to the chassis, the burner being fed through a rubber tube — a system that enabled both front and rear lights to be run from one generator. The burners were of ceramic and provided two impinging gas streams, supplemented by air from a side entry to give a flat flame that did not form a carbon deposit on the burner jets.

A later generator was of the diving bell type, in which carbide was held in a container covered by a deep cap allowing water in an outer container to seep under the cap skirt. When the gas pressure rose, it prevented the water seepage and stopped generation.

In 1897, Claude and Hess discovered that compressed acetylene which is explosive, could be stored and handled safely when it was dissolved in acetone, which could hold

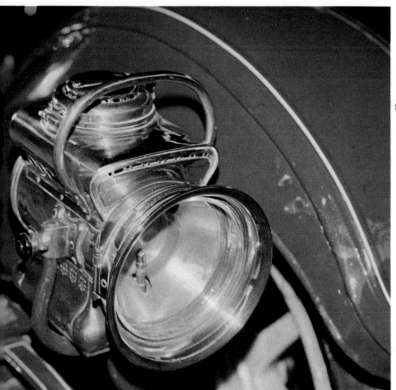

The 1960 Plymouth Valiant had four headlamps, two for main and two for dipped beams.

*Left: Horse-carriage-type candle lights of 1898. The long tube underneath held a spring to push the candle up and keep the flame in front of the reflector.
Centre: In 1901, railway practice was used in lamps where a wick dipped into oil.
Right: Acetylene gas, produced by dripping water onto calcium carbide, gave an intense white light in this 1914 lamp.*

many times its own volume of gas. By filling steel cylinders containing porous material, with the dissolved acetylene, a rechargeable source of clean gas became available.

Acetylene lamps were large and made of brass. They had to provide enough air passageways for both combustion air and the products of the flame and at the same time to keep cool. The hinged front cover usually had a plain glass. Round the inside of the lamp was a parabolic strip reflector, with a smaller mirror set behind the flame.

These lamps gave so good a light that oncoming drivers began to complain of dazzle from the parallel beams produced by the optical system. This was combated in several ways, one of which was the use of thin slats, blackened on top and silvered underneath, across the glass.

A rival to the acetylene lamp, with its replaceable gas cylinder, was the petrol-oxygen lamp. In this lamp, oxygen was passed through a mixing device containing petrol. The mixed inflammable gas was led to a burner, where the flame impinged on a thorium oxide disc, which incandesced to give a brilliant light source.

TUNGSTEN FILAMENT LAMPS

By this time, around 1910, the electric light bulb using robust tungsten filaments in place of the original delicate carbon filament, was at last capable of withstanding the vibrations of the car and road surfaces. The electric bulb could fairly easily be substituted for the oil or gas burner in existing lamps, and a number of these conversion sets became available.

Most of these used four-volt bulbs and relied on rechargeable accumulators. Soon these were being charged on the vehicle by a dynamo, belt or chain driven from some convenient part of the engine or transmission, such as the propeller shaft or the shaft which was between the gearbox and clutch.

The use of a single filament bulb enabled a much better design of reflector to be used, since there was no need to provide an escape path for hot gas. The parabolic reflector was brought right round the bulb and also formed the rear reflector.

For dipping the lamps to prevent dazzle, W. T. G. Fenson devised a mechanism in 1921 in which the lamps were mounted on hinges underneath. A lever operated by the driver could tilt the whole lamp downwards. This was overtaken by the pneumatic dip, where small pistons connected to swivelling reflectors moved under the influence of engine suction applied to cylinders inside the headlamp shells.

In 1924, A. Graves devised a bulb having two filaments, one of which was placed at the focus of the optical system to provide a long straight beam. The other was placed ahead of, or above, the first filament to provide an out-of-focus spread of light. The filaments had individual contacts

214

By 1913 electric lamps began to be fitted.

in the base of the bulb and could be switched alternately by a foot-operated dipping switch provided for the driver.

Five years later, W. H. Lund and W. C. Howard designed a headlamp which had an extra conical reflector above the bulb to produce a wide fan of light downwards to illuminate the immediate road surface. The lower part of the reflector gave a long beam with a flat top which would not upset an approaching driver.

About this time much more attention was given to the function of the glass. Many forms of partial lenses and prisms were used to control the spread of light and to intensify the beam in the required areas. By 1931, the double dipping system began to have a rival in the dip and switch system, where the nearside lamp reflector was swung down as the offside lamp was extinguished.

By the late 1930s, the optical system was responsible for most of the increased efficiency of lamps. To retain this efficiency, accurate focusing of the filaments and cleanliness of the reflector were essential.

A sealed beam unit was designed by the British Thompson-Houston Company in 1937 and later developed by the General Electric Company in America. This unit was, in effect, a large bulb, in which the filament was sealed into the back of a glass reflector and the front glass was sealed to the reflector rim, the whole being filled with an inert gas.

Although the sealed beam unit provides optimum light for its entire life, it suffers from high production costs and expensive replacement. Another design to give an accurate

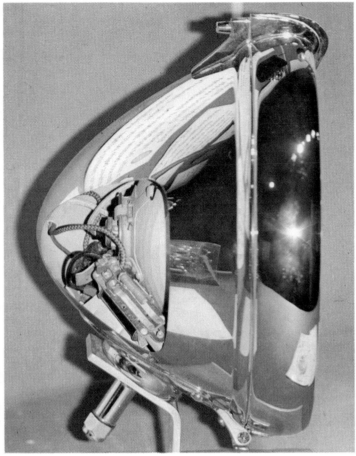

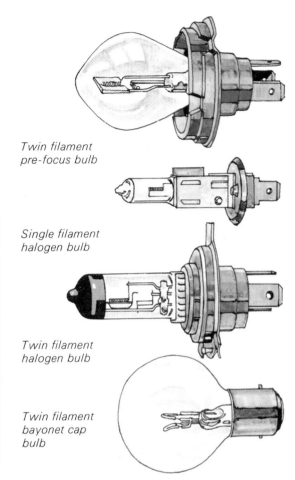

Twin filament pre-focus bulb

Single filament halogen bulb

Twin filament halogen bulb

Twin filament bayonet cap bulb

One method of dipping was to tilt the reflector by an electromagnet.

focus is the prefocus bulb, which has a radial flange on the cap, the flange being spring-held against an annular seating on the back of the reflector.

Another dipping arrangement pioneered by Cadillac and Lincoln in 1957 is the use of four headlamps, two for main long range beam and two for dipped beam, the pairs of lamps being switched alternately.

HALOGEN LAMPS

Although tungsten, of which filaments have been made for many years, has a melting temperature of 3,500 degrees Centigrade, it begins to vaporize when heated to some 2,300 degrees Centigrade in the vacuum that exists within a bulb. This reduces the thickness of the wire, and consequently its life, and causes blackening of the inside of the glass. By filling the bulb with an inert gas, such as argon, this temperature can be raised, since the vaporizing point rises under pressure and the gas conducts the heat away from the filament.

Gas-filled bulbs are nearly half as efficient again as vacuum bulbs and, since their working temperature is higher, they give a whiter light. In 1959, G.E.C. discovered that if the bulbs were filled with one of the halogens — bromine, chlorine, fluorine or iodine — the vaporizing tungsten formed a halide compound, which split under high temperature and deposited its tungsten on the filament.

By using this phenomenon, the operating temperature could be raised considerably and the light output about doubled for a given consumption of electricity. The raised temperature and the necessity of having the envelope near the filament were, however, sufficient to soften or melt the glass of the bulb. So an envelope of quartz, resistant to the higher temperatures, had to be used. These bulbs became known as quartz-iodine, or quartz-halogen bulbs, as iodine was the original halogen used.

Owing to the recycling nature of these bulbs, it is difficult to use two filaments within a single envelope. Their first use for main lights was restricted to cars with four headlamps, such systems being produced by Bosch in 1963 and Cibié in 1965. Three years later the same firm produced a single lamp with two separate quartz-halogen bulbs for two headlamp cars. The Bosch H4 headlamps have overcome the difficulties of twin filament halogen bulbs.

MOVING LAMPS

The long range beams and softer suspensions at this period highlighted the need for a method of keeping the beams parallel to the road, regardless of suspension movement or fore-and-aft tilting of the body with different loads.

Many devices to move the lamps in a vertical plane according to the mean deflection between the wheels and the chassis had been suggested. These included the mechanical linkwork of Kern in 1927; the pendulum tilted reflectors of Madsen in 1932, which could also be susceptible to gradient, acceleration and braking; the mechanical suspension-actuated device of Pierron in 1935 and the electrical axle-deflection sensing device of Bosch in 1955. In 1955, Citroën also offered the D series with self-levelling lamps controlled hydraulically from the self-levelling suspension.

Lamps which were secured to mudguards turned with the wheels and so enabled the drivers to see where they were going. The problem of turning body-mounted lights was solved by an Argentinian, W. Rae in 1917, by mounting the lamps on stalks and coupling them by linkwork to the steering drop arm, though W. S. Schuyler had thought of this eighteen years earlier. This idea reappeared in a much more advanced form in the Citroën Pallas of 1966 and again in the Citroën S.M., which was the first car to have halogen lights which were both self-levelling and also turned with the steering.

Simpler forms of levelling using manual levers are similar to the manual mechanical dipping systems of 50 or 60 years ago. Renault, on the 4L in 1961, provided a lever by the headlight to allow load compensation without movement of the primary beam position adjustment.

FUTURE LAMPS

One form of anti-dazzle which has not yet reached production is the Autosensor of Lucas, devised in 1964 to sense approaching lights and move a shutter across the lamp progressively to prevent light meeting the oncoming vehicle. Another is the use of polarized light. By passing light through a special light polarizing glass, all the light except that vibrating in one plane will be stopped. The use of headlamp glasses and windscreens which polarize light in planes relatively at right angles would eliminate dazzle. Unfortunately, such a system requires all vehicles to be so fitted with it to work. There is a loss of around 75 per cent of light through the polarizing glass, and toughened windscreen glass changes the plane of polarization so that with such screens the system becomes ineffective.

To overcome this great loss of light, Bosch have gone back to a nineteenth-century discovery by Brewster that when light is reflected from a polished surface of a transparent material at a particular angle, the reflected light is polarized and the remainder goes through the material.

By using very thin laminations of different materials as a multi-layer polarizer and a plane mirror to reflect the remaining light, Bosch have achieved a practical efficiency of 60 per cent. At the same time they have overcome the drawback of heat absorption in the filter. The use of polarizing screens on the windscreen has brought the use of polarized light to a possibility for future anti-dazzle.

The increase in motorway driving and higher front glass temperatures of halogen and other lamps has led to a greater build-up of mud on headlamp glasses. Two women, Eileen Smith in 1933 and Estelle Lake in 1965, saw the need for cleaning the lamp glasses, and in 1967 Bosch devised a system similar to windscreen wipers for clearing mud from the headlamps. Such a system was fitted to the Saab 99 in 1973.

Headlamp wipers on the Mercedes-Benz ESV of 1974.

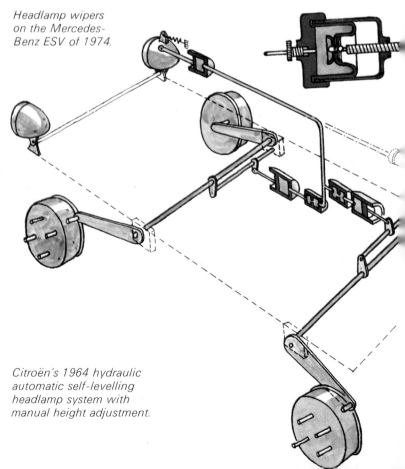

Citroën's 1964 hydraulic automatic self-levelling headlamp system with manual height adjustment.

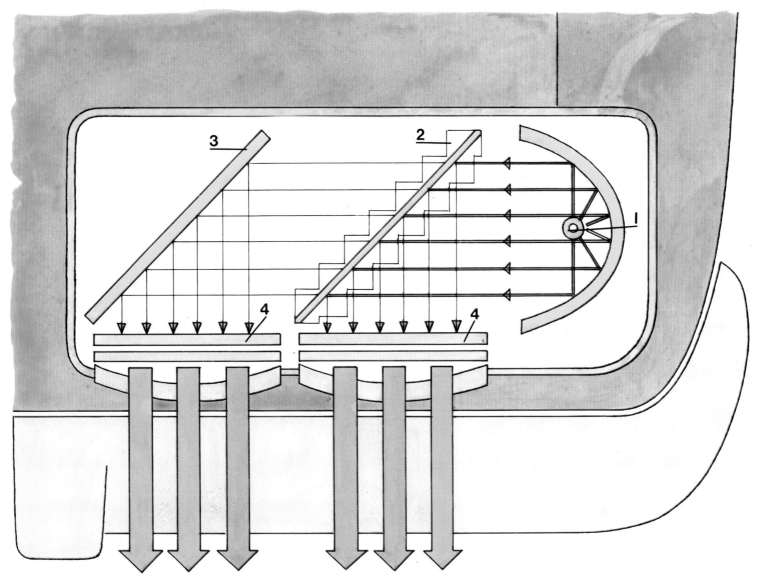

3

2

1

4   4

Bosch two-stage
polarization twin-
headlamp unit.
1 Light source
2 Multi-layer
   polarizing
   filter
3 Plane mirror
4 Polarizing
   filters

The lamps on the
Citroën SM moved with
the steering and were
self-levelling.

ANCILLARY EQUIPMENT – Helpful

As soon as the motor car became available to the general public, owners began to think of ancillary equipment that would make driving easier, journeying more comfortable or simply make one car look different from another.

Laws were soon passed that demanded the fitting of accessories, such as audible warning devices, speedometers, rear view mirrors, windscreen wipers and, later, signalling systems and passenger-protection equipment. Many of these were modifications of accessories that had already been used on other forms of transport.

Comfort was largely a matter of suspension, body and seating design, but it was not long before the cold winds of progress could be felt and otherwise unwanted exhaust heat from the engine was diverted to warm the passengers.

Of the remaining accessories, many became fashionable for short periods according to current taste, more were designed in an attempt to give an impression of speed to badly designed cars and some were even useful.

WARNING DEVICES

When the roads were traffic free as they were in the days of stage coaches, a long horn was used to warn innkeepers and passengers of the approach of the coach. This was a musical instrument that required skill on the part of the guard to produce a note at all. Although the horn disappeared with the coach, it left its name to be used by the motor car.

Most of the early powered vehicles gave warning of approach by bell and sometimes by whistle. In 1884 J. Riedel designed a bell mechanism operated by movement of the axle on application of the brakes. Other bells were sounded when the driver stamped on a foot button to swing weighted levers against the bell.

Five years later J. Ashton and A. Wormald produced a whistle, blown by air supplied by foot bellows. Others made whistles worked by diverting the exhaust gases into a short brass organ pipe. Some of these had multiple pipes that gave a chime reminiscent of the steam locomotive.

The most usual horn of the early days was the bulb horn dating back to 1871. This was nothing more than a musical instrument, in which a reed was made to vibrate a column of air produced by squeezing a rubber bulb. The frequency of the note was determined by the length and shape of the trumpet. These trumpets, which increased in cross-sectional area away from the reed, came in all shapes and sizes. The short ones gave high pitched squeaks and the long ones gave deep resonant notes. These long horns were sometimes ornate flexible brass tubes flowing along the curve of the front mudguard and ending in dragons heads, whose open mouths gave forth the sound. Others had their trumpets coiled round and round to confine the length into a smaller space.

The position of the horn bulb was the subject of much thought. In 1891 W. J. Chesterton placed his at the bottom of the whip socket. (It took a number of years for carriage builders to realize that the petrol engine did not need a

whip!) In 1894 E. Dickens clamped the bulb horn to the steering handlebar and in 1896 Fredrick Simms built a piston and cylinder into the vertical handle of the steering tiller. He also suggested the use of an electric switch in the handle and thus began the idea of steering wheel rim switches. Just what kind of warning device he intended to switch he did not disclose.

Although A. B. Woakes had thought of vibrating a diaphragm electrically in 1892, the invention of the electric horn is credited to Miller Reese Hutchinson of New York. In 1905 he designed a horn which had a flexible diaphragm vibrated by an electro-magnet. When the current was supplied to the magnet, its armature hit the centre of the diaphragm. At the same time contacts through which the magnetic current was flowing were opened to break the circuit. A spring returned the armature to close the contacts and so the diaphragm was vibrated at a high frequency. By providing a screw adjustment for the contacts, Hutchinson made his horn tuneable.

He also had two other ideas at this time. Firstly, the use of several diaphragm units feeding different frequency pulses of air into a common trumpet to produce either a

The millionth Bosch electric horn in section.

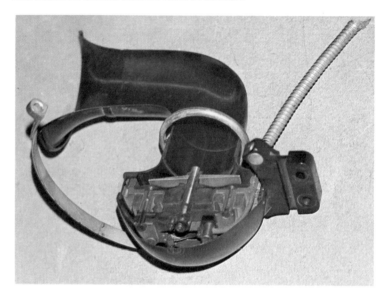

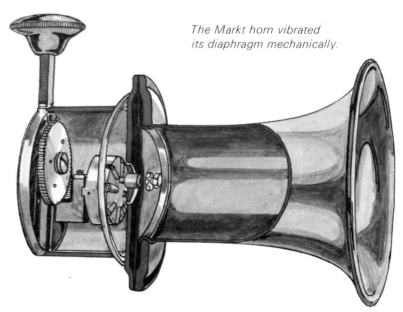

The Markt horn vibrated its diaphragm mechanically.

extras

chord or, by sequence switching, a succession of different notes. His second idea was the use of a fairly rigid diaphragm to give an "unpleasant" noise and make itself heard above any surrounding din.

A. N. Pierman and W. P. Phillips had ideas of vibrating a diaphragm by rotating a toothed wheel against a peg at the diaphragm centre in 1899. This toothed wheel was driven by contact with a bicycle tyre. Eight years later Hutchinson turned his attention to this type of mechanical vibrator and drove his toothed wheel by a flexible shaft in the same manner as the early speedometers. In 1909 he decided to use an electric motor for the drive. G. F. Long employed a rack and pinion to rotate the wheel when an external button was pressed manually.

This type of horn, in which a raucous noise was generated by the wheel and diaphragm, became known as a Klaxon, although the Klaxon Company of New Jersey and their designer John Ferreol Monnot of London did not appear on the scene until several years later. The word "klakson" became the French word for motor horn.

Bosch suggested the town and country horn in 1921, when they provided a damper, in the form of a choke, that

could be switched into the electrical circuit. Later versions of this theme had a rocking switch that sounded one or two horns depending on which way the switch dolly had been moved.

By 1922 the good mannered tones of the electric horn were not penetrating the sound barriers that appear to enclose the cabs of heavy lorries. To get the message through, Bosch devised a horn in which a rigid disc as well as a diaphragm was attached to the armature. The armature was arranged to hit against the magnet core at the end of the stroke. This caused the disc to vibrate at a high frequency that would penetrate into a noisy vehicle driving compartment.

Later electric horns combined the features of the diaphragm and the trumpet of the reed horn. This produced its more mellow tone by using the diaphragm as a reed to vibrate the air column in the tuned length of the trumpet. These were known as windtone horns and usually had a spiral passage above the diaphragm to increase the effective length of the air column.

The Sparks and Withington Company took Hutchinson's idea of separate notes and produced a tune playing

International Charette of 1901 with its long bulb horn.

instrument in 1929. This had an electric motor-driven air compressor feeding three or more different note horns. Valves opened by a camshaft, also driven by the motor, determined which note was to be played and its duration. These "Colonel Bogy" horns became popular again in the 1950s, with drivers if not pedestrians.

SPEEDOMETERS

The speedometer is concerned with two related variables, the distance travelled by the car and the speed at which the car is moving. The instrument that shows the first of these is correctly called an odometer but more usually known as the total, or trip, mileage recorder. The second is recorded by the speedometer, which is really a device indicating the speed of rotation of the wheels, or something in the transmission connected to them, calibrated in miles or kilometres per hour. Although both these readings come from one instrument, the two devices are only connected at the input end of the drive from the wheels.

The odometer is a very old device. It was first described by Vitruvius in the first century B.C. as a means of showing how far a taxi-chariot had travelled. Leonardo da Vinci had a similar idea around 1500. In this a disc was geared to one of the road wheels and had a series of holes near its edge. Each hole held a stone, which was kept in the hole in the disc by a stationary plate underneath. The plate had a hole in it so that as the two holes came together the stone fell into a box. The number of stones in the box showed the distance travelled.

The use of the odometer as a taxi meter continued and the design became more sophisticated, the gearing having dials, and later, drums that actually gave a reading, in miles or kilometres, of the distance covered. When fitted to motor vehicles the total distance that could be recorded rose to five figures. Usually a second, or trip set of figures was added to give a record of one journey. These figures could be reset to zero at will.

Early odometers had a series of dials on parallel axes, each dial being geared to turn at one tenth of the speed of the one before. The numbers on the dials appeared at windows in the face of the instrument. This system had two disadvantages. It was difficult to read the numbers since often they were either on their way into or out of a window. Secondly it was difficult to produce a mechanism that would let the numbers be zeroed for a trip mechanism.

The solution to these problems was the drum type recorder. In this the numbers 0 to 9 are engraved around the periphery of a drum having two sets of internal gear teeth. Usually there are six drums mounted together on a central spindle. The right hand part of the inside of the drum has twenty teeth and the left hand part has two teeth. The two-teeth gear is actually a twenty-tooth gear in which all but two adjacent teeth have been left out. When the drums are mounted on the spindle the two teeth of the right hand drum are next to the twenty teeth of the next drum on the left. These two sets of teeth engage a pinion

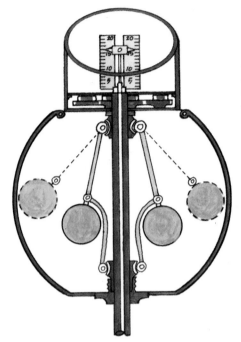

Prew's centrifugal speedometer of 1896 had a linear speed scale and total distance recording dials.

with five or six teeth (this number is not important) so that every time the right hand drum makes one revolution the two teeth will move the next left drum through one tenth of a revolution.

This results in the drum numbers appearing at the windows, without moving, for nine-tenths of a revolution. Moreover, by moving the spindles supporting the pinions backwards through one revolution, all the drums can be reset to zero if the gear teeth are designed to interlock in the reverse direction. Earlier methods of resetting the trip mechanism included winding all the drums backwards and using one-way clutches between the drums and their spindle.

The speed-measuring devices are of four main types, most of which are older than the motor car. Originally they were fitted to railway locomotives and not to road wheels — everybody knew how fast a horse could move. An early locomotive speedometer was designed by A. W. Forde in 1855 and was a modification of the centrifugal governor. Instead of connecting the governor to the throttle it was connected to a pointer that registered speed.

T. W. Harding and R. Willis thought of the second type in 1877. In this a fan produced a current of air that impinged on a blade wheel. The wheel could rotate against a spring and had a pointer on its spindle. As the fan rotated faster, the air current blew the wheel round farther against its spring and so indicated the speed.

Nine years later T. Horn used a similar system, but replaced the air by a magnetic field. A copper drum, driven by a drive shaft, rotated between stationary magnets and dragged a soft iron disc round by the magnetic eddy currents produced.

The third type is known as the chronometric since it depends on the indication of the number of revolutions that occur in a fixed time as determined by a clock

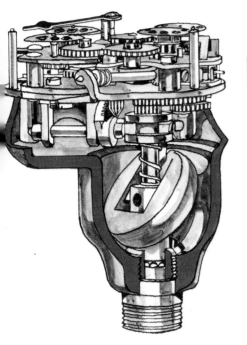

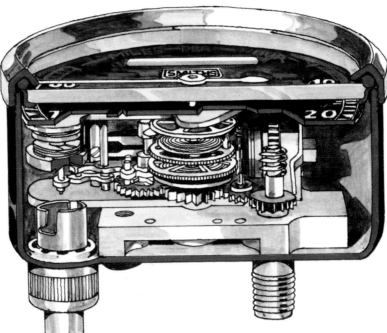

Left: The centrifugal Watford speedometer of 1919 had a circular weight on the driving shaft and both total distance and trip dials.

Right: The Smiths Chronometric speedometer measured the distance travelled in fixed time intervals.

mechanism. This system was suggested by M. J. R. Jacquemir, also in 1877.

An electrical generator was used for the fourth type. This was driven by the transmission and since the voltage of a dynamo is proportional to the speed at which it rotates, the indicating part of the speedometer was merely a specially calibrated voltmeter.

A Yorkshire schoolmaster, Edward Prew, designed a centrifugal-type speedometer for the motor car in 1896. In this a vertical shaft was driven from the front wheels and carried two pivoted arms with ball weights at their ends. As the balls swung outwards under centrifugal force, with increasing speed, they pulled up a ring loose on the shaft. This ring was connected, by an inward projection through a slot in the shaft, to a central rod. The rod had a pointer at its top, which gave the indication of the speed of the car on a vertical scale.

The shaft had gears at the top end to rotate four separate pointers that indicated the distance travelled in quarters, miles, and tens and hundreds of miles.

A better known speedometer, the Bowden of 1908, was designed by Charles Spratt and Francis Shenton. Their design used a horizontal paddle with balls in the spaces between the spokes. These balls ran round inside a saucer-shaped track so that the faster they ran the further up the curve of the dish they moved. This movement lifted a flat plate above the balls and rotated a pointer spindle through a rack and pinion gearing.

Albert Rutherford in 1909 used a ring mounted on pivots at right angles to the drive shaft. The ring swung against a spring so that, as speed increased, the diameter of the ring moved towards a perpendicular position to the shaft axis. In this – the forerunner of the Watford speedometer – a second, tell-tale, needle was fitted to show the maximum speed obtained. Also the mileage recorder was

driven by a pawl and ratchet mechanism so that numbers jumped into and out of their windows as every new unit was turned over.

One of the most popular speedometers of the early 1920s was the Stewart magnetic, invented by John K. Stewart of Chicago in 1910. The only moving part of this was a circular magnet driven by a flexible shaft from a front wheel or the propeller shaft. Fitted over the magnet, but not touching it, was an inverted aluminium cup on the rim of which was printed the figures indicating the car's speed. The cup was urged to a zero position by a spiral hair spring. As the magnet revolved there was a magnetic pull on the cup, which rotated against the spring to present the figure of the speed in a window in the instrument dial. Well over a million were made and, at the American factory alone, production was 2,000 a day.

Internal illumination of an eddy drum speedometer, for use in a car dashboard at night, was suggested by L. Casgrain in 1909.

In the chronometric speedometer designed by Leonard Cowey in 1904 a disc was rotated by a pawl mechanism intermittently against the force of a spring. The duration of the intermittent drive was proportional to the speed of the driving shaft and the speed at which the disc tried to move in the opposite direction was dependent on the stressing of the spring. These two motions would balance each other with the disc in a particular position for each speed, so by gearing a pointer to the disc spindle an indication of speed was given.

Other chronometric types used a watch-type escapement mechanism to couple a spring-returned pointer to the drive for a predetermined and fixed time interval. The faster the drive, the further the pointer would travel in the fixed time. One snag with this mechanism was that the pointer used three intervals for each reading: one when it moved up to the speed indication, a second when it remained stationary so that it could be read and a third when it was returned to zero ready for the next movement.

In 1912 Bahne Bonniksen of Coventry overcame these troubles by using two pointers. These worked alternately to show the speed and while one was stationary, the other was driven forwards to the zero position. This provided a speed reading all the time and did away with the return spring and reverse motion of the pointer.

Later, in 1915, E. Jaeger of France introduced a chronometric with only one pointer. This was moved by two time-wheels to show the reading of each alternately. The pointer could be seen jerking from one speed to another, both up and down, at the intervals of the operation of the time wheels. The Jaeger design was produced by British Jaeger who, in 1927, became part of what is now Smiths Industries Limited, a firm that began making centrifugal speedometers in 1904.

Modern speedometers are mostly of the magnetic eddy current type and their message is shown either by a pointer or by a two coloured ribbon moving in a straight line past a row of figures, the junction between the colours, generally red and black, indicating the reading. The future will probably be a head-up display in front of the driver, a

system developed by Smiths in the early 1970s from the war time fighter aircraft gunsight.

REV. COUNTERS

The revolution or rev. counter owes its incorrect name to the days of the slow-speed, steam engines used for powering great factories and ships. In those days the actual number of revolutions was counted and, if necessary, timed with a clock. With the coming of high speed engines this was impracticable and instruments indicating engine speed in revolutions per minute were used. The correct name of these instruments is "tachometers".

The tachometer works on the same principle as the speedometer, except that the dial is graduated in revolutions per minute (r.p.m.) instead of miles, or kilometres, per hour. The chronometric movement is still used for a large number of instruments, but in recent years the electric impulse type has become more accurate and done away with the complication of flexible shaft drives.

With the coming of electronic circuits containing transistors it became possible to design instruments that would measure the frequency of the low-tension electrical impulses in the coil ignition circuit. The lead between the contact-breaker and coil is passed through an iron core on the back of the tachometer. The voltage in each pulse is sensed and amplified and the meter, which is actually a voltmeter, indicates the engine speed.

INSTRUMENT DRIVES

Except for the electrical speedometers and tachometers that need only wires, the drive has invariably been through flexible shafts. In these an outer casing of steel wire, often of rectangular section, is wound into a helix with its coils touching. Some outer casings had two wound layers of triangular or D-section wire to give a smooth inner surface and to keep the lubricant within. End fittings screwed on to the back of the instrument and the drive gearing.

The inner driving cable, or shaft, was a similar tightly coiled spring, forged to a square section at the ends to fit into square holes in the speedometer drive shaft and the driving gear. The Stewart drive had hardened steel links hooked together, which made for easy length adjustment and repair.

The drive was taken from either a front wheel or from the propeller shaft. In the former case a gear ring was clamped to the hub of the wheel spokes and drove a pinion that was either coupled to the flexible shaft or, in the better constructions, to a swivel joint. The pinion shaft carried a skew gear meshing with a second skew gear on a vertical shaft. On the bottom of the vertical shaft was a bevel gear in mesh with a second bevel on the drive shaft. When the wheel turned to steer the car, the upper part of the gear casing could pivot about the vertical axis and allow the skew and bevel gears to walk round each other without disturbing the drive.

The other form of drive from the propeller shaft relied on

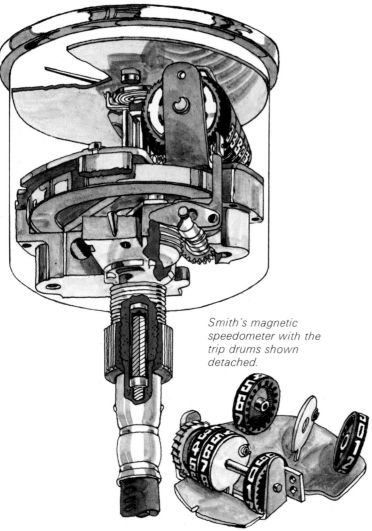

Smith's magnetic speedometer with the trip drums shown detached.

a split pulley that clamped round the shaft and drove a second pulley through a light belt. The second pulley was carried in an arm attached to the chassis and spring loaded to tension the belt. The drive was taken from the second pulley.

When the speedometer became a legal necessity instead of an optional extra, a drive shaft was added to the gearbox. This shaft had a gear that meshed with a gear on the output shaft of the gearbox. Usually the latter gear is now a skew gear and the speedometer drive comes off the gearbox at right angles to the gearbox centre line.

PRESSURE GAUGES

Once the lubrication system became pressurized, drivers began to be worried about the pressure of the oil in the system so pressure gauges or pressure indicators were fitted.

The indicators were simple devices comprising no more than a spring-loaded plunger, or diaphragm, that would move a tell-tale rod out from a hole when the pressure was sufficient to overcome the spring. The present oil pressure warning light operates in much the same way by a diaphragm closing a switch in the lamp circuit when the pressure is too low to hold the switch open.

Gauges that actually indicate the pressure are based on

the discovery that Eugène Bourdon of France made around 1840. He found that a circular arc of flattened tube would attempt to straighten out when pressure was applied inside. The paper roll that straightens out with a squeak when blown into on festive occasions works on just the same idea.

One end of the flattened tube is connected to an oil pressure pipe and the other, closed, end by linkwork to a pointer. As the pressure increases the tube tries to straighten and the pointer shows the pressure. Gauges of this kind can be used to show the pressure of coolant in a closed system or the suction in an inlet manifold.

To stop a loss of oil and a mess on the garage floor if a gauge or its pipeline should break, the engine oil pressure acts on a diaphragm, the other side of which acts on a servo fluid that fills the pressure gauge and its pipework.

TEMPERATURE GAUGES

The two most useful temperatures for the driver to know are those of the oil in the sump and the coolant in the radiator. The outside air temperature can tell the driver if there is a chance of ice on the road in near freezing conditions.

The temperatures of the oil and water were often taken by an adaptation of a common thermometer — the water

The 1909 Vauxhall speedometer drive.

Bourdon tube pressure gauge with sector and pinion movement.

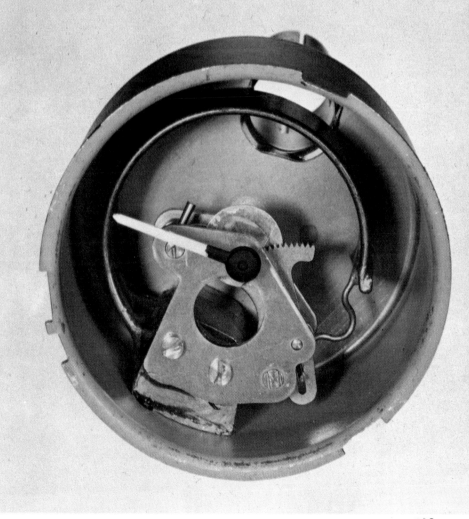

223

Water thermometer mounted in the radiator cap.

temperature being taken by a device mounted in the radiator filler cap which showed an ascending red line of coloured alcohol as the water temperature increased. A similar device was used for oil temperatures, with a long capillary tube leading from a thermometer bulb in the sump to a glass tube mounted in an instrument on the dash.

The expansion of liquids with a rise in temperature was also used to actuate a pointer moving over a calibrated circular scale. This was done by using the increasing pressure, caused by the expansion, to work a Bourdon tube pressure gauge. Again these could be mounted on the filler cap or on the dash.

These liquid, or vapour, pressure-sensitive instruments are still in use and have been joined by electric remote-reading thermometers. The electric instrument depends on the fact that most substances increase their electrical resistance as they get hotter. A tiny voltage stabilizer, which, through vibrating contacts, holds the voltage constant below the twelve volts of the battery, passes current through a heater coil surrounding a bimetallic strip in the instrument and through a sensitive pellet in the thermometer bulb. As the pellet resistance increases, less current passes and the coil cools. Since the two metals of the bimetallic strip expand at different rates, the strip bends to move the instrument pointer in accordance with the strip temperature.

FUEL GAUGES

Throughout the entire life of the motor car the quantity of fuel in the tank has always been a matter of concern. The oldest and most obvious, way of finding out how much petrol was in the tank was to take off the filler cap and look.

This was not always easy, particularly in poor light or when the cap was not too accessible; moreover the car had to be stationary. A dipstick, often with graduations for gallons, or litres, was more accurate than guess work but still had drawbacks, even if it was cheap. The dipstick was used on a lot of cars for a long time.

The next idea was borrowed, once again, from the days of steam and consisted of a glass tube, mounted outside the tank and connected at its bottom end to the bottom of the tank. The level of fuel in the tube indicated the quantity of fuel in the tank and providing that the top of the tube was left open, or vented back to the top of the tank, it worked well as long as the tank was in view of the driver. With scuttle-mounted fuel tanks the glass tube was fixed to the dash and piped to the tank.

Once the tank was positioned under the seat or at the back of the car, better devices were called for. In 1904 G. P. B. Smith thought of using a float on the end of a swinging arm. The rocking movement of the arm was translated into rotation of a pointer spindle. The pointer moved over a scale, mounted under glass, on the tank top or side to show the contents. Later the same year G. W. Gregory thought of using an Archimedes screw, rotated by a nut in the rising and falling float, in order to move the contents pointer.

To develop a remote reading gauge, thoughts turned to the glass tube type, but this time a slave fluid was used to measure the pressure at the bottom of the tank due to the

Smith's bimetallic strip water temperature gauge.

height of fuel above. The fluid was led to a tube on the dash, but since the dash was higher than the tank it was necessary to close the top of the tube and provide a partial vacuum above the fluid.

An alternative system was to lead a small bore tube from the bottom of the tank to one end of a syphon tube on the dash. The other end of the syphon dipped into coloured fluid. As the air pressure in the small tube rose it forced the fluid back round the syphon and the fluid level thus indicated the fuel content of the tank.

Another, and now common, system was to use the float to move a contact over a coil of resistance wire. Thus the resistance of the coil varied with the level of fuel and with a steady voltage through the coil the current in the circuit was proportioned to the fuel contents. This was easily indicated on an appropriately calibrated ammeter, or on a hot wire or bimetallic meter as used for temperature.

ELECTRICAL INSTRUMENTS

Drivers have always been worried over the functioning of the electrical system, particularly as a slowly discharging battery can bring a car to a halt on a dark night. With the increasing reliability and high current generating rates of modern alternator and transistor circuits, the worry has largely disappeared and so have the instruments that show the working of the system.

Two things were of importance. Firstly, the battery needed to be in a state of full charge and, secondly, the

dynamo had to be in command of the situation by providing slightly more current than was being used.

Battery charge is shown by the voltage across the terminals. Actually the voltmeter so installed was usually calibrated to show the state of the battery from discharged to charged, rather than the actual voltage in figures.

The other meter connected in the charging circuit was an ammeter that measured the current flowing. The car ammeter has its zero, or no current, marking in the centre. Movement to the left shows a discharge when current is being taken from the battery, and to the right a charge when the dynamo is charging at a rate higher than that at which the electrical components are trying to discharge the battery. This can be seen in older cars when at idling speed with the lights on there is a discharge. As the engine is speeded up, the dynamo begins to charge and the ammeter needle swings to the charge condition. If the battery is well charged the regulator will cut the charging rate down to provide a just positive balance. On the other hand if the battery is discharged, the charging rate will be much higher and fall off as the battery voltage builds up.

Both instruments are similar in construction and working. The main difference is that as the voltmeter is connected in parallel across the battery it has a very high resistance so that virtually no current flows through its windings. The ammeter is, on the other hand, connected in series with the charging circuit and has a very low resistance so that it does not produce a voltage drop.

Moving coil high resistance voltmeter movement.

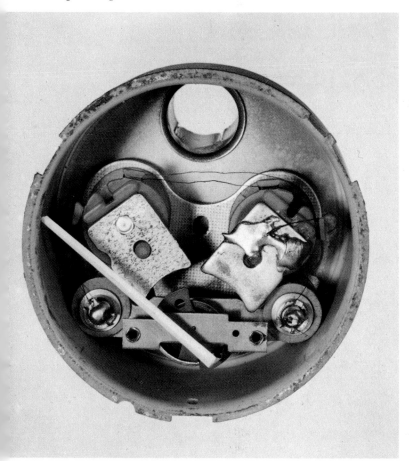

Smith's permanent magnet type ammeter has a low resistance.

The meter movement comprises a small permanent magnet and an electromagnet between which is pivoted a piece of soft iron attached to the needle. When a current flows through the magnet coil the soft iron is attracted away from the permanent magnet. The soft iron and needle find a point of balance between the two opposing magnetic forces, proportional to the strength of the current.

WARNING LIGHTS

The present day car has relatively few instruments because of the cost of installing them and the probable inability of the majority of drivers to benefit from the information the dials could give. Instead there are a series of warning lights that light up when the driver's attention needs to be drawn to a condition of some part of the car.

The ignition warning light is a universal fitment. It lights up to show that the ignition is switched on and then goes out as the dynamo, or alternator, takes over the ignition current supply from the battery. If the light comes on again when the engine is running, it shows the generator is not keeping pace with the needs of the ignition system, usually because the driving belt has broken or a wire become disconnected.

Other warning lights show a lack of, or low, oil pressure, low fuel level, headlamps on main beam and which side flashers are working. Some sophisticated systems have been developed that will show many more malfunctions such as low brake fluid level, worn brake pads, broken lamp filaments, high coolant temperatures and whether the seat belts are fastened. An early example of such warning lights was the low oil pressure warning on the 1926 Talbot.

MIRRORS

It was not long before the motorist, like the coach and cart drivers before him, wanted to know what was happening behind. In 1896 J. W. Cockerill produced a mirror mounted on a ball joint suitable for attachment to a vehicle. This gave the driver the opportunity to adjust the mirror to the position best suited to him, so that he could see what he wanted to in the rear.

Thereafter, except for improvements in mirror mountings, both for outside and inside use, and the use of convex parabolic mirrors for a wider view, there was little improvement in mirror design.

Mirrors that could be adjusted from the driving seat were suggested by Marcel Buyse of Brussels in 1932. He employed Bowden cables to move the externally mounted mirror and relied on friction between the inner and outer cables to hold the mirror adjusted. Several other people toyed with the idea in following years, but it was not until the 1960s that the idea turned into a production fitment. This followed the design of the Jervis Corporation of Michigan, in which the mirror was moved vertically by a push-pull movement and horizontally by turning the single adjusting knob.

By 1937, dazzle caused by the main beams from the lights of following cars began to be a problem. The first cure for this, apart from swinging the mirror out of the path of the light, was to use back-to-back mirrors that could be turned round. This scheme of Esca William Puckert, of Croydon, had a plain mirror on one side for day use and a darkened mirror on the other for night use. An alternative to this was a coloured transparent shield that hinged down in front of the day mirror.

The Libby-Owens-Ford Glass Company of Ohio had a better idea in 1943. Their mirror comprised of a piece of transparent material with two sides at a slight angle to each other. The front surface, nearest the driver, had a semi-transparent mirror film that would not reflect more than 30 per cent. of the light for night use. The rear surface was covered with a normal mirror coating for day use. By slight tilting of the mirror in its holder either surface could be made the one through which the view was obtained, while the reflection from the other surface passed above, or below, the driver's eyes.

Joseph Lucas Limited produced an automatic dipping mirror in 1963. A light-sensitive cell in the corner of the mirror was activated by a following bright light and

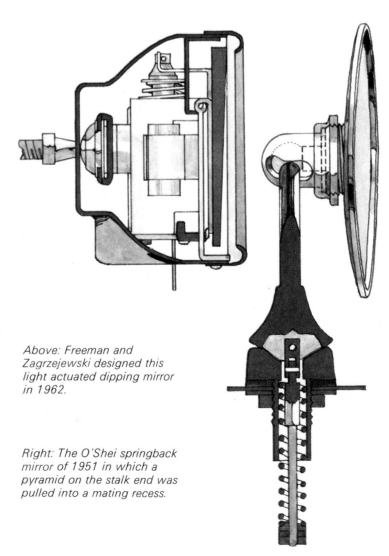

Above: Freeman and Zagrzejewski designed this light actuated dipping mirror in 1962.

Right: The O'Shei springback mirror of 1951 in which a pyramid on the stalk end was pulled into a mating recess.

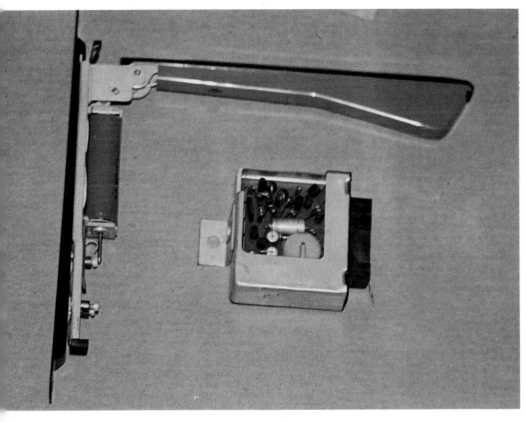

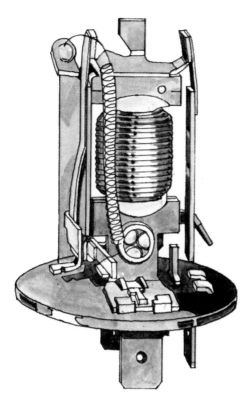

Semaphore type direction indicator and transistorized flasher unit.

triggered a solenoid to move the glass to the night driving position. This did not become popular and now the majority of interior mirrors have a manual dip mechanism.

One of the troubles of external mirrors, particularly when mounted out on the wings, was their vulnerability to blows putting them out of adjustment. William Edward O'Shei of America, a prolific inventor, particularly in the windscreen wiper field, who earlier spelt his name Oishei, had the idea of a spring-back mounting in 1951. By making the bottom end of the arm in the shape of a truncated pyramid and forming the base to a complementary shape, a strong vertical spring could allow the mirror arm to rotate to four positions and still locate itself accurately. A small movement merely made the arm rotate slightly and then spring back to its original position.

DIRECTION INDICATORS

Not only did drivers want to know what was happening behind, but they needed to tell following traffic just what they intended to do. As long ago as 1889 E. Martin thought of using a board mounted at the back of his vehicle. When he applied the brakes, flaps opened to reveal the word STOP on the board.

The mechanical brake signals continued to be suggested until the coming of four-wheel brakes and electrical systems. Then a switch was connected to a brake rod so that application of the brakes caused a red lamp at the rear to light. Later, with hydraulic brakes, the switch was made sensitive to the pressure in the brake line.

By 1893 J. B. Freeman added to the earlier idea by using a roller at the back. This roller was worked by a cord

to show STOP, LEFT and RIGHT. Other people followed with mechanical arms that swung out on the appropriate side of the car when the driver moved a control. By 1905 such semaphore signals had become pneumatically operated and self-cancelling to the design of F. Berger.

Three years later Alfredo Giansanti Barrachini, of Rome, used separate semaphore arms with internal illumination by electric bulbs. Although he originally operated the arms by cables, provision was made for raising them electrically.

An electric switch that cancelled the indicators when the steering wheel was moved to straight ahead after a turn was designed in 1916 by Herbert Faulkner. Two years after this the Naillik Motor Signal Company of Boston marketed a pair of translucent hands with internal lighting bulbs. These were raised by electric motors, whose armatures rotated through only one quarter of a revolution.

It was not until 1923 that a linear solenoid was employed by two Frenchmen Gustave Deneef and Maurice Boisson. They did not fit their bulb in the arm but in the stationary casing. Max Ruhl and Ernst Neumann of Berlin produced the linear solenoid and internal bulb type of semaphore in 1927. This was developed and used on very many cars until the coming of the flasher that Fiat fitted to the 1500 of 1935.

Before that a number of people had used flashing lights in the older semaphore and illuminated arrow types of indicators. H. G. Wheeler employed a motor-driven interrupter and the Winooski Electrical Manufacturing Company of Vermont preferred a pneumatic device worked from engine suction.

The thermal interrupter switch dates back to at least

1914, but was not thought of for car use until 1935 and then by the United Lens Corporation of Delaware. The next year Trico Products of New York fitted a thermal switch into a brake light circuit.

One form of thermal switch depends on the expansion of a tension wire when it is heated by the passage of current. Switching on a lamp sends current through the wire and through a ballast resistance to the lamp filament. This current is not sufficient to light the lamp, due to the resistance, but will heat the wire. As the wire expands it allows a clicker spring to move over and close contacts that pass current to the bulb and, at the same time, to short circuit the wire. The wire cools and the clicker spring opens the contacts to extinguish the light and start the sequence again.

In 1962 John Charlesworth Ridout and Frank Hill made a flasher circuit in which transistors were used to feed the solenoid of a relay. The following year saw the whole circuit was transistorised.

WINDSCREEN WIPERS

As soon as the windscreen appeared it was realized that rain would obstruct the view if the water drops were not wiped away. One of the earliest car wipers – they had been used on other transport before – were brushes on each side of the glass. J. H. Apjohn thought of this in 1903 and moved his wipers up and down the screen frame.

Pivoting in the top of the frame became the popular method of mounting hand-operated wipers, which soon changed their brushes into rubber strips that acted as "squeegees" over the flat glass. Using one hand to work the wiper was considered dangerous by Ormond Edgar Wall, an Hawaiian dentist, so in 1917 he mounted an electric motor on a stay in the middle of the screen and used a crank mechanism to oscillate a long rubber-edged blade about its centre. In doing this he not only set the pattern of a crank drive for the future, but also that of the multiblade wiper that cleared the passenger's side. The next multi-blade, having two parallel blades, was designed by Frank Stewart of Chicago in 1922. In 1924 Bosch began production of electric motor driven wipers.

Meanwhile William Mitchel Folberth, a Cleveland automobile mechanic, designed a wiper in 1920 powered by the suction in the inlet manifold. This suction wiper had a horizontal piston reciprocated by atmospheric pressure when first one end and then the other of the cylinder was connected to the suction. A trip valve mechanism changed the suction and atmospheric connections at the end of each stroke.

John R. Oishei of Buffalo hit a cyclist on a rainy night and soon after, in 1917, founded the Tri-Continental Corporation to manufacture wipers. Later the name was shortened to Trico, and Folberth was aquired by the company. By 1937 the vacuum motor was standard on American cars.

In the early twenties suction wipers worked on the same principle but had a semi-circular cylinder and a swinging

228

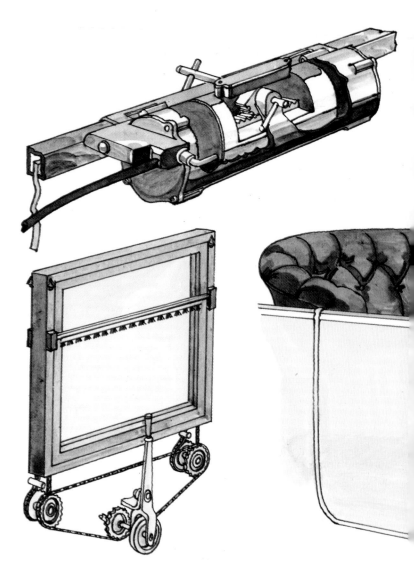

flap as the piston. This gave the partial rotation needed for the blade without the need for a rack and pinion gearing.

Although by 1932 two Australian inventors R. A. Powell and R. W. Newton had added a self-parking feature and four years later Lucas a multispeed control, the suction wiper was doomed. Its great fault was that, being dependent on engine suction, it would speed up when the car was slowing down and slow down when the car accelerated. This was somewhat mitigated by the use of a vacuum reservoir as used on the Ford Popular.

Although the electric wiper had been fitted with a self-parking mechanism by 1930, it was some years later before it acquired a variable speed circuit to deal with the conditions between a light drizzle and a heavy storm.

The coming of the curved windscreen posed problems for the designers of wiper blades since the curvature of the blade rubber had to change as the blade moved across the screen. Vauxhall produced a blade composed of a number of short blades in T-shaped holders, all pivoted to a main curved arm in 1933. The next year they were followed by Lucas who had a single curved blade in a flexible holder, connected to the wiper arm by a bridge pivoted to the ends of the holder. In 1944 Trico produced the whiffletree-type

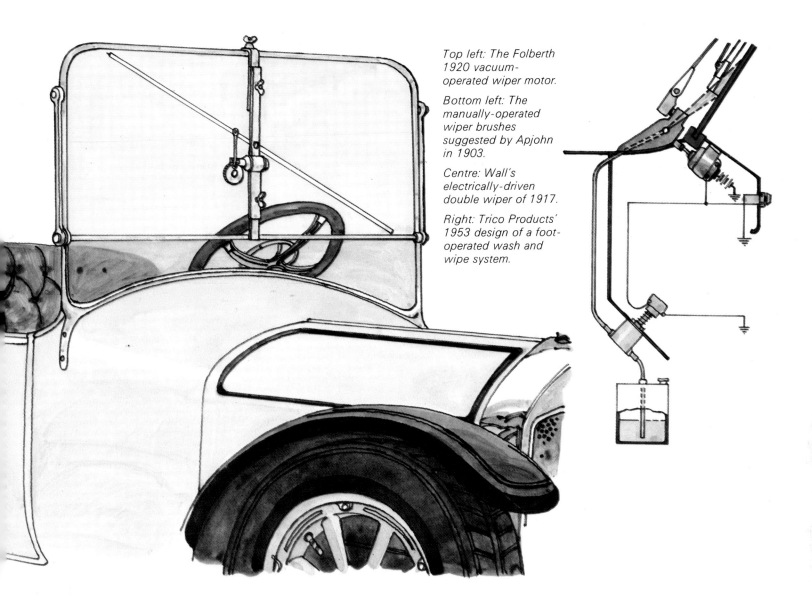

blade that used a flexible blade holder connected to a bridge member at points a third of the length from each end. Later blade holders had two or more curved levers for balanced pressure distribution following the Trico design of 1948.

WINDSCREEN WASHERS

Although several people had had ideas of keeping screens clean by continually spraying water on to the surface, collecting the water, filtering it and pumping it on again, it was not until 1930 that a washer was used with a wiper. In that year John Henry Derby of Rugby designed a simple manual pump that would spray water through a nozzle on to the area swept by the wiper blade.

Three years later Fenwick Hutton Hedley of Newcastle realized that the spray would be more effective if it moved with the blade. This idea lasted for nearly forty years.

Triumph fitted a manual screen washer in 1935 onto the Gloria Vitesse as standard equipment, and by 1936 Trico had produced a suction-actuated washer that sprayed at the touch of a button. Another button-operated washer that had an electric-motor-driven centrifugal pump submerged in the water container was made by Lucas in 1953. Volkswagen had the ingenious idea to use the

pressure in the spare tyre in order to work their washer.

The powered washers allowed Trico to design an automatic washer in 1953. This had a foot switch that worked both the washer and wiper together for a quick clean when mud from a vehicle in front dirtied the glass. A second switch provided the usual wiper action. Later variations of this by Fiat had timed washes and moved the control to a steering column stalk.

Early and late electric wiper motors and blade for curved windscreen.

HEATING AND VENTILATING

Supplying fresh air to the inside of a vehicle was no problem in the days of open cars nor, even, the earlier closed bodies with their poorly fitting doors and windows. Warming the interior was another matter.

Where there was no source of heat from the engine, as with the horse carriage, foot warmers supplied the comfort. Beginning with hot bricks wrapped in cloth and stone hot-water bottles, they evolved into portable solid-fuel burners. Even as late as the 1920s Clark foot warmers were being made. These had a metal casing covered with thick Brussels carpet and a drawer in the side to hold bricks of special coal. These bricks would last for about twelve hours.

As soon as there was some waste heat available from the engine cooling system or the exhaust, many people tried to deflect the heat to the passengers benefit. It is reported that this was done as early as 1897 in a Canstatt-Daimler. Since the radiator was under the seat it would not have been all that difficult to lead a hot water pipe across the rear of the toe board.

Although there was no dearth of ideas, and many were used on long distance coaches, it was a long time before a heating device became even an optional fitting. Most of the early designs ducted the radiator air into the closed body-

work and at times further assisted its progress with a fan.

By 1930 Albert Henry Bates of Illinois had thought of taking hot water from the cooling system to a radiator fitted in the car and circulating the warm air with an electric fan. The following year Clayton Dewandre of Lincoln produced a drum-shaped heater that could be fitted as an optional accessory. This had two coils of finned tubes carrying the hot water and an electric fan in the centre. Air was drawn in from slots in the periphery of the drum and blown out through flaps at the rear face. Moving the flaps controlled the direction and amount of air circulating in the body. This formed the pattern of recirculating air heaters that became popular in the early post Second World War era.

When Porsche designed the Mercedes-Benz 130H in 1933, he took the cylinder cooling air through the central tubular chassis backbone to controllable vents inside the body. The central duct was carried on to the front of the car and fitted with a throttling flap. By adjusting the flap the temperature and volume of air to the passengers could be varied. The fundamentals of this idea are still in use on some Volkswagen and Fiat cars.

To overcome the temperature changes in this system when the engine changed from idling to full power, the 1954 Dyna-Panhard and later Volkswagen and Porsche cars had separate petrol burning heaters. These were, in effect, enclosed blowlamps which had fans in order to

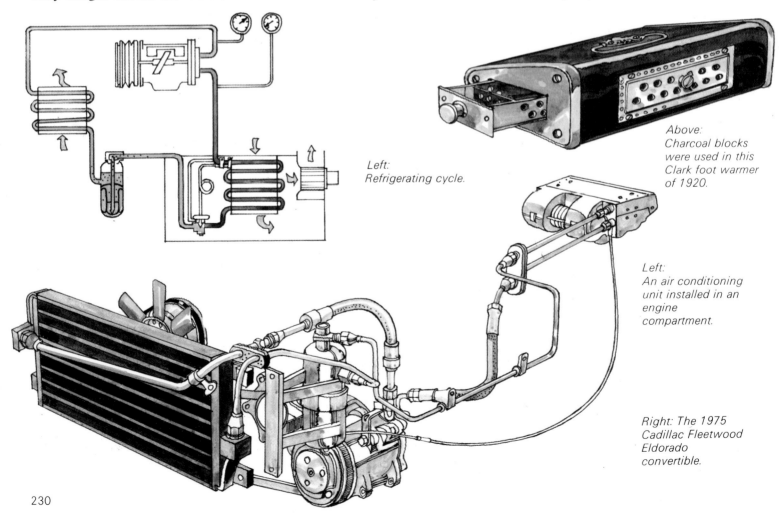

Left:
Refrigerating cycle.

Above:
Charcoal blocks were used in this Clark foot warmer of 1920.

Left:
An air conditioning unit installed in an engine compartment.

Right: The 1975 Cadillac Fleetwood Eldorado convertible.

direct the air through ducts to the interior of the car.

When the heater became a "designed-in" part of the modern car, with its radiator, or heat exchanger, and fan mounted in front of the dash, fresh air was obtained from outside the car. The need to take the air from a high point such as just in front of the screen, to stop blowing dangerous exhaust fumes into the car was soon realized. Further, with the heater ducts under the scuttle, it was obvious to make provision for windscreen de-misting and de-icing by diverting some or indeed all of the warm air in the way that Vauxhall did in 1954.

At this time the air pumped into the car was left to find its own way out, usually through the door seals. Humber provided a special vent in the lower pressure area at the base of the rear window in 1960. However, the pattern for the following years was set by Ford when the Cortina was presented in 1963 with the Aeroflow system.

In the Aeroflow a grill in the high pressure area at the base of the screen fed air to the heater and to two eye-ball vents at the ends of the fascia. These vents contained valves that controlled the volume of air and they could be swivelled to direct the flow to the front occupants faces or to the door windows. The heater air could be directed to the interior at foot level or the screen, or somewhere between them, and the temperature could be regulated by a valve in the water system. The pattern of the through flow of air, whether warm or cool, was ensured by non-return flap valves which were mounted in the rear quarters of the car.

Keeping the interior cool was, and still is, a problem in hot climates. William Whiteley in 1884 thought of placing trays of ice blocks in a box under a carriage body and using an axle driven fan to blow cold air where it was needed. Nash fitted their "Weather Eye" system of air conditioning in 1938.

This was, in effect, a small refrigerator in the ventilating air stream. Air conditioning gained momentum in America where temperatures were higher and greater use was made of the automobile.

The Delanair system installed in the XJ12 Jaguar provides full thermostat-controlled temperatures from cooling to warming. This control of the ventilating air flow from multiple vents for both front and rear passengers is maintained at the desired temperature irrespective of outside conditions. With such systems refrigerator gas, Freon, is compressed in an engine driven compressor and then cooled to liquid state in a separate condenser radiator. The liquid is expanded to gas again in an evaporator and in so doing extracts heat from the ventilating air being blown through the evaporator.

Before the introduction of heaters, windscreens were kept free from mist and ice by small electric heater elements mounted at the bottom of the glass. Eventually these gave way to heated glass which had filaments of gold foil that were actually buried within the glass.

CAR RADIO

As soon as wireless emerged from its amateur status in the late 1920s, receiving sets were mounted in cars. These were not a great success since the equipment was bulky and suffered from valves that picked up the vibrations of the car like microphones. These valves were later supplemented by ones which had indirectly heated cathodes and were mounted in anti-vibration holders.

A Blaupunkt portable radio was fitted in a Ford Köln making a journey across the Sahara Desert and this revealed a number of drawbacks. From this knowledge Blaupunkt developed the A.S.5 radio, which was first fitted in a Studebaker in 1932. Enclosed in a metal box of some ten litres (2·2 cubic feet) volume, compared with the present 0·8 litres (0·18 cubic feet), this five valve set had a remote control unit. The control unit for tuning and switching was clamped on the steering column and operated the radio through flexible shafts similar to speedometer cables.

Meanwhile Motorola in America had been producing radios since 1928 and held much the same advanced position in America that Blaupunkt had in Europe. Motorola introduced the use of a vibrator and transformer for the H.T. supply in 1932 and followed this with a cold cathode re-rectifier valve the same year.

Wireless became an optional extra in Crossley in 1933, Hillman in 1934 and the Triumph Dolomite in 1937. To avoid the shielding of the metal bodies the aerials were mounted under the wooden running boards between the mudguards. This was standard in the 1500 Fiat of 1935.

After the Second World War, car radios benefited from the knowledge gained in the previous years and they appeared as three connected units. The tuning stage was mounted in the dash panel, or just underneath, the power stage was fitted under the bonnet or above the passenger's foot well, and the loudspeaker either under the fascia or behind the rear seats. All these sets were amplitude modulated and used medium and long wave bands.

By 1952 Germany had the first reasonably full coverage of its area with FM (frequency modulation), and consequently Blaupunkt was able to offer the first FM car radio in that year. To save the driver the distraction of manual station selection by using a rotating knob, Blaupunkt and Motorola introduced push-button tuning. At first this was done by an electromagnet attracting a tuning carriage that moved in a straight path. The speed of the carriage was regulated by a rotating wind vane governor, similar to the folliot of early clocks. When a selection button was pressed the carriage moved from one end as far as the button. This mechanism was relatively heavy and when a spring returned the carriage to its starting point the "clunk" could be felt in the car.

Later push-button radios had an interlocking bar mechanism that released all the other buttons and allowed the depressed button to connect a tuned circuit to the detector stage. This was an improvement on the 1954

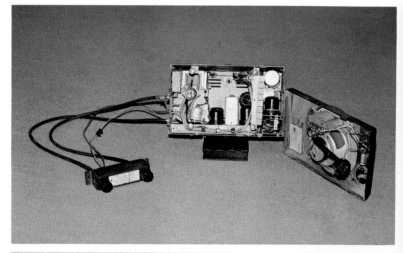

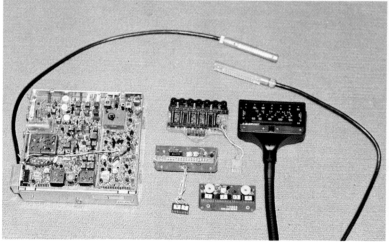

Blaupunkt electric motor drive for the tuner, the desired station impulse triggering an electro-magnetic stop.

By 1968 the Blaupunkt Coburg model was fitted with an electronic self seeker circuit that automatically tuned, and kept tuned, the set to the desired frequency by gauging that station's signal strength.

1957 saw the first semi-conductor radio on the market, but this soon disappeared when it was found that car motion generated static electricity and driving near transmitters put the point-contact transistors out of action. Another difficulty was that of getting early transistors to work at radio frequencies. This led to the use of valves in the radio-frequency input stages and transistors in the lower audio-frequency output stages. The first fully transistorized receiver was marketed by Blaupunkt in 1961.

Stereo radio, originated in America by Motorola, was the logical follower to the use of stereo tape and disc players.

The latest Berlin radio has gone back to the early days by having a remote control unit mounted on a flexible stalk so that it may be positioned near the steering wheel rim. This control unit has touch-sensitive buttons to select one long, two medium, one short wave and two FM stations and a further button for Automobile Road Information (ARI). When ARI is engaged, the radio will automatically relay road information from the nearest and therefore, most appropriate local station irrespective of the

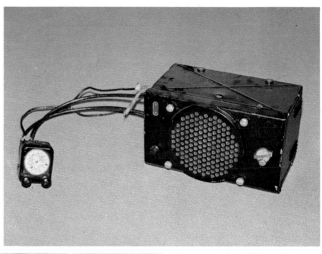

Far left, top:
In 1935 the Blaupunkt radio used massive components cased in a stout steel box that also held the speaker.

Far left, bottom:
The Berlin radio of 1974 is a mass of tiny components connected to a control head on a flexible stalk.

Left: The modern radio and cassette player occupies only a small volume compared to the bulk of 1935.

Blaupunkt's 1932 radio was tuned through a flexible shaft from a dial on the steering column.

Frequency modulation for car radios was introduced by Blaupunkt in this 1952 set.

programme that has been otherwise selected. It can also record such information on the cassette unit if the car is left unattended. It has touch controls for volume and tone and illumination of station seeking is arranged by light-emitting diodes.

Another feature introduced in 1974 was the Automatic Interference Limiter (AIL). In this the peaks of spurious signals produced by unsuppressed electric motors and neon signs are sensed, reversed and fed back to the system so that the high level noises are cancelled out.

RECORDED MUSIC

Not content with the programmes relayed by radio stations, the American public began to demand their own choice of recorded music by the mid-1950s. Helped by the introduction of the extended play (45 r.p.m.) and long play ($33\frac{1}{3}$ r.p.m.) microgroove records that would allow much longer playing time than the older 78 r.p.m. records, Motorola produced a disc player. This was fitted in Chrysler cars in America in 1956.

Three years later Philips of Holland introduced the Auto Mignon record player for Europe. These disc players soon faded from the scene as they were overtaken by tape recorders and as drivers became annoyed at feeding different records every few minutes.

By 1964 small tape recorders with reel to reel tape

feeds were being fitted for automobile use. Feeding the tape round the drive capstan and replay heads was only possible for a passenger. To ease the procedure for changing the tape RCA and SABA developed large cassettes that contained both of the tape reels and also led the tape automatically into its correct playing position.

Philips, in conjunction with the Japanese electronic industry, developed the compact cassette introduced in 1964 to oust the large cassette. This compact cassette is now leading the market, its only competition being the cartridge.

In a design to overcome the bulk problem of the large cassette, the cartridge was also produced. Unlike the cassette that contains two reels the cartridge relies on the tape being drawn from one end of the plastics box and returned to the other end. As the interior height of the box is the same as the tape width and the tape is moving in a smooth volume it does not tangle even though it is not wound on to a reel. The first cartridge providing eight recorded tracks, for stereo reproduction, was produced about the same time as the compact cassette.

Advances in electronic devices to maintain the tape speed constant and the Dolby system of unwanted tape noise suppression have resulted in the modern tape cassette or cartridge providing high fidelity reproduction with tape speeds as low as 23·8 mm (0·94 inches) per second.

SERVICING - Keeping in shape

Like all machinery, the motor car must receive attention from time to time if it is to continue working efficiently. Also, on occasion, there is a need for the repair or replacement of worn or broken parts. As the car increased in popularity, the motor servicing industry grew to keep the cars running.

The pioneers who made their own cars were not only experimenters but engineers, capable of looking after their new inventions. Soon they began to sell to wealthy enthusiasts with no such skills. These pioneer owners built themselves well-equipped motor-houses where hired chauffeurs could maintain the horseless-carriage.

Cars breaking down on short runs could easily be towed home by horse, but gradually, as cars became used for longer journeys, the bicycle repairers and village blacksmiths found their mechanics' knowledge could be put to profitable use by doing small repair jobs. This led to the advertisement of their services as "Motor Engineers", although most of them learned their additional trade at the expense of the car owners.

In 1902 the word "garage" was first used for places where cars could be stored and later maintained. These establishments grew in number rather than size, except in the larger cities where garages able to deal with more than half a dozen cars at a time were built.

The rapid increase in the motoring public after the First World War was responsible for the emergence of the skilled motor-fitter as a tradesman in his own right. Due to the relative simplicity of automobile design at this period, these men were able to tackle a wide range of repair work, limited only by skill and equipment, on practically any motor car.

By the middle 1930s design for more production and better performance complicated matters and reduced the scope of repair possible at small garages. To deal with this situation firms specializing in the repair of particular units came into being. These firms dealt with main assemblies such as engines, transmissions and electrical components.

This led obviously to the exchange replacement service, where the customer received a reconditioned unit in exchange for his existing one. The old unit was then reconditioned for later exchange. The first manufacturer to give this service was Ford. In 1930 they would replace the engine of their eight-horse power model for £9·50, including labour.

The growth of replacement rather than repair reduced the necessary skills of the motor mechanic since he was no longer expected to perform metal-working operations. Instead, his knowledge had to expand towards a more accurate and faster diagnosis of faults and the rapid replacement of parts. This has led to the introduction of complex diagnostic equipment and, in recent years, a tendency towards production-line methods of servicing.

LUBRICATION

The aim of the early manufacturers was to provide constant

234

lubrication in the engine. Although their lubrication systems were not always efficient, the engine was better treated than the other moving parts of the car.

The gears and bearings of the transmission were designed to run in a bath of oil held in the bottom of their casings and thrown about by the gear teeth. Since this oil, unlike the oil in the engine, was not contaminated by the products of combustion, the only attention necessary was an occasional change of oil. This removed most of the small metallic particles produced by wear between the moving surfaces.

With the coming of smoother surfaces on machined components, better materials to withstand wear and a greater knowledge of the mechanics and chemistry of lubrication, the oil change intervals increased. These intervals have now reached a state where the assembly can be lubricated and sealed for life. This has been done on some rear axles, notably by Ford.

Although there have been devices for oil-draining by poking a tube down the dipstick hole since the early 1920s, this has never become popular. Changing oil is still carried out in the time-honoured way of taking a screwed plug out of the bottom of the engine, or transmission, for the purpose of draining.

For bearings where there was no means for sealing oil into the rubbing areas, grease was used. Such bearings included the spring shackles, steering joints as well as the universal joints.

From the beginning until the early 1920s grease cups with screw-down lids, known as Stauffer lubricators, were fitted to each bearing. These lids usually had small click-springs inside to prevent them unscrewing with the vibration. A turn of the lid at frequent intervals pushed a little more grease into the bearing.

A slightly more positive grease cup had a small spring-loaded plunger to keep the grease under pressure. On the top of the plunger was a small rod that poked through the cap to show the amount of grease left in the cup.

In 1919 Edward Coe Critchlow, the production superintendent of the Union Oil Company of California, invented a system in which a pressure gun forced grease into a nipple screwed into the bearing. The grease was kept under pressure in the gun by a screw thread on the plunger, and the ball valve on the outlet prevented grease emerging except when the ball was pressed off its seat by the nipple. When it was not in use the nipple was covered for protection with a rubber cap.

A typical country garage of the early 1930s displayed at the Stratford Motor Museum.

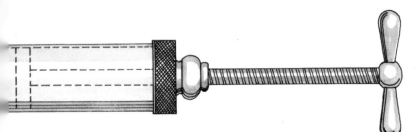   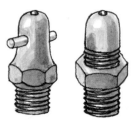

E. C. Chritchow's 1919 grease gun and five of the different types of grease nipples of later years.

Later the same year, the Alemite Die-Casting and Manufacturing Company of Chicago produced a screw gun with a flexible pipe ending in a bayonet connection. The grease nipple on the bearing was formed as the complementary bayonet connection and provided with a spring-loaded ball valve to stop grease coming back out of the bearing. This bayonet connection was still in use on military vehicles in the Second World War.

Other nipple types followed. Tecalemit used a hexagonal head over which the end of the grease gun could slide transversely to lock in position. Benton and Stone, of Birmingham, trading as Enots, had a simpler nipple with a hemispherical end to allow the gun to be applied at a slight angle. This was later modified to a taper with a small, flat, circular end. The circular end could give a pressure-tight seal against a hollow hemispherical end on the gun with the two parts at a much greater angle.

Within a year or two of the coming of the grease gun, the business of filling the gun was made less messy by the introduction of a cartridge of grease such as that devised by Kevitt Rotheram in 1922.

Meanwhile, in 1920, Siegmund Sokal, a Pole living in London, thought of using a force feed lubricator coupled to the various bearings by small pipes. A distributing valve in the base of this chassis-mounted lubricator allowed the selection of which bearing was to receive the grease.

This centralized system developed into an automatic "one-shot" system, where a pump drew oil from a container and fed all the chassis lubrication points. A few manufacturers fitted this system in which the pump was either connected to the clutch pedal, (Rolls Royce), to a separate pedal on the passenger's foot board, (Riley), or to the steering column, (Guy).

Other cars, such as the M.Gs., had grouped grease nipples feeding the bearings through long small-bore pipes.

Meanwhile, the grease guns were improved by the addition of a small diameter pump that raised the pressure to the region of 5,000 pounds per square inch. These pumps were operated either by a separate lever or by a telescoping of the tubes leading from the container to the nipple engaging nozzle.

Within the past twenty years the grease-lubricated bronze bush has been replaced by rubber bushes, particularly in independent suspension systems, and by nylon or similar plastic bearings. These do not need grease, and the bearings that do have been designed to be lubricated and sealed for life. The days of the grease gun are almost over – it now appears a clumsy instrument.

TOOLS

The responsibility of keeping a motor car running efficiently and in a safe condition has given rise to a greater number of specialized tools than any other technical advance. The great number of cars and the complexity of their design has resulted in separate tools and pieces of equipment for every job and, in many cases, for different models.

The tools carried and used by the pioneers were the standard spanners, screwdrivers and pliers of the time. The kits suggested in the first motor manuals were sufficient for major repairs on the relatively simple designs. As the owner-driver probably knew as much, or as little, about his car as the nearest blacksmith, the driver just got on with repairs at the roadside when the car broke down. It was the earliest and most common form of "do-it-yourself".

Soon the tool and accessory makers realized that the motor market was a profitable one. They began to provide extra and special tools for the motor car. One of the first was an adjustable spanner known as a "motor wrench". This was supposed to be able to deal with all the different

sizes of nut and to be usable as a hammer if needed. In practice the loose sliding jaw could be almost guaranteed to remove the essential corners from the nuts and using it as a hammer made things even worse.

The adjustable spanner came in many forms but most of them suffered from a lack of rigidity in the moving jaw. Some, however, such as the Lucas "Girder", the Abingdon "King Dick" and the "Master" followed the idea of the horse era double-bar coach wrench in having a long guide-bearing for the jaw. These could, and did, give years of useful service.

Other universal spanners blossomed and faded over the years. They varied in design from nut pliers to fixed serrated jaws, not all of which were for the true mechanic. Apart from the nut pliers, gripping tools remained relatively static in design except for two. These were the Bernard pliers of the early 1920s where the jaws were constrained to remain parallel in action for a better grip, and the Mole vice-grip wrench. This originated in Germany in the late 1930s and re-appeared in America in 1942 before flooding into Europe.

The fixed, or set, spanners were originally the same as those used in general engineering where the bolts had the coarse threads of the cast iron age. These spanners were also short shanked so that the average mechanic could not break the bolt by using too much torque. The combined advents of chrome-alloy steels and tool stylists produced

Michelin tyre repair outfit which was used as shown to remove the tube from a beaded edge tyre.

thinner spanners of twice the length in the 1930s. At the same time the threads became finer and this, by strengthening the bolts, partially offset the excessive length of the spanners.

At about the same time the ring spanner was produced with a second hexagonal opening within the first. This was used from the beginning for large nuts such as hub caps and where space was tight. These bi-hex ring spanners had twice the number of positions round a nut and could be used in the more confined spaces with only 30 degrees of shank movement as against a set spanner that needs to be turned over.

Tube spanners, originally forged from the solid and later from thin-wall tube, were always useful for sparking plugs and other parts set deep in recesses. But all these gave pride of place to the square drive socket set. Sockets with only one driving device were available in small numbers from the 1920s, but they came into mass use after the Second World War. The modern set of sockets in its special metal box and provided with extension bars, T-handles, ratchet handles, speed braces and universal joints looks very imposing but can take time to fit together.

The simple screwdriver has progressed from the oval, pear-shaped, beechwood handle and forged blade to the yellow transparent plastic handle and straight blade. Although the plastic may allow the screwdriver to be wrongly used as a chisel by being able to stand up to hammer blows, the handle is far less pleasant to grip. In the intervening years the motor-tool kit usually contained a driver with a slim, integral, forged handle. To help hand grip, wood panels were recessed into and rivetted to the handle sides. This strong tool was useful as a chisel, tyre lever or even to strengthen a weak part if necessary.

TYRE REMOVAL

Early motorists who fitted pneumatic tyres onto the wheels of their cars initially found them a source of trouble. This trouble was threefold. Firstly the road surfaces consisted of loose sharp-edged stones with a liberal sprinkling of horseshoe nails. Secondly, the beaded-edge tyres were difficult to remove and replace. Thirdly, the materials of the inner tubes, patches and rubber solution were poor and the whole operation was rather a chancy do-it-yourself kind of business.

The removal of a beaded-edge tyre was a matter of brute strength. Two long tyre levers, looking like mediaeval instruments of torture, were needed. Their ends were forced under the tyre bead about ten inches (250 mm.) apart and then that section of the tyre was levered up over the edge of the rim. This meant the use of great force since the bead rubber had to stretch to go over the larger outer diameter of the rim. Once one section was over the rest was levered off until the inner tube could be pulled between the tyre wall and the rim.

The changing shapes of hand tools over 70 years.

Inner tube patches and outer cover repair kits of the early 1920s.

To provide enough space to be able to pull the tube valve through its hole in the rim, a forked lever was used to hold up a section of tyre wall.

Putting the tube and tyre back on the rim needed the same amount of strength and a great deal of care not to pinch the tube between the lever end and the rim. This would mean starting again in order to mend the self-inflicted puncture.

The well-base rim and wired-edge tyre did not need strength. The inextensible wired bead would slip down into the well on the opposite side of the rim and let the bead come over the rim edge. These tyres could often be replaced by laying the wheel on the ground and just walking on the tyre wall. This saved a great deal of tube-nip punctures.

Tubeless tyres needed a clamping band round the outer diameter to force the beads against the rim edge and so provide enough initial sealing to keep the inflating air within the tyre and rim assembly.

PUNCTURE REPAIR

The usual cause of tyre puncture is a hard object making a hole in the cover and, if there is one fitted, the inner tube. It has always been so.

The pioneers' tyres were particularly vulnerable because of flints and pieces of iron on the road. These not only made holes for the air to escape from the tube, but cut and tore holes in the soft, weak, outer covers. These weakened the tyre and also exposed the tube, allowing it to come in

The K.C. No-stretch Tire Boot.

direct contact with the road, producing yet another puncture to harass the motorist.

To overcome this two kinds of patches were used. The first, a multi-layer cord fabric and rubber patch was cemented to the inner surface of the cover. This patch had the layers of different sizes to give tapered edges and so prevent tube chafing.

More serious damage needed the second type of patch. This consisted of an inner patch to stop the tube entering the split and an outer boot or gaiter to take the load from the damaged area of the cover. One such inner patch was the Dur-a-Bul Wire-Knit Blow-Out of the early 1920s which had a layer of wire mesh embedded in layers of cushioning rubber and five plies of fabric. Some of the plies extended sideways from the near circular section patch to clamp under tyre beads and to keep the patch in place.

The outer patches were of leather or rubber and fabric, often with metal studs. These were strapped or laced over

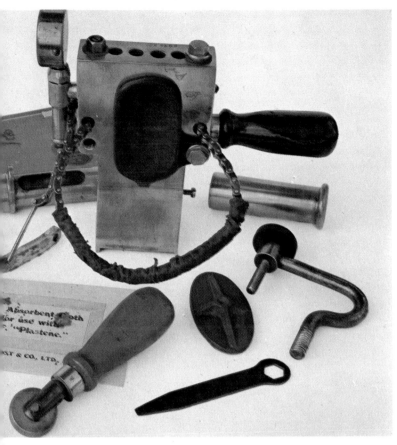

A Harvey-Frost Baby vulcanizer kit for tube and tyre repairs.

While the garages used steam- and later electrically-heated vulcanizers, small devices were sold for road-side repairs. These had two flat areas between which the tube and patch could be clamped. The exact amount of heat needed was supplied by a combustible disc or fuse, or a measured quantity of petrol.

To avoid the use of heat, a cold cure based on the Parkes curing process was developed as an alternative. In this the two surfaces were cement-covered and allowed to dry. Then a cold-curing solution, containing sulphur chloride and carbon bisulphide, was applied and the patch put over the puncture.

Later patches had one surface coated with a raw gum and a cement layer protected by fabric. These only required softening with petrol and relied on the heat generated in the tyre to complete the vulcanizing. With the coming of butyl tubes, roadside puncture repair ceased.

TYRE GAUGES

Soon after the pneumatic tyre was introduced it was realized that it needed inflating to a pressure commensurate with the load carried. Kicking the tyre to see if it was hard

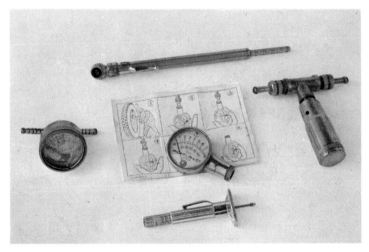

Four tyre pressure gauges and a tread depth gauge.

the outside of the tyre. The Kimball Steel Tire Armour consisted of a band of two inch (50 mm.) wide steel plates linked together to wrap round the tyre and then to be hooked to the rim.

The hole in the inner tube was an easier matter to mend. Puncture outfits were always carried in the tool kit and these contained a thin metal rasp, rather like a nutmeg grater, scissors, rubber solution and french chalk. The rasp was used to rough-up the surface of the tube and a piece of patching rubber was cut with the scissors from a roll. The solution was used to fix the patch to the tube and the chalk was finally dusted over the repair to stop any sticking between tube and cover if too much cement had been used.

Later patches were sold in assorted shapes and sizes with feathered edges and a linen liner to keep the pre-roughened surface clean.

The original cement was a solution of raw rubber in naptha. This would stick for a while and then, being raw rubber, would lose its adhesive properties when subject to heat and oxidization. The properties were later improved by the addition of a gum, such as shellac or rosin, with sulphur as a drier.

To give a permanent repair it was necessary to vulcanize the patch in position. The heat and pressure in the vulcanizing process baked the cement and stabilized the rubber in the solution to give similar properties to that of the tube rubber. This repair treatment was suggested by H. Harvey Frost in 1902.

enough did not give an accurate answer. The B. F. Goodrich Company designed a sliding caliper with two sets of graduations. The top, unloaded, width was measured and this measurement, transferred to the other scale, gave the caliper jaw setting for the tyre width at the bottom when properly inflated.

The proper measurement is, however, the pressure in the tube. Tyre pumps were fitted with Bourdon tube gauges, but these were not satisfactory. They indicated the pressure of air being used to open the valve against the existing tube pressure and they soon wore out since the needle flickered to its reading at each pump stroke.

In 1909, a pressure gauge which could be applied to the valve was invented. A pin in the gauge end opened the valve by pressing the core centre and the air acted against a spring-loaded piston. The piston movement was proportional to the pressure and was indicated by move-ment of a separate calibrated plunger held at its reading by light friction even after the gauge had been removed. This type of gauge has remained in use ever since.

WHEEL BALANCING

It is almost impossible to build a tyre that is of uniform weight throughout. Consequently every tyre has a circumferential portion that is heavier than other similar portions. When fitted on a wheel and rotated at a good speed this heavier, or out of balance, portion causes vibrations, which tend to reduce the life of both vehicle and tyre, as well as annoying the passengers.

With the higher wheel speeds of racing cars this vibration was met much earlier than it was with touring cars. At first the only concern was with static balance, in which a wheel has weight added to the light portion so that when free to rotate about its bearings it can be stopped in any position. With an unbalanced wheel the heavier portion will eventually, after a certain amount of pendulum swinging, come to rest at the bottom.

High speed cars began to have their wheels balanced by winding lead wire round the rim ends of the spokes. By the 1930s the faster touring and sports cars were capable of speeds where a lack of wheel balance could be felt. Such cars had their wheels balanced by lead washers on bolts that passed through the well of the rim.

Waiting for the wheel to come to rest with the heaviest part at the bottom each time weight was added to the rim was a time consuming business. In 1928 the Goodyear Tire and Rubber Company had the idea of supporting a wheel, or a tyre on a dummy wheel, horizontally on a point pivot. Since the wheel could immediately tilt with its heaviest portion down, it was much easier just to add weight to the rim until the wheel remained horizontal. Apparatus of this kind was also used to find the lightest part of new tyres. This part was marked with a red dot and, if the tyre was fitted with the red dot in line with the inner tube valve, some degree of balance was obtained.

By the end of the 1940s it became apparent that static balancing was not enough to prevent wheel wobble. This became a greater problem as the spring rates of independent suspensions were lowered and the weights of the wheels and their rotational speeds increased. Dynamic unbalance was caused by the heavy portion being on one side of the centre plane of the wheel. This unbalance had, in effect, two causes. Firstly, the centre plane may not have been at right angles to the wheel axis. Secondly, the out-of-balance weight was not equally distributed on each side of the centre plane.

Dynamic unbalance caused a rocking movement in the wheel and this became very apparent when the frequency of the oscillation approximated to the natural frequency of the steering system. This caused the car to deviate from a straight line as the wheels took over from the steering.

In 1949 Jack Hardman and Tom French of the Dunlop Rubber Company modified the horizontal wheel static balancing machine by adding a device to produce an opposing rocking force when the wheel was rotated. This device consisted of two weights at the ends of an arm pivotable on a tube passing through the wheel hub. By altering the angle of the arm, and thereby changing the distance of the weight from the rotational axis of the wheel, and by altering the rotational position of the device in relation to the wheel, a figure of the dynamic unbalance could be obtained.

Correction of the dynamic unbalance was, and still is, made by clipping lead weights to the edge of the rim on the appropriate side. It is, of course, necessary that wheels should be both statically and dynamically balanced for vibration-free running. Normally, a wheel is balanced statically and then dynamically.

A simple apparatus for this was designed by Hermann Beissbarth of Munich in 1953. The wheel was mounted on a dummy hub supported on a shaft for rotation about a horizontal axis. The shaft bearing was supported on a vertical pivot and could oscillate horizontally against springs on each side. A recording disc on the other end of the shaft was marked by a fixed stylus. When the wheel was spun, the vibration due to the unbalance caused the spindle to oscillate in a horizontal plane. The stylus marked the disc to show the position of the greatest lack of balance

and the amplitude of the vibration indicated how much compensating weight was needed.

Within the following few years the apparatus became easier to use as electro-mechanical devices took the place of the stylus to show the weight required. The position of the weight was shown by making a mark on the wheel and viewing it in the light of a stroboscopic lamp.

By the end of the decade, balancing apparatus had been designed to avoid the need to remove the wheels and mount them on special hubs. A trolley was brought to a jacked-up wheel and a friction roller on the trolley rotated the car wheel. An electro-mechanical device mounted between the suspension and the ground recorded the frequency and strength of vibration due to the imbalance. This device was also coupled to the timer of the stroboscopic lamp so that the apparent stationary chalk mark on the tyre could indicate the heaviest, or lightest, part of the wheel. To overcome the natural damping of the sprung system, the wheel was rotated in each direction and the mean of the two heaviest positions was used to determine the location of the weight.

WHEEL ALIGNMENT

Pneumatic tyres have always been an expensive wearing part of motoring. To reduce the rate of wear it is essential that the wheels are kept in proper alignment and that the various steering angles are maintained. Failure to do this results in needless scrubbing away of rubber and also in poor steering performance.

Michelin produced a gauge in 1904 that measured the amount of toe-in of the front wheels. Gauges of this type were essentially large calipers which compared the distances between the front wheel rims, on the horizontal centre lines of the wheels, at the front and back. Since this measurement was made difficult by the presence of the chassis and engine, the gauge consisted of a long bar on which two arms with inward projecting ends were clamped in such a way that they could be made to slide. The arms were adjusted along the bar until their ends just touched the two rims at the rear of their horizontal diameters. The gauge was then moved forward and the difference in spacing at the front of the rims was measured. This measurement showed the amount by which the front wheels were out of parallel.

The other dimension that was checked was the distance between the wheel centres on each side of the car. Since most, although not all cars, have equal wheelbases on the two sides, this would show if the axles were parallel.

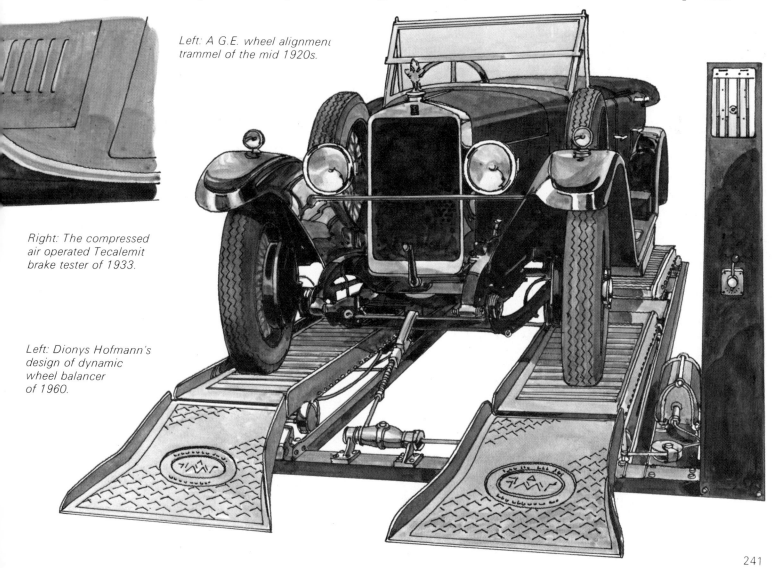

Left: A G.E. wheel alignment trammel of the mid 1920s.

Right: The compressed air operated Tecalemit brake tester of 1933.

Left: Dionys Hofmann's design of dynamic wheel balancer of 1960.

With the advent of independent suspension systems, both at the front and the rear, such simple tests became insufficient and often inadequate. This was largely caused by the lack of connection between the wheels. When one wheel rises, the linkwork of the suspension causes that wheel to tilt or to change the track and this makes the previous simple tests of little value.

Bosch produced a wheel alignment indicator which would show the horizontal alignment of a pair of front wheels irrespective of their relative vertical angle or track. This indicator relies on two thin beams of light reflected from mirrors attached to the wheels. The front wheels are run on to two dished turntables that allow the wheels to be centred and to pivot without friction between the tyres and their supporting surfaces.

Two light projectors are mounted exactly opposite the centres of the turntables. The light beams from these projectors are emitted from holes in the centres of white screens which are marked with horizontal and vertical lines. When there is no car between them, the light from each projector meets the vertical line on the screen of the other projector.

The first headlamp beam-setter built by Bosch in 1917.

Two mirrors are mounted on holders, which are clamped on to the rim or the hub of each wheel. These mirrors are located exactly parallel to the plane containing the ends of the three rim-engaging legs of the holder, or at right angles to the axis of a hub adaptor.

The car steering is turned until the beam from one projector is reflected back from the mirror to shine exactly on the vertical line on that projector's screen. If the car wheels are parallel then the other light beam will also fall on its projector's vertical line. Any deviation from this indicates the degree of toe-in or toe-out of the wheels. Tilting of the wheels in a vertical plane, or track changes due to the independence of the suspension, have no effect on the alignment indication although such tilting will be

shown by the light striking the screen above or below the horizontal line.

A further benefit of this optical alignment indicator is its ability to check that the wheels turn the same amount on each side of the straight ahead position. This is done by using three-piece mirrors in which the central mirrors are flanked by two more mirrors mounted at an angle. When the steering is turned to align the light beam in an angled mirror on one side, the amount of deviation of the other side is noted. The steering is then turned to align the corresponding mirror on the other side of the car and, if the steering geometry is correct, the deviation should be the same. The three mirrors allow this to be checked for both steering locks.

BRAKE TESTING

Early braking systems were considered satisfactory if they locked the wheels of the motor car or caused the passengers to be thrown forwards with obviously painful results. But soon it was realized that the true measure of efficiency was the actual rate of retardation. H. E. Wimperis and G. K. B. Elphinstone took some of the earlier ideas of acceleration-measuring instruments and in 1909 produced a meter that could be clamped to a part of the bodywork.

This later became known as the Tapley meter and consisted of a pendulum free to swing in a plane, parallel to the car's direction of movement. The pendulum was an eccentrically-mounted disc, having liquid or magnetic damping means to reduce unwanted oscillations. The disc was coupled to a drum with numbers round the periphery, these numbers being visible through a window in the casing. The casing was rotatable about the pendulum axis, so that the reading could be set to zero when the vehicle was stationary on a level road. Application of the brakes when the car was moving caused the pendulum to swing forwards and the number at the window casing indicated the deceleration as a decimal of "g", the earth's gravitational attraction (32 feet or 9·81 metres per second, per second).

The Tapley required the car to be driven on a relatively traffic-free, level road, which was not always convenient. To allow brake testing to be carried out in the garage and to measure the amount of braking at each wheel, the car was held stationary and the force needed to rotate the wheels against the brakes was measured.

One system used in the early 1930s was that of Tecalemit, where the four road wheels were supported on four separate rough-surfaced trolleys. The trolleys were mounted on rollers running on ramps having a special profile, which offered a resistance to forward movement proportional to the weight on each trolley. Once on the tester, the brakes were applied and the car was pulled forward by a pneumatic cylinder through a steel cable. This caused the rollers to ride up the ramps until the brakes began to slip and the wheels rotate. The reading of

the distance that the rollers had moved up the ramps gave an indication of the braking force at each wheel.

Within a few years the roller and ramp idea was replaced by two pairs of corrugated rollers that engaged either the front or the rear wheels. The power needed to drive these rollers at a predetermined speed, usually three miles (five kilometres) per hour, against the retardation of the brakes gave a measure of the brake efficiency. Bosch have devised a system whereby the rollers are driven through an hydraulic transmission system and the fluid pressure needed is proportional to the braking force.

DIAGNOSTIC EQUIPMENT

The drivers of the first motor cars and the cycle mechanics and blacksmiths who repaired them soon became experienced in the diagnosis of faults. They had to learn the hard way — by experience. As the car grew in popularity and became more complicated, the driver's knowledge grew less and the garage trade increased. The complexity of the mechanism and the higher speed stresses made the diagnosis of incipient faults a necessity. No longer were sight, sound, smell and a sixth sense sufficient.

By 1904 Serge Berditschewsky Apostoloff, of London, had come to the conclusion that subjective feelings of lack of performance were insufficient for accurate diagnosis. He devised a rolling road test bed on which the car was mounted with its driving wheels in contact with a drum. The front wheels rested against a stop. The car was run to drive the drum, which was coupled to a dynamo and to a fan that blew cooling air over the engine compartment. The power generated by the dynamo could be measured and used to judge the car's performance. Apostoloff went on to suggest that by giving the car a rocking motion and using the drum to drive a model car against a cinema screen background, people could be taught to drive.

While these rolling road test beds could give a reliable guide to the performance of the engine and were useful for tuning, they could only indicate the presence of a fault. Since it was necessary to know the actual cause of poor performance, diagnostic equipment was evolved which could be attached to various components and so pinpoint the trouble or show an under-standard performance. Probably the simplest of these devices was the neon tube sparking-plug tester. In this a glass tube filled with neon gas and with a contact in each end was connected at one end to a suspect plug. If the tube lit up red in synchronism with the engine firing strokes the plug was working. If not, the plug or its feeding lead was suspect.

Other devices were the vacuum gauge, the compression tester and the ignition timing light. The vacuum gauge was connected to the inlet manifold to measure the suction produced by the pistons on the inlet stroke. If the suction was weak this would be due to a leak either in the manifold joints, a badly seating valve, broken, or worn, piston rings or a cylinder in need of reboring. The compression tester was screwed into a sparking-plug hole and, when the engine was turned slowly by hand, indicated the pressure produced in the cylinder.

The ignition timing light was an extension of the neon indicator, in which the flashes were used to illuminate a mark on the flywheel or the fan pulley. This mark was usually level with the top centre crankshaft position for number one cylinder. When the engine was running the mark would appear stationary as it would only light each time the plug fired. This stroboscopic effect was used to check and adjust the timing of the ignition and to observe the action of the advance and retard mechanism.

In instruments such as the Bosch timing light, an electronic circuit receives the electrical impulse from the sparking-plug lead and uses it to trigger a stronger light from a discharge tube. This gives a better illumination of the crankshaft mark. By further manually-controlled circuitry the time between the ignition pulse and the light flash can be varied. This allows the apparent position of the mark to be lined up with a fixed mark and, at the same time, an appropriately calibrated meter shows the time difference as the angle of ignition advance. The Bosch ESAW timing light of 1967 was the first to provide this

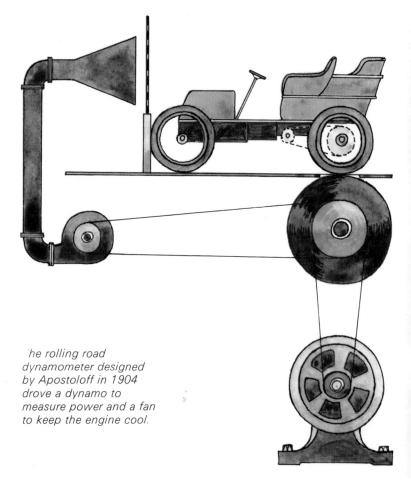

he rolling road dynamometer designed by Apostoloff in 1904 drove a dynamo to measure power and a fan to keep the engine cool.

useful feature as well as an indication of the dwell angle.

The dwell-angle tester is another electronic device which indicates the angle through which the contact breaker cam turns while the breaker points are closed. This gives an indication not only of the contact breaker gap but also of any wear that has taken place in the cam or, more likely, in its follower. For the most efficient ignition system, the dwell period must be as long as possible to allow full build-up of electrical energy in the ignition primary system.

Bosch timing light and dwell-angle meter.

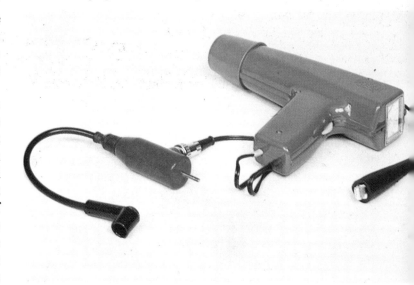

A modern fully-equipped diagnostic test bay including rolling road and brake test equipment.

Starting in 1925 Bosch began a range of test equipment. This range expanded and in 1968 the separate instruments were brought together to give a diagnostic unit. Flexible leads were taken to connections on the car and by switching at the single console, that held five meters and a cathode-ray oscilloscope, the operator could perform a rapid check on the vehicle's health. The first of these diagnostic units was installed by the Ford main agent in Weiden/Oberpfalz in August 1968 and shortly Volkswagen had installed some 6000 in their home and overseas dealers' premises.

The work of making all the connections to the ignition, generator, carburettor and exhaust systems was time consuming and in 1971 Bosch introduced their break-through, using computer techniques. Cars were fitted with a multi-pin socket in the engine compartment. The pins of this socket were wired to the appropriate points of the car, so that the only connection was a single plug from the diagnostic unit.

Further advanced thinking provided plastic programme sheets, one for each model, that fed into the computer the standard values of the conditions being measured. In addition to some 30 objective tests a further 50 subjective examinations, such as tyre condition and brake pipe damage, were interlaced into the programme. The interlacing was such that the operator had to perform all the checks in the correct order for the full cycle to be completed.

Battery voltage was measured both on no-load and with a 100 amp discharge to indicate condition. Cylinder compressions were compared by examining the fluctuations in the starter current as it rotated the engine, the battery condition and oil viscosity being taken into account by the computer. The latter then proceeded with a series of tests on the ignition equipment and checked the resistances of all the lighting circuits to seek for poor connections or broken bulb filaments. The wheel alignment checks from the Bosch optical device were also fed to the computer.

By this advanced diagnostic unit some 80 different checks can be made on the car in half an hour and the results printed out on a sheet that also gives the manufacturers' standard figures. More advanced units incorporate a rolling road performance and brake test and exhaust emission checks.

In some countries, federal regulations lay down maximum percentages of certain exhaust emissions, particularly carbon monoxide. In the first Bosch gas analyser the proportion of carbon monoxide was determined by measuring the temperature rise of a platinum-rhodium catalyst as the carbon monoxide was changed to carbon dioxide by oxygen from the atmosphere. This type was taken into general use in Germany in mid-1969, to check conformity with the laws. Bosch exhaust gas analysers employing an infra-red gas analysis system were first used in Germany and later introduced for this purpose in Austria and Switzerland.

SAFETY–Self-protection

From the moment the first motor car began to move it became a potential source of accidents. Every moving thing possesses energy, the magnitude of which is dependent on the mass of the body and the speed at which it is moving. An accident causes the sudden and unpremeditated release of this energy in an unwanted place.

Safety precautions to minimize the destructive dangers of this energy can be practised in two ways. Primary safety is achieved by keeping the released energy and damageable areas apart as in the case of a seat belt that stops a passenger from being thrown against the car fascia. An example of providing secondary safety is padding the fascia to reduce an unbelted occupant's injury.

BUMPERS

In 1904, Frederick Simms applied buffers to the ends of a motor car, taking the idea from railway engines. Curved buffers, padded with solid or inflated rubber, were mounted on leaf springs to guard the corners of the car from damage. In one suggested form these bumpers were able to telescope against helical springs to absorb the energy of the accident. This idea has lately been reapplied to E.S.V.s – experimental safety vehicles.

The bumpers were not immediately accepted because traffic in towns was light and small bumps were easily taken by the tyres or chassis frame at the front and rear, and by running-boards at the sides. Bumper protection was not necessary until the coming of wheel-enveloping mudguards and bodywork.

Early bumpers were stout tubes or steel springs mounted away from the body and feeding bump loads back to the chassis frame. Later they became more decorative than useful as they were smoothed into the body line. Often a blow at walking speed was enough to bend the chromium-plated, pressed-steel bumper back into the very areas it was supposed to protect.

Two protective devices were then added. Vertical over-riders were fitted because the different bumper heights were not standardized and the shining finish was protected by inserting rubber strips.

A fringe benefit of the full width transverse bumper of the 1930s was an anti-shimmy device. The bumper consisted of flat springs mounted, with their width horizontal, on rubber bushes from the dumbirons. The ends of a further spring blade were bent round to form cylindrical chambers closed at the top by a cap, and by the flat springs at the bottom. The chambers contained heavy weights, whose inertia damped torsional oscillations at the front of the car.

With increasing world concern about the ever-rising accident rate, safety engineers took a closer look at the bumpers' safety standards. In some countries the amount of energy absorption was stipulated by law. One method of meeting the requirements was to use soft bumpers of considerable thickness, as on the Volvo 144. These gave body protection for both car and pedestrian.

Another solution was an energy-absorbing bumper mounting that could be used with flexible bumper bars. Dunlop designed a triangular mounting of rubber and plastics, fusion-bonded together. It would gradually fold inside the channel section of the bumper under impact and then return to its original shape. A variation was a piston and cylinder mounting. The cylinder was fitted with a fluent plastics material that was extruded at a controlled rate on impact. This type of energy-absorbing device had other applications in passive restraint systems.

Thinking more of pedestrian protection and of the body-catching scoops fitted to electric trams many years before, British Leyland developed a lifter bar. This bar was mounted above the bumper and spring-loaded to pivot upwards when the bumper met an obstruction. The movement of the bar lifted the pedestrian and held him on

Above: Frederick Simms'
impact absorbing bumper
of 1904.

Below: Volvo's bumper
designed to absorb impacts
at slow speeds.

the padded top of the bonnet to avoid injuries caused if the victim was thrown on to the road surface.

BODY STRENGTHENING

While the bumper will cope with minor impacts, stronger body structures and greater dissipation of destructive energy are needed for major collisions. Bodywork was designed with crumpling areas at the front and rear. These areas allowed for a certain amount of controlled crushing of bonnet and boot.

When a car body crumples at a controlled rate, it lengthens the time in which the energy is dissipated. This considerably reduces the acceleration on the occupants when a car suddenly stops and they continue forward under their own momentum. In other words a longer time is allowed for the forward movement of the passengers to be slowed from the speed of the car before the accident to the speed, if any, afterwards.

The space required for this crushability is relatively long and cannot be provided at the sides of the bodywork. So bodies were built, such as the Jaguar XJ12, with W-sectioned steel reinforcement within the door and wall thickness. This kind of strengthening is carried out to a greater extent with the E.S.V.s.

Legislation is also beginning to require a degree of non-crushability in the roof. Strong members are taken up in the area of the door pillars and windscreen frame across the roof to provide a roll-over cage and prevent the roof collapsing if the car is inverted.

Since the doors form a part of the strengthening frame it is essential that they stay shut, not only for protection but to prevent the occupants being thrown out. Present

The Volvo 244 was built with both primary and secondary safety in mind.

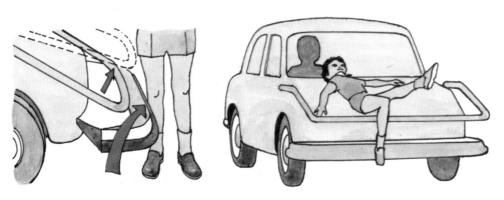

British Leyland's bumper bar that lifts a pedestrian to safety onto a soft bonnet top.

cars have anti-burst locks, which secure the opening edge of the door to the door frame and prevent body distortion pulling the lock tongue from its hasp. The simplest form is a T-headed member on the door engaging a slotted plate on the pillar. More complex forms with greater strength are coming into use. In the E.S.V.s more interlocking devices are used and on some the door and pillar are designed to act as one structure when closed.

As well as being provided with a strong shell to shield from the external effects of a collision, passengers should be protected from injury caused by contact with the interior. One way is to cushion all the objects on which a passenger could be injured. Another is to restrain the passengers from being thrown around within the body.

CUSHIONING

In many collisions passengers will be thrown against the steering wheel, fascia or windscreen, unless restrained.

To reduce the chest-crushing force the steering wheel can have a large, padded boss to spread the load. It can also be provided with a column that collapses at a controlled rate to reduce the peak chest load. In 1956, Ferdinand Porsche invented a collapsible shaft that telescoped into the bore of the steering worm after it had contracted a spring ring. Control of the movement was given by the escape of fluid through holes successively closed as the column slid into the worm.

General Motors introduced a collapsible outer tube of perforated metal two years later. The tube would concertina under end load and allow the steering shaft to telescope after shearing frangible plastics pins. Mercedes-Benz developed a large steering wheel hub in the shape of a stepped cone. This hollow metal hub was well padded and would concertina under chest loads.

In a front collision there is also a risk of the steering column being forced back into the driver's chest. One way of preventing this is to use a short column with the steering box on the bulkhead, or a shaft in two parts hinged by a universal joint. The hinged shaft folds on endwise impact. The Rover 2000 was designed to have both systems, while the Vale of 1934 gave the maximum danger with its long shaft extending from a steering box mounted on the extreme front of the chassis.

Other forms of cushioning are found in the padded fascia and sun visors, the recessed or padded dash knobs and the padded areas in front of the passengers' knees. Some makers have removed all knobs from the dash and placed them on the steering column or a central console.

RESTRAINT SYSTEMS

With the direct tiller steering of the pioneers, it was all too easy for the driver to be thrown out when a front wheel met a bump. In 1903, G. Pounce suggested drivers should be held in their seats by belts or harness in the same way that a child is kept safely restrained in a perambulator.

The introduction of wheel steering, windscreens and

Wilmot-Breeden disc-latch anti-burst latch that resists the door pulling away from the door pillar.

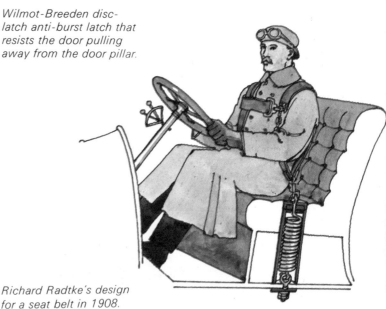

Richard Radtke's design for a seat belt in 1908.

enclosed driving seats appeared to obviate the need for seat belts. But in the mid-1950s it was realized, particularly in Sweden, that many injuries could be prevented if the occupants were kept in their seats during an accident.

Considerable development had already taken place in seat belts for aircraft. Pacific Scientific Products produced a reel in 1956 that would allow the belt or strap to pay out slowly but would lock solid when the strap began to move quickly. This fitting helped to overcome the dislike some people felt in being belted into the seat.

Another inertia locking system was devised by Irving Air Chute of Great Britain. In this, a ball was free to roll on a dished plate. As long as the acceleration forces on the car were normal the ball kept to the centre of the dish. When these forces exceeded a predetermined figure owing to the car hitting, or being hit by, something, the ball rolled up the dish and jammed the reel on which the belt was coiled. To keep these belts reasonably tidy, a light spring tended to reel up the belt slack, except when the reel was locked.

The fitting of belts to the front seats became a legal requirement in some countries in spite of personal dislikes.

Fiat experimental safety vehicles came in three sizes in 1974.

In 1961, Arnold Kent of England had the idea of fitting inflatable cushions in front of the occupants. They were stowed until a collision caused them to be inflated automatically from a container of compressed air or inert gas.

Three or four years later this idea was taken up by Eaton, Yale and Towne in America and some complex air bag systems evolved. The air cushions were stored in the steering wheel hub, under the fascia and in the backs of the front seats. Triggering devices located in the bumpers inflated the bags from compressed gas bottles, sometimes through a frangible diaphragm broken by a small cartridge. To prevent an air pressure build-up within the car body, which could cause injuries, one scheme included a further explosive charge to blow out the windscreen.

Another form of passive restraint which does not need any action by the passenger is the self-applying seat belt. In 1966, Ford developed a shoulder and lap strap belt with two ends attached to the rear of the door and the third to an arm between the seats. As the door shut, the belt moved to its correct position and was tightened by rearward movement of the arm. In other designs one of the belt mountings in the door moved to set the belt. The belt ends were moved by electric motors having limit switches that prevented engine starting unless the belts were fixed.

Realizing that the restraint systems gave little or no protection to small children, Jean Ames of England produced a special child seat and harness in 1962. This padded seat was held on the rear seat by straps passing to strong points in the car body. A full harness retained the child comfortably and safely. Later development included a system allowing for child growth from cot to adult by changing the straps.

While these restraint systems save the occupants from the forward acceleration of front impacts, they give no protection from the effects of those from the rear. In the mid-1960s, Saab and Volvo of Sweden, and Rover of England began to fit headrests to the tops of the front seats.

These prevented "whip-lash" injuries where the head was suddenly accelerated backwards over the back of the seat. These built-in head rests were made narrower than the seat back to allow some rearward vision for the driver and forward vision for the rear passengers.

FUTURE TRENDS—Improving all the

Concern over the preservation of world fuel supplies and of the environment leads to the questions, not only of what will be the car of the future, but also what will be the future of the car? Smooth and effortless journeyings have always been one of man's greatest ambitions, particularly the owning of personal transport. It is, therefore, unlikely that the private car will cease to exist. No other system has yet been suggested to give such facility for door-to-door journeys.

The reduction in both energy use and noxious fume emission will result in the development of internal combustion engines for economy rather than power. The reduction of maximum permitted speeds, even on special motorways, will encourage such a trend.

One modification to the engine being developed by Honda and likely to appear in the near future is the stratified charge combustion chamber. In this system a small volume of normal strength mixture is admitted to, and ignited in, a separate combustion chamber. The burning gas is led to the main combustion chamber, where it ignites a weak mixture to provide the greater part of the power. This type of burning results in a reduction of both fuel consumption and unpopular emissions.

By reverting to the external combustion engine where, as in the steam engine, the fuel is used only to heat the

The Bersey electric car was more of an electrically driven horse cab.

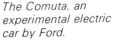

The Comuta, an experimental electric car by Ford.

working fluid and does not become part of that fluid, the choice of fuel increases. Fuels can be burnt more efficiently under steady combustion conditions. Further, there is no necessity for high volatility or anti-knock properties.

The steam engine could come back, either in multi-cylinder reciprocating or steam turbine form. Working fluids, other than water, may prove easier and suitable to use in a closed circuit that includes a condensing system. There is no reason why the eventual fuel for such an engine should not be nuclear, in which case the car could be charged for life.

Another form of engine is the hot-air engine. In this the fluid air and the heating and cooling cycle is based on the work of Dr. Robert Stirling in 1816. Though Sir George Cayley, the grandfather of aerodynamics, built an engine in 1807 it is the Stirling cycle that has been the subject of considerable development. A great deal of work has been done on this engine by Phillips of Holland and its use in automobiles may well come about.

Gaseous fuels may take the place of hydrocarbons. One such fuel that shows promise is liquid hydrogen. This can be obtained from water and, when it is burnt in air, it returns to water and nitrogen, which have no ecological effect. Since it needs to be stored at high pressures, there is a penalty in the weight of the necessary containers.

As long ago as 1866, E. Poitevin designed an electro-magnetically-driven road vehicle deriving its power from batteries. Many more electric cars followed, particularly in the early years of this century. These were smooth, quiet and easy to control, but they again suffered a weight penalty.

Recent demands for commuter cars for short journeys and the growing need for road space has led to rethinking on the electric car. Modern thinking is to reduce the running losses, such as road and air friction resistances, to the absolute minimum and to increase the energy storage of the battery as well as reducing its weight and size.

Although the lead-acid battery has developed to a good state of reliability, it has had little reduction in specific weight. More advanced batteries, such as the alkali-metal high temperature batteries of the sodium-sulphur type, increase the range or power by anything up to ten times.

On long distance roads there is the possibility of feeding current by induction from a conductor buried under the road surface. Alternatively, a battery of photo-cells on the roof could provide a current from solar energy. Both of these are alternatives or supplements to recharging at meters when parked.

To obtain the benefits of the pollution-free and silent working of an electric motor in towns and the long range performance of the internal combustion engine in the

The Minissima town car designed by Bill Towns round Mini components.

country, Bosch are developing a hybrid drive system. An electric motor is built into the transmission between the clutch and the differential.

For out-of-town driving the clutch is engaged to allow the internal combustion engine to drive the rear wheels. When driving downhill, at a constant speed in flat country and under braking, the excess power output of the engine is used to drive the motor as a generator.

In city traffic the clutch is disengaged and the car is driven by the electric motor, the engine being stopped. If needed, the engine power can be supplemented by the motor for acceleration and hill climbing. This enables a smaller internal combustion engine to be used to obtain the desired performance.

A conventional Ford Escort Estate car had its gearbox replaced by an electric motor. The batteries were placed under the rear seats and under the load platform. The additional equipment added 880 lbs (400 kg) to the original weight of 1936 lbs (880 kg). Even so acceleration was improved, emission was reduced, yet fuel consumption remained the same as that for the unmodified Escort.

With increasing use of the car, particularly in urban areas, there will be more economical use of road area.

While the passenger and luggage space will remain the same, there will be a reduction in the overall dimensions.

Such a size reduction is in opposition to the provision of safety devices as seen in current E.S.Vs. Damage-reducing bumpers, crushable zones and body strengthening all use extra road space. This conflict will highlight the need for automatic prevention of collisions, rather than reliance on the driver's skill.

By using radar techniques to sense the proximity of other vehicles in front, overriding control of the throttle and brakes can prevent most impacts. A further stage in automatic control is the use of buried cables, or radio waves, not only to determine the speed and separation of vehicles, but to programme the steering for at least the correct turn-offs from motorways. This could be extended to routes for door-to-door journeys. Under such circumstances the driver would play the same part as the driver of an automatically-controlled train.

There seem to be strong arguments for a two-tier car system. A manually-controlled town car of simple construction and a very sophisticated distance car with a high degree of automation.

The town car would be most efficient as a unit of a communal fleet. These town cars would be available to all subscribers and would be picked up and left at the points of use. The design of these simple transports would be based on a rugged, electrically-powered moulded plastics box. Controls and ancillary fittings, even of the simplest kind, would be reduced to a minimum. With limited range and speed they would be no more than powered brief cases, prams or baskets!

On the other hand, the sophisticated long-distance or inter-town car would be individually owned. Using nuclear energy to provide power from a closed circuit turbine, the majority of services would be driven from a hydraulic ring main charged by a pump driven by the turbine. This main would feed power not only to individual motors in each wheel and to an anti-lock retarding system throttling the motors for braking, but also to a self-levelling suspension system and constant horizontal seating platform.

With an automatic control system programmed for speed and route, at least on motorways, the driver would have little to do. Accident prevention of such advanced cars would rely mainly on radar obstacle detection systems and visibility in fog would be provided by closed circuit television. Its appearance will be that of a futuristic crystal ball.

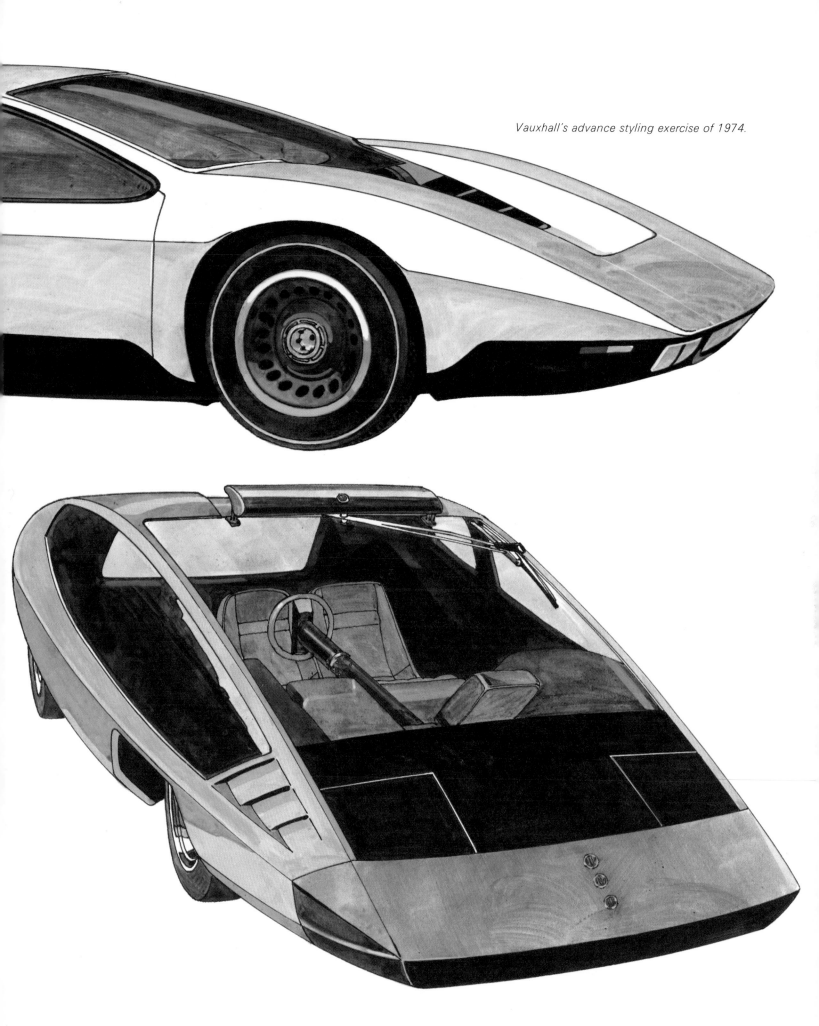

Vauxhall's advance styling exercise of 1974.

The Coins designed for Ford by Ghia in 1974 for the 1990s.

INDEX

Entries in bold indicate a sub-section
Numerals in bold italics indicate an illustration